SCOTT FORESMAN · ADDISON WESLEY

Mathematics

Grade 3

Answer Key
for Reteaching, Practice, Enrichment and Problem Solving

PEARSON

Scott
Foresman

Editorial Offices: Glenview, Illinois • Parsippany, New Jersey • New York, New York

Sales Offices: Parsippany, New Jersey • Duluth, Georgia • Glenview, Illinois
Coppell, Texas • Ontario, California • Mesa, Arizona

ISBN 0-328-04941-7

4 5 6 7 8 9 10 V084 12 11 10 09 08 07 06 05 04

Name_____

Ways to Use Numbers
P 1-1

Tell if each number is used to locate, name, measure, or count.

1.

Measure

2.

Name

Sal Yon Frank Joe Kym Lia

3. Who is fourth in line?

Joe

4. Write the ordinal number for Sal's place in line.

1st or first

5. **Reasoning** If Joe leaves to find another book, who will be fifth in line?

Lia

Test Prep

6. Which ordinal number comes next? 42nd, 43rd, 44th,

A. 54th   B. 41st   C. 45th   D. 55th

7. **Writing in Math** Explain how a number can name something.

Sample answer: The number on a baseball shirt names the player.

_____

© Pearson Education, Inc. 3

Use with Lesson 1-1. **1**

Name_____

Ways to Use Numbers
R 1-1

Numbers can be used to locate, to name, to measure, and to count.

Locate   Name   Measure   Count

Numbers can also be used to show the order of people or objects. These are called ordinal numbers.

Tell if each number is used to locate, name, measure, or count.

1.

Count

2.

Name

3.

Measure

Use the picture below for 4–7.

Striped   Dotted   Gray   Starred   White

4. Which ball is third in line?

Gray

5. Write an ordinal number for the white ball's place in line.

Fifth

6. Which ball is second in line?

Dotted

7. Which ball is fourth in line?

Starred

8. **Number Sense** What ordinal number would come next in the following list? 10th, 11th, 12th, . . .

13th

© Pearson Education, Inc. 3

Use with Lesson 1-1. **1**

Name_____

Calendar Days
E 1-1
CRITICAL THINKING

Mandy and her friends are adding new holidays to the calendars shown below. Find the date for each new holiday, and write the date next to each holiday's name.

February
S	M	T	W	T	F	S
					1	2
3	4	5	6	7	8	9
10	11	12	13	14	15	16
17	18	19	20	21	22	23
24	25	26	27	28		

March
S	M	T	W	T	F	S
					1	2
3	4	5	6	7	8	9
10	11	12	13	14	15	16
17	18	19	20	21	22	23
24	25	26	27	28	29	30
31						

April
S	M	T	W	T	F	S
	1	2	3	4	5	6
7	8	9	10	11	12	13
14	15	16	17	18	19	20
21	22	23	24	25	26	27
28	29	30				

May
S	M	T	W	T	F	S
		1	2	3	4	
5	6	7	8	9	10	11
12	13	14	15	16	17	18
19	20	21	22	23	24	25
26	27	28	29	30	31	

1. **Best Friend Day:** the third Friday in April:

April 19

2. **Exercise Day:** the first Tuesday in February:

February 5

3. **Favorite Animal Day:** the fifth Thursday in May:

May 30

4. **Game Day:** the third Friday in March:

March 15

5. **Letter Writing Day:** the second Monday in February:

February 11

6. **Sports Day:** the fourth Wednesday in May:

May 22

7. **Storytelling Day:** the second Thursday in March:

March 14

© Pearson Education, Inc. 3

Use with Lesson 1-1. **1**

Name_____

Ways to Use Numbers
PS 1-1

Birdhouses Carmen and her mother are building birdhouses. First, they measured 6 ft of wood. Second, they cut the wood. Third, they nailed the pieces of wood together. Carmen and her mother made three birdhouses.

1. What ordinal numbers are in the story about building birdhouses?

First, second, third

2. What number is used as a measurement in the story?

6 ft

3. What number is used as a count in the story?

3 birdhouses

Lunch Time Four students were in line in the lunch room. Martha was not first or fourth. Cory was ahead of Martha but behind Ricci. Greg was behind Martha.

4. What ordinal numbers are mentioned in the lunch time story?

First, fourth

5. Write the order of the students in line from first to fourth.

Ricci, Cory, Martha, Greg

6. **Writing in Math** Write a sentence about a time you used a number to measure.

Sample answer: I filled a measuring cup with 8 oz of milk.

© Pearson Education, Inc. 3

Use with Lesson 1-1. **1**

© Pearson Education, Inc. 3

Name_____

Numbers in the Hundreds

P 1-2

Write each number in standard form.

1. **261** 2. **245** 3. **137**

4. $700 + 30 + 6$ **736**

5. two hundreds, five tens, nine ones **259**

Write the word name for each number.

6. 212 **Two hundred twelve**

7. $600 + 3$ **Six hundred three**

Algebra Find each missing number.

8. $200 + 10 +$ **2** $= 212$

9. **900** $+ 70 + 1 = 971$

Test Prep

10. Which is the missing number? $100 +$ _____ $+ 9 = 139$

   A. 3   B. 13   C. 30   D. 33

11. **Writing in Math** Explain how the digit 7 can have different values.

   Sample answer: The value of the number depends on its place. A seven can be worth 700, 70, or 7 depending on whether it is in the hundreds, tens, or ones place.

© Pearson Education, Inc. 3

Name_____

Numbers in the Hundreds

R 1-2

Here are different ways to show 612.

place-value blocks:

expanded form: $600 + 10 + 2$

standard form: 612

word form: six hundred twelve

Write each number in standard form.

1. **308** 2. **559**

3. $400 + 30 + 7$ **437**

4. six hundred twenty **620**

5. $200 + 50 + 1$ **251**

6. three hundred forty-five **345**

Write the word form for each number.

7. 285 **Two hundred eighty-five**

8. 892 **Eight hundred ninety-two**

9. 146 **One hundred forty-six**

10. 378 **Three hundred seventy-eight**

11. **Number Sense** Write a three-digit number with a 2 in the hundreds place and a 4 in the tens place. **Answers will vary from 240 to 249.**

© Pearson Education, Inc. 3

Name_____

Show Time!

E 1-2
NUMBER SENSE

Use the data given to write the number of tickets that were sold each day in standard form, expanded form, and word form.

Ticket Code

☐ = 100 tickets   ▨ = 10 tickets   ▭ = 1 ticket

Ticket Sales

Opening Night—
Day 2—
Day 3—
Day 4—
Day 5—

1. Opening Night ticket sales **512; $500 + 10 + 2$; five hundred twelve**

2. Day 2 ticket sales **433; $400 + 30 + 3$; four hundred thirty-three**

3. Day 3 ticket sales **221; $200 + 20 + 1$; two hundred twenty-one**

4. Day 4 ticket sales **344; $300 + 40 + 4$; three hundred forty-four**

5. Day 5 ticket sales **415; $400 + 10 + 5$; four hundred fifteen**

© Pearson Education, Inc. 3

Name_____

Numbers in the Hundreds

PS 1-2

Art Museum Jefferson Elementary students took a field trip to the art museum. At the museum, there are paintings and pencil drawings.

166 paintings

16 pencil drawings

1. What digit is in the ones place of both of these numbers? **6**

2. Both of the numbers contain the digits 1 and 6. Are the numbers equal? Explain.
   No, because they have different values.

Endangered Species The table below shows the number of endangered plants and animals in 2001.

Endangered Species in 2001	
Plants	737
Animals	507

3. What is the word form for the number of endangered animals? **Five hundred, seven**

4. What digit is in the hundreds place of the number of endangered plants? **7**

5. **Writing in Math** Explain how you know that the number of endangered plants is different from the number of endangered animals.
   Sample answer: The digits in the tens and hundreds places are different.

© Pearson Education, Inc. 3

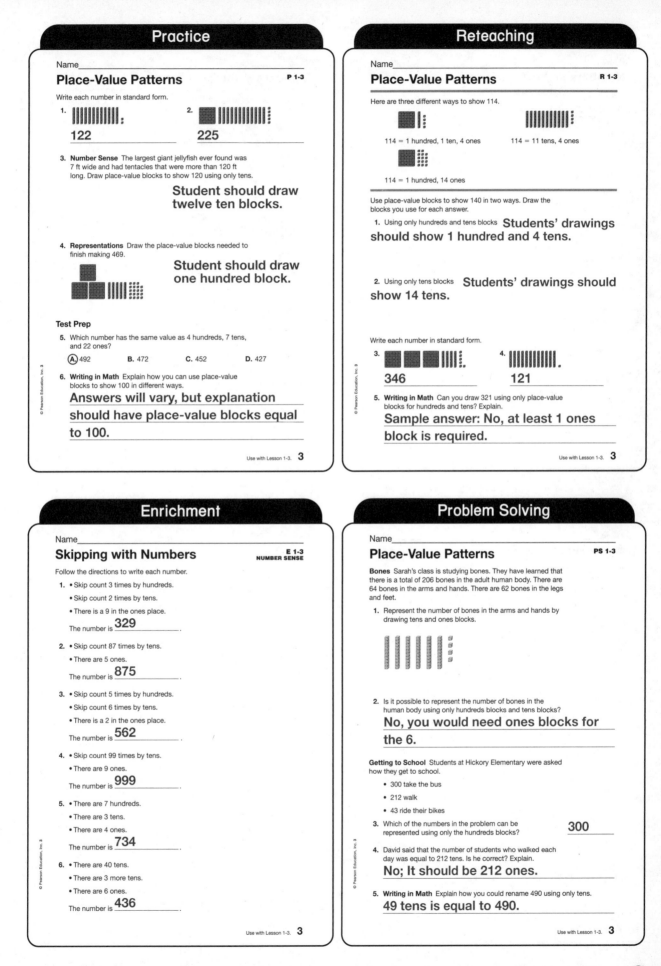

Practice

Name_____

Place-Value Patterns   P 1-3

Write each number in standard form.

1. **122**

2. **225**

3. **Number Sense** The largest giant jellyfish ever found was 7 ft wide and had tentacles that were more than 120 ft long. Draw place-value blocks to show 120 using only tens.

   Student should draw twelve ten blocks.

4. **Representations** Draw the place-value blocks needed to finish making 469.

   Student should draw one hundred block.

Test Prep

5. Which number has the same value as 4 hundreds, 7 tens, and 22 ones?

   (A.) 492   **B.** 472   **C.** 452   **D.** 427

6. **Writing in Math** Explain how you can use place-value blocks to show 100 in different ways.

   Answers will vary, but explanation should have place-value blocks equal to 100.

Use with Lesson 1-3. **3**

Reteaching

Name_____

Place-Value Patterns   R 1-3

Here are three different ways to show 114.

114 = 1 hundred, 1 ten, 4 ones   114 = 11 tens, 4 ones

114 = 1 hundred, 14 ones

Use place-value blocks to show 140 in two ways. Draw the blocks you use for each answer.

1. Using only hundreds and tens blocks **Students' drawings should show 1 hundred and 4 tens.**

2. Using only tens blocks **Students' drawings should show 14 tens.**

Write each number in standard form.

3. **346**

4. **121**

5. **Writing in Math** Can you draw 321 using only place-value blocks for hundreds and tens? Explain.

   Sample answer: No, at least 1 ones block is required.

Use with Lesson 1-3. **3**

Enrichment

Name_____

Skipping with Numbers   E 1-3
NUMBER SENSE

Follow the directions to write each number.

1. • Skip count 3 times by hundreds.
   • Skip count 2 times by tens.
   • There is a 9 in the ones place.
   The number is **329**

2. • Skip count 87 times by tens.
   • There are 5 ones.
   The number is **875**

3. • Skip count 5 times by hundreds.
   • Skip count 6 times by tens.
   • There is a 2 in the ones place.
   The number is **562**

4. • Skip count 99 times by tens.
   • There are 9 ones.
   The number is **999**

5. • There are 7 hundreds.
   • There are 3 tens.
   • There are 4 ones.
   The number is **734**

6. • There are 40 tens.
   • There are 3 more tens.
   • There are 6 ones.
   The number is **436**

Use with Lesson 1-3. **3**

Problem Solving

Name_____

Place-Value Patterns   PS 1-3

Bones Sarah's class is studying bones. They have learned that there is a total of 206 bones in the adult human body. There are 64 bones in the arms and hands. There are 62 bones in the legs and feet.

1. Represent the number of bones in the arms and hands by drawing tens and ones blocks.

2. Is it possible to represent the number of bones in the human body using only hundreds blocks and tens blocks?

   No, you would need ones blocks for the 6.

Getting to School Students at Hickory Elementary were asked how they get to school.
   • 300 take the bus
   • 212 walk
   • 43 ride their bikes

3. Which of the numbers in the problem can be represented using only the hundreds blocks? **300**

4. David said that the number of students who walked each day was equal to 212 tens. Is he correct? Explain.

   No; It should be 212 ones.

5. **Writing in Math** Explain how you could rename 490 using only tens.

   49 tens is equal to 490.

Use with Lesson 1-3. **3**

Name_____

Numbers in the Thousands

P 1-4

Write each number in standard form.

1.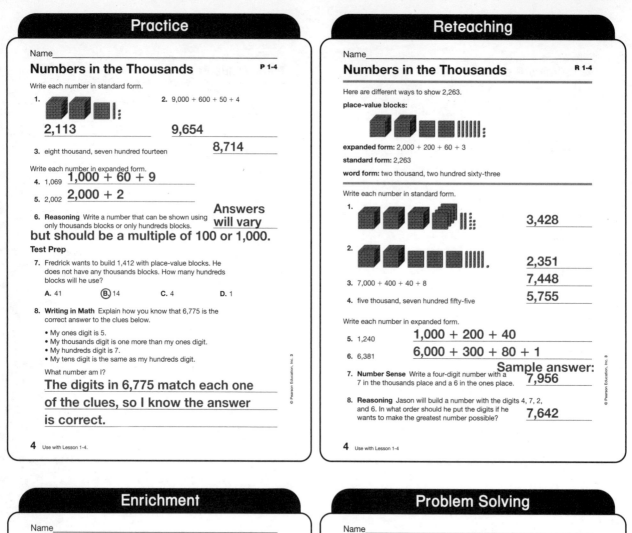

2,113

2. $9,000 + 600 + 50 + 4$

9,654

3. eight thousand, seven hundred fourteen

8,714

Write each number in expanded form.

4. 1,069   **$1,000 + 60 + 9$**

5. 2,002   **$2,000 + 2$**

6. **Reasoning** Write a number that can be shown using only thousands blocks or only hundreds blocks.

Answers will vary but should be a multiple of 100 or 1,000.

Test Prep

7. Fredrick wants to build 1,412 with place-value blocks. He does not have any thousands blocks. How many hundreds blocks will he use?

A. 41   **(B.) 14**   C. 4   D. 1

8. **Writing in Math** Explain how you know that 6,775 is the correct answer to the clues below.

• My ones digit is 5.
• My thousands digit is one more than my ones digit.
• My hundreds digit is 7.
• My tens digit is the same as my hundreds digit.

What number am I?

The digits in 6,775 match each one of the clues, so I know the answer is correct.

© Pearson Education, Inc. 3

Name_____

Numbers in the Thousands

R 1-4

Here are different ways to show 2,263.

place-value blocks:

expanded form: $2,000 + 200 + 60 + 3$

standard form: 2,263

word form: two thousand, two hundred sixty-three

Write each number in standard form.

1.   **3,428**

2.   **2,351**

3. $7,000 + 400 + 40 + 8$ **7,448**

4. five thousand, seven hundred fifty-five   **5,755**

Write each number in expanded form.

5. 1,240   **$1,000 + 200 + 40$**

6. 6,381   **$6,000 + 300 + 80 + 1$**

7. **Number Sense** Write a four-digit number with a 7 in the thousands place and a 6 in the ones place.

Sample answer: 7,956

8. **Reasoning** Jason will build a number with the digits 4, 7, 2, and 6. In what order should he put the digits if he wants to make the greatest number possible?

7,642

© Pearson Education, Inc. 3

Name_____

Fun with Thousands

E 1-4
REASONING

Asian Elephant	Giraffe	Hippopotamus
8,818 lb	2,646 lb	4,409 lb

Kodiak Bear	Saltwater Crocodile	White Rhinoceros
1,764 lb	2,425 lb	4,850 lb

Write the name of each animal.

1. The weight of this animal is equal to 2 thousands, 4 hundreds, 2 tens, and 5 ones.

Saltwater crocodile

2. The weight of this animal is equal to 4 thousands, 40 tens, and 9 ones.

Hippopotamus

3. The weight of this animal is equal to 176 tens and 4 ones.

Kodiak bear

4. The weight of this animal is equal to 88 hundreds and 18 ones.

Asian elephant

5. The weight of this animal is equal to 2 thousands, 64 tens, and 6 ones.

Giraffe

6. The weight of this animal is equal to 48 hundreds and 5 tens.

White rhinoceros

© Pearson Education, Inc. 3

Name_____

Numbers in the Thousands

PS 1-4

Backpacks A store ordered one thousand, four hundred ninety-seven backpacks to sell at their back-to-school sale.

1. Write the number of backpacks in standard form.

1,497

2. Jeremy represented the number of backpacks as shown. Is his work correct? Explain.

No; Jeremy forgot 9 tens blocks.

3. The store manager wants to display 1,000 backpacks on shelves. Each shelf holds 100 backpacks. How many shelves will the store manager need?

10 shelves

4. Last year, the store sold a total of 1,421 pencils. Hannah said the store sold more than 14 hundred pencils. Is she correct? Explain.

Yes; 14 hundred is 1,400, which is less than 1,421.

5. **Writing in Math** What is the least possible number you can write with a 1 in the thousands place? How can you be sure your answer is correct?

1,000; All other numbers with a 1 in the thousands place are greater than 1,000.

© Pearson Education, Inc. 3

Practice

Name_____

Greater Numbers

P 1-5

Write each number in standard form.

1. seventy-five thousand, three hundred twelve   **75,312**

2. one hundred fourteen thousand, seven   **114,007**

3. 20,000 + 7,000 + 600 + 90 + 3   **27,693**

4. 100,000 + 40,000 + 2,000 + 500 + 30 + 2   **142,532**

Write each number in expanded form.

5. 73,581   **70,000 + 3,000 + 500 + 80 + 1**

6. 100,317   **100,000 + 300 + 10 + 7**

7. **Number Sense** Write a six-digit number in which the digit 4 has the value of 40,000.   **Sample answer: 743,268**

8. The area of Ethiopia is 437,600 square miles. Write the area of Ethiopia in expanded form.

   400,000 + 30,000 + 7,000 + 600

9. The area of Israel is 8,550 square miles. Write the area of Israel in word form.

   Eight thousand, five hundred fifty

Test Prep

10. Which is the value of 3 in 328,469?

    A. 300   B. 3,000   C. 30,000   (D) 300,000

11. **Writing in Math** Explain how 8 ten thousands can be equal to 80 thousands.

    Sample answer: There are 10 thousands in 1 ten thousand so 8 ten thousands is 80,000.

Reteaching

Name_____

Greater Numbers

R 1-5

A period is a group of three digits in a number, starting from the right. A comma is used to separate two periods.

Thousands Period			Ones Period		
hundred thousands	ten thousands	thousands	hundreds	tens	ones
2	4	7,	3	6	2

Here are different ways to show 247,362.

expanded form: 200,000 + 40,000 + 7,000 + 300 + 60 + 2

standard form: 247,362

word form: two hundred forty-seven thousand, three hundred sixty-two

Write each number in standard form.

1. 60,000 + 8,000 + 200 + 50 + 1   **68,251**

2. 30,000 + 600 + 30 + 2   **30,632**

3. four hundred one thousand, four hundred fifty-four   **401,454**

4. five hundred twenty-nine thousand, three hundred seventy-eight   **529,378**

5. Write 522,438 in expanded form.

   500,000 + 20,000 + 2,000 + 400 + 30 + 8

6. Write 349,281 in expanded form.

   300,000 + 40,000 + 9,000 + 200 + 80 + 1

7. **Number Sense** What is the value of the 7 in 86,752?   **700**

8. Lake Erie is 32,630 square miles. Write the area of Lake Erie in expanded form.

   30,000 + 2,000 + 600 + 30

Enrichment

Name_____

A Pile of Bricks

E 1-5

NUMBER SENSE

The apartment building where Hannah lives was built with 213,854 bricks.

1. How many groups of 100,000 bricks can you make with 213,854?

   2 groups of 100,000

2. How many bricks are left over if you place 213,854 bricks in groups of 10,000?

   3,854 bricks

3. The apartment building where James lives was built with bricks that total 41 ten thousands. Write this number in standard form.

   410,000

4. How is the value of the *hundred-thousands place* different in the number of bricks in Hannah's building and the number of bricks in James's building?

   2 hundred thousands are in the number of bricks in Hannah's building and 4 hundred thousands are in the number of bricks in James's building.

5. A garage is going to be built behind James's building. This building will need two hundred eighty-four thousand one hundred eighty-seven bricks. Write the number of bricks that will be used to build the garage in expanded form.

   200,000 + 80,000 + 4,000 + 100 + 80 + 7

Problem Solving

Name_____

Greater Numbers

PS 1-5

State	Population
Alaska	634,892
Montana	904,433
North Dakota	634,448
Vermont	613,090

1. Write the population of Vermont in expanded form.

   600,000 + 10,000 + 3,000 + 90

2. Which states have a population with a 4 in the thousands place?

   Alaska, Montana, and North Dakota

3. What is the value of the digit 8 in the population of Alaska?   **800**

Ocean	Depth
Pacific Ocean	15,215 ft
Atlantic Ocean	12,881 ft
Indian Ocean	13,002 ft

4. Which ocean has a depth with the same digit in the ten-thousands place and in the ones place?

   Atlantic Ocean

5. Write the depth of the Indian Ocean in expanded form.

   10,000 + 3,000 + 2

6. **Writing in Math** Give the value of the 2 in each ocean's depth. Which value is the greatest?

   200; 2,000; 2; 2,000 is the greatest

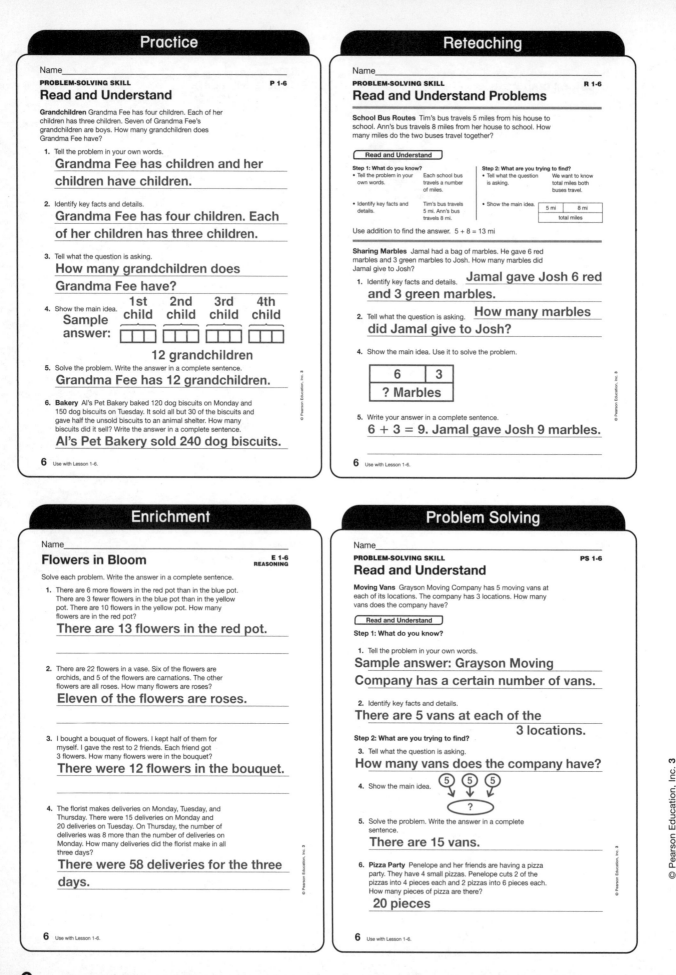

Practice

PROBLEM-SOLVING SKILL   P 1-6
Read and Understand

Grandchildren Grandma Fee has four children. Each of her children has three children. Seven of Grandma Fee's grandchildren are boys. How many grandchildren does Grandma Fee have?

1. Tell the problem in your own words.

   Grandma Fee has children and her

   children have children.

2. Identify key facts and details.

   Grandma Fee has four children. Each

   of her children has three children.

3. Tell what the question is asking.

   How many grandchildren does

   Grandma Fee have?

4. Show the main idea.

	1st child	2nd child	3rd child	4th child

   Sample answer:

   12 grandchildren

5. Solve the problem. Write the answer in a complete sentence.

   Grandma Fee has 12 grandchildren.

6. **Bakery** Al's Pet Bakery baked 120 dog biscuits on Monday and 150 dog biscuits on Tuesday. It sold all but 30 of the biscuits and gave half the unsold biscuits to an animal shelter. How many biscuits did it sell? Write the answer in a complete sentence.

   Al's Pet Bakery sold 240 dog biscuits.

6 Use with Lesson 1-6.

Reteaching

PROBLEM-SOLVING SKILL   R 1-6
Read and Understand Problems

School Bus Routes Tim's bus travels 5 miles from his house to school. Ann's bus travels 8 miles from her house to school. How many miles do the two buses travel together?

Read and Understand

Step 1: What do you know?		Step 2: What are you trying to find?	
• Tell the problem in your own words.	Each school bus travels a number of miles.	• Tell what the question is asking.	We want to know total miles both buses travel.
• Identify key facts and details.	Tim's bus travels 5 mi. Ann's bus travels 8 mi.	• Show the main idea.	5 mi / 8 mi / total miles

Use addition to find the answer. 5 + 8 = 13 mi

Sharing Marbles Jamal had a bag of marbles. He gave 6 red marbles and 3 green marbles to Josh. How many marbles did Jamal give to Josh?

1. Identify key facts and details. **Jamal gave Josh 6 red**

   and 3 green marbles.

2. Tell what the question is asking. **How many marbles**

   did Jamal give to Josh?

4. Show the main idea. Use it to solve the problem.

6	3
? Marbles	

5. Write your answer in a complete sentence.

   6 + 3 = 9. Jamal gave Josh 9 marbles.

6 Use with Lesson 1-6.

Enrichment

Flowers in Bloom   E 1-6
                                             REASONING

Solve each problem. Write the answer in a complete sentence.

1. There are 6 more flowers in the red pot than in the blue pot. There are 3 fewer flowers in the blue pot than in the yellow pot. There are 10 flowers in the yellow pot. How many flowers are in the red pot?

   There are 13 flowers in the red pot.

2. There are 22 flowers in a vase. Six of the flowers are orchids, and 5 of the flowers are carnations. The other flowers are all roses. How many flowers are roses?

   Eleven of the flowers are roses.

3. I bought a bouquet of flowers. I kept half of them for myself. I gave the rest to 2 friends. Each friend got 3 flowers. How many flowers were in the bouquet?

   There were 12 flowers in the bouquet.

4. The florist makes deliveries on Monday, Tuesday, and Thursday. There were 15 deliveries on Monday and 20 deliveries on Tuesday. On Thursday, the number of deliveries was 8 more than the number of deliveries on Monday. How many deliveries did the florist make in all three days?

   There were 58 deliveries for the three

   days.

6 Use with Lesson 1-6.

Problem Solving

PROBLEM-SOLVING SKILL   PS 1-6
Read and Understand

Moving Vans Grayson Moving Company has 5 moving vans at each of its locations. The company has 3 locations. How many vans does the company have?

Read and Understand

Step 1: What do you know?

1. Tell the problem in your own words.

   Sample answer: Grayson Moving

   Company has a certain number of vans.

2. Identify key facts and details.

   There are 5 vans at each of the

   3 locations.

Step 2: What are you trying to find?

3. Tell what the question is asking.

   How many vans does the company have?

4. Show the main idea.

   ⑤ ⑤ ⑤
      ?

5. Solve the problem. Write the answer in a complete sentence.

   There are 15 vans.

6. **Pizza Party** Penelope and her friends are having a pizza party. They have 4 small pizzas. Penelope cuts 2 of the pizzas into 4 pieces each and 2 pizzas into 6 pieces each. How many pieces of pizza are there?

   20 pieces

6 Use with Lesson 1-6.

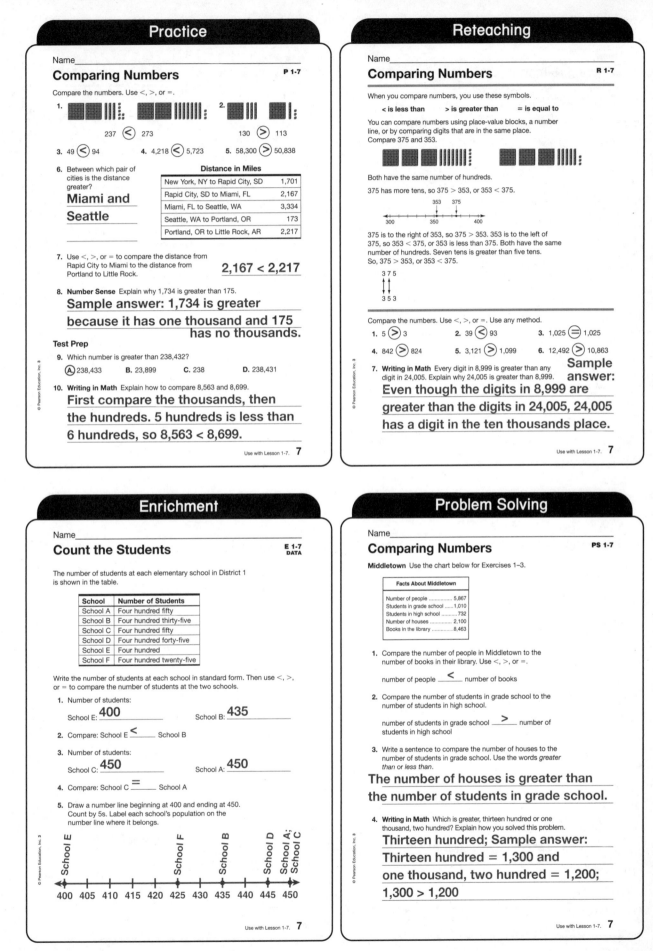

Practice

Name_____

Comparing Numbers   P 1-7

Compare the numbers. Use <, >, or =.

1. 237 ⊙< 273   2. 130 ⊙> 113

3. 49 ⊙< 94   4. 4,218 ⊙< 5,723   5. 58,300 ⊙> 50,838

6. Between which pair of cities is the distance greater?

Distance in Miles	
New York, NY to Rapid City, SD	1,701
Rapid City, SD to Miami, FL	2,167
Miami, FL to Seattle, WA	3,334
Seattle, WA to Portland, OR	173
Portland, OR to Little Rock, AR	2,217

Miami and Seattle

7. Use <, >, or = to compare the distance from Rapid City to Miami to the distance from Portland to Little Rock.

2,167 < 2,217

8. **Number Sense** Explain why 1,734 is greater than 175.

Sample answer: 1,734 is greater because it has one thousand and 175 has no thousands.

Test Prep

9. Which number is greater than 238,432?

Ⓐ 238,433   B. 23,899   C. 238   D. 238,431

10. **Writing in Math** Explain how to compare 8,563 and 8,699.

First compare the thousands, then the hundreds. 5 hundreds is less than 6 hundreds, so 8,563 < 8,699.

Use with Lesson 1-7. **7**

Reteaching

Name_____

Comparing Numbers   R 1-7

When you compare numbers, you use these symbols.

< is less than   **> is greater than**   **= is equal to**

You can compare numbers using place-value blocks, a number line, or by comparing digits that are in the same place. Compare 375 and 353.

Both have the same number of hundreds.

375 has more tens, so 375 > 353, or 353 < 375.

375 is to the right of 353, so 375 > 353. 353 is to the left of 375, so 353 < 375, or 353 is less than 375. Both have the same number of hundreds. Seven tens is greater than five tens. So, 375 > 353, or 353 < 375.

3 7 5
↑ ↑ ↑
3 5 3

Compare the numbers. Use <, >, or =. Use any method.

1. 5 ⊙> 3   2. 39 ⊙< 93   3. 1,025 ⊙= 1,025

4. 842 ⊙> 824   5. 3,121 ⊙> 1,099   6. 12,492 ⊙> 10,863

7. **Writing in Math** Every digit in 8,999 is greater than any digit in 24,005. Explain why 24,005 is greater than 8,999.

Sample answer: Even though the digits in 8,999 are greater than the digits in 24,005, 24,005 has a digit in the ten thousands place.

Use with Lesson 1-7. **7**

Enrichment

Name_____

Count the Students   E 1-7
                                                          DATA

The number of students at each elementary school in District 1 is shown in the table.

School	Number of Students
School A	Four hundred fifty
School B	Four hundred thirty-five
School C	Four hundred fifty
School D	Four hundred forty-five
School E	Four hundred
School F	Four hundred twenty-five

Write the number of students at each school in standard form. Then use <, >, or = to compare the number of students at the two schools.

1. Number of students:

   School E: **400**   School B: **435**

2. Compare: School E **<** School B

3. Number of students:

   School C: **450**   School A: **450**

4. Compare: School C **=** School A

5. Draw a number line beginning at 400 and ending at 450. Count by 5s. Label each school's population on the number line where it belongs.

School E — 400
School F — 425
School B — 435
School D — 445
School A; School C — 450

400 405 410 415 420 425 430 435 440 445 450

Use with Lesson 1-7. **7**

Problem Solving

Name_____

Comparing Numbers   PS 1-7

Middletown Use the chart below for Exercises 1–3.

Facts About Middletown	
Number of people	5,867
Students in grade school	1,010
Students in high school	732
Number of houses	2,100
Books in the library	8,463

1. Compare the number of people in Middletown to the number of books in their library. Use <, >, or =.

   number of people **<** number of books

2. Compare the number of students in grade school to the number of students in high school.

   number of students in grade school **>** number of students in high school

3. Write a sentence to compare the number of houses to the number of students in grade school. Use the words *greater than* or *less than*.

   The number of houses is greater than the number of students in grade school.

4. **Writing in Math** Which is greater, thirteen hundred or one thousand, two hundred? Explain how you solved this problem.

   Thirteen hundred; Sample answer: Thirteen hundred = 1,300 and one thousand, two hundred = 1,200; 1,300 > 1,200

Use with Lesson 1-7. **7**

Name_____

Ordering Numbers

P 1-8

Write the numbers in order from least to greatest.

1. 216 208 222 **208, 216, 222**

2. 210 219 211 **210, 211, 219**

Write the numbers in order from greatest to least.

3. 633 336 363 **633, 363, 336**

4. 5,000 50 500 **5,000, 500, 50**

5. **Representations** Draw a number line. Make sure the following numbers are on your number line: 1,472; 1,560; 1,481.

Number lines will vary, but numbers should be in order.

6. Write the river lengths in order from least to greatest.

3,740; 3,964; 4,000; 4,145

World's Longest Rivers

River	Length (miles)
Amazon	4,000
Yangtze	3,964
Mississippi-Missouri	3,740
Nile	4,145

Test Prep

7. In which number does 4 have the greatest value?

A. 9,499   (B) 4,391   C. 2,240   D. 1,944

8. **Writing in Math** Sara says the number with the most digits is always greatest. Do you agree? Explain.

Yes. A four-digit number is greater than a three-digit number because it has thousands not only hundreds.

Name_____

Ordering Numbers

R 1-8

To order numbers from greatest to least or least to greatest, you can use a number line.

These numbers, in order from least to greatest, are 505, 535, and 560.

You can also use place value to order numbers. First, you compare pairs of numbers to find the greatest number. Then you compare the other numbers.

National Monument	Total Height
Statue of Liberty	305 ft
Washington Monument	555 ft
Gateway Arch	630 ft

630 > 305
Is 630 also greater than 555?
630 > **555**
Yes, so 630 is greatest.
555 > **305**
So, 305 is least.

Write the numbers in order from least to greatest.

1. 560 583 552 **552, 560, 583**

2. 583 575 590 **575, 583, 590**

3. 576 580 557 **557, 576, 580**

Write the numbers in order from greatest to least.

4. 973 1,007 996 **1,007; 996; 973**

5. 5,626 5,636 5,616 **5,636; 5,626; 5,616**

6. 445 455 450 **455; 450; 445**

7. **Representations** Jamie is 9 years old, Al is 12 years old, David is 3 years old, and Naomi is 6 years old. Draw a number line from 1 to 12. Put these ages on the number line from least to greatest.

D N J A
0 1 2 3 4 5 6 7 8 9 10 11 12

Name_____

Mail Ordering

E 1-8
NUMBER SENSE

A mail carrier dropped his bag and the mail he was delivering got all mixed up. Help him to put the addresses in order.

4815 Elm St.
4721 Elm St.
4913 Elm St.

1. Put the addresses on Elm St. in order from least to greatest.

4721, 4815, 4913

2511 Maple St.
2502 Maple St.
2499 Maple St.
2437 Maple St.
2498 Maple St.
2516 Maple St.

2. Put the addresses on Maple St. that end in an even number in order from least to greatest.

2498, 2502, 2516

3. Put the addresses on Maple St. that end in an odd number in order from greatest to least.

2511, 2499, 2437

854 Pine St.
851 Pine St.
814 Pine St.
843 Pine St.
862 Pine St.
890 Pine St.
867 Pine St.
839 Pine St.
802 Pine St.
824 Pine St.

4. Write the numbers of the letters addressed to Pine St. in order from least to greatest in the correct mail bags.

Mail 801–850
**802 814
824
839 843**

Mail 851–900
**851 854
862
867 890**

Name_____

Ordering Numbers

PS 1-8

Penny Count Mr. Smith's third-grade class collected pennies in a jar. After 3 months, the students guessed the number of pennies in the jar. After they had guessed, Mr. Smith and the students counted the pennies and wrote 1,365 on a sign.

1. Five of the guesses were 999; 1,500; 1,250; and 1,025. Write these numbers from least to greatest.

999; 1,025; 1,250; 1,500

2. Of the four guesses listed in Exercise 1, which were less than the actual number of pennies?

999; 1,025; and 1,250

3. Write two numbers greater than 1,200 but less than the number of pennies in the jar.

Sample answer: 1,201; 1,364

Great Lakes The Great Lakes are in the Midwest of the United States and in Canada. They are the largest lakes in the world.

Lake	Depth (in feet)
Superior	483
Michigan	279
Huron	195
Erie	62
Ontario	283

4. Write the names of all five lakes in order of their depths from least to greatest.

Erie, Huron, Michigan, Ontario, Superior

5. **Writing in Math** If two numbers have different numbers of digits, which one is greater? Explain how you know.

Sample answer: The number with more digits because its place value is greater.

© Pearson Education, Inc. 3

Name_____

Number Patterns

Continue each pattern.

1. 15, 30, 45, **60** , **75**

2. 30, 24, 18, **12** , **6**

3. 3, 6, 9, **12** , 15

4. 220, 230, 240, **250** , **260**

Use place-value patterns to find each sum or difference.

5. 890 − 300 = **590**

6. 150 + 200 = **350**

7. 470 − 350 = **120**

8. 340 + 220 = **560**

9. Joshua is raising fruit flies for a science project. At the beginning of the first day, he had 4 fruit flies. His fruit flies double in number each day. How many fruit flies does he have at the end of three days?

32 fruit flies

10. **Representations** Choose your own pattern. Draw a number line to show your pattern.

Sample answer:

20 40 60 80

Test Prep

11. Which is 100 more than 7,399?

A. 7,400 **(B)** 7,499 C. 8,399 D. 8,499

12. **Writing in Math** Mrs. Bradner has 30 tomato plants. She wants to plant the same number of plants in each row of her garden. Explain how she could decide the number of rows to plant.

Sample answer: Mrs. Bradner could use skip counting, number lines, and patterns to decide the number of rows and the number of plants in each row.

© Pearson Education, Inc. 3

Use with Lesson 1-9. **9**

Name_____

Number Patterns

You can use a number line to find a number pattern.

Find the pattern. Find the next two numbers.

17, 14, 11, 8, **5** , **2**

−3 −3 −3 −3

A hundred chart can help you find 39 − 12 using place-value patterns. Start at 39 and move up one row to subtract 10. Then move two columns to the left to subtract 2 ones. 39 − 12 = 27.

Continue each pattern.

1. 4, 8, 12, **16** **20**

2. 90, 80, 70, **60** **50**

3. 7, 14, 21, **28** **35**

4. 25, 50, 75, **100** **125**

Use place-value patterns to find each sum or difference.

5. 18 + 20   **38**

6. 21 + 17   **38**

7. 46 − 12   **34**

8. **Writing in Math** Explain how you can use a hundred chart to subtract 12 from 46.

Sample answer: You find 46 and move up one row to subtract 10; that is 36. Then move two columns to the left to subtract 2; that is 34.

© Pearson Education, Inc. 3

Use with Lesson 1-9. **9**

Name_____

Other Number Patterns

Jeremy and Belinda made up a challenging pattern problem for their class. They made three rules:

Rule 1: Take the first number and subtract something to get the second number.

Rule 2: Take the second number and add something to get the third number.

Rule 3: Repeat Rule 1 and Rule 2 to continue the pattern.

This is what they wrote on the board:

13, 9, 15, 11, 17, 13, 19

1. How did Jeremy and Belinda change the first number, 13, to the second number, 9?

They subtracted 4 from 13 to get 9.

2. How did they change the second number, 9, to the third number, 15?

They added 6 and 9 to get 15.

3. Write the next four numbers in the pattern.   **15, 21, 17, 23**

In 4–5, write the next three numbers to continue the pattern. Write a rule or rules to describe the pattern.

4. $3.20, $2.90, $2.60, **$2.30** , **$2.00** , **$1.70**

Rule(s): **Subtract $0.30**

5. 6, 11, 8, 13, 10, **15** **12** **17**

Rule(s): **Add 5 and then subtract 3.**

© Pearson Education, Inc. 3

Use with Lesson 1-9. **9**

Name_____

Number Patterns

Census A census is a count of all of the people in a country. The United States takes a census once every 10 years.

1. The first United States census was taken in the year 1790. Name the years that the next four censuses were taken.

1800, 1810, 1820, 1830

2. The United States took a census in the year 2000. Name the years that the four previous censuses were taken.

1990, 1980, 1970, 1960

Leap Year Once every 4 years, an extra day is added to the calendar. This helps the seasons match up with our calendars. When it is a leap year, there is a 29th day in February.

3. There was a leap year in 1968. Continue this pattern.

1968, 1972, 1976, **1980** **1984** **1988**

4. There was a leap year in the year 2000. Name the years that the four previous leap years occurred.

1996, 1992, 1988, 1984

5. **Writing in Math** What are the next three numbers in the pattern? 33, 30, 27, 24, _____, _____, _____ What is the number before 33? Explain how you know.

21, 18, 15; 36; Sample answer: The number goes down by 3.

© Pearson Education, Inc. 3

Use with Lesson 1-9. **9**

Name_____

Rounding Numbers

P 1-10

Round to the nearest ten.

1. 37
40

2. 92
90

3. 133
130

4. 2,219
2,220

Round to the nearest hundred.

5. 172
200

6. 929
900

7. 8,438
8,400

8. 5,555
5,600

9. **Number Sense** Tyrell says $750 is about $800. Sara says $750 is about $700. Who is correct? Explain.

Tyrell is correct. In $750 the tens digit is 5, so you round up to $800.

10. Which two lakes have the same depth when rounded to the nearest hundred?

Huron and Ontario

11. Which lake has a depth of about 900 ft?

Michigan

Depths of the Great Lakes

Lake	Depth (feet)
Erie	210
Huron	750
Michigan	923
Ontario	802
Superior	1,333

Test Prep

12. Round 7,468 to the nearest hundred.

A. 7,400　　**B.** 7,460　　**C.** 7,470　　**D.** 7,500

13. **Writing in Math** Explain how you would use a number line to round 148 to the nearest ten.

Sample answer: I would look at a number line and see that 148 is closer to 150 than 140. So, 148 rounds to 150.

© Pearson Education, Inc. 3

Name_____

Rounding Numbers

R 1-10

You can use place value to round to the nearest ten or hundred.

Find the rounding place. If the digit in the ones or the tens place is 5, 6, 7, 8, or 9, then round to the next greater number. If the digit is less than 5, do not change the digit in the rounding place.

Round 17 to the nearest ten: **20**

Explain. **7 is in the ones place. Round to the next greater ten.**

Round 153 to the nearest ten. **150**

Explain. **Because 3 is in the ones place and 3 is less than 5, the digit in the tens place doesn't change.**

Round 1,575 to the nearest hundred. **1,600**

Explain. **Because the 7 in the tens place is 5 or greater, round to the next greater hundred.**

1. Round 63 to the nearest ten: **60**

Explain. **Three is in the ones place, so the 6 stays the same.**

Round each number to the nearest ten.

2. 58
60

3. 71
70

4. 927
930

5. 3,121
3,120

Round each number to the nearest hundred.

6. 577
600

7. 820
800

8. 2,345
2,300

9. 8,750
8,800

10. **Reasoning** If you live 71 mi from a river, does it make sense to say you live about 80 mi from the river? Explain.

No. To the nearest ten, 71 rounds to 70.

© Pearson Education, Inc. 3

Name_____

And the Answer Is?

E 1-10
ESTIMATION

1. If 1,569 rounds to 1,570, what is the rounding place?

Tens place

2. When this 3-digit number is rounded to the nearest ten, the sum of its digits is 16. The hundreds digit of this number is 8 and the ones digit is 5. What is the number?

875

3. When this 4-digit number is rounded to the nearest ten, it rounds to 2,350. The number is less than 2,360 and greater than 2,350. The ones digit is an even number that you count after 2. What is the number?

2,354

4. When this 3-digit number is rounded to the nearest hundred, it rounds to 200. Rounded to the nearest ten, this number rounds to 200. The sum of the digits of this number is 19. What is the number?

199

5. When this 4-digit number is rounded to the nearest ten or hundred, the numbers round up. All of the digits in this number are the same. The sum of the digits is 20. What is the number?

5,555

6. When this 4-digit number is rounded to the nearest thousand, it rounds up to 3,000. The hundreds digit is less than 6. The digits in the tens and ones place add to a sum of 8 and they are the same. What is the number?

2,544

7. When this 3-digit number is rounded to the nearest hundred it rounds down to 900. The digit in the ones place is the fifth odd number that you count beginning with 1. The sum of the digits is 22. What is the number?

949

© Pearson Education, Inc. 3

Name_____

Rounding Numbers

PS 1-10

School Spirit In September, several events took place at Southside School: 155 people went to the band concert, 247 people went to the softball game, and 321 people went to the art show.

1. Round the number of people that attended each event to the nearest ten.

160, 250, 320

2. Which event had about 100 people more than the band concert?

Softball game

Car Show José attended a car show to see many types of antique cars. He saw 239 cars at the show. Gina arrived at the car show later and saw only 101 cars.

3. Round the number of cars José saw to the nearest hundred.

200

4. Round the number of cars José saw to the nearest ten.

240

5. Round the number of cars Gina saw to the nearest hundred.

100

6. **Writing in Math** Write a 4-digit number that rounds to 1,000 when rounded to the nearest hundred. Explain how you got your answer.

Sample answer: 1,022; The number is closer to 1,000 than to 1,100.

© Pearson Education, Inc. 3

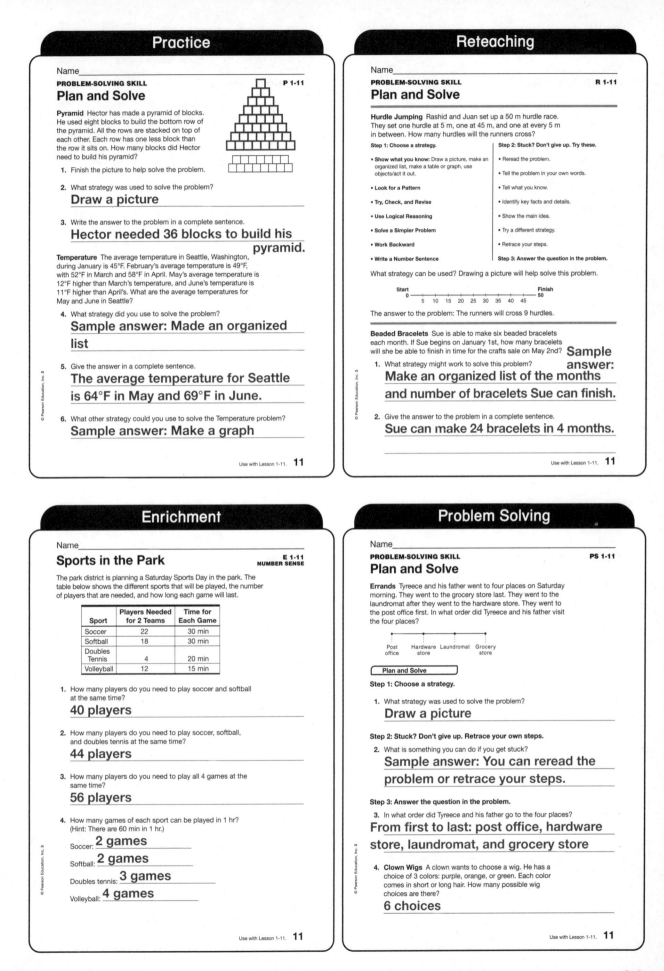

Practice

Name_____

PROBLEM-SOLVING SKILL   P 1-11
Plan and Solve

Pyramid Hector has made a pyramid of blocks. He used eight blocks to build the bottom row of the pyramid. All the rows are stacked on top of each other. Each row has one less block than the row it sits on. How many blocks did Hector need to build his pyramid?

1. Finish the picture to help solve the problem.

2. What strategy was used to solve the problem?
   Draw a picture

3. Write the answer to the problem in a complete sentence.
   Hector needed 36 blocks to build his pyramid.

Temperature The average temperature in Seattle, Washington, during January is 45°F. February's average temperature is 49°F, with 52°F in March and 58°F in April. May's average temperature is 12°F higher than March's temperature, and June's temperature is 11°F higher than April's. What are the average temperatures for May and June in Seattle?

4. What strategy did you use to solve the problem?
   Sample answer: Made an organized list

5. Give the answer in a complete sentence.
   The average temperature for Seattle is 64°F in May and 69°F in June.

6. What other strategy could you use to solve the Temperature problem?
   Sample answer: Make a graph

Reteaching

Name_____

PROBLEM-SOLVING SKILL   R 1-11
Plan and Solve

Hurdle Jumping Rashid and Juan set up a 50 m hurdle race. They set one hurdle at 5 m, one at 45 m, and one at every 5 m in between. How many hurdles will the runners cross?

Step 1: Choose a strategy.
- Show what you know: Draw a picture, make an organized list, make a table or graph, use objects/act it out.
- Look for a Pattern
- Try, Check, and Revise
- Use Logical Reasoning
- Solve a Simpler Problem
- Work Backward
- Write a Number Sentence

Step 2: Stuck? Don't give up. Try these.
- Reread the problem.
- Tell the problem in your own words.
- Tell what you know.
- Identify key facts and details.
- Show the main idea.
- Try a different strategy.
- Retrace your steps.

Step 3: Answer the question in the problem.

What strategy can be used? Drawing a picture will help solve this problem.

Start										Finish
0	5	10	15	20	25	30	35	40	45	50

The answer to the problem: The runners will cross 9 hurdles.

Beaded Bracelets Sue is able to make six beaded bracelets each month. If Sue begins on January 1st, how many bracelets will she be able to finish in time for the crafts sale on May 2nd?

1. What strategy might work to solve this problem?
   Sample answer: Make an organized list of the months and number of bracelets Sue can finish.

2. Give the answer to the problem in a complete sentence.
   Sue can make 24 bracelets in 4 months.

Enrichment

Name_____

Sports in the Park
                                         E 1-11
                                         NUMBER SENSE

The park district is planning a Saturday Sports Day in the park. The table below shows the different sports that will be played, the number of players that are needed, and how long each game will last.

Sport	Players Needed for 2 Teams	Time for Each Game
Soccer	22	30 min
Softball	18	30 min
Doubles Tennis	4	20 min
Volleyball	12	15 min

1. How many players do you need to play soccer and softball at the same time?
   40 players

2. How many players do you need to play soccer, softball, and doubles tennis at the same time?
   44 players

3. How many players do you need to play all 4 games at the same time?
   56 players

4. How many games of each sport can be played in 1 hr?
   (Hint: There are 60 min in 1 hr.)
   Soccer: **2 games**
   Softball: **2 games**
   Doubles tennis: **3 games**
   Volleyball: **4 games**

Problem Solving

Name_____

PROBLEM-SOLVING SKILL   PS 1-11
Plan and Solve

Errands Tyreece and his father went to four places on Saturday morning. They went to the grocery store last. They went to the laundromat after they went to the hardware store. They went to the post office first. In what order did Tyreece and his father visit the four places?

Post office	Hardware store	Laundromat	Grocery store

┌─────────────────┐
│ **Plan and Solve** │
└─────────────────┘

Step 1: Choose a strategy.

1. What strategy was used to solve the problem?
   Draw a picture

Step 2: Stuck? Don't give up. Retrace your own steps.

2. What is something you can do if you get stuck?
   Sample answer: You can reread the problem or retrace your steps.

Step 3: Answer the question in the problem.

3. In what order did Tyreece and his father go to the four places?
   From first to last: post office, hardware store, laundromat, and grocery store

4. **Clown Wigs** A clown wants to choose a wig. He has a choice of 3 colors: purple, orange, or green. Each color comes in short or long hair. How many possible wig choices are there?
   6 choices

© Pearson Education, Inc. 3

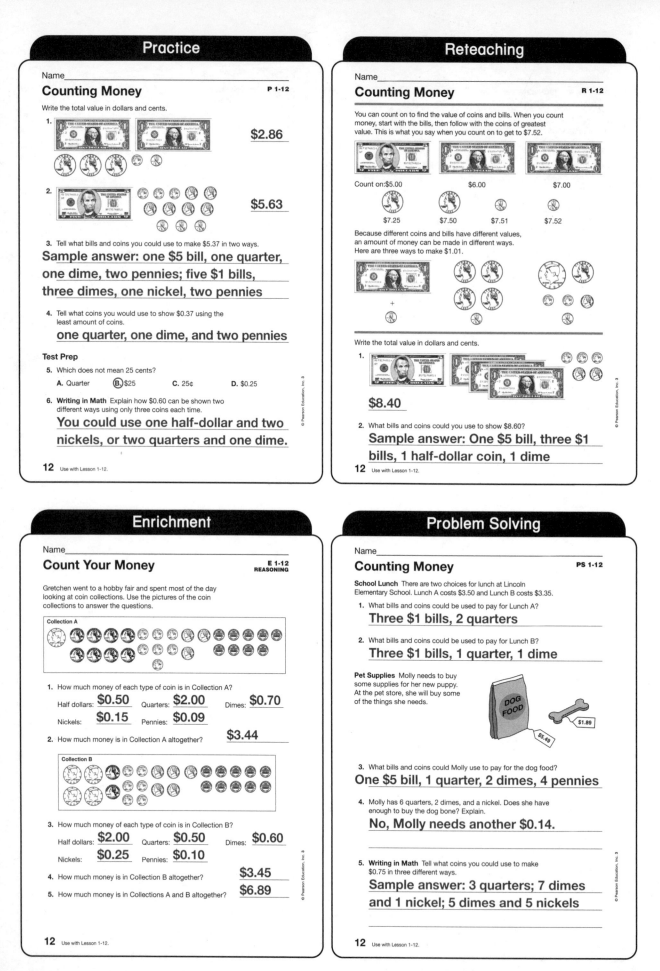

Practice

Name_____

Counting Money   P 1-12

Write the total value in dollars and cents.

1.   **$2.86**

2.   **$5.63**

3. Tell what bills and coins you could use to make $5.37 in two ways.

Sample answer: one $5 bill, one quarter, one dime, two pennies; five $1 bills, three dimes, one nickel, two pennies

4. Tell what coins you would use to show $0.37 using the least amount of coins.

one quarter, one dime, and two pennies

Test Prep

5. Which does not mean 25 cents?

   A. Quarter   **B.** $25   C. 25¢   D. $0.25

6. **Writing in Math** Explain how $0.60 can be shown two different ways using only three coins each time.

You could use one half-dollar and two nickels, or two quarters and one dime.

12   Use with Lesson 1-12.

© Pearson Education, Inc. 3

Reteaching

Name_____

Counting Money   R 1-12

You can count on to find the value of coins and bills. When you count money, start with the bills, then follow with the coins of greatest value. This is what you say when you count on to get to $7.52.

Count on: $5.00 $6.00 $7.00

$7.25 $7.50 $7.51 $7.52

Because different coins and bills have different values, an amount of money can be made in different ways. Here are three ways to make $1.01.

+

Write the total value in dollars and cents.

1.   **$8.40**

2. What bills and coins could you use to show $8.60?

Sample answer: One $5 bill, three $1 bills, 1 half-dollar coin, 1 dime

12   Use with Lesson 1-12.

© Pearson Education, Inc. 3

Enrichment

Name_____

Count Your Money   E 1-12 REASONING

Gretchen went to a hobby fair and spent most of the day looking at coin collections. Use the pictures of the coin collections to answer the questions.

Collection A

1. How much money of each type of coin is in Collection A?

Half dollars: **$0.50**   Quarters: **$2.00**   Dimes: **$0.70**

Nickels: **$0.15**   Pennies: **$0.09**

2. How much money is in Collection A altogether?   **$3.44**

Collection B

3. How much money of each type of coin is in Collection B?

Half dollars: **$2.00**   Quarters: **$0.50**   Dimes: **$0.60**

Nickels: **$0.25**   Pennies: **$0.10**

4. How much money is in Collection B altogether?   **$3.45**

5. How much money is in Collections A and B altogether?   **$6.89**

12   Use with Lesson 1-12.

© Pearson Education, Inc. 3

Problem Solving

Name_____

Counting Money   PS 1-12

School Lunch There are two choices for lunch at Lincoln Elementary School. Lunch A costs $3.50 and Lunch B costs $3.35.

1. What bills and coins could be used to pay for Lunch A?

Three $1 bills, 2 quarters

2. What bills and coins could be used to pay for Lunch B?

Three $1 bills, 1 quarter, 1 dime

Pet Supplies Molly needs to buy some supplies for her new puppy. At the pet store, she will buy some of the things she needs.

DOG FOOD

$1.89

$5.49

3. What bills and coins could Molly use to pay for the dog food?

One $5 bill, 1 quarter, 2 dimes, 4 pennies

4. Molly has 6 quarters, 2 dimes, and a nickel. Does she have enough to buy the dog bone? Explain.

No, Molly needs another $0.14.

5. **Writing in Math** Tell what coins you could use to make $0.75 in three different ways.

Sample answer: 3 quarters; 7 dimes and 1 nickel; 5 dimes and 5 nickels

12   Use with Lesson 1-12.

© Pearson Education, Inc. 3

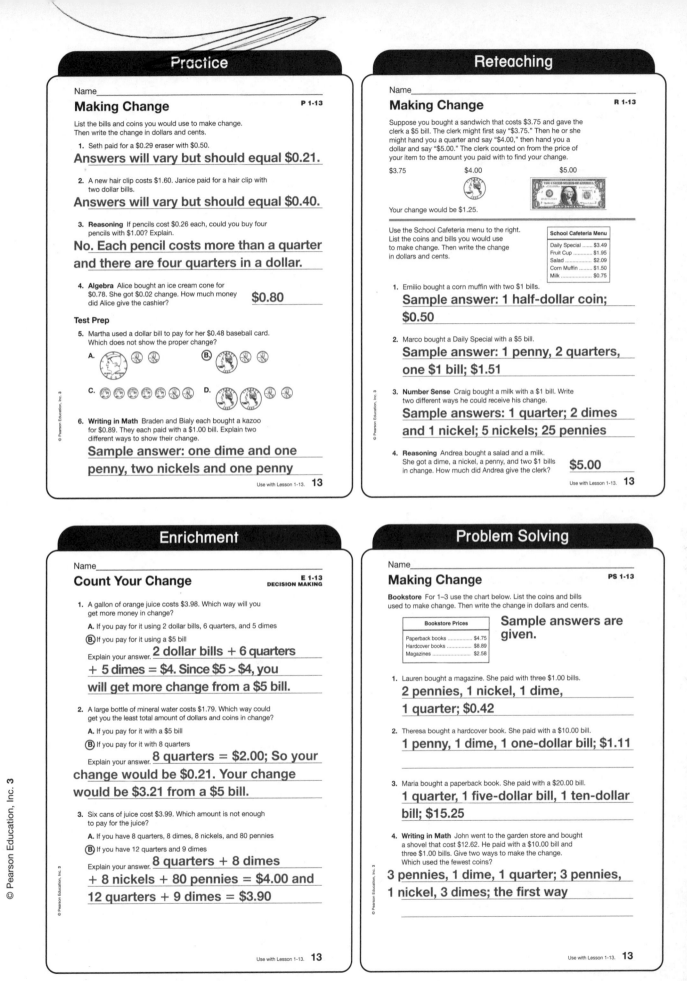

Name_____

Making Change

P 1-13

List the bills and coins you would use to make change.
Then write the change in dollars and cents.

1. Seth paid for a $0.29 eraser with $0.50.

Answers will vary but should equal $0.21.

2. A new hair clip costs $1.60. Janice paid for a hair clip with two dollar bills.

Answers will vary but should equal $0.40.

3. Reasoning If pencils cost $0.26 each, could you buy four pencils with $1.00? Explain.

No. Each pencil costs more than a quarter and there are four quarters in a dollar.

4. Algebra Alice bought an ice cream cone for $0.78. She got $0.02 change. How much money did Alice give the cashier? $0.80

Test Prep

5. Martha used a dollar bill to pay for her $0.48 baseball card. Which does not show the proper change?

A.   B.

C.   D.

6. Writing in Math Braden and Bialy each bought a kazoo for $0.89. They each paid with a $1.00 bill. Explain two different ways to show their change.

Sample answer: one dime and one penny, two nickels and one penny

Use with Lesson 1-13.   **13**

Name_____

Making Change

R 1-13

Suppose you bought a sandwich that costs $3.75 and gave the clerk a $5 bill. The clerk might first say "$3.75." Then he or she might hand you a quarter and say "$4.00," then hand you a dollar and say "$5.00." The clerk counted on from the price of your item to the amount you paid with to find your change.

$3.75 $4.00 $5.00

Your change would be $1.25.

Use the School Cafeteria menu to the right. List the coins and bills you would use to make change. Then write the change in dollars and cents.

School Cafeteria Menu	
Daily Special	$3.49
Fruit Cup	$1.95
Salad	$2.09
Corn Muffin	$1.50
Milk	$0.75

1. Emilio bought a corn muffin with two $1 bills.

Sample answer: 1 half-dollar coin; $0.50

2. Marco bought a Daily Special with a $5 bill.

Sample answer: 1 penny, 2 quarters, one $1 bill; $1.51

3. Number Sense Craig bought a milk with a $1 bill. Write two different ways he could receive his change.

Sample answers: 1 quarter; 2 dimes and 1 nickel; 5 nickels; 25 pennies

4. Reasoning Andrea bought a salad and a milk. She got a dime, a nickel, a penny, and two $1 bills in change. How much did Andrea give the clerk? $5.00

Use with Lesson 1-13.   **13**

Name_____

Count Your Change

E 1-13
DECISION MAKING

1. A gallon of orange juice costs $3.98. Which way will you get more money in change?

A. If you pay for it using 2 dollar bills, 6 quarters, and 5 dimes

B If you pay for it using a $5 bill

Explain your answer. **2 dollar bills + 6 quarters + 5 dimes = $4. Since $5 > $4, you will get more change from a $5 bill.**

2. A large bottle of mineral water costs $1.79. Which way could get you the least total amount of dollars and coins in change?

A. If you pay for it with a $5 bill

B If you pay for it with 8 quarters

Explain your answer. **8 quarters = $2.00; So your change would be $0.21. Your change would be $3.21 from a $5 bill.**

3. Six cans of juice cost $3.99. Which amount is not enough to pay for the juice?

A. If you have 8 quarters, 8 dimes, 8 nickels, and 80 pennies

B If you have 12 quarters and 9 dimes

Explain your answer. **8 quarters + 8 dimes + 8 nickels + 80 pennies = $4.00 and 12 quarters + 9 dimes = $3.90**

Use with Lesson 1-13.   **13**

Name_____

Making Change

PS 1-13

Bookstore For 1–3 use the chart below. List the coins and bills used to make change. Then write the change in dollars and cents.

Bookstore Prices	
Paperback books	$4.75
Hardcover books	$8.89
Magazines	$2.58

Sample answers are given.

1. Lauren bought a magazine. She paid with three $1.00 bills.

2 pennies, 1 nickel, 1 dime, 1 quarter; $0.42

2. Theresa bought a hardcover book. She paid with a $10.00 bill.

1 penny, 1 dime, 1 one-dollar bill; $1.11

3. Maria bought a paperback book. She paid with a $20.00 bill.

1 quarter, 1 five-dollar bill, 1 ten-dollar bill; $15.25

4. Writing in Math John went to the garden store and bought a shovel that cost $12.62. He paid with a $10.00 bill and three $1.00 bills. Give two ways to make the change. Which used the fewest coins?

3 pennies, 1 dime, 1 quarter; 3 pennies, 1 nickel, 3 dimes; the first way

Use with Lesson 1-13.   **13**

© Pearson Education, Inc. 3

PROBLEM-SOLVING SKILL   P 1-14
Look Back and Check

Pumpkin Seeds Ricardo planted 22 pumpkin seeds in hills.
He planted 2 seeds in each hill. How many hills did he plant
seeds in?

Esther solved the Pumpkin Seed problem. Check her work.

| 2 | 2 | 2 | 2 | 2 | 2 | 2 | 2 | 2 | 2 | 2 |
11 hills

1. Did Esther answer the right question? Explain.

   Yes. She told how many hills.

2. Is her work correct? Explain.

   Yes. She counted by twos correctly.

Gardening Tedo makes $0.75 an hour weeding gardens.
How much will he make if he works for four hours?

Joshua solved the Gardening problem. Check his work.

Tedo's Pay	
Hours	Pay
1	$0.75
2	$1.50
3	$2.00
4	$2.75

He will make $2.75 in
four hours.

3. Did Joshua answer the right question? Explain.

   Yes. He figured how
   much Tedo would earn.

4. Is his answer correct? Explain.

   No. He did not add correctly;
   day 3 should be $2.25 and
   day 4 should be $3.00.

PROBLEM-SOLVING SKILL   R 1-14
Look Back and Check

Planting Flowers Max had 120 bulbs to plant in
the fall. There were 48 daffodil bulbs, and the rest
were tulip bulbs. How many tulip bulbs did Max
have to plant?

Paige's Work	
120	
48	?

$120 - 48 = 72$
Max planted 72 tulip bulbs.

You are not finished with the problem until you
look back and check your answer.

Step 1: Check your answer.
Did Paige answer the right question?
Yes, she found the number of tulip bulbs Max
planted.

Step 2: Check your work.
Paige could use place-value patterns to check if
her answer is correct.
She can use a number line to skip count by 10s.

Did Paige use the correct operation?
Paige used subtraction to find the number of tulip
bulbs Max planted.

Camera Sales A camera company
wants to sell at least 130 cameras each
week. One week they sold 38 cameras
with zoom lenses and 86 regular
cameras. Did they sell at least 130
cameras that week?

Martin's Work

I know that 38 can be rounded to 40 and
86 can be rounded to 90.

$40 + 90 = 130$; Yes, the camera store sold
enough cameras.

1. Did Martin answer the right question? Explain.

   Yes, Martin found how many cameras
   were sold that week and compared
   the answer to 130.

2. Is his work correct? Explain.

   No, Martin added incorrectly. The sum
   should be 124, so the store did not sell
   at least 130 cameras that week.

Always Check Your Answer
                                                    E 1-14
                                                    REASONABLENESS

A teacher is planning a field trip to the zoo. A total of 73 people,
including students and adults, will go to the zoo. Each bus has
14 rows. Only 2 people can sit on each side of a row. The
teacher says that 2 buses must be ordered. Is this reasonable?

1. How many people can sit in each row?

   4 people can sit in each row.

2. How many people can sit in 1 bus?

   56 people can sit in one bus.

3. Is the teacher's decision to order 2 buses reasonable? Explain.

   Yes, 56 people can sit in each bus.
   So 2 buses are needed.

Margot feeds her dog 2 cups of food each day. There are
10 cups of dog food in each small bag of dog food. Margot
says that she needs to buy 3 small bags of dog food to feed her
dog for 20 days. Is this reasonable?

4. How many cups of food does Margot feed her dog in 20 days?

   40 cups in 20 days

5. How many cups of dog food are in 3 small bags of dog food?

   30 cups

6. Is Margot's decision to buy 3 small bags of dog food
   reasonable? Explain.

   No, she will only have 30 cups for
   20 days and she needs 40 cups.

PROBLEM-SOLVING SKILL   PS 1-14
Look Back and Check

Leaf Collections Two students have leaf
collections. Frederick has 26 leaves. Yumi has
11 more leaves than Frederick. How many leaves
does Yumi have?

Conchita solved the problem as shown.

26	11		26
37			+ 11
			37

Step 1: Check your answer.

1. Was the correct question answered? Explain.

   Yes; The number of leaves Yumi has
   was found.

Step 2: Check your work.

2. Is the work shown correct? Explain.

   Yes; Conchita added correctly.

3. Did Conchita use the right operation? Explain.

   Yes; Addition was correctly used.

School Store The school store sells school supplies. A pencil
costs $0.35. A ruler sells for a dime more than a pencil. A pen
costs 2 quarters. How much more does a pen cost than a ruler?

Drew solved the problem as shown.

4. Was the correct question answered?
   Explain.

   Yes; Drew found the
   difference.

cost of ruler:
$0.35 - $0.10 = $0.25

cost of pen:
$0.25 + $0.25 = $0.50

difference in cost:
$0.50 - $0.25 = $0.25

5. Was Drew's final answer correct? Explain.

   No; It should have been $0.50 − $0.45
   = $0.05.

Name_____

PROBLEM-SOLVING APPLICATIONS   P 1-15

Great Heights

There are many very tall mountains in the United States. The table shows the heights of a few of the tallest mountains.

Mountains in the United States

Mountain	Height (feet)
Mount McKinley	20,320
Mount Massive	14,421
Mount Rainier	14,410

1. Write the word form of the height of Mount Rainier.

   Fourteen thousand, four hundred ten

2. Write the expanded form of the height of Mount Massive.

   10,000 + 4,000 + 400 + 20 + 1

3. Order the heights from greatest to least.

   20,320; 14,421; 14,410

4. Leonard would like to buy a fruit juice that costs $0.95. Leonard has five coins that equal that amount exactly. Tell what coins Leonard has.

   Three quarters and two dimes

Reba would also like to buy a fruit juice. She decides to buy one for herself and one for her friend Yvonne.

5. The two juices cost $1.90. If Reba pays for them with $10.00, how much change should she receive?   **$8.10**

6. Tell two different ways Reba could receive her change.

   Sample answer: $5 bill, three $1 bills, one dime; eight $1 bills, two nickels

© Pearson Education, Inc. 3

Use with Lesson 1-15. **15**

Name_____

PROBLEM-SOLVING APPLICATIONS   R 1-15

White-Tailed Deer

White-tailed deer that live in the desert weigh less than their eastern relatives. The average weight of an adult male Desert White-tailed deer is about 200 pounds. The females have an average weight of about 125 pounds. Use place value to compare.

200

2 hundreds is greater than 1 hundred.

125

You could say 200 > 125, or 125 < 200.

So, the male white-tailed deer weighs more than the female white-tailed deer.

White-tailed deer can run as fast as 40 miles per hour. Suppose the speed of one deer is recorded at 37 miles per hour. The speed of another deer is recorded at 23 miles per hour.

1. Compare the speeds of the two deer, using the > and < symbols.

   23 < 37; 37 > 23

2. How much faster did the first deer run than the second deer? Show your work and write your answer in a complete sentence.

   37 − 23 = 14; The first deer ran 14 miles per hour faster than the second deer.

3. Nena paid $4.75 to hike in a state park for one day. She paid with a $20 bill. How much change did she receive?

   $15.25

© Pearson Education, Inc. 3

Use with Lesson 1-15. **15**

Name_____

Fish in the Lake

E 1-15
DATA

Number of Fish in the Lake

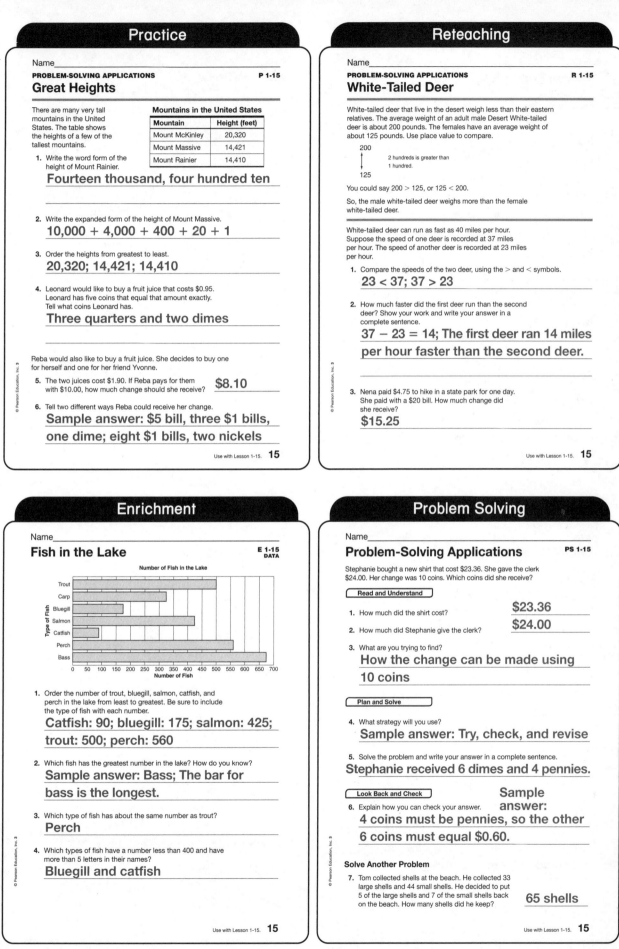

1. Order the number of trout, bluegill, salmon, catfish, and perch in the lake from least to greatest. Be sure to include the type of fish with each number.

   Catfish: 90; bluegill: 175; salmon: 425; trout: 500; perch: 560

2. Which fish has the greatest number in the lake? How do you know?

   Sample answer: Bass; The bar for bass is the longest.

3. Which type of fish has about the same number as trout?

   Perch

4. Which types of fish have a number less than 400 and have more than 5 letters in their names?

   Bluegill and catfish

© Pearson Education, Inc. 3

Use with Lesson 1-15. **15**

Name_____

Problem-Solving Applications

PS 1-15

Stephanie bought a new shirt that cost $23.36. She gave the clerk $24.00. Her change was 10 coins. Which coins did she receive?

Read and Understand

1. How much did the shirt cost?   **$23.36**

2. How much did Stephanie give the clerk?   **$24.00**

3. What are you trying to find?

   How the change can be made using 10 coins

Plan and Solve

4. What strategy will you use?

   Sample answer: Try, check, and revise

5. Solve the problem and write your answer in a complete sentence.

   Stephanie received 6 dimes and 4 pennies.

Look Back and Check

6. Explain how you can check your answer.   **Sample answer: 4 coins must be pennies, so the other 6 coins must equal $0.60.**

Solve Another Problem

7. Tom collected shells at the beach. He collected 33 large shells and 44 small shells. He decided to put 5 of the large shells and 7 of the small shells back on the beach. How many shells did he keep?   **65 shells**

© Pearson Education, Inc. 3

Use with Lesson 1-15. **15**

© Pearson Education, Inc. 3

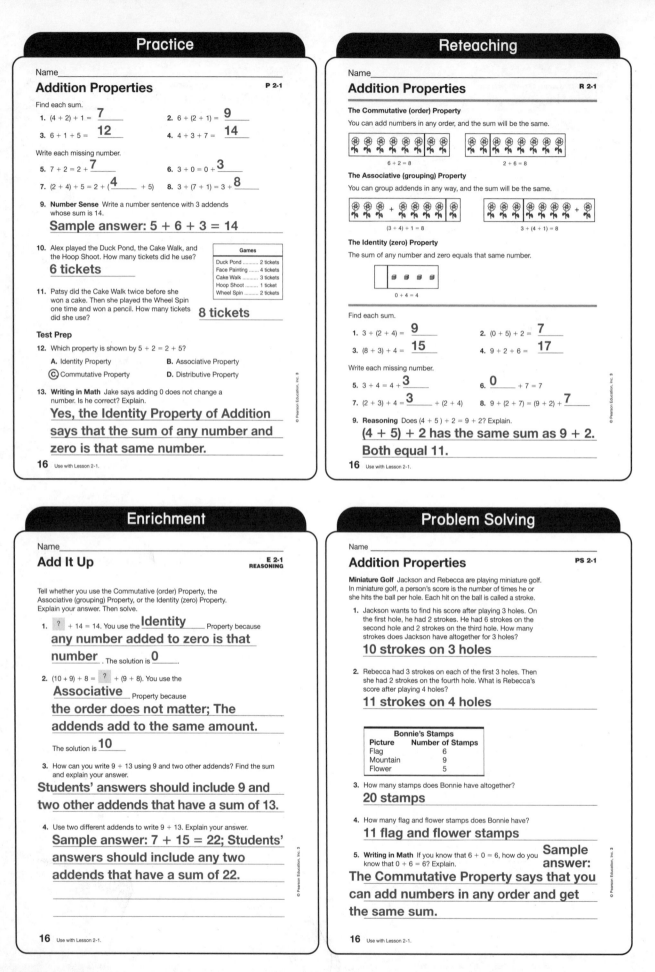

Practice

Name_____

Addition Properties   P 2-1

Find each sum.

1. (4 + 2) + 1 = **7**   2. 6 + (2 + 1) = **9**

3. 6 + 1 + 5 = **12**   4. 4 + 3 + 7 = **14**

Write each missing number.

5. 7 + 2 = 2 + **7**   6. 3 + 0 = 0 + **3**

7. (2 + 4) + 5 = 2 + (**4** + 5)   8. 3 + (7 + 1) = 3 + **8**

9. **Number Sense** Write a number sentence with 3 addends whose sum is 14.

Sample answer: 5 + 6 + 3 = 14

10. Alex played the Duck Pond, the Cake Walk, and the Hoop Shoot. How many tickets did he use?

6 tickets

Games	
Duck Pond	2 tickets
Face Painting	4 tickets
Cake Walk	3 tickets
Hoop Shoot	1 ticket
Wheel Spin	2 tickets

11. Patsy did the Cake Walk twice before she won a cake. Then she played the Wheel Spin one time and won a pencil. How many tickets did she use?

8 tickets

Test Prep

12. Which property is shown by 5 + 2 = 2 + 5?

A. Identity Property   B. Associative Property

C. Commutative Property   D. Distributive Property

13. **Writing in Math** Jake says adding 0 does not change a number. Is he correct? Explain.

Yes, the Identity Property of Addition says that the sum of any number and zero is that same number.

© Pearson Education, Inc. 3

Reteaching

Name_____

Addition Properties   R 2-1

The Commutative (order) Property

You can add numbers in any order, and the sum will be the same.

6 + 2 = 8   2 + 6 = 8

The Associative (grouping) Property

You can group addends in any way, and the sum will be the same.

(3 + 4) + 1 = 8   3 + (4 + 1) = 8

The Identity (zero) Property

The sum of any number and zero equals that same number.

0 + 4 = 4

Find each sum.

1. 3 + (2 + 4) = **9**   2. (0 + 5) + 2 = **7**

3. (8 + 3) + 4 = **15**   4. 9 + 2 + 6 = **17**

Write each missing number.

5. 3 + 4 = 4 + **3**   6. **0** + 7 = 7

7. (2 + 3) + 4 = **3** + (2 + 4)   8. 9 + (2 + 7) = (9 + 2) + **7**

9. **Reasoning** Does (4 + 5) + 2 = 9 + 2? Explain.

(4 + 5) + 2 has the same sum as 9 + 2. Both equal 11.

© Pearson Education, Inc. 3

Enrichment

Name_____

Add It Up   E 2-1
                              REASONING

Tell whether you use the Commutative (order) Property, the Associative (grouping) Property, or the Identity (zero) Property. Explain your answer. Then solve.

1. **?** + 14 = 14. You use the **Identity** Property because **any number added to zero is that number**. The solution is **0**.

2. (10 + 9) + 8 = **?** + (9 + 8). You use the **Associative** Property because **the order does not matter; The addends add to the same amount.**

The solution is **10**.

3. How can you write 9 + 13 using 9 and two other addends? Find the sum and explain your answer.

Students' answers should include 9 and two other addends that have a sum of 13.

4. Use two different addends to write 9 + 13. Explain your answer.

Sample answer: 7 + 15 = 22; Students' answers should include any two addends that have a sum of 22.

© Pearson Education, Inc. 3

Problem Solving

Name_____

Addition Properties   PS 2-1

Miniature Golf Jackson and Rebecca are playing miniature golf. In miniature golf, a person's score is the number of times he or she hits the ball per hole. Each hit on the ball is called a stroke.

1. Jackson wants to find his score after playing 3 holes. On the first hole, he had 2 strokes. He had 6 strokes on the second hole and 2 strokes on the third hole. How many strokes does Jackson have altogether for 3 holes?

10 strokes on 3 holes

2. Rebecca had 3 strokes on each of the first 3 holes. Then she had 2 strokes on the fourth hole. What is Rebecca's score after playing 4 holes?

11 strokes on 4 holes

Bonnie's Stamps	
Picture	Number of Stamps
Flag	6
Mountain	9
Flower	5

3. How many stamps does Bonnie have altogether?

20 stamps

4. How many flag and flower stamps does Bonnie have?

11 flag and flower stamps

5. **Writing in Math** If you know that 6 + 0 = 6, how do you know that 0 + 6 = 6? Explain.

Sample answer: The Commutative Property says that you can add numbers in any order and get the same sum.

© Pearson Education, Inc. 3

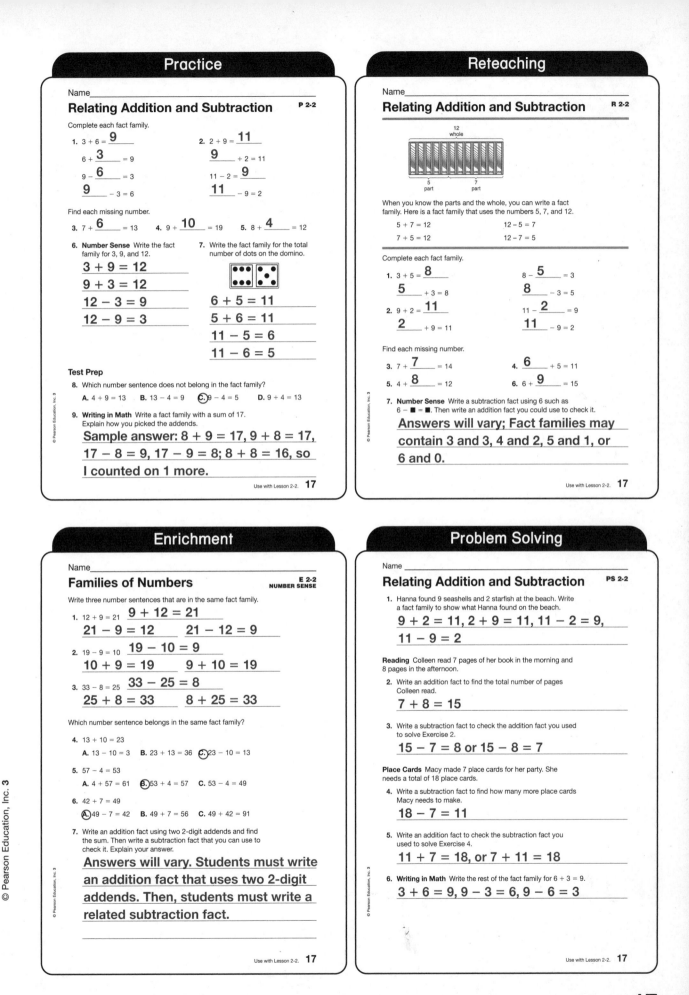

Practice

Name_____

Relating Addition and Subtraction P 2-2

Complete each fact family.

1. 3 + 6 = **9**
   6 + **3** = 9
   9 − **6** = 3
   9 − 3 = 6

2. 2 + 9 = **11**
   9 + 2 = 11
   11 − 2 = **9**
   11 − 9 = 2

Find each missing number.

3. 7 + **6** = 13   4. 9 + **10** = 19   5. 8 + **4** = 12

6. **Number Sense** Write the fact family for 3, 9, and 12.

   3 + 9 = 12
   9 + 3 = 12
   12 − 3 = 9
   12 − 9 = 3

7. Write the fact family for the total number of dots on the domino.

   6 + 5 = 11
   5 + 6 = 11
   11 − 5 = 6
   11 − 6 = 5

Test Prep

8. Which number sentence does not belong in the fact family?

   A. 4 + 9 = 13   **B.** 13 − 4 = 9   **C.** 9 − 4 = 5   **D.** 9 + 4 = 13

9. **Writing in Math** Write a fact family with a sum of 17. Explain how you picked the addends.

   Sample answer: 8 + 9 = 17, 9 + 8 = 17,
   17 − 8 = 9, 17 − 9 = 8; 8 + 8 = 16, so
   I counted on 1 more.

Use with Lesson 2-2. **17**

Reteaching

Name_____

Relating Addition and Subtraction R 2-2

```
            12
           whole
  ┌─────────────────────┐
  └─────────────────────┘
    5              7
   part           part
```

When you know the parts and the whole, you can write a fact family. Here is a fact family that uses the numbers 5, 7, and 12.

   5 + 7 = 12   12 − 5 = 7
   7 + 5 = 12   12 − 7 = 5

Complete each fact family.

1. 3 + 5 = **8**
   5 + 3 = 8

   8 − **5** = 3
   8 − 3 = 5

2. 9 + 2 = **11**
   2 + 9 = 11

   11 − **2** = 9
   11 − 9 = 2

Find each missing number.

3. 7 + **7** = 14   4. **6** + 5 = 11

5. 4 + **8** = 12   6. 6 + **9** = 15

7. **Number Sense** Write a subtraction fact using 6 such as 6 − ■ = ■. Then write an addition fact you could use to check it.

   Answers will vary; Fact families may
   contain 3 and 3, 4 and 2, 5 and 1, or
   6 and 0.

Use with Lesson 2-2. **17**

Enrichment

Name_____

Families of Numbers E 2-2 NUMBER SENSE

Write three number sentences that are in the same fact family.

1. 12 + 9 = 21   9 + 12 = 21
   21 − 9 = 12   21 − 12 = 9

2. 19 − 9 = 10   19 − 10 = 9
   10 + 9 = 19   9 + 10 = 19

3. 33 − 8 = 25   33 − 25 = 8
   25 + 8 = 33   8 + 25 = 33

Which number sentence belongs in the same fact family?

4. 13 + 10 = 23
   A. 13 − 10 = 3   **B.** 23 + 13 = 36   **C.** 23 − 10 = 13

5. 57 − 4 = 53
   A. 4 + 57 = 61   **B.** 53 + 4 = 57   **C.** 53 − 4 = 49

6. 42 + 7 = 49
   A. 49 − 7 = 42   **B.** 49 + 7 = 56   **C.** 49 + 42 = 91

7. Write an addition fact using two 2-digit addends and find the sum. Then write a subtraction fact that you can use to check it. Explain your answer.

   Answers will vary. Students must write
   an addition fact that uses two 2-digit
   addends. Then, students must write a
   related subtraction fact.

Use with Lesson 2-2. **17**

Problem Solving

Name_____

Relating Addition and Subtraction PS 2-2

1. Hanna found 9 seashells and 2 starfish at the beach. Write a fact family to show what Hanna found on the beach.

   9 + 2 = 11, 2 + 9 = 11, 11 − 2 = 9,
   11 − 9 = 2

Reading Colleen read 7 pages of her book in the morning and 8 pages in the afternoon.

2. Write an addition fact to find the total number of pages Colleen read.

   7 + 8 = 15

3. Write a subtraction fact to check the addition fact you used to solve Exercise 2.

   15 − 7 = 8 or 15 − 8 = 7

Place Cards Macy made 7 place cards for her party. She needs a total of 18 place cards.

4. Write a subtraction fact to find how many more place cards Macy needs to make.

   18 − 7 = 11

5. Write an addition fact to check the subtraction fact you used to solve Exercise 4.

   11 + 7 = 18, or 7 + 11 = 18

6. **Writing in Math** Write the rest of the fact family for 6 + 3 = 9.

   3 + 6 = 9, 9 − 3 = 6, 9 − 6 = 3

Use with Lesson 2-2. **17**

Name_____

Find a Rule

P 2-3

Complete each table. Then write a rule for the table.

1.

In	7	13	4	12	0
Out	11	17	8	**16**	**4**

Add 4

2.

In	16	9	4	18	3
Out	13	6	1	**15**	**0**

Subtract 3

3.

In	16	31	27	62	99
Out	26	41	37	**72**	**109**

Add 10

4.

In	57	39	71	22	19
Out	46	28	60	**11**	**8**

Subtract 11

5. **Number Sense** Lako put in 12 and got out 17. Then she put in 1 and got out 6. What rule was she using?

Add 5

6. Elton uses the rule Subtract 6 for his table. If he puts in 18, what will he get out?

12

Test Prep

7. The rule for Stan's table is Subtract 4. Which number should he put in to get out 7?

A. 13   Ⓑ 11   C. 9   D. 3

8. **Writing in Math** Angel says the rule for this table is Add 0. Frank says the rule is Subtract 0. Who is correct? Explain.

In	6	14	31	29	0
Out	6	14	31	29	0

They are both correct, because whether you add or subtract 0, the number remains the same.

Name_____

Find a Rule

R 2-3

In	1	3	2	4	8	6
Out	0	2	1	3	7	

Each number in the top row, **In,** of the table is related to the number in the bottom row, **Out,** by the same rule. The rule in this table is **subtract 1.** A rule explains what to do to the numbers that you put **In,** like those on the top row of the table, to get the numbers that come **Out.**

Complete the table.

1.

In	4	3	1	5	2	7
Out	7	6	4	8	**5**	**10**

2. Write the rule, such as **subtract 1.**

Add 3

Complete each table. Then write a rule for the table.

3.

In	5	20	15	10	30
Out	10	25	20	**15**	**35**

Rule: Add 5

4.

In	16	17	10	13	11
Out	9	10	3	**6**	**4**

Rule: Subtract 7

5. **Writing in Math** The rule is **add 4.** Make your own table with an In and Out pattern to match the rule.

Answers will vary; Check students' work to be sure the rule add 4 is used consistently.

Name_____

Line Rules

E 2-3
NUMBER SENSE

Each type of line stands for a different rule. Follow the directions of the arrows, and use the rules with the line codes to find the missing numbers.

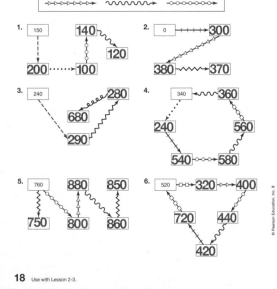

Name_____

Find a Rule

PS 2-3

1. Heather put 14 in her table and got out 6. Then she put in 9 and got out 1. What rule was she using?

Subtract 8

2. The rule for Austin's table is add 12. What number should Austin put in to get out 15?

3

3. The rule for Benji's table is subtract 7. What number should Benji put in to get out 2?

9

John's Garden John planted his flower boxes in an In and Out pattern.

In	✳ ✳ ✳	✳	✳ ✳	✳ ✳ ✳ ✳	✳ ✳ ✳ ✳ ✳ ✳
Out	✳ ✳ ✳ ✳ ✳	✳ ✳ ✳	✳ ✳ ✳ ✳	✳ ✳ ✳ ✳ ✳ ✳	✳ ✳ ✳ ✳ ✳ ✳ ✳ ✳

4. Write the rule for John's In and Out pattern.

Add 2

5. Use the rule to finish drawing the flowers in John's flower boxes.

6. **Writing in Math** Write your own rule for a table. Then write a complete sentence telling what number would come out if you put in 20.

Students should write an addition or a subtraction rule. Check students' work to make sure that they found the correct answer when 20 was put in.

© Pearson Education, Inc. **3**

Name_____

P 2-4
Write a Number Sentence

Write a number sentence. Then solve. Write the answer in a complete sentence.

1. Hector bought 9 lb of dog food. His dog ate 3 lb in one week. How much dog food was left?

$9 - 3 = n$; 6 lb of dog food were left.

2. Janice pulled weeds for 2 hr on Saturday and 1 hr on Sunday. She watered the garden for 1 hr. How much time did she spend pulling weeds?

$1 + 2 = n$; Janice spent 3 hr pulling weeds.

Heather has a new bead kit. It has directions for many different crafts. Help her decide how many beads to use. For 3–6, use the craft chart. Write your answer in a complete sentence.

Craft	Red Beads	Blue Beads
Necklace	10	12
Ankle chain	9	11
Key chain	24	16

3. How many beads in all does Heather need to make an ankle chain?

Heather needs 20 beads.

4. Heather will make a key chain and a necklace. How many blue beads will she use?

Heather will use 28 blue beads.

5. Heather has 17 blue beads. If she makes an ankle chain, how many blue beads will she have left?

Heather will have 6 blue beads left.

6. How many beads in all does Heather need to make a key chain?

Heather needs 40 beads.

Use with Lesson 2-4. **19**

© Pearson Education, Inc. 3

Name_____

R 2-4
Write a Number Sentence

Suppose you do two tasks today. How much money would you earn if you walked the dog and made your bed?

Task	Pay
Walk Dog	$2.00
Do Dishes	$1.25
Make Bed	$1.00

To write a number sentence to solve a problem, follow these four steps:

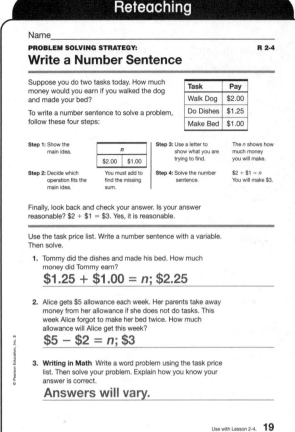

Step 1: Show the main idea.

n	
$2.00	$1.00

Step 2: Decide which operation fits the main idea.

Step 3: Use a letter to show what you are trying to find.

You must add to find the missing sum.

Step 4: Solve the number sentence.

The n shows how much money you will make.

$2 + $1 = n$
You will make $3.

Finally, look back and check your answer. Is your answer reasonable? $2 + $1 = $3. Yes, it is reasonable.

Use the task price list. Write a number sentence with a variable. Then solve.

1. Tommy did the dishes and made his bed. How much money did Tommy earn?

$1.25 + $1.00 = n$; $2.25

2. Alice gets $5 allowance each week. Her parents take away money from her allowance if she does not do tasks. This week Alice forgot to make her bed twice. How much allowance will Alice get this week?

$5 - $2 = n$; $3

3. **Writing in Math** Write a word problem using the task price list. Then solve your problem. Explain how you know your answer is correct.

Answers will vary.

Use with Lesson 2-4. **19**

© Pearson Education, Inc. 3

Name_____

Sal's Super Sale

E 2-4
DECISION MAKING

Sal's Superstore had a weekend sale with discounts on many store items. The table shows the price of sale items (including tax).

Sal's Super Sale	
Paperback books:	$3.00
Computer games:	$21.00
100-minute calling cards:	$19.00
Hardcover books:	$11.00
Running shoes:	$49.00

1. Angelo had $35 to spend. He bought a 100-minute calling card and 2 paperback books. How much money does he have left?

$10

Carla bought 2 items. She gave her money to the cashier and received $1 in change.

2. Which 2 items did Carla buy?

Paperback books and computer games; paperback books and hardcover books

3. How much money did she give the cashier? Explain.

The amount must be $1 more than the total cost for Exercise 2; $24, $14.

4. Juan bought 2 computer games and 1 other item. What is the least amount that the items could cost altogether? Explain your answer.

$45 for 2 computer games and a paperback book

5. Write a word problem using the items from Sal's Super Sale. Solve your problem. Then explain your answer.

Check students' problems, answers, and explanations.

Use with Lesson 2-4. **19**

© Pearson Education, Inc. 3

Name_____

PS 2-4
Write a Number Sentence

Baseball Simon bought a baseball for $4, a bat for $12, and a cap for $3. How much money did he spend altogether?

Read and Understand

1. How much did the baseball cost? $4

2. How much did the bat cost? $12

3. How much did the cap cost? $3

4. What are you trying to find?

How much money Simon spent

Plan and Solve

5. Which operation will you use? Addition

6. Write a number sentence. $4 + $12 + $3 = n$

7. Solve the number sentence. $n = 19$

8. Write the answer in a complete sentence.

Simon spent $19 altogether.

Look Back and Check

9. Explain how you can check your answer.

Sample answer: Use estimation, 4 + 10 + 3 = 17

Solve Another Problem

10. The length of Naoko's bedroom is 8 ft shorter than the length of the living room. If the living room is 21 ft long, what is the length of Naoko's bedroom?

13 ft

Use with Lesson 2-4. **19**

© Pearson Education, Inc. 3

Name_____

Mental Math: Break Apart Numbers

P 2-5

Find each sum using mental math.

1. $12 + 36 =$ __48__
2. $42 + 37 =$ __79__
3. $15 + 23 =$ __38__
4. $17 + 42 =$ __59__
5. $84 + 11 =$ __95__
6. $52 + 35 =$ __87__

7. **Number Sense** Ashton broke apart a number into $30 + 7$. What number did she start with? __37__

For 8 and 9, use the menu and mental math.

8. How much would an Orange Smoothie and a Peach Parfait cost?

$0.77

Drink Menu	
Strawberry Fizz	$0.45
Orange Smoothie	$0.31
Banana Blast	$0.11
Apple Cider Slush	$0.24
Peach Parfait	$0.46

9. Sarah wants two Apple Cider Slushes. How much will she pay?

$0.48

Test Prep

10. To break apart the number 42, which two numbers would you use?

 A. $40 + 20$ **B.** $35 + 3$ Ⓒ $40 + 2$ **D.** $20 + 4$

11. **Writing in Math** Explain how you would use mental math to add $14 + 71$.

Break apart the numbers. Add the tens: $10 + 70 = 80$. Then add the ones: $4 + 1 = 5$. Then add the tens and ones: $80 + 5 = 85$.

© Pearson Education, Inc. 3

Name_____

Mental Math: Break Apart Numbers

R 2-5

You can break apart numbers to make them easier to add mentally.

Find $31 + 45$ using mental math. There are two ways.

First, break apart the numbers into tens and ones.

	tens		ones
$31 =$	30	$+$	1
$45 =$	40	$+$	5

Add the tens together: $30 + 40 = 70$.

Add the ones together: $1 + 5 = 6$.

Finally, add the tens and the ones together: $70 + 6 = 76$.

So, $31 + 45 = 76$.

or

Break apart only one number.

$45 = 40 + 5$

Then add $40 + 31 = 71$.

Next add the 5 to 71:

$71 + 5 = 76$

So, $31 + 45 = 76$.

Find each sum using mental math.

1. $52 + 12 =$ __64__
2. $24 + 71 =$ __95__
3. $36 + 43 =$ __79__
4. $47 + 50 =$ __97__
5. $54 + 23 =$ __77__
6. $24 + 72 =$ __96__
7. $33 + 46 =$ __79__
8. $22 + 64 =$ __86__
9. $34 + 53 =$ __87__

10. **Number Sense** To add $32 + 56$, Juanita first added $32 + 50$. What numbers should she add next? __$82 + 6$__

11. In June, 46 cars were sold. There were 12 cars sold in April. How many more cars were sold in June than in April?

34 more cars

© Pearson Education, Inc. 3

Name_____

Break It Up and Add

E 2-5
NUMBER SENSE

1. Which choice helps the most to solve $43 + 8$?

 A. think of 8 as $4 + 4$

 B. think of 43 as $44 - 1$

 Ⓒ think of 8 as $10 - 2$

 Explain.

 Add $43 + 10 = 53$, then subtract 2.

 $43 + 8 =$ __51__

2. Which choice helps the most to solve $67 + 29$?

 A. think of 67 as $63 + 4$

 Ⓑ think of 29 as $30 - 1$

 C. think of 29 as $25 + 4$

 Explain.

 Add $67 + 30 = 97$, then subtract 1.

 $67 + 29 =$ __98__

3. Which choice does *not* help you solve $63 + 28$ using mental math?

 A. think of 63 as $60 + 3$

 B. think of 28 as $30 - 2$

 Ⓒ think of 28 as $25 + 3$

 Explain.

 You should find the sum using tens. 25 is not a tens number.

 $63 + 28 =$ __91__

© Pearson Education, Inc. 3

Name_____

Mental Math: Break Apart Numbers

PS 2-5

America's Garbage Each year Americans throw away millions of pounds of garbage. The table shows what type of garbage might be in 100 lb of garbage.

100 Pounds of Garbage in the United States	
Paper products	36 lb
Yard waste	20 lb
Food waste	9 lb
Metal	9 lb
Glass	8 lb
Plastic	7 lb
Other waste	11 lb

1. Of the 100 lb of garbage, how many pounds are paper products and yard waste? **56 lb**

2. How much does the glass and metal garbage weigh? **17 lb**

3. How much does the plastic, glass, metal, and paper products garbage weigh? **60 lb**

4. Explain how you could use mental math to figure out the combined weight of all of the garbage listed on the table.

 Sample answer: Add the one-digit numbers until they are two-digit numbers. Then add the two-digit numbers by breaking them apart.

5. **Writing in Math** Explain how to solve $28 + 13$ using mental math.

 Sample answer: Add the tens: $20 + 10 = 30$. Then add the ones: $8 + 3 = 11$. $30 + 11 = 41$, so $28 + 13 = 41$.

© Pearson Education, Inc. 3

Name_____

Mental Math: Using Tens to Add

P 2-6

Find each sum using mental math.

1. $72 + 19 =$ **91**

2. $36 + 28 =$ **64**

3. $14 + 26 =$ **40**

4. $17 + 49 =$ **66**

5. $4 + 27 =$ **31**

6. $55 + 37 =$ **92**

7. **Number Sense** Jonah wants to add $43 + 19$.
He added $43 + 20$. What step should he take next? **Subtract 1**

In the United States House of Representatives, the number of representatives a state has depends on the number of people living in the state. Use mental math to find each answer.

State	Representatives
California	52
New York	31
Texas	30
Florida	23

8. How many representatives do California and Texas have altogether?

82 representatives

9. How many representatives do Florida and New York have altogether?

54 representatives

10. **Reasonableness** Miles says $47 + 36$ is the same as $50 + 33$. Is this reasonable? Explain.

Yes. $36 = 30 + 3 + 3$; $47 + 3 = 50$; $50 + 30 + 3 = 83$

Test Prep

11. Find the sum of $27 + 42$ using mental math.

Ⓐ 69　　**B.** 67　　**C.** 62　　**D.** 15

12. **Writing in Math** How does knowing $30 + 7 = 37$ help you find $37 + 23$?

You can add $30 + 7 + 23$ to find the answer: 60.

Use with Lesson 2-6. **21**

© Pearson Education, Inc. 3

Name_____

Mental Math: Using Tens to Add

R 2-6

To add mentally, you can break numbers apart to make a ten.

For example, to find $26 + 17$, you can break the numbers apart like this:

A.
$26 + 17$

B. You can break 17 into $4 + 13$.
$4 + 13$

C. Add $26 + 4 = 30$.
$26 + 4 = 30$

D. Then add $30 + 13 = 43$.
$30 + 13 = 43$

So, $26 + 17 = 43$.

To find $46 + 9$, you could first find $46 + 10 = 56$. Then you can subtract 1 from the answer. $56 - 1 = 55$. This is the same sum as $46 + 9$.

Find each sum using mental math.

1. $67 + 9 =$ **76**

2. $35 + 8 =$ **43**

3. $46 + 7 =$ **53**

4. $25 + 49 =$ **74**

5. $37 + 56 =$ **93**

6. $87 + 13 =$ **100**

7. **Reasonableness** Marcie says, "To find $87 + 7$, I can find $87 + 10$ and then subtract 3." Do you agree? Explain?

Marcie's strategy is correct. She added 3 to 7 to get 10. Then she needs to subtract 3 after she adds $87 + 10$. Both expressions equal 94.

Use with Lesson 2-6. **21**

© Pearson Education, Inc. 3

Name_____

Adding Stories

E 2-6
MENTAL MATH

The table at the right shows the number of stories for the five tallest buildings in New Orleans, Louisiana.

Use mental math to solve each problem.

Building	Number of Stories
Place St. Charles	53
One Shell Square	51
Plaza Tower	45
Energy Centre	39
LL&E Tower	36

1. How many stories would each building have if 17 stories were added?

Place St. Charles: **70**　One Shell Square: **68**

Plaza Tower: **62**　Energy Centre: **56**

LL&E Tower: **53**

2. What is the total number of stories in Place St. Charles and LL&E Tower?

89 stories

3. What is the total number of stories in One Shell Square and Plaza Tower?

96 stories

4. The owners of the Place St. Charles plan to add 10 stories, and the owners of One Shell Square plan to add 14 stories. After the new stories are built, which building will have the greatest number of stories?

One Shell Square

5. If the number of stories in Energy Centre were doubled, would the building have a greater number of stories than LL&E Tower and Plaza Tower combined?

No, it would have 78 stories and the 2 buildings would have 81 stories.

Use with Lesson 2-6. **21**

© Pearson Education, Inc. 3

Name_____

Mental Math: Using Tens to Add

PS 2-6

1. How many feet of space would you need for a 16 ft long saltwater crocodile to sit before a 27 ft long anaconda? **43 ft**

2. An elephant can run at a speed of 25 mi per hour. A wild turkey can travel 15 mi per hour. If the two animals started at the same point and ran in opposite directions for one hour, how many miles apart would they be? **40 mi**

Fliers Odie handed out fliers advertising the school fair. He kept track of the number of fliers he handed out during the week.

Number of Fliers
Monday—37
Tuesday—61
Wednesday—49
Thursday—26
Friday—38

3. How many fliers did Odie hand out on Wednesday and Thursday? **75 fliers**

4. How many fliers did Odie hand out on Monday, Thursday, and Friday? **101 fliers**

5. Odie handed out 64 fliers over the course of two days. Which two days were they?

Thursday and Friday

6. **Writing in Math** Use Odie's table to write your own problem that can be solved using mental math. Write the answer to your problem in a complete sentence.

Check students' problems and answers. The problem should be solved by mental math and the answer should be written in a complete sentence.

Use with Lesson 2-6. **21**

© Pearson Education, Inc. 3

Estimating Sums

P 2-7

Round to the nearest hundred to estimate each sum.

1. 236 + 492 $200 + 500 = 700$

2. 126 + 223 $100 + 200 = 300$

Round to the nearest ten to estimate each sum.

3. 18 + 36 $20 + 40 = 60$

4. 145 + 239 $150 + 240 = 390$

Use any method to estimate each sum. **Sample answers.**

5. 167 + 449 $170 + 450 = 620$

6. 387 + 285 $400 + 300 = 700$

7. Number Sense April needs to estimate the sum of 427 and 338. Should she round to the nearest ten or to the nearest hundred to get the closer answer? Explain.

Rounding to the nearest ten is closer because 427 is closer to 430 than to 400 and 338 is closer to 340 than to 300.

8. The flower shop just received a shipment of 432 roses. They need to fill an order for 273 roses. Use any method to estimate how many roses they will have left.

Sample answer: 430 − 270 = 160

Test Prep

9. Which of the following shows estimating 287 + 491 by using compatible numbers?

A. 200 + 500   **B.** 300 + 500   **C.** 280 + 400   Ⓓ 290 + 490

10. Writing in Math How can you use rounding to estimate 331 + 193?

I can round each number to the nearest ten: 330 + 190 = 520.

Estimating Sums

R 2-7

Suppose your class is saving 275 cereal box tops for a fundraising project. Your class has 138 Fruity Cereal box tops and 152 Bran Cereal box tops. Does your class have enough box tops for the project? Since you only need to know if you have enough, you can estimate.

Here are some ways you can estimate.

Rounding: Round each addend to the nearest hundred or to the nearest ten. Then add and compare.

Round to the nearest *hundred*.

$152 \Rightarrow 200$
$+138 \Rightarrow 100$
$= 300$

Since 300 > 275, you have enough.

Round to the nearest *ten*.

$152 \Rightarrow 150$
$+138 \Rightarrow 140$
$= 290$

Since 290 > 275, you have enough.

Front-end estimation: Use the front digit of each number and zeroes for the rest.

$152 \Rightarrow 100$
$+138 \Rightarrow 100$
$= 200 < 275$

Compatible numbers: Use numbers that are close but easy to add.

$152 \Rightarrow 150$
$+138 \Rightarrow 140$
$= 290 > 275$

Round to the nearest ten to estimate each sum.

1. 37 + 117   **160**   **2.** 42 + 98   **140**

Round to the nearest hundred to estimate each sum.

3. 240 + 109   **300**   **4.** 87 + 588   **700**

5. Reasonableness Sun-Yi estimated 270 + 146 and got 300. Is this reasonable? Explain.

No. Rounding by tens would give an estimate of 420 (270 + 150). Rounding by hundreds would give an estimate of 400 (300 + 100).

Picture Puzzles

E 2-7
VISUAL THINKING

Write a sentence to tell how you would solve each puzzle. Then draw a picture that shows each new arrangement.

1. The triangle of marbles is pointing to the left. Move only 2 marbles to make the triangle point to the right.

Sample answer: Move 4 above 1 and 6 below 1.

2. the toothpick house faces right. Move only 1 toothpick to make the house face left.

Sample answer: Move 3 to connect 2 and 6.

3. The 12 toothpicks make 4 diamonds. Remove only 4 toothpicks to make 2 diamonds that are the same size.

Sample answer: Remove 5, 6, 7, 8.

Estimating Sums

PS 2-7

Cars Passing Sanchez lives on a busy street. One morning he counted 246 cars that went by his apartment building in 1 hour. That afternoon he counted 187 cars that went by in 1 hour.

1. Estimate to the nearest hundred the number of cars that went by the apartment building during the 2 hours Sanchez was counting.   **400 cars**

2. Estimate to the nearest ten the number of cars that went by the apartment building.   **440 cars**

Animal Species Many different animals live on Earth. The chart shows the number of species of some animals.

Animal Species

Animal Group	Number of Species
Birds of prey	307
Parrots	353
Sharks	330
Whales and dolphins	83

3. Estimate the number of species of birds on the chart to the nearest hundred.

700 species of birds

4. Estimate the number of species of sharks, whales, and dolphins to the nearest hundred.

400 species of sharks, whales, and dolphins

5. Writing in Math Use the Animal Species chart to write your own problem using estimation. Write the answer in a complete sentence.

Students' problems should use estimation.

Name_____

Overestimates and Underestimates

Estimate each sum by rounding. Then tell whether each estimate is an overestimate or an underestimate.

1. $17 + 49$ $20 + 50 = 70$; Overestimate

2. $71 + 13$ $70 + 10 = 80$; Underestimate

3. $818 + 139$ $820 + 140 = 960$; Overestimate

4. $162 + 72$ $160 + 70 = 230$; Underestimate

Grand Rapids — Lansing — Detroit — Kalamazoo — St. Joseph
63 mi, 84 mi, 135 mi, 49 mi

5. Estimate the distance from Grand Rapids to Detroit by rounding.

$60 + 80 = 140$ mi

6. Did you underestimate or overestimate?

Underestimate

7. Stanton needs to travel from Detroit to St. Joseph. He says he will drive more than 190 mi. Do you agree? Explain.

No. $140 + 50 = 190$; I overestimated, so Stanton will drive less than 190 mi.

Test Prep

8. Which is an underestimate?

A. $89 + 139$ is about 230.
B. $104 + 212$ is about 310.
C. $58 + 77$ is about 140.
D. $437 + 15$ is about 460.

9. **Writing in Math** Is it reasonable to say the sum of 146 and 149 is less than 300? Explain.

Yes, because $150 + 150 = 300$ and I overestimated, the sum is less than 300.

Name_____

Overestimates and Underestimates

Overestimate: An overestimate happens when you round up.

Gina has 36 tomato plants and 57 pepper plants. If she has 100 pots, does she have enough for the plants? Round to the nearest ten to estimate the sum.

     36 rounds up to 40
+ 57 rounds up to 60
              100   She has enough pots.

Each addend was rounded *up* so the estimated sum is *greater than* the actual sum. It is an overestimate.

Underestimates: An underestimate happens when you round down.

Gerry is in charge of seating for the school show. She has set up 34 seats in the center and 23 seats on each side. She is expecting 70 people. Has she set up enough chairs? Round to the nearest ten to estimate the sum.

     34 rounds down to 30
     23 rounds down to 20
+ 23 rounds down to 20
             70 seats is the estimated sum.

Each addend was rounded *down*, so the estimated sum, 70, is *less than* the actual sum. It is an underestimate.

Estimate each sum by rounding to the nearest ten. Then tell whether each estimate is an overestimate or an underestimate.

1. $36 + 47$ 90; Overestimate

2. $11 + 44$ 50; Underestimate

3. **Number Sense** Liz wants to send two packages. The shipping cost for one package will be $42, and the other will cost $38. Liz has $100. Estimate the total cost of shipping the packages. Does Liz have enough money? Explain.

Yes. Liz has $100, and the estimate to mail her packages is $80.

Name_____

Art Supplies

The Art Club is planning to buy new supplies. There are 12 students in the club. The list at the right shows the different packages and the price for each package. The club only plans to buy 2 packages from the list.

Supply Packages	Price
1 dozen paintbrushes	$24
6 watercolor sets	$54
2 dozen pads of paper	$72
4 sets of colored pencils	$18
12 tubes of oil paint	$33

1. Which two packages on the list are the least expensive?

Paintbrushes and colored pencils

2. Which two packages are the most expensive?

Watercolor sets and paper

3. Which two packages on the list cost about $40 altogether?

Paintbrushes and colored pencils

4. Which two packages on the list cost about $75 altogether?

Watercolor sets and oil paint

5. Besides the cost of the items, what are two questions that the Art Club should ask before purchasing supplies?

Sample answers: What supplies does the club need the most? What supplies do members use the most?

6. Without a spending limit, which two packages should the Art Club buy? Explain your answer.

Sample answer: Paper and watercolor sets; They contain the most supplies.

Name_____

Overestimates and Underestimates

Sports Day Pine Wood School is having an all-sports day. Any student can gather members to form teams for the sporting events. A list of the events and the number of players needed is posted on the gymnasium door.

All-Sports Day

Sport	Number of Players
Field hockey	11
Australian football	18
Rugby	15
Soccer	11
Volleyball	6

1. Frank wants to enter the soccer and field hockey events. He estimates he will need 20 people to form the 2 teams. Will that be enough? Explain.

No; Frank rounded down, and he needs more than 20 people.

2. Sheila plans to form teams for Australian football and rugby. Estimate the number of players she will need to find.

Sample answer: About 35 players

3. Payton found 30 people for teams. Estimate to find if that is enough for one Australian football team and one volleyball team.

Yes, 30 is enough.

4. **Writing in Math** Use the All-Sports Day chart above and explain how you could estimate the number of students needed to form one of each team.

Sample answer: Round each number to the nearest 10, and then add them.

Mental Math:
Using Tens to Subtract

Find each difference using mental math.

1. $63 - 19 = $ __44__   **2.** $47 - 18 = $ __29__

3. $72 - 38 = $ __34__   **4.** $61 - 25 = $ __36__

5. $84 - 29 = $ __55__   **6.** $80 - 11 = $ __69__

7. Number Sense Gillian started solving $88 - 29$.
This is what she did.

$$88 - 29 = ?$$
$$88 - 30 = 58$$

What should she do next?   __Add 1.__

8. Mary has $84 in her bank account. She withdraws $67. Use mental math to find out how much she has left in her bank account.

__$17__

9. Tiffany needs 63 tiles for her art mosaic. She has already collected 46 tiles. Use mental math to find how many more tiles she needs.

__17 tiles__

Test Prep

10. To solve $35 - 19$, Jack used $35 - 20$ and then

Ⓐ added 1.   **B.** subtracted 1.   **C.** subtracted 9.   **D.** added 9.

11. Writing in Math Tell how to find $81 - 36$ using mental math.

__Think $81 - 40 = 41$. Then add 4__
__because $36 + 4 = 40$. $41 + 4 = 45$, so__
__$81 - 36 = 45$.__

Mental Math:
Using Tens to Subtract

You can change numbers to tens to make subtraction problems easier.

There are two ways we can subtract $42 - 28$.

One way to make this problem simpler is to change 28 to 30, because it is easier to subtract 30 from 42.

Then, add 2 to the answer because you subtracted 2 too many.
$42 - 28 = (42 - 30) + 2 = 14$

Another way is to add the same amount to each number.

$$42 \quad - \quad 28$$
$$\Downarrow \qquad \Downarrow$$
$$+2 \quad +2$$
$$\Downarrow \qquad \Downarrow$$
$$44 \quad - \quad 30 = 14$$

So, $42 - 28 = 14$.

Find each difference using mental math.

1. $32 - 17 = $ __15__   **2.** $51 - 46 = $ __5__   **3.** $42 - 17 = $ __25__

4. $29 - 17 = $ __12__   **5.** $63 - 56 = $ __7__   **6.** $78 - 19 = $ __59__

7. $94 - 18 = $ __76__   **8.** $55 - 33 = $ __22__   **9.** $87 - 24 = $ __63__

10. Number Sense To solve $39 - 27$, Anika changed it to $(40 - 27) + 1$. Is this a simpler problem? Explain.

__No. $(40 - 27) + 1$ is not easy to do__
__mentally. $42 - 30$ is easier.__

Timing Tasks

One weekend Gloria recorded the amount of time it took her to do her weekend tasks. Use the times she recorded in the table to answer the questions. Remember: There are 60 min in 1 hr.

Weekend Task	Minutes to Complete
Clean room	58
Rake lawn	34
Pull weeds	29
Practice piano	31
Do homework	73
Walk dog	27

1. About how many hours does it take Gloria to clean her room?

__About 1 hr__

2. Which tasks take Gloria about $\frac{1}{2}$ hr to complete?

__Rake the lawn; pull weeds; practice__
__piano; walk dog__

3. Which task takes Gloria more than 1 hr to complete?

__Do homework__

4. Which tasks take more than $\frac{1}{2}$ hr but less than 1 hr to complete?

__Clean room; rake lawn; practice piano__

5. List the greatest number of tasks that Gloria can complete in 2 hr.

__Rake lawn; pull weeds; practice piano;__
__walk dog__

6. About how many hours does it take Gloria to complete all of her weekend tasks?

__About 4 hr__

Mental Math: Using Tens to Subtract

The table shows how fast some animals can run.

Speeds of Animals

Animal	Speed (miles per hour)
Cheetah	65
Squirrel	12
Giraffe	32
Coyote	43
Rabbit	35
Wild turkey	15

1. How much faster is a giraffe than a squirrel?

__20 mi per hour faster__

2. How much slower is a rabbit than a coyote?

__8 mi per hour slower__

3. The difference in speed between a rabbit and another animal is 20 mi per hour. What is the other animal? __Wild turkey__

4. What is the difference in speed between the fastest and slowest animal on the chart? __53 mph__

5. Writing in Math Explain how you would use mental math to solve $43 - 18$.

__Sample answer: You would add 2 to__
__both numbers so you could subtract__
__20 instead of 18: $45 - 20 = 25$.__

Name_____

Mental Math: P 2-10
Counting On to Subtract

Count on to find each difference mentally.

1. $43 - 16 =$ **27**   2. $81 - 67 =$ **14**

3. $72 - 16 =$ **56**   4. $21 - 9 =$ **12**

5. $33 - 18 =$ **15**   6. $65 - 12 =$ **53**

Algebra Count on to find the value of the missing number.

7. $37 + x = 59$ **22**   8. $17 + n = 72$ **55**   9. $48 + y = 67$ **19**

Victoria has saved 73 tokens from the toy store. The tokens can be turned in for prizes. Victoria checked the toy store's Web site to see what prizes were available. The chart at the right shows her choices.

Flying disc	19 tokens
Beach ball	26 tokens
Sunglasses	39 tokens
Beach towel	58 tokens

10. How many tokens will Victoria have left if she gets the beach towel?

15 tokens

11. How many tokens would Victoria have left if she got the beach ball and the sunglasses?

8 tokens

Test Prep

12. Which subtraction problem could be solved by thinking of

$28 + \_\_\_ = 45$?

A. $28 - 45$ (B.) $45 - 28$ C. $28 - 9$ D. $45 - 10$

13. **Writing in Math** Write a missing addend addition sentence to help solve $78 - 49$. Explain how you would use it.

49 + ■ = 78; From 49, count up to the next 10. From 50, count by tens to 70. Then count up to 78. I counted 1 + 20 + 8 = 29.

Use with Lesson 2-10. **25**

Name_____

Mental Math: R 2-10
Counting On to Subtract

Erica wanted to find a new way to subtract mentally. She wondered if counting on would help her to subtract. When you count on, you change a subtraction problem into an addition problem that is missing an addend.

Erica thought that to find $86 - 47$, she would change the problem into $47 + ■ = 86$.

First, she would count by ones up to the nearest ten: $47 + 3 = 50$.

Then, she would count by tens up to 80: $50 + 30 = 80$.

Then she counted up to 86: $80 + 6 = 86$.

Finally Erica added all the numbers she counted up by: $3 + 30 + 6 = 39$.

So, $86 - 47 = 39$.

Count on to find each difference mentally.

1. $60 - 32 =$ **28**   2. $48 - 12 =$ **36**   3. $53 - 17 =$ **36**

4. $69 - 24 =$ **45**   5. $76 - 37 =$ **39**   6. $42 - 28 =$ **14**

7. $96 - 85 =$ **11**   8. $56 - 28 =$ **28**   9. $84 - 69 =$ **15**

Algebra Count on to find the value of the missing number.

10. $37 +$ **22** $= 59$ 11. $76 +$ **14** $= 90$ 12. $48 +$ **17** $= 65$

13. **Number Sense** Rob wants to spend $60 on birthday presents for Samir. Rob buys Samir a hat that costs $37. How much money does Rob have left to buy Samir another birthday present? Write the number sentence you would use to solve the problem. Then solve.

$60 − $37 = n; Rob has $23 left.

Use with Lesson 2-10. **25**

Name_____

Number Patterns E 2-10
NUMBER SENSE

The students at Parker Elementary School raised money to help pay for new musical instruments. The music store where they purchased the instruments donated $10 for every $1 that the students raised. The students' goal was to raise $700. Complete the chart and use it to answer the questions below.

Group	Week 1	Week 2	Week 3	Week 4	Week 5
Students	$10	$20	$25	$15	$5
Music Store	$100	$200	$250	$150	$50

1. How many weeks did it take the students to reach their goal?

4 weeks

2. At the end of 5 weeks, how much money did the students raise?

$75

3. How much did the music store donate in total?

$750

4. How much money, including the donations from the music store, was raised altogether after 5 weeks?

$825

5. Make a new chart to show how the students could have raised $700 in 3 weeks by changing the amounts raised in the first and second weeks.

Sample answer:

Group	Week 1	Week 2	Week 3
Students	$25	$25	$20
Music store	$250	$250	$200

Use with Lesson 2-10. **25**

Name_____

Mental Math: Counting On to PS 2-10
Subtract

1. Polly has made 16 posters for back-to-school night. She needs 32 posters altogether. How many more does she need to make?

16 posters

2. Austin is only allowed to watch 45 min of television each day. One afternoon, he watched 36 min of television. How many more minutes of television is Austin allowed to watch for the rest of the day?

9 min

3. Manuel plans to read a total of 50 pages of his book on Monday and Tuesday. He read 29 pages on Monday. How many more pages does he need to read on Tuesday?

21 pages

4. To solve $84 - 43$, Davis thought of $43 + 7 = 50$. Explain what Davis should do to finish solving the problem.

Next, Davis can find 84 − 50 = 34. Then he should add 7: 34 + 7 = 41, so 84 − 43 = 41.

5. Write two number sentences with a difference of 17.

Sample answer: 18 − 1 = 17; 20 − 3 = 17

6. Write two number sentences with a difference of 33.

Sample answer: 34 − 1 = 33; 43 − 10 = 33

7. **Writing in Math** Explain how you would count on to find $62 - 39$.

Sample answer: You would count on 39 + 1 = 40, and 40 + 22 = 62. 22 + 1 = 23, so 62 − 39 = 23.

Use with Lesson 2-10. **25**

Estimating Differences

P 2-11

Round to the nearest hundred to estimate each difference.

1. 236 − 119 **100**   **2.** 558 − 321 **300**

Round to the nearest ten to estimate each difference.

3. 677 − 421 **260**   **4.** 296 − 95 **200**

Use any method to estimate each difference. **Sample answers.**

5. 667 − 329

$700 − 300 = 400; 670 − 330 = 340$

6. 882 − 651

$900 − 700 = 200; 880 − 650 = 230$

7. Number Sense Fern rounded to the nearest ten to find 548 − 132. She thought 540 − 130 = 410. Do you agree? Explain.

No, 548 should be rounded to 550.
So, 550 − 130 = 420.

8. Hector's music teacher requires 450 min of practice each month. Hector practiced 239 min the first three weeks this month. Estimate how many minutes he has left to practice.

Sample answer: 450 − 240 = 210 min

Test Prep

9. Which is not a compatible number for 76?

A. 80   **B.** 75   **C.** 70   **(D)** 60

10. Writing in Math Below are Kate's and Kirk's estimates for 177 − 129. Whose answer is closer to the actual answer? Explain.

Kate: 180 − 130 = 50
Kirk: 200 −100 = 100

Kate's; She rounded to the nearest ten.

Estimating Differences

R 2-11

Members of the Biology Club caught 136 grasshoppers and 188 butterflies in nets. How many more butterflies than grasshoppers did the club catch?

Here are four different ways to estimate differences.

Round to the nearest hundred:

188 rounds to 200
− 136 rounds to 100
About 100 more butterflies than grasshoppers

Round to the nearest ten:

188 rounds to 190
− 136 rounds to 140
About 50 more butterflies than grasshoppers

Use compatible numbers:

188 is close to 185
− 136 is close to 135
About 50 more butterflies than grasshoppers

Use front-end estimation:

188 ⇒ 100
− 136 ⇒ 100
About the same number of butterflies and grasshoppers

Use any method to estimate each difference.

1. 68 − 42 **30**   **2.** 88 − 17 **70**

3. 442 − 112 **300**   **4.** 346 − 119 **230**

5. 692 − 87 **600**   **6.** 231 − 109 **120**

Sample answers are given for 1–6.

7. Writing in Math Chuck estimated 287 − 29 and got a difference of about 200. Is this a reasonable estimate? Explain.

No. In this case, Chuck should have used a different method to estimate. Rounding to tens would give an estimate of 260, which is much closer to the exact difference.

How Are They Alike?

E 2-11
VISUAL THINKING

1. These are Group A shapes.   These are not Group A shapes.

How are the shapes in Group A alike?

The shapes all have a circle around them.

2. These are Group B shapes.   These are not Group B shapes.

How are the shapes in Group B alike?

The shapes all have 1 dot in each angle.

3. These are Group C shapes.   These are not Group C shapes.

How are the shapes in Group C alike?

Each pair of congruent shapes is joined together.

Estimating Differences

PS 2-11

Highest Roller Coasters

Location	Height (ft)
Valencia, California	415
Gold Coast, Australia	380
Mie, Japan	318
Sandusky, Ohio	310
Yamanashi, Japan	259

1. About how much higher is the roller coaster in California than the roller coaster in Ohio?

About 110 ft higher, or about 100 ft higher

2. About how much is the difference between the heights of the two roller coasters in Japan?

About 60 ft difference

3. About how much is the difference between the height of the roller coaster in Australia and the height of the roller coaster with the least height?

About 120 ft, or about 100 ft difference

4. Micah's family spent a day at the amusement park. It took them 48 min to drive to the park and 39 min to drive home. About how much time did it take Micah's family to drive to and from the park?

About 90 min

5. Writing in Math Should you round to the nearest ten or the nearest hundred in order to get the closest estimate? Explain.

Sample answer:
Nearest ten; Rounding 463 to 460 is closer than rounding to 500.

Practice

Name_____

PROBLEM-SOLVING SKILL   P 2-12
Writing to Explain

Snacks The school is going to give each student at Rose Elementary School a granola bar for a snack during field day. There are 758 students. They have already purchased 439 granola bars. About how many more granola bars do they need?

1. Is an exact answer or an estimate needed for this problem? Explain.

   Estimate; The problem asks about how many more.

2. What operation is needed to solve this problem? Why?

   Subtract; You need to find a difference.

3. What is the answer?

   About 320 granola bars; I rounded to the nearest ten: 760 − 440 = 320.

4. Use mental math to find the exact number of granola bars they still need to purchase.

   319 granola bars

5. Draw a picture to show why you subtracted to solve the problem.

   Sample answer:

758	
439	?

6. **Writing in Math** Explain how the digit 1 can have different values in 111.

   A digit's value depends on its place in the number. The 1 in the hundreds place is worth 100, the 1 in the tens place is worth 10, and the 1 in the ones place is worth 1.

Use with Lesson 2-12. **27**

Reteaching

Name_____

PROBLEM-SOLVING SKILL   R 2-12
Writing to Explain

You can explain your answer to a problem by breaking the problem into steps. For example:

If you wanted to go on the pony ride and the Ferris wheel, would you need more than 40 tickets?

Carnival Ride Costs

Ferris Wheel	23 tickets
Pony Ride	24 tickets
Water Slide	18 tickets
Moonwalk	12 tickets

Ask yourself if an exact answer or an estimate is needed.

The problem asks if you need more than 40 tickets. An exact answer is not needed. An estimate is enough.

Then, decide which operation you should use and why.

To solve this problem, you should add because you are putting together the number of tickets needed.

Finally, find the answer and explain how you found it.

Step 1: Round 24 down to 20

Step 2: Round 23 down to 20

Step 3: 20 + 20 = 40

Step 4: Both numbers were rounded down, so more than 40 tickets are needed.

1. Joe wants to go on the water slide and the pony ride. How many tickets will he need? Explain how he can find the exact number of tickets using mental math.

   42 tickets; 24 + 20 = 44, then 44 − 2 = 42.   Sample answer:

2. Renaldo read a book that has 286 pages. Roz read 179 pages of a different book. About how many more pages did Renaldo read than Roz? Show the problem you used to find the answer.

   110 pages; 290 − 180 = 110   Sample answer:

Use with Lesson 2-12. **27**

Enrichment

Name_____

Flower Sale   E 2-12
                                    DECISION MAKING

Miss Richards's Flower Shop is having a week-long sale.

Flower Sale

One dozen roses:	$24
Mixed flower bouquet:	$19
Wedding display:	$72
Potted plant:	$8

1. Marisa wants to buy one dozen roses and one bouquet. She has $50 to spend. Can she buy both items? Use estimation to explain your answer.

   Yes; $24 rounds to $20. $19 rounds to $20. $20 + $20 = $40

2. Gary has $100, and he wants to buy one of each of the four items. Does he have enough money? Explain your answer.

   No; The total estimated cost for one of each item is $120. $20 + $20 + $70 + $10 = $120

3. Which three items have costs that add up the closest to $100? Explain how you solved this problem.

   Sample answer: I used trial and error. The bouquet, wedding display, and potted plant add up to $99.

4. Explain why it is better to round to the nearest ten than to the nearest hundred when solving problems about the sale at Miss Richards's Flower Shop.

   It does not make sense to round to hundreds when you have prices that are between $8 and $72.

Use with Lesson 2-12. **27**

Problem Solving

Name_____

PROBLEM-SOLVING SKILL   PS 2-12
Writing to Explain

Shells Ned and Mya collected shells on the beach. Ned found 82 shells and Mya found 56 shells. How many more shells did Ned find than Mya?

Read and Understand

1. What are you trying to find?

   How many more shells Ned found

Plan and Solve

2. Is an exact answer or an estimate needed?

   Sample answer: Exact answer

3. What operation should you use?

   Subtraction

4. Write the answer in a complete sentence.

   Ned found 26 more shells than Mya.

5. Explain how you found your answer. **Sample answer: You subtract 56 from 82 to find the difference.**

Look Back and Check

6. Explain how you can check your answer. **Sample answer: I can add the answer to the number of shells Mya found. 56 + 26 = 82**

Solve Another Problem

7. Kyle read that there are 170 species of animals at the Little Rock Zoo in Arkansas. Catherine read that there are 229 species of animals at the Miami Metrozoo. About how many fewer species of animals live at the Little Rock Zoo?

   About 60 fewer species

Use with Lesson 2-12. **27**

Name_____

Fire Trucks

For 1–3, use the Key Facts: Ladder Trucks chart.

KEY FACTS
Ladder Trucks

• Truck width	8 ft
• Truck length	37 ft
• Maximum ladder height	105 ft
• Water spray per minute	1,500 gal
• Seating	6 people
• Hose length	1,000 ft
• Hose width	5 in.

1. Use mental math to find the number of people who can sit in three fire trucks.

   6 + 6 + 6 = 18 people

2. Write the word name for the length of the hose on a ladder truck.

   One thousand

3. Estimate the difference between the maximum ladder height and the truck length. Explain how you estimated.

   The maximum ladder height is about 70 ft longer than the truck length. I rounded each number to the tens place.

For 4 and 5, use the Firefighting Models chart.

Firefighting Models

Model	Price
Pumper	$5
Aerial ladder	$8
Fire chief car	$4
Rescue unit	$6

4. Marcy has $10. Does she have enough money to buy an aerial ladder and a fire chief car? Why or why not?

   No. An aerial ladder and a fire chief car cost $12.

5. Diego bought one of each type of model. How much money did he spend?

   Diego spent $23.

© Pearson Education, Inc. 3

Name_____

Big Cats

The tiger is the largest animal in the cat family and the only cat that consistently has stripes.

There used to be 8 kinds of tigers. Three of the kinds have become extinct, or disappeared.

How many kinds of tigers are left?

You can subtract to find the answer.

8 − 3 = 5

So, there are 5 kinds of tigers left.

Suppose a tiger eats 33 lb of meat one night and 39 lb of meat on another night.

1. Round 33 and 39 to the nearest tens place.

   30; 40

2. Find the sum of the rounded numbers.

   70

3. How many pounds of meat did the tiger eat in the two nights? Show your work and write your answer in a complete sentence.

   The tiger ate 72 lb of meat in the two nights.

Suppose Country A has 288 tigers in zoos and Country B has 171 tigers in zoos. How many more tigers does Country A have than Country B?

4. Find an estimate by rounding each number to the nearest ten.

   120

5. Find the actual difference. Write your answer in a complete sentence.

   Country A has 117 more tigers than Country B.

© Pearson Education, Inc. 3

Name_____

Tony's Car Care

Tony's Car Care Service is owned by Mr. Coffaro. He has 5 mechanics who work for him. The table to the right shows how much he pays each mechanic per hour.

Mechanic	$ per Hour
Jose	$14
Jane	$13
Nikki	$11
Gabriella	$17
Robert	$12

1. During 1 hr, Jose and Gabriella worked on a car. Write a number sentence to show the amount Mr. Coffaro paid the 2 mechanics for 1 hr of work.

   $14 + $17 = $31

2. During another hour, Mr. Coffaro paid 2 mechanics a total of $29 to work on a car. Which 2 mechanics worked on the car? Explain.

   Gabriella and Robert worked on the car. Their hourly pay adds up to exactly $29. $17 + $12 = $29.

3. Write an addition sentence to show the amount of money Mr. Coffaro would pay Gabriella for 3 hr of work.

   $17 + $17 + $17 = $51

4. Robert and Nikki worked on a car for 1 hr. To estimate how much Mr. Coffaro paid them, round the hourly wages of Robert and Nikki to the nearest ten. Then find the total amount.

   Robert: $12 rounds to $10. Nikki: $11 rounds to $10. $10 + $10 = $20. About $20 for 1 hour

© Pearson Education, Inc. 3

Name _____

How Many Bones?

Bones Babies have 300 bones in their bodies at birth. As people grow, some of the bones fuse together. An adult's body has 206 bones. How many more bones does a baby's body have than an adult's body?

Read and Understand

1. What are you trying to find?

   How many more bones a baby's body has than an adult's body

Plan and Solve

2. Which operation will you use?

   Subtraction

3. Write and solve a number sentence.

   300 − 206 = 94

4. Write the answer in a complete sentence.

   A baby's body has 94 more bones.

Look Back and Check

5. Explain how you can check your answer.

   Sample answer: You could add 94 + 206 to see if the answer is 300.

Solve Another Problem

6. Dawson has 372 postcards in his collection. His Aunt Sally sent him 432 postcards that had collected during her travels. Does he have at least 800 postcards altogether?

   Yes, 370 + 430 = 800 or 400 + 400 = 800

© Pearson Education, Inc. 3

Name_____

Adding Two-Digit Numbers

P 3-1

1. $\begin{array}{r} 73 \\ +\ 19 \\ \hline 92 \end{array}$	2. $\begin{array}{r} 16 \\ +\ 48 \\ \hline 64 \end{array}$	3. $\begin{array}{r} 52 \\ +\ 39 \\ \hline 91 \end{array}$	4. $\begin{array}{r} 28 \\ +\ 8 \\ \hline 36 \end{array}$
5. $\begin{array}{r} 62 \\ +\ 19 \\ \hline 81 \end{array}$	6. $\begin{array}{r} 14 \\ +\ 32 \\ \hline 46 \end{array}$	7. $\begin{array}{r} 59 \\ +\ 27 \\ \hline 86 \end{array}$	8. $\begin{array}{r} 36 \\ +\ 26 \\ \hline 62 \end{array}$

9. $58 + 28 =$ __86__   10. $13 + 72 =$ __85__

11. **Number Sense** Tad's place-value blocks are shown at the right. What two numbers is he adding?

__66 and 17__

12. What is the answer to Tad's problem?

__83__

13. Esther swam 18 laps on Monday and 13 laps on Tuesday. How many laps did she swim in all?

__31 laps__

14. Write an addition sentence with the sum of 42. One of the addends must have a 4 in the ones column.

Sample answer: 24 + 18 = 42

Test Prep

15. Which is the sum of $72 + 25$?

A. 99   (B.) 97   C. 90   D. 79

16. **Writing in Math** How can estimating help you add two-digit numbers?

By estimating, you can tell if your answer is reasonable.

Name_____

Adding Two-Digit Numbers

R 3-1

To find $27 + 57$, first estimate. 27 is close to 30. 57 is close to 60. $30 + 60 = 90$, so the answer should be about 90.

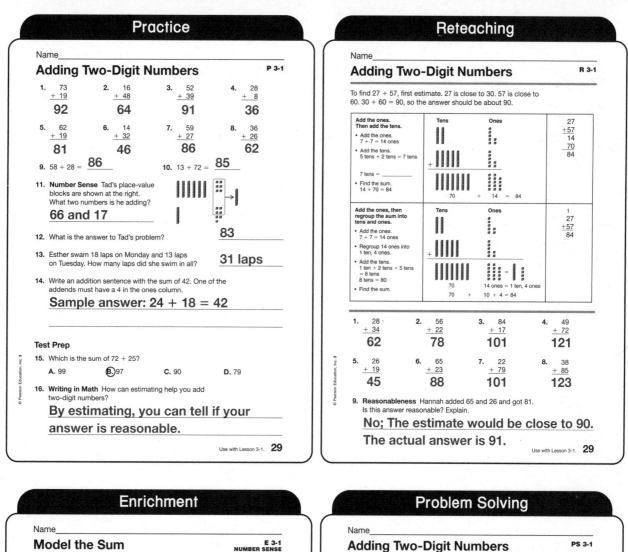

1. $\begin{array}{r} 28 \\ +\ 34 \\ \hline 62 \end{array}$	2. $\begin{array}{r} 56 \\ +\ 22 \\ \hline 78 \end{array}$	3. $\begin{array}{r} 84 \\ +\ 17 \\ \hline 101 \end{array}$	4. $\begin{array}{r} 49 \\ +\ 72 \\ \hline 121 \end{array}$
5. $\begin{array}{r} 26 \\ +\ 19 \\ \hline 45 \end{array}$	6. $\begin{array}{r} 65 \\ +\ 23 \\ \hline 88 \end{array}$	7. $\begin{array}{r} 22 \\ +\ 79 \\ \hline 101 \end{array}$	8. $\begin{array}{r} 38 \\ +\ 85 \\ \hline 123 \end{array}$

9. **Reasonableness** Hannah added 65 and 26 and got 81. Is this answer reasonable? Explain.

__No; The estimate would be close to 90.__
__The actual answer is 91.__

Name_____

Model the Sum

E 3-1
NUMBER SENSE

Draw the missing tens and ones for each sum.
For 1–4, sample answers are given.

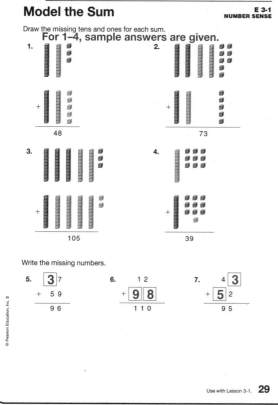

Write the missing numbers.

5. $\begin{array}{r} \boxed{3}\,7 \\ +\ \ 5\ 9 \\ \hline 9\ 6 \end{array}$ 6. $\begin{array}{r} 1\ 2 \\ +\ \boxed{9}\,\boxed{8} \\ \hline 1\ 1\ 0 \end{array}$ 7. $\begin{array}{r} 4\,\boxed{3} \\ +\ \boxed{5}\,2 \\ \hline 9\ 5 \end{array}$

Name_____

Adding Two-Digit Numbers

PS 3-1

1. Harley's mother bought a dozen whole-wheat muffins at the market. Then she stopped at the neighborhood bakery to purchase blueberry muffins. She bought a baker's dozen. How many muffins did she purchase in all?

Measurement Chart		
dozen	=	12
baker's dozen	=	13
foot	=	12 in.
yard	=	36 in.

__25 muffins__

2. Sara planted cucumbers in her garden. She planted each cucumber plant 2 ft apart. How many inches apart were Sara's cucumbers?

__24 in.__

3. At a track-and-field day, Joshua jumped 2 yd and 1 ft in the long jump. How many inches did Joshua jump? __84 in.__

4. Austin says 3 ft is the same as 1 yd. Do you agree? Explain.

Sample answer:
Yes, because 1 yd and 3 ft are both 36 in.

5. Choose two of the numbers from the list that will have the highest sum, then add.

49, 27, 34

$49 + 34 = 83$

6. **Writing in Math** Madison counted 43 chickens at her uncle's farm. She also counted 24 turkeys. How many chickens and turkeys did Madison count? Explain how Madison might have estimated the total.

__67 chickens and turkeys; Sample answer:__
__Madison might have estimated 40__
__chickens and 25 turkeys, or 65 chickens__
__and turkeys.__

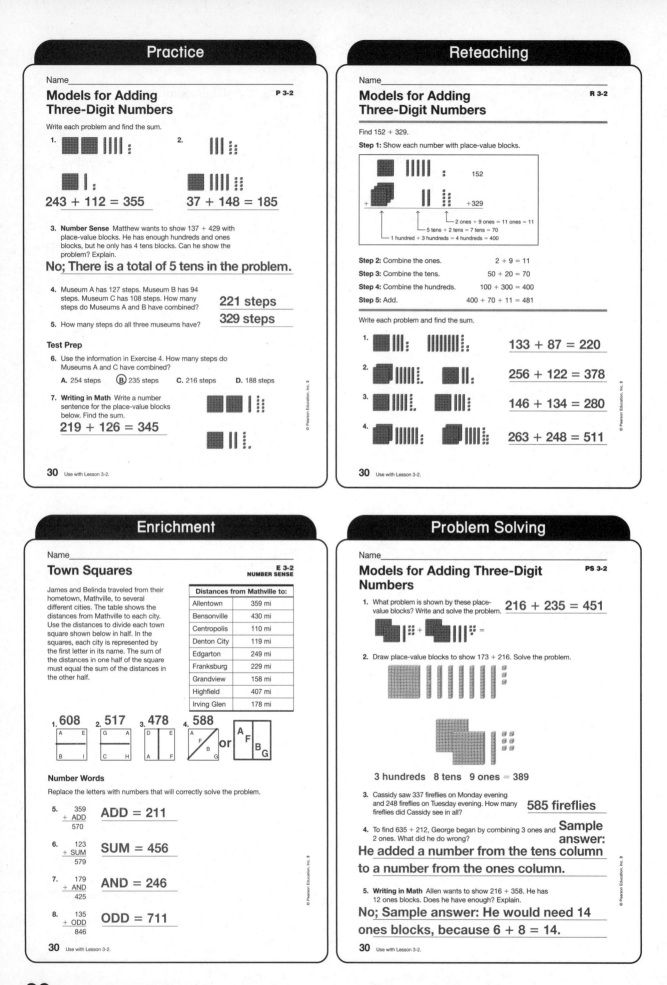

Practice

Name_____

Models for Adding Three-Digit Numbers

P 3-2

Write each problem and find the sum.

1. $243 + 112 = 355$

2. $37 + 148 = 185$

3. **Number Sense** Matthew wants to show $137 + 429$ with place-value blocks. He has enough hundreds and ones blocks, but he only has 4 tens blocks. Can he show the problem? Explain.

No; There is a total of 5 tens in the problem.

4. Museum A has 127 steps. Museum B has 94 steps. Museum C has 108 steps. How many steps do Museums A and B have combined?

221 steps

5. How many steps do all three museums have?

329 steps

Test Prep

6. Use the information in Exercise 4. How many steps do Museums A and C have combined?

A. 254 steps **B.** 235 steps C. 216 steps D. 188 steps

7. **Writing in Math** Write a number sentence for the place-value blocks below. Find the sum.

$219 + 126 = 345$

© Pearson Education, Inc. 3

Reteaching

Name_____

Models for Adding Three-Digit Numbers

R 3-2

Find $152 + 329$.

Step 1: Show each number with place-value blocks.

- 152
- +329
- 2 ones + 9 ones = 11 ones = 11
- 5 tens + 2 tens = 7 tens = 70
- 1 hundred + 3 hundreds = 4 hundreds = 400

Step 2: Combine the ones. $2 + 9 = 11$

Step 3: Combine the tens. $50 + 20 = 70$

Step 4: Combine the hundreds. $100 + 300 = 400$

Step 5: Add. $400 + 70 + 11 = 481$

Write each problem and find the sum.

1. $133 + 87 = 220$

2. $256 + 122 = 378$

3. $146 + 134 = 280$

4. $263 + 248 = 511$

© Pearson Education, Inc. 3

Enrichment

Name_____

Town Squares

E 3-2
NUMBER SENSE

James and Belinda traveled from their hometown, Mathville, to several different cities. The table shows the distances from Mathville to each city. Use the distances to divide each town square shown below in half. In the squares, each city is represented by the first letter in its name. The sum of the distances in one half of the square must equal the sum of the distances in the other half.

Distances from Mathville to:	
Allentown	359 mi
Bensonville	430 mi
Centropolis	110 mi
Denton City	119 mi
Edgarton	249 mi
Franksburg	229 mi
Grandview	158 mi
Highfield	407 mi
Irving Glen	178 mi

1. 608
2. 517
3. 478
4. 588

Number Words

Replace the letters with numbers that will correctly solve the problem.

5. $359 + ADD = 570$ **ADD = 211**

6. $123 + SUM = 579$ **SUM = 456**

7. $179 + AND = 425$ **AND = 246**

8. $135 + ODD = 846$ **ODD = 711**

© Pearson Education, Inc. 3

Problem Solving

Name_____

Models for Adding Three-Digit Numbers

PS 3-2

1. What problem is shown by these place-value blocks? Write and solve the problem.

$216 + 235 = 451$

2. Draw place-value blocks to show $173 + 216$. Solve the problem.

3 hundreds 8 tens 9 ones = 389

3. Cassidy saw 337 fireflies on Monday evening and 248 fireflies on Tuesday evening. How many fireflies did Cassidy see in all?

585 fireflies

4. To find $635 + 212$, George began by combining 3 ones and 2 ones. What did he do wrong?

Sample answer: He added a number from the tens column to a number from the ones column.

5. **Writing in Math** Allen wants to show $216 + 358$. He has 12 ones blocks. Does he have enough? Explain.

No; Sample answer: He would need 14 ones blocks, because $6 + 8 = 14$.

© Pearson Education, Inc. 3

Practice

Name_____

Adding Three-Digit Numbers   P 3-3

1. 329
  + 468
  797

2. 148
  + 231
  379

3. 555
  + 777
  1,332

4. 718
  + 29
  747

5. 152
  + 535
  687

6. 396
  + 428
  824

7. 592
  + 168
  760

8. 633
  + 210
  843

9. 536 + 399 = **935**

10. 319 + 791 = **1,110**

Long Jumpers

Animal	Distance (feet)
Flying dragon	100
Flying fish	328
Sugar glider	300

11. What is the total maximum distance that the flying dragon and the flying fish can jump together?   **428 ft**

12. What is double the sugar glider's maximum gliding distance?   **600 ft**

Test Prep

13. Find the sum of 163 + 752.

   A. 895   (B.) 915   C. 925   D. 929

14. **Writing in Math** Write an addition story for two 3-digit numbers. Write the answer to your story.

   Sample answer: Bob has 611 stamps. He gets 134 new stamps. How many stamps does Bob have now? 745 stamps

Reteaching

Name_____

Adding Three-Digit Numbers   R 3-3

Find 237 + 186.

Step 1: Add the ones. 7 ones + 6 ones = 13 ones

Regroup. 13 ones = 1 ten, 3 ones

Step 2: Add the tens. 1 ten + 3 tens + 8 tens = 12 tens

Regroup. 12 tens = 1 hundred, 2 tens

Step 3: Add the hundreds.

1 hundred + 2 hundreds + 1 hundred = 4 hundreds

Add together the hundreds, tens, and ones.

400 + 20 + 3 = 423

1. 118
  + 146
  264

2. 283
  + 147
  430

3. 542
  + 109
  651

4. 220
  + 479
  699

5. Find the sum of 456 and 38.   **494**

6. Add 109 and 656.   **765**

7. **Estimation** Estimate to decide which sum is less than 600: 356 + 292 or 214 + 356.   **214 + 356**

Enrichment

Name_____

Baseball by the Numbers   E 3-3
NUMBER SENSE

In this math baseball game, each position is marked with a number value. If the ball lands on any of the positions shown, you will score points. Which two position number values would the ball have to land on in order to get the sums listed below?

1. sum = 332   **231 + 101**

2. sum = 884   **441 + 443**

3. sum = 665   **222 + 443**

4. sum = 543   **442 + 101**

5. sum = 769   **668 + 101**

6. sum = 453   **222 + 231**

7. The sum of which two numbers would equal a home run?   **443 + 556**

8. The sum of which two numbers would equal more than a home run?   **Sample answer: 556 + 668**

9. What is the lowest score for two numbers?   **222 + 101 = 323**

Problem Solving

Name_____

Adding Three-Digit Numbers   PS 3-3

1. The Boeing 747 jumbo jet weighs as much as 386 tons at takeoff. It can carry 674 people. How many people could two of these jets carry?   **1,348 people**

2. How many first- and second-grade students attend Jackson Elementary? Find the sum.   **591 students**

Jackson Elementary School	
Grade	Number of Students
1	312
2	279
3	370
4	327
5	296

3. Which two grades have the least number of students? How many students do they have combined?   **Second grade, fifth grade; 575 students**

4. Which two grades combined have 682 students?   **First grade, third grade**

5. Choose two grade levels and write an addition sentence that shows regrouping of ones.   **Sample answer: 312 + 279 = 591**

6. **Writing in Math** To find the sum of 286 + 134, would you regroup once or twice? Explain.   **Twice; Sample answer: Because there are more than 10 in both the ones column and the tens column**

Name_____

Adding Three or More Numbers
P 3-4

1.	2.	3.	4.
36 29 + 12 **77**	142 297 + 116 **555**	524 97 + 190 **811**	716 12 + 149 **877**

5.	6.	7.	8.
156 561 + 213 **930**	241 421 + 124 **786**	98 312 + 175 **585**	420 318 + 196 **934**

9. **Estimation** Estimate the sum of 327 + 419 + 173.
Sample answer: 900

10. **Number Sense** Justine has 162 red buttons, 98 blue buttons, and 284 green buttons. She says she knows she has more than 500 buttons without adding. Do you agree? Explain.
Yes; Sample answer: If you estimate, it is 160 + 100 + 280 = 540.

11. Carlos ate 1 oz bran flakes, 1 banana, 1 c whole milk, and 1 c orange juice. How many calories did he eat?
455 calories

Breakfast

Food	Amount	Calories
Bran flakes	1 oz	90
Banana	1	105
Orange juice	1 c	110
Whole milk	1 c	150

Test Prep

12. Kyle has 378 pennies, 192 nickels, and 117 dimes. How many coins does he have altogether?

A. 495   B. 570   C. 677   (D) 687

13. **Writing in Math** Write an addition problem with 3 addends in which you regroup once to solve.
Sample answer: 241 + 132 + 365 = 738

Name_____

Adding Three or More Numbers
R 3-4

Find 137 + 201 + 109.

First, estimate. The number 137 is close to 100. The number 201 is close to 200, and the number 109 is close to 100. 100 + 200 + 100 = 400, so the answer should be about 400.

Step 1	Step 2	Step 3	Step 4
Line up the ones, tens, and hundreds.	Add the ones. Regroup as needed.	Add the tens. Regroup as needed.	Add the hundreds.
137 201 + 109	1 137 201 + 109 7	1 137 201 + 109 47	1 137 201 + 109 447
All the numbers are in neat columns so you can add them easily.	Regroup 17 ones into 1 ten and 7 ones.	No need to regroup.	So, 137 + 201 + 109 = 447.

Check to see if the answer is reasonable. Your estimate was 400. 447 is close to 400, so the answer is reasonable.

1.	2.	3.	4.
32 64 + 71 **167**	127 39 + 87 **253**	17 68 + 32 **117**	358 427 + 27 **812**

5. 382 + 45 + 181 = **608**

6. 12 + 138 + 98 = **248**

7. **Number Sense** Ranier has 37 baseball cards, 65 football cards, and 151 hockey cards. How many sports cards does he have in all?
253 sports cards

Name_____

Chairs for the Teachers
E 3-4
REASONING

Math teachers from many schools held a meeting at the Hotel Grand. In preparation, the planning committee placed chairs in the rooms according to the floor plan.

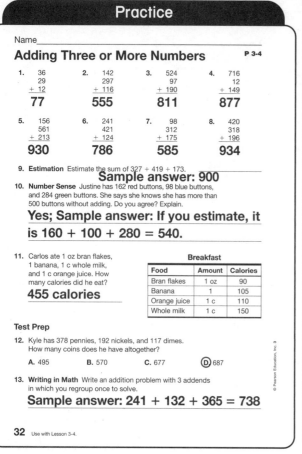

1. Which room could hold 100 teachers from Clinton School, 20 students from Rogers School, and 7 principals?
Blue Room

2. Which room was used for 77 third-grade teachers from Boone School, 2 student teachers, and 21 second-grade teachers from St. Paul School?
Green Room

3. When all of the sixth-grade teachers met, 2 doors had to be opened between rooms so that 3 rooms could be connected. Which meeting room arrangement held the most teachers?
Blue, Red, and Green rooms

4. When all the meeting rooms were filled, only 3 rooms of people would fit into the chairs already in the Grand Room. Which 3 rooms of people fit?
Blue, Red, and Green rooms; or Red, Green, and Yellow rooms

Name_____

Adding Three or More Numbers
PS 3-4

Nation	Number of Square Miles
Andorra	174
Bahrain	240
Barbados	165
Dominica	290
Grenada	130
Kiribati	280

1. What is the combined square mileage of Andorra, Bahrain, and Barbados?
579 mi^2

2. What is the combined square mileage of Dominica, Grenada, and Kiribati?
700 mi^2

3. What is the combined square mileage of the three smallest countries on the chart?
469 mi^2

4. What is the combined square mileage of the three largest countries on the chart?
810 mi^2

5. Estimate the combined square mileage of all six countries to the nearest hundred.
1,300 mi^2

6. Write an addition problem with three addends. Make the problem so the sum is greater than 400 but less than 600.
Sample answer: 310 + 120 + 102 = 532

7. **Writing in Math** How can you use mental math to find 353 + 50 + 27? Explain.
Sample answer: You could add compatible numbers: 350 + 50 = 400. Then find 3 + 27 = 30. Finally, find 400 + 30 = 430.

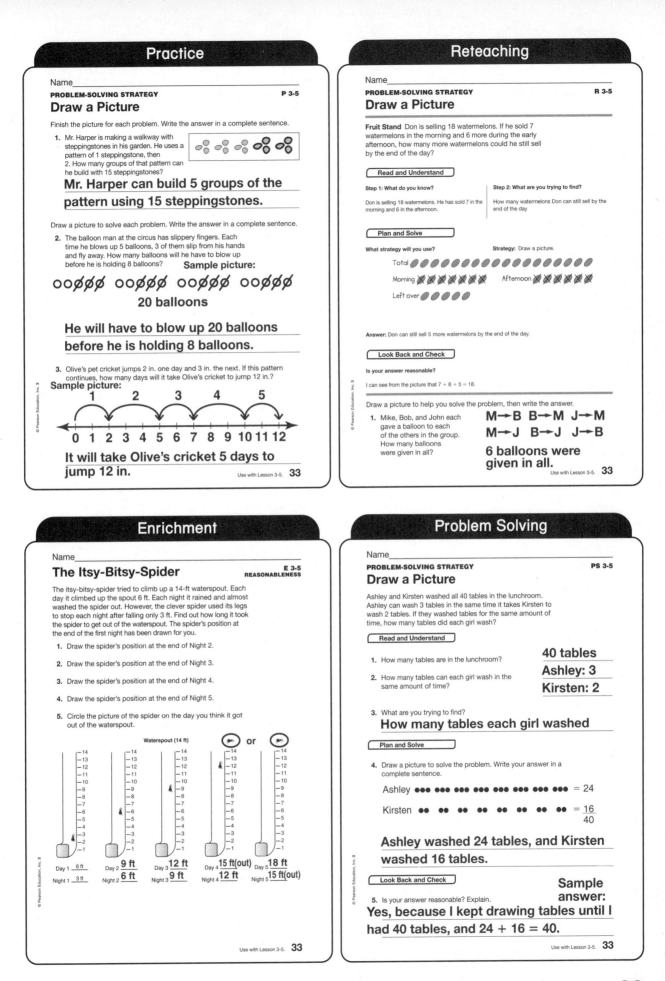

Practice

Name _____

PROBLEM-SOLVING STRATEGY   P 3-5

Draw a Picture

Finish the picture for each problem. Write the answer in a complete sentence.

1. Mr. Harper is making a walkway with steppingstones in his garden. He uses a pattern of 1 steppingstone, then 2. How many groups of that pattern can he build with 15 steppingstones?

Mr. Harper can build 5 groups of the pattern using 15 steppingstones.

Draw a picture to solve each problem. Write the answer in a complete sentence.

2. The balloon man at the circus has slippery fingers. Each time he blows up 5 balloons, 3 of them slip from his hands and fly away. How many balloons will he have to blow up before he is holding 8 balloons?

Sample picture:

○○∅∅ ○○∅∅ ○○∅∅ ○○∅∅
20 balloons

He will have to blow up 20 balloons before he is holding 8 balloons.

3. Olive's pet cricket jumps 2 in. one day and 3 in. the next. If this pattern continues, how many days will it take Olive's cricket to jump 12 in.?

Sample picture:

It will take Olive's cricket 5 days to jump 12 in.

Use with Lesson 3-5. **33**

© Pearson Education, Inc. 3

Reteaching

Name _____

PROBLEM-SOLVING STRATEGY   R 3-5

Draw a Picture

Fruit Stand Don is selling 18 watermelons. If he sold 7 watermelons in the morning and 6 more during the early afternoon, how many more watermelons could he still sell by the end of the day?

Read and Understand

Step 1: What do you know?

Don is selling 18 watermelons. He has sold 7 in the morning and 6 in the afternoon.

Step 2: What are you trying to find?

How many watermelons Don can still sell by the end of the day

Plan and Solve

What strategy will you use?   **Strategy:** Draw a picture.

Answer: Don can still sell 5 more watermelons by the end of the day.

Look Back and Check

Is your answer reasonable?

I can see from the picture that 7 + 6 + 5 = 18.

Draw a picture to help you solve the problem, then write the answer.

1. Mike, Bob, and John each gave a balloon to each of the others in the group. How many balloons were given in all?

M→B B→M J→M
M→J B→J J→B

6 balloons were given in all.

Use with Lesson 3-5. **33**

© Pearson Education, Inc. 3

Enrichment

Name _____

The Itsy-Bitsy-Spider

E 3-5
REASONABLENESS

The itsy-bitsy-spider tried to climb up a 14-ft waterspout. Each day it climbed up the spout 6 ft. Each night it rained and almost washed the spider out. However, the clever spider used its legs to stop each night after falling only 3 ft. Find out how long it took the spider to get out of the waterspout. The spider's position at the end of the first night has been drawn for you.

1. Draw the spider's position at the end of Night 2.

2. Draw the spider's position at the end of Night 3.

3. Draw the spider's position at the end of Night 4.

4. Draw the spider's position at the end of Night 5.

5. Circle the picture of the spider on the day you think it got out of the waterspout.

Use with Lesson 3-5. **33**

© Pearson Education, Inc. 3

Problem Solving

Name _____

PROBLEM-SOLVING STRATEGY   PS 3-5

Draw a Picture

Ashley and Kirsten washed all 40 tables in the lunchroom. Ashley can wash 3 tables in the same time it takes Kirsten to wash 2 tables. If they washed tables for the same amount of time, how many tables did each girl wash?

Read and Understand

1. How many tables are in the lunchroom?

2. How many tables can each girl wash in the same amount of time?

40 tables
Ashley: 3
Kirsten: 2

3. What are you trying to find?

How many tables each girl washed

Plan and Solve

4. Draw a picture to solve the problem. Write your answer in a complete sentence.

Ashley ••• ••• ••• ••• ••• ••• ••• ••• = 24

Kirsten •• •• •• •• •• •• •• •• = 16/40

Ashley washed 24 tables, and Kirsten washed 16 tables.

Look Back and Check

5. Is your answer reasonable? Explain.

Sample answer:

Yes, because I kept drawing tables until I had 40 tables, and 24 + 16 = 40.

Use with Lesson 3-5. **33**

© Pearson Education, Inc. 3

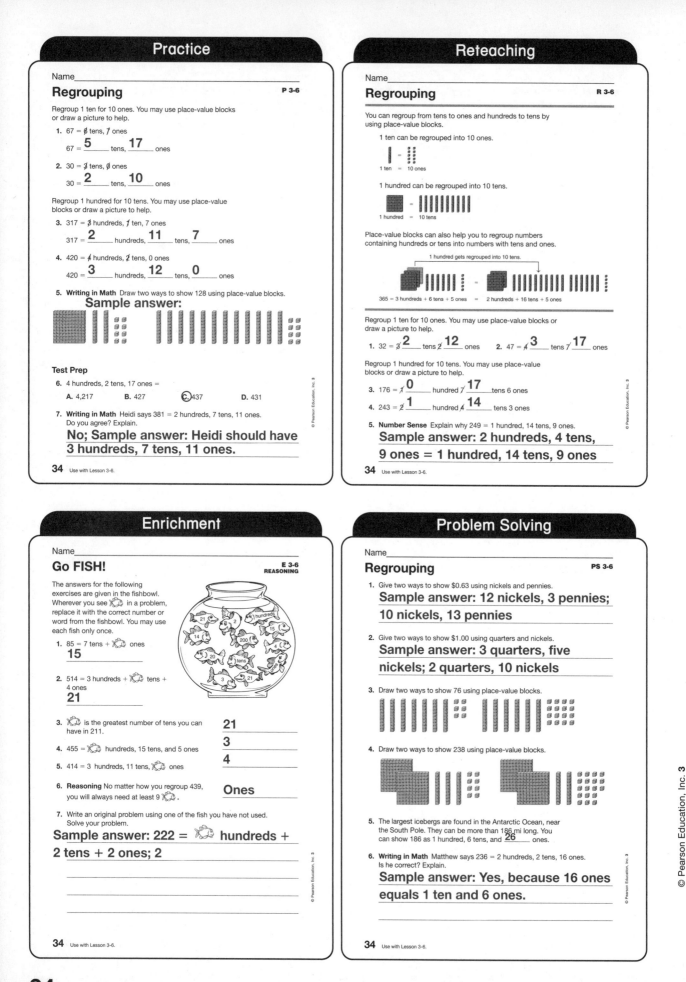

Practice

Regrouping   P 3-6

Regroup 1 ten for 10 ones. You may use place-value blocks or draw a picture to help.

1. 67 = 6 tens, 7 ones
    67 = **5** tens, **17** ones

2. 30 = 3 tens, 0 ones
    30 = **2** tens, **10** ones

Regroup 1 hundred for 10 tens. You may use place-value blocks or draw a picture to help.

3. 317 = 3 hundreds, 1 ten, 7 ones
    317 = **2** hundreds, **11** tens, **7** ones

4. 420 = 4 hundreds, 2 tens, 0 ones
    420 = **3** hundreds, **12** tens, **0** ones

5. **Writing in Math** Draw two ways to show 128 using place-value blocks.
    Sample answer:

Test Prep

6. 4 hundreds, 2 tens, 17 ones =
    A. 4,217   **B.** 427   **C.** 437   **D.** 431

7. **Writing in Math** Heidi says 381 = 2 hundreds, 7 tens, 11 ones. Do you agree? Explain.
    No; Sample answer: Heidi should have 3 hundreds, 7 tens, 11 ones.

Reteaching

Regrouping   R 3-6

You can regroup from tens to ones and hundreds to tens by using place-value blocks.

1 ten can be regrouped into 10 ones.

1 ten = 10 ones

1 hundred can be regrouped into 10 tens.

1 hundred = 10 tens

Place-value blocks can also help you to regroup numbers containing hundreds or tens into numbers with tens and ones.

1 hundred gets regrouped into 10 tens

365 = 3 hundreds + 6 tens + 5 ones = 2 hundreds + 16 tens + 5 ones

Regroup 1 ten for 10 ones. You may use place-value blocks or draw a picture to help.

1. 32 = 3 **2** tens 2 **12** ones   2. 47 = 4 **3** tens 7 **17** ones

Regroup 1 hundred for 10 tens. You may use place-value blocks or draw a picture to help.

3. 176 = 1 **0** hundred 7 **17** tens 6 ones

4. 243 = 2 **1** hundred 4 **14** tens 3 ones

5. **Number Sense** Explain why 249 = 1 hundred, 14 tens, 9 ones.
    Sample answer: 2 hundreds, 4 tens, 9 ones = 1 hundred, 14 tens, 9 ones

Enrichment

Go FISH!   E 3-6 REASONING

The answers for the following exercises are given in the fishbowl. Wherever you see 🐟 in a problem, replace it with the correct number or word from the fishbowl. You may use each fish only once.

1. 85 = 7 tens + 🐟 ones
    15

2. 514 = 3 hundreds + 🐟 tens + 4 ones
    21

3. 🐟 is the greatest number of tens you can have in 211.
    21

4. 455 = 🐟 hundreds, 15 tens, and 5 ones
    3

5. 414 = 3 hundreds, 11 tens, 🐟 ones
    4

6. **Reasoning** No matter how you regroup 439, you will always need at least 9 🐟.
    Ones

7. Write an original problem using one of the fish you have not used. Solve your problem.
    Sample answer: 222 = 🐟 hundreds + 2 tens + 2 ones; 2

(fishbowl contains: 21, 2, hundreds, 15, 14, 200, tens, 20, 3, 21, ones)

Problem Solving

Regrouping   PS 3-6

1. Give two ways to show $0.63 using nickels and pennies.
    Sample answer: 12 nickels, 3 pennies; 10 nickels, 13 pennies

2. Give two ways to show $1.00 using quarters and nickels.
    Sample answer: 3 quarters, five nickels; 2 quarters, 10 nickels

3. Draw two ways to show 76 using place-value blocks.

4. Draw two ways to show 238 using place-value blocks.

5. The largest icebergs are found in the Antarctic Ocean, near the South Pole. They can be more than 186 mi long. You can show 186 as 1 hundred, 6 tens, and **26** ones.

6. **Writing in Math** Matthew says 236 = 2 hundreds, 2 tens, 16 ones. Is he correct? Explain.
    Sample answer: Yes, because 16 ones equals 1 ten and 6 ones.

Name_____

Subtracting Two-Digit Numbers

P 3-7

1. 71
− 10
61

2. 65
− 18
47

3. 19
− 17
2

4. 35
− 11
24

5. 91
− 38
53

6. 40
− 26
14

7. 21
− 17
4

8. 83
− 56
27

9. 89 − 66 = **23**

10. 52 − 38 = **14**

11. 63 − 35 = **28**

12. Stanton used the addition sentence 21 + 16 = 37 to check his work. Write two subtraction problems that Stanton could have been checking.

37 − 16 = 21 and 37 − 21 = 16

13. The tree farm had 65 shade trees for sale. It sold 39 of the trees. How many trees did it have left?

The tree farm had 26 trees left.

Test Prep

14. Find the difference of 76 − 38.

A. 42   B. 38   C. 36   D. 32

15. **Writing in Math** Bethany has 40 apples. Write a subtraction story about the apples that would require regrouping. Then write the answer in a complete sentence.

Sample answer: Bethany gives 21 apples to Joel. How many apples does Bethany have left? Bethany has 19 apples.

Use with Lesson 3-7. **35**

© Pearson Education, Inc. 3

Name_____

Subtracting Two-Digit Numbers

R 3-7

Here is how to subtract two-digit numbers.

Find 55 − 36.

Estimate: 60 − 40 = 20, so the answer should be about 20.

What You Think	What You Show	What You Write
Step 1 Subtract the ones. Regroup if you need to. Since you can't subtract 6 from 5, regroup.	Regroup 1 ten into 10 ones. / 15 ones − 6 ones = 9 ones.	4 15 $5\!\!\!/5$ −36 9
Step 2 Subtract the tens.	4 tens − 3 tens = 1 ten.	4 15 $5\!\!\!/5$ −36 19

Add to check your answer. 19 + 36 = 55

It checks.

1. 86
− 51
35

2. 47
− 18
29

3. 62
− 35
27

4. 41
− 11
30

5. 28 − 17 **11**

6. 53 − 38 **15**

7. **Number Sense** To subtract 91 from 99, do you need to regroup? Explain.

Sample answer: No. 9 > 1, so no regrouping is needed.

8. Felicia has 67 paperback books in her collection. She sold 48 of them. How many books does she have left?

19 books

Use with Lesson 3-7. **35**

© Pearson Education, Inc. 3

Name_____

Seesaw Subtraction

E 3-7
NUMBER SENSE

In order for the seesaw to be balanced, the total of both sides must be equal. Draw the ball half, cube, cylinder, or pyramid on the right side of the seesaw to make it balanced. You may use the figures more than once. Then write the subtraction problem that helped you figure out the correct answer. The first one has been started for you.

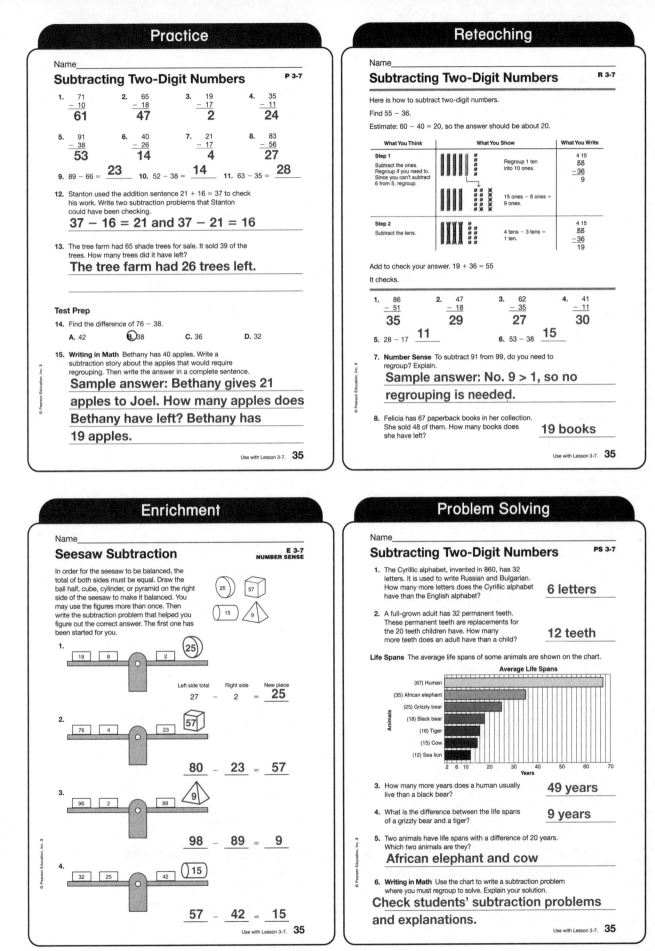

1.
19   8   2   (25)

Left side total   Right side   New piece
27   −   2   =   **25**

2.
76   4   23   [57]

80 − **23** = **57**

3.
96   2   89   △9

98 − **89** = **9**

4.
32   25   42   (15)

57 − **42** = **15**

Use with Lesson 3-7. **35**

© Pearson Education, Inc. 3

Name_____

Subtracting Two-Digit Numbers

PS 3-7

1. The Cyrillic alphabet, invented in 860, has 32 letters. It is used to write Russian and Bulgarian. How many more letters does the Cyrillic alphabet have than the English alphabet?

6 letters

2. A full-grown adult has 32 permanent teeth. These permanent teeth are replacements for the 20 teeth children have. How many more teeth does an adult have than a child?

12 teeth

Life Spans The average life spans of some animals are shown on the chart.

Average Life Spans

(67) Human
(35) African elephant
(25) Grizzly bear
(18) Black bear
(16) Tiger
(15) Cow
(12) Sea lion

Animals / Years
2 6 10   20   30   40   50   60   70

3. How many more years does a human usually live than a black bear?

49 years

4. What is the difference between the life spans of a grizzly bear and a tiger?

9 years

5. Two animals have life spans with a difference of 20 years. Which two animals are they?

African elephant and cow

6. **Writing in Math** Use the chart to write a subtraction problem where you must regroup to solve. Explain your solution.

Check students' subtraction problems and explanations.

Use with Lesson 3-7. **35**

© Pearson Education, Inc. 3

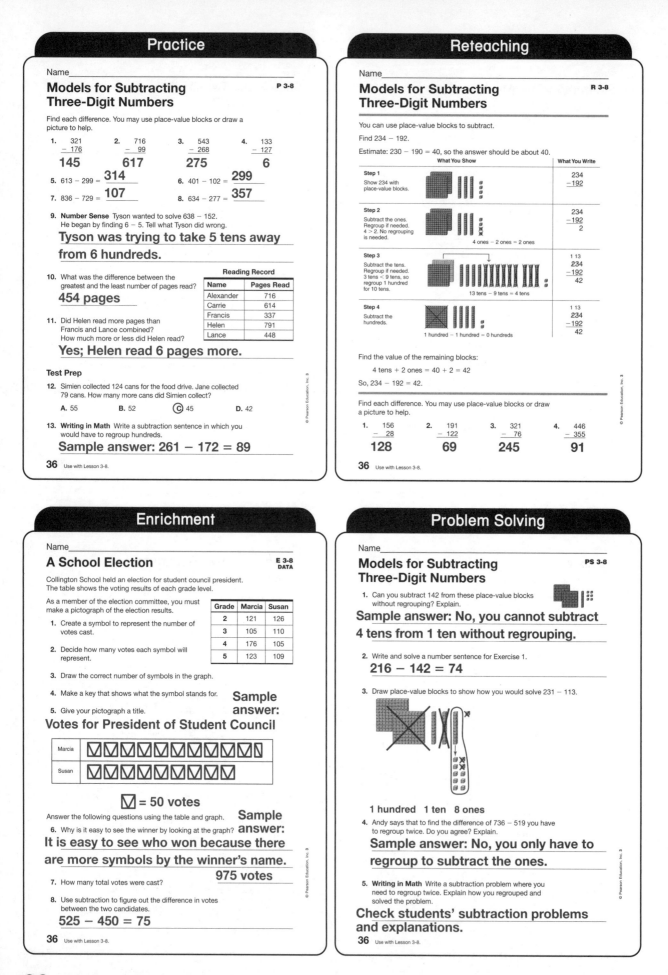

Practice

Name_____

Models for Subtracting Three-Digit Numbers

P 3-8

Find each difference. You may use place-value blocks or draw a picture to help.

1. 321
   − 176
   145

2. 716
   − 99
   617

3. 543
   − 268
   275

4. 133
   − 127
   6

5. 613 − 299 = **314**

6. 401 − 102 = **299**

7. 836 − 729 = **107**

8. 634 − 277 = **357**

9. **Number Sense** Tyson wanted to solve 638 − 152. He began by finding 6 − 5. Tell what Tyson did wrong.
Tyson was trying to take 5 tens away from 6 hundreds.

10. What was the difference between the greatest and the least number of pages read?
454 pages

Reading Record	
Name	Pages Read
Alexander	716
Carrie	614
Francis	337
Helen	791
Lance	448

11. Did Helen read more pages than Francis and Lance combined? How much more or less did Helen read?
Yes; Helen read 6 pages more.

Test Prep

12. Simien collected 124 cans for the food drive. Jane collected 79 cans. How many more cans did Simien collect?

A. 55   B. 52   **C.** 45   D. 42

13. **Writing in Math** Write a subtraction sentence in which you would have to regroup hundreds.
Sample answer: 261 − 172 = 89

36 Use with Lesson 3-8.

© Pearson Education, Inc. 3

Reteaching

Name_____

Models for Subtracting Three-Digit Numbers

R 3-8

You can use place-value blocks to subtract.

Find 234 − 192.

Estimate: 230 − 190 = 40, so the answer should be about 40.

What You Show		What You Write
Step 1 Show 234 with place-value blocks.		234 −192
Step 2 Subtract the ones. Regroup if needed. 4 > 2. No regrouping is needed.	4 ones − 2 ones = 2 ones	234 −192 2
Step 3 Subtract the tens. Regroup if needed. 3 tens < 9 tens, so regroup 1 hundred for 10 tens.	13 tens − 9 tens = 4 tens	1 13 234 −192 42
Step 4 Subtract the hundreds.	1 hundred − 1 hundred = 0 hundreds	1 13 234 −192 42

Find the value of the remaining blocks:

4 tens + 2 ones = 40 + 2 = 42

So, 234 − 192 = 42.

Find each difference. You may use place-value blocks or draw a picture to help.

1. 156
   − 28
   128

2. 191
   − 122
   69

3. 321
   − 76
   245

4. 446
   − 355
   91

36 Use with Lesson 3-8.

© Pearson Education, Inc. 3

Enrichment

Name_____

A School Election

E 3-8
DATA

Collington School held an election for student council president. The table shows the voting results of each grade level.

As a member of the election committee, you must make a pictograph of the election results.

Grade	Marcia	Susan
2	121	126
3	105	110
4	176	105
5	123	109

1. Create a symbol to represent the number of votes cast.

2. Decide how many votes each symbol will represent.

3. Draw the correct number of symbols in the graph.

4. Make a key that shows what the symbol stands for.

5. Give your pictograph a title.

Sample answer:

Votes for President of Student Council

Marcia	☑☑☑☑☑☑☑☑☑☑
Susan	☑☑☑☑☑☑☑☑

☑ = 50 votes

Answer the following questions using the table and graph.

6. Why is it easy to see the winner by looking at the graph? **Sample answer:**
It is easy to see who won because there are more symbols by the winner's name.

7. How many total votes were cast? **975 votes**

8. Use subtraction to figure out the difference in votes between the two candidates.
525 − 450 = 75

36 Use with Lesson 3-8.

© Pearson Education, Inc. 3

Problem Solving

Name_____

Models for Subtracting Three-Digit Numbers

PS 3-8

1. Can you subtract 142 from these place-value blocks without regrouping? Explain.
Sample answer: No, you cannot subtract 4 tens from 1 ten without regrouping.

2. Write and solve a number sentence for Exercise 1.
216 − 142 = 74

3. Draw place-value blocks to show how you would solve 231 − 113.

1 hundred 1 ten 8 ones

4. Andy says that to find the difference of 736 − 519 you have to regroup twice. Do you agree? Explain.
Sample answer: No, you only have to regroup to subtract the ones.

5. **Writing in Math** Write a subtraction problem where you need to regroup twice. Explain how you regrouped and solved the problem.
Check students' subtraction problems and explanations.

36 Use with Lesson 3-8.

© Pearson Education, Inc. 3

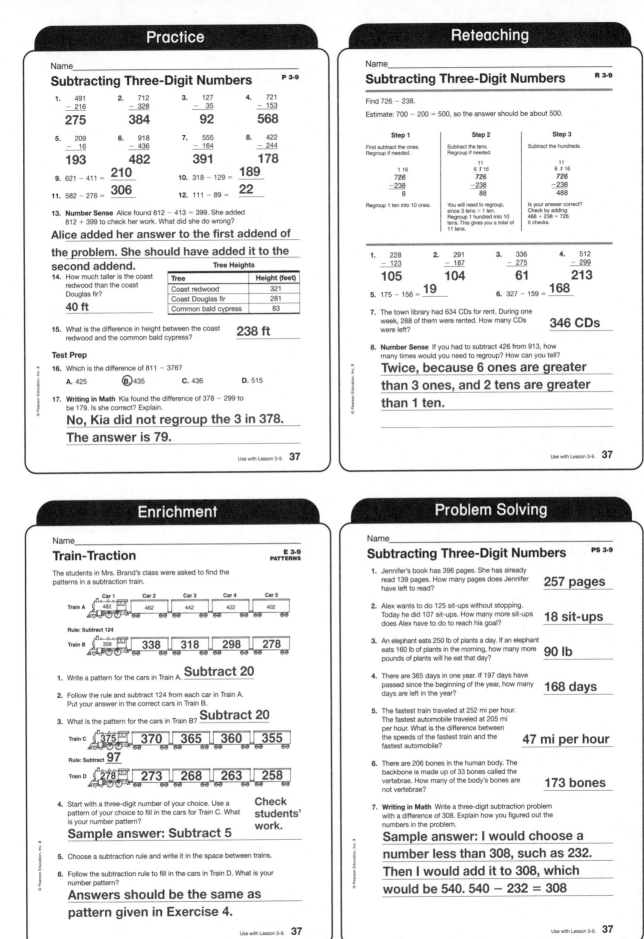

Practice

Name_____

Subtracting Three-Digit Numbers   P 3-9

| 1. | 491
− 216
275 | 2. | 712
− 328
384 | 3. | 127
− 35
92 | 4. | 721
− 153
568 |

| 5. | 209
− 16
193 | 6. | 918
− 436
482 | 7. | 555
− 164
391 | 8. | 422
− 244
178 |

9. 621 − 411 = **210**   10. 318 − 129 = **189**

11. 582 − 276 = **306**   12. 111 − 89 = **22**

13. **Number Sense** Alice found 812 − 413 = 399. She added 812 + 399 to check her work. What did she do wrong?

Alice added her answer to the first addend of the problem. She should have added it to the second addend.

14. How much taller is the coast redwood than the coast Douglas fir?

40 ft

Tree Heights

Tree	Height (feet)
Coast redwood	321
Coast Douglas fir	281
Common bald cypress	83

15. What is the difference in height between the coast redwood and the common bald cypress?   **238 ft**

Test Prep

16. Which is the difference of 811 − 376?

A. 425   **B.** 435   C. 436   D. 515

17. **Writing in Math** Kia found the difference of 378 − 299 to be 179. Is she correct? Explain.

No, Kia did not regroup the 3 in 378. The answer is 79.

Use with Lesson 3-9. **37**

Reteaching

Name_____

Subtracting Three-Digit Numbers   R 3-9

Find 726 − 238.

Estimate: 700 − 200 = 500, so the answer should be about 500.

Step 1	Step 2	Step 3
First subtract the ones. Regroup if needed.	Subtract the tens. Regroup if needed.	Subtract the hundreds.
1 16 726 −238 8	11 6 1 16 726 −238 88	11 6 1 16 726 −238 488
Regroup 1 ten into 10 ones.	You will need to regroup, since 3 tens > 1 ten. Regroup 1 hundred into 10 tens. This gives you a total of 11 tens.	Is your answer correct? Check by adding: 488 + 238 = 726. It checks.

| 1. | 228
− 123
105 | 2. | 291
− 187
104 | 3. | 336
− 275
61 | 4. | 512
− 299
213 |

5. 175 − 156 = **19**   6. 327 − 159 = **168**

7. The town library had 634 CDs for rent. During one week, 288 of them were rented. How many CDs were left?   **346 CDs**

8. **Number Sense** If you had to subtract 426 from 913, how many times would you need to regroup? How can you tell?

Twice, because 6 ones are greater than 3 ones, and 2 tens are greater than 1 ten.

Use with Lesson 3-9. **37**

Enrichment

Name_____

Train-Traction   E 3-9 PATTERNS

The students in Mrs. Brand's class were asked to find the patterns in a subtraction train.

Train A: Car 1: 482, Car 2: 462, Car 3: 442, Car 4: 422, Car 5: 402

Rule: Subtract 124

Train B: 358, **338**, **318**, **298**, **278**

1. Write a pattern for the cars in Train A.   **Subtract 20**

2. Follow the rule and subtract 124 from each car in Train A. Put your answer in the correct cars in Train B.

3. What is the pattern for the cars in Train B?   **Subtract 20**

Train C: 375, **370**, **365**, **360**, **355**

Rule: Subtract **97**

Train D: 278, **273**, **268**, **263**, **258**

4. Start with a three-digit number of your choice. Use a pattern of your choice to fill in the cars for Train C. What is your number pattern?

Check students' work.

Sample answer: Subtract 5

5. Choose a subtraction rule and write it in the space between trains.

6. Follow the subtraction rule to fill in the cars in Train D. What is your number pattern?

Answers should be the same as pattern given in Exercise 4.

Use with Lesson 3-9. **37**

Problem Solving

Name_____

Subtracting Three-Digit Numbers   PS 3-9

1. Jennifer's book has 396 pages. She has already read 139 pages. How many pages does Jennifer have left to read?   **257 pages**

2. Alex wants to do 125 sit-ups without stopping. Today he did 107 sit-ups. How many more sit-ups does Alex have to do to reach his goal?   **18 sit-ups**

3. An elephant eats 250 lb of plants a day. If an elephant eats 160 lb of plants in the morning, how many more pounds of plants will he eat that day?   **90 lb**

4. There are 365 days in one year. If 197 days have passed since the beginning of the year, how many days are left in the year?   **168 days**

5. The fastest train traveled at 252 mi per hour. The fastest automobile traveled at 205 mi per hour. What is the difference between the speeds of the fastest train and the fastest automobile?   **47 mi per hour**

6. There are 206 bones in the human body. The backbone is made up of 33 bones called the vertebrae. How many of the body's bones are not vertebrae?   **173 bones**

7. **Writing in Math** Write a three-digit subtraction problem with a difference of 308. Explain how you figured out the numbers in the problem.

Sample answer: I would choose a number less than 308, such as 232. Then I would add it to 308, which would be 540. 540 − 232 = 308

Use with Lesson 3-9. **37**

© Pearson Education, Inc. 3

Name_____

Subtracting Across Zero

P 3-10

1. 406
  − 28
378
	2. 300
	  − 211
	89
		3. 501
		  − 268
		233
			4. 707
			  − 77
			630

5. 605
  − 219
386
	6. 800
	  − 579
	221
		7. 901
		  − 728
		173
			8. 704
			  − 95
			609

9. 404 − 305 = **99** _____

10. 501 − 223 = **278** _____

11. Patricia estimated that 439 − 186 would be close to 300.
Do you agree? Explain and solve the problem.

No, 439 rounds to 400 and 186 rounds

to 200. 400 − 200 = 200

12. There are 600 ears of corn for sale at the produce market.
At the end of the day there are 212 ears left. How many
ears of corn were sold?

388 ears of corn

13. Party Palace has an order for 505 party favors. It packaged 215
favors in the morning and 180 favors in the afternoon. How
many party favors does it still need to package to fill the order?

110 party favors

Test Prep

14. 3 hundreds, 10 tens, 6 ones =

   A. 316   B. 306   C. 416   (D) 406

15. **Writing in Math** Explain how you can estimate to tell **Sample**
whether 433 − 147 = 286 is reasonable. **answer:**
433 rounds to 400 and 147 rounds to 100;
400 − 100 = 300; 300 is close to 286, so
the answer is reasonable.

Name_____

Subtracting Across Zero

R 3-10

To subtract from a number with a zero in the tens place, you
need to first regroup a hundred into tens.

Find 207 − 98.

Step 1	Step 2	Step 3
Subtract the ones. Regroup if necessary.	Regroup the hundreds.	Regroup the tens and subtract.
207 − 98	1 10 2̶0̶7 − 98	9 17 1 10 2̶0̶7̶ − 98 109
Normally you would regroup 1 ten into 10 ones. Since there are no tens, you must first regroup hundreds.	2 hundreds and 0 tens is equal to 1 hundred and 10 tens. Now you can regroup the tens.	10 tens and 7 ones is the same as 9 tens and 17 ones. Now you can subtract.

1. 302 − 72 **230**	2. 105 − 36 **69**	3. 300 − 228 **72**	4. 500 − 223 **277**

5. 105 − 37 = **68** _____

6. 301 − 192 = **109** _____

7. Dave and Chris went bowling. Dave knocked down
300 pins and Chris knocked down 187 pins. How
many fewer pins did Chris knock down than Dave? **113 pins**

8. **Writing in Math** Use place-value blocks to draw a picture
showing one way to find 406 − 202.

Drawings should show 3 hundreds,

10 tens, 6 ones and 1 hundred,

10 tens, 2 ones.

Name_____

Quilt Quest

E 3-10
VISUAL THINKING

Marianne is making two samples each of her award-winning
quilts. She plans to keep one quilt and donate the other to a
local charity. She is almost finished with the second quilt of
each type except for one detail.

Finish the quilt on the right to match the quilt on the left.

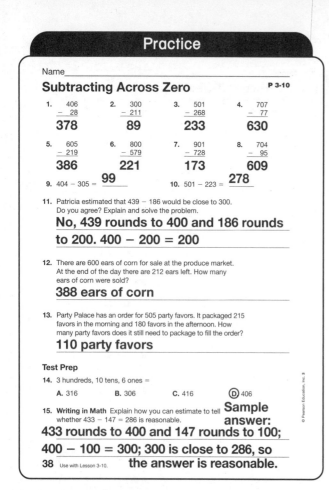

Name_____

Subtracting Across Zero

PS 3-10

1. Heather's book has 100 pages. She has 37 pages
left to read. How many pages has Heather
already read? **63 pages**

2. Mrs. Healy's class needs 250 points to earn their
next field trip. They have already earned 107 points.
How many points do they still need to earn? **143 points**

3. A box of paper has 500 sheets. Mr. Paton's class
used 426 sheets of paper during the last six
months. How many sheets are left in the box? **74 sheets less**

4. The Sears Tower in Chicago, Illinois, has 110 stories.
The Jin Mao Building in Shanghai, China, has 88
stories. How many stories taller is the Sears Tower? **22 stories**

Everglades Everglades National Park is home to 300 species
of birds, 120 kinds of trees, and 25 types of orchids.

5. Mikayla was able to find 87 different trees
during a two-day hike with her family. How
many more trees can she find? **33 more trees**

6. How many more types of trees are there
than types of orchids? **95 more trees**

7. Badlands National Park has 56 species of grass. Is this more
or less than the kinds of trees found in Everglades National
Park? Write a number sentence to show your answer.

Less; 120 − 56 = 64 trees

8. **Writing in Math** Write your own word problem about the
birds that live in the Everglades. Then solve the problem.

Check students' problems and solutions.

_____

_____

Name_____

PROBLEM-SOLVING SKILL   P 3-11

Exact Answer or Estimate?

Were less than 50 sack lunches eaten
during the week?

Sack Lunches	
Monday:	▢▢▢▢
Tuesday:	▢
Wednesday:	▢▢▢▢▢
Thursday:	▢▢
Friday:	▢▢◣

Each ▢ = 2 sack lunches.
Each ◣ = 1 sack lunch.

1. What do you know?

**The number of sack
lunches eaten
each day**

2. What are you trying to find?

**If 50 sack lunches or less were eaten
during the whole week**

3. What operation will you use? **Addition**

4. Is an estimate enough? Explain.

**Yes; You only need to find if there
were more than or less than 50 sack
lunches.**

5. Solve the problem. Give your answer in a complete sentence.

Less than 50 sack lunches were eaten.

6. How many more sack lunches were eaten on Wednesday
than on Thursday?

4 more sack lunches

Name_____

PROBLEM-SOLVING SKILL   R 3-11

Exact Answer or Estimate?

There are times when an estimate is enough to solve a problem.
Sometimes an exact answer is needed.

Reading Competition Sanjay and Teresa
are having a reading competition. The
table shows how many books each
has read. How many more books has
Sanjay read than Teresa?

Month	Sanjay	Teresa
January	12 books	15 books
February	27 books	21 books
March	22 books	8 books
April	6 books	13 books

The problem asks for an exact answer.
To find out the exact answer, you need
to add the books read by Sanjay and the books read by Teresa.
Sanjay read 67 books. Teresa read 57 books. Then you need to
subtract the number of books read by Teresa from the number
of books read by Sanjay. $67 - 57 = 10$. Sanjay read exactly
10 more books than Teresa.

If the question had been "Who has read more books, Sanjay or
Teresa?" an estimate would be enough.

Water Park Crowd On a sunny day, 108 people were at the water
park. After an hour, 36 people had left. A little bit later, 24 people came
back to the water park. How many people are now at the water park?

1. What operations will you use? Explain.

**Sample answer: I will use both
addition and subtraction.**

2. Is an estimate enough? Explain.

**No; The question requires an exact
answer of how many people.**

3. Solve the problem. Write your answer in a complete sentence.

**There are 96 people at the water park
right now.**

Name_____

E 3-11
ESTIMATION

Be Prepared

David is helping his teacher plan for the school picnic. Decide
if he needs to find an exact answer or an estimate. Write the
estimate or exact answer on David's picnic list.

David's Picnic List	
Estimate	**Exact Amount**
1.—	1. **24 yd**
2. **2 bolts**	2.—
3. **4 spools**	3.—
4. **10 boxes**	4.—
5.—	5. **16 badges**

1. David needs fabric for 8 picnic tables. Each table will need
3 yd of checkered fabric. How many yards are needed?

2. If checkered fabric is sold only in bolts of 20 yd, how many
bolts should David buy?

3. Each of the 8 classes requires a banner that will identify
its class. Each banner should be 24 in. long. Banners
come in 50-in. spools. How many spools of banner does
David need?

4. Granola bars are served as snacks at the picnic. David
figures that 96 students will come and each will eat about
2 granola bars. One box has 20 granola bars. How many
boxes does he need?

5. Every teacher must wear an identification badge. Two
teachers will represent each of the 8 classes. How many
badges will David need?

Name_____

PROBLEM-SOLVING SKILL   PS 3-11

Exact Answer or Estimate?

Coat Drive The third-grade classes collected used coats and
jackets to give to a clothing drive. Their goal was to collect at
least 55 coats. Did they meet their goal?

Coat Drive	
Class	**Number of Coats**
3 A	○○○○○○○○○○○○
3 B	○○○○○○○○○□
3 C	○○○○○○○○○○□

Each ○ = 2 coats.
Each □ = 1 coat.

Read and Understand

1. How many coats were collected by each class?

3A: 24 coats; 3B: 19 coats; 3C: 21 coats

2. What are you trying to find?

If the classes collected at least 55 coats

Plan and Solve

3. Is an estimate enough? Explain.

Yes, because it says *at least* 55 coats.

4. Solve the problem. Write your answer in a complete
sentence.

The classes collected at least 55 coats.

Look Back and Check

5. How do you know your estimate is reasonable?

**Sample
answer:
Each number rounds to 20, and 20 + 20
+ 20 = 60. 60 is greater than 55.**

Practice

Name_____

Adding and Subtracting Money P 3-12

| 1. $7.29
− 1.03
$6.26 | 2. $3.50
+ 2.91
$6.41 | 3. $6.00
− 2.59
$3.41 | 4. $17.99
− 13.86
$4.13 |

| 5. $20.00
− 18.42
$1.58 | 6. $12.04
+ 3.16
$15.20 | 7. $4.21
+ 3.99
$8.20 | 8. $6.18
− 3.19
$2.99 |

9. $7.83 + $0.62 = **$8.45** 10. $16.02 − $5.19 = **$10.83**

11. $18.21 + $14.36 = **$32.57** 12. $27.36 − $15.29 = **$12.07**

13. Liz gets paid $4.75 each day for delivering newspapers. How much money will she have after delivering newspapers for 3 days?

Liz will have $14.25.

14. Liz saved her money for 3 days to buy new tennis shoes for $16.98. Tell how much money she still needs or how much she will have left over.

Liz still needs $2.73.

Test Prep

15. Sam paid for a notebook that costs $0.76 with a $1.00 bill. What was his change?
(A.) $0.24   B. $0.42   C. $0.75   D. $0.34

16. **Writing in Math** Austin paid for $4.77 worth of groceries with a $5.00 bill. Could he have received a quarter with his change? Explain.

No; He gets $0.23 in change, and a quarter is worth $0.25.

40 Use with Lesson 3-12.

Reteaching

Name_____

Adding and Subtracting Money R 3-12

Find $12.50 + $9.25.

Estimate: $13 + $9 = $22.

Step 1	Step 2
Add as you would with whole numbers. Make sure to line up the decimal points before adding.	Write the answer in dollars and cents. Be sure to include the decimal point.
1 $12.50 + 9.25 21 75	1 $12.50 + 9.25 $21.75

$12.50 + $9.25 = $21.75

| 1. $2.87
+ 1.09
$3.96 | 2. $15.31
− 2.27
$13.04 | 3. $ 3.67
+ 13.22
$16.89 | 4. $10.07
− 0.88
$9.19 |

5. $7.65 + $0.82 **$8.47**   6. $17.21 − $12.33 **$4.88**

7. $14.31 + $36.29 **$50.60**   8. $9.27 − $8.85 **$0.42**

9. Wallace bought a model airplane for $6.93. He paid with a $20 bill. How much change did Wallace get back? **$13.07**

10. **Writing in Math** Samina wants to pay for some balloons with a $10 bill. The balloons cost $1.79. Samina estimates that she will get $7.00 back in change. Do you agree with her estimate? Explain.

Sample answer: No, $1.79 is about $2.00, so her estimate should have been about $8.00.

40 Use with Lesson 3-12.

Enrichment

Name_____

Book Sale E 3-12
DECISION MAKING

Best Price Books is having a sale on new books. The newspaper ad shows the regular price and the sale price. You have $25.00 saved for gifts. Decide how you might spend your money to buy presents for the 5 other people in your family.

Book Type	Regular Price	Sale Price
Sports	$10.35	$9.20
Cooking	$8.75	$6.35
Mystery	$5.95	$3.25
Easy reading	$3.42	$2.50
Travel	$6.99	$2.95

1. Put the books in order from least expensive to most expensive according to their regular price.

Easy reading, mystery, travel, cooking, sports

2. Put the books in order from least expensive to most expensive according to their sale price. What was the difference in the order?

Easy reading, travel, mystery, cooking, sports; Travel and mystery changed places.

3. Which kind of book had its price reduced the most? By what amount?
Travel; $4.04

4. You have made a list of your family and their favorite books. Decide how you could spend the $25.00 so that each one receives a book. How much change would you get back?

Older brother—sports Younger brother—easy reading and sports
Sister—travel and sports Mom—cooking and mystery
Dad—travel and cooking

Sample answer: Older brother: sports, younger brother: easy reading, sister: travel, mom: mystery, dad: travel; $4.15

40 Use with Lesson 3-12.

Problem Solving

Name_____

Adding and Subtracting Money PS 3-12

1. Hillary paid a $3.75 admission fee to tour the zoo. She paid with a $5.00 bill. How much change did she get? **$1.25**

2. Hillary ate lunch at the zoo's snack shop. She paid $1.98 for a ham sandwich and $1.03 for a large fruit juice. How much money did she spend for lunch? **$3.01**

3. Hillary would like to treat her younger brother and sister to a day at the zoo. How much will she have to save to pay for all three admissions? **$11.25**

Gift Shop Hillary stopped at the zoo's gift shop before returning home. The chart shows a price list of items for sale.

Elephant puzzle	$3.95
Postcard pack	$1.87
Lion mug	$2.89
Zoo blocks	$4.80
Monkey puppet	$3.75

4. Hillary paid for the postcard pack with two $1.00 bills. How much change did she get?
$0.13

5. How much would a monkey puppet and zoo blocks cost? **$8.55**

6. If a customer paid for 2 items with a $10.00 bill and had $2.31 left over, what 2 items did he buy?
Lion mug and zoo blocks

7. **Writing in Math** Joe estimates that since he has only $5.00, he can't buy 2 different items as gifts for his parents. Do you agree with his estimate? Explain.

No; The postcard pack is < $2.00 and the lion mug is < $3.00, so he could buy 2 gifts with $5.00.

40 Use with Lesson 3-12.

© Pearson Education, Inc. 3

Name_____

Choose a Computation Method   P 3-13

Use mental math, paper and pencil, or a calculator to solve.

1.	716	2.	11,234	3.	$4.76	4.	720
	− 310		− 2,378		+ 2.25		− 319
	406		**8,856**		**$7.01**		**401**

5.	$32.61	6.	780	7.	400	8.	204,516
	+ 19.86		− 298		− 312		+ 307,629
	$52.47		**482**		**88**		**512,145**

9. 158 + 269 = **427**   10. $13.00 − $9.57 = **$3.43**

11. **Number Sense** Would you use mental math to solve
2,984 + 1,997 + 406? Explain.

No; The numbers are too big, and I would need to regroup.

12. Pauline subtracted 3,162 − 1,498 as shown.   3,162
What did Pauline do wrong?   −1,498
                                                   2,664

Pauline forgot to change the 3 to a 2 when she regrouped 1 thousand for 10 hundreds.

Test Prep

13. Find 650 − 298.

A. 352   B. 350   C. 302   D. 358

14. **Writing in Math** Solve this problem with pencil and paper:
2,593 + 1,389. Tell one way you could check your answer.

3,982; Sample answer: I could estimate to see if I am close: 3,000 + 1,000 = 4,000. That is close to 3,928.

Use with Lesson 3-13. **41**

Name_____

Choose a Computation Method   R 3-13

Use mental math to solve problems that are simple.

Example: 250 + 200

Use paper and pencil, and make estimates to solve problems
with two or more regroupings.

Example: 524 + 217   1
I estimate 524 to be 500. I estimate 217   524
to be 200. So, my answer should be about 700.   + 217
My estimate of 700 is close to 741.   741

Use a calculator to solve problems with many regroupings.
Example: 23,142 − 17,565
First I'll estimate by rounding to the nearest thousand:
23,000 − 18,000 = 6,000.
23,142 − 17,565 = 5,577
My estimate of 6,000 is close to 5,577.

Use mental math, paper and pencil, or a calculator to solve.

1.	1,200	2.	$26.91	3.	300	4.	96,346
	+ 800		+ 42.03		− 109		− 18,982
	2,000		**$68.94**		**191**		**77,364**

5. Backbone Mountain in Maryland is 3,360 ft high. Mount
Washington in New Hampshire is 6,288 ft high. How much
higher is Mount Washington than Backbone Mountain?
Write your answer in a complete sentence.

Mount Washington is 2,928 ft higher than Backbone Mountain.

Use with Lesson 3-13. **41**

Name_____

The Best Method   E 3-13
                                  MENTAL MATH

You can choose different methods to solve different kinds of
problems. Answer the questions. Then place the letter clue into
the riddle that matches the sum or difference.

1.	380	2.	220
	+ 210		+ 770
	590 T		**990** N

Write two mental math addition problems that equal the sums given.

3. **320** + **215** = 535 A

4. **1,190** + **910** = 2,100 E

Sample answers given for 3–7.

Solve the following problems by using either mental math,
paper and pencil, or a calculator. Use each method only once.
Explain why you chose that method to solve the problem.

5. 89,808
   − 83,999
   5,809 N

There are many regroupings, so a calculator works best.

6. 748
   − 119
   629 E

It would be hard to subtract mentally, so paper and pencil work well.

7. 470
   − 310
   160 I

It is easy to do this problem mentally because there are no regroupings.

8. Riddle Question: Why was the number 6 afraid of the number 7?

Answer:

Because s e v e n **A T E   N I N E**!
                    535 590 2,100 990 160 5,809 629

Use with Lesson 3-13. **41**

Name_____

Choose a Computation Method   PS 3-13

1. Tell how you could use mental math to solve 368 − 199.

Sample answer: Subtract 200 from 368 = 168. Then add 1 because 1 was added to 199. 168 + 1 = 169

Languages Many different
languages are spoken all over the
world. The most widely spoken
languages are shown on the table.

2. How many people speak
English and Spanish? What
computation method did
you use?

802 million people; Pencil and paper

| World Languages | |
Language	Number of People (in millions)
Mandarin Chinese	885
Hindustani	461
English	450
Spanish	352

3. How many more people speak Hindustani than Spanish?
What computation method did you use?

109 million more people; Pencil and paper

4. **Writing in Math** Explain when you would choose to use a
calculator to solve a math problem.

Sample answer: When the problem has a lot of large numbers, or when there is a lot of regrouping

Use with Lesson 3-13. **41**

© Pearson Education, Inc. 3

Name_____

Equality and Inequality

P 3-14

Compare. Write <, >, or = for each $\bigcirc$.

1. $20 \;\boxed{<}\; 13 + 9$

2. $14 - 7 \;\boxed{<}\; 16 - 8$

3. $32 + 5 + 3 \;\boxed{=}\; 40$

4. $268 - 112 \;\boxed{<}\; 112 + 268$

5. $\$3.29 + \$7.16 \;\boxed{<}\; \$10.50$

6. $1 + 2 + 3 \;\boxed{=}\; 3 + 2 + 1$

Find three whole numbers that make each number **Sample answers:**
sentence true.

7. $15 + x > 18$ $x =$ **4, 5, 6, 7**

8. $375 - n < 200$ $n =$ **176, 177, 178, 179**

9. Which two animals are able to spend an equal number of minutes under water?

The hippopotamus

and the porpoise

Average Breath-Holding Time Underwater

Animal	Minutes
Hippopotamus	15
Muskrat	12
Platypus	10
Porpoise	15
Sea otter	5

10. The muskrat can hold its breath for a greater amount of time than which two animals?

The platypus and the sea otter

Test Prep

11. Which number does not make the number sentence

$26 + y > 30$ true?

A. 10   (B) 4   C. 7   D. 100

12. **Writing in Math** Write a number sentence with two expressions that equal each other.

Sample answers: $3 + 7 = 4 + 6$,

$12 - 6 = 3 + 3$

Name_____

Equality and Inequality

R 3-14

A number sentence that uses < (less than) or > (greater than) is an inequality. Example: $8 > 1 + 6$. This equation is read as 8 is *greater than* $1 + 6$.

You can add or subtract on each side of a number sentence to decide if the sentence is true or false.

$$9 + 7 > 8 + 6 \qquad 9 - 2 > 8 + 1$$
$$16 \quad > \quad 14 \qquad\quad 7 \quad > \quad 9$$
True   False

Find a number to make the number sentence true.

$3 + \underline{\hspace{1cm}} > 8$

Try 2. $3 + 2 > 8$

        $5 > 8$ False

Try 7. $3 + 7 > 8$

        $10 > 8$ True

Compare. Write <, >, or = for each $\bigcirc$.

1. $13 + 7 \;\boxed{=}\; 20$

2. $14 + 22 \;\boxed{<}\; 37 + 1$

3. $42 - 18 \;\boxed{<}\; 27 + 6$

4. $28 - 14 \;\boxed{=}\; 5 + 9$

Find three whole numbers that make each number sentence true.

5. $5 + \underline{\hspace{1cm}} < 15$ **Answers may vary.**

Any numbers from zero through 9

6. $19 - \underline{\hspace{1cm}} < 12$

Any numbers greater than 7

7. $27 + \underline{\hspace{1cm}} > 30$

Any numbers greater than 3

Name_____

A Question of Balance

E 3-14
ALGEBRA

If you answer the questions correctly, the beam will get balanced.

☐ Weight

- If the problem has a < sign, draw the weight on the left side of the balance.

- If the problem has a > sign, draw the weight on the right side.

- If the problem has an = sign, draw a weight on both sides.

Write >, <, or = in each circle to make the statement true. Then draw the weight in the correct position on the balance beam.

| 8 |
| 6 |
| 3 |
| 2 |
| 1 |

| 7 |
| 5 |
| 4 |
| 3 |
| 1 |

1. 24 copies of a newspaper $\boxed{=}$ 2 dozen copies of the same newspaper

2. $100 \;\boxed{<}\; 77 + 77$

3. $202 - 198 \;\boxed{=}\; 303 - 299$

4. $8 + 297 \;\boxed{>}\; 300$

5. $333 - 325 \;\boxed{>}\; 5$

6. $200 + 57 + 502 \;\boxed{<}\; 902$

7. $135 - 49 \;\boxed{>}\; 456 - 381$

8. $27 + 32 \;\boxed{<}\; 74 + 68$

Name_____

Equality and Inequality

PS 3-14

1. Krista, Carol, and Ben all solved the problem $1 + 7 < 10 - \underline{\hspace{1cm}}$. Krista says the answer is 1. Carol says the answer is 2. Ben says the answer is 0. Are their answers correct? Explain.

Krista is correct because 8 is less than 9. Carol is wrong because 8 is not less than 8. Ben is correct because 8 is less than 10.

2. Find three whole numbers that make $106 + x > 212$ true.

Correct answers are numbers greater than 106.

3. Harper thinks there is more than one whole number that will make $16 - x = 9$ true. Do you agree? Explain.

No, only $16 - 7 = 9$.

4. The number sentence $17 + 2 = 15$ is false. Find two ways you could change it to make it true.

Sample answer: $17 + 2 = 19$; $17 - 2 = 15$

5. **Writing in Math** Write a number sentence that makes the expressions $11 + x$ and $16 - 3$ equal. Explain how you would find what numbers and symbols would make it true.

Sample answer: $11 + 2 = 16 - 3$. Adding 2 to 11 makes the expressions equal.

Name_____

PROBLEM-SOLVING APPLICATIONS   P 3-15

Bow-Wow Facts

The American Kennel Club (AKC) is a national group that has lots of information about dogs, including ways to keep dogs healthy, facts about different kinds of dogs, and rules in dog shows.

1. The AKC says that a male Alaskan malamute show dog should weigh about 85 lb and that a female should weigh about 10 lb less. About how much should a female weigh?

About 75 lb

2. The average female St. Bernard show dog weighs about 145 lb. The average male St. Bernard weighs about 20 lb more. About how much does the average male St. Bernard show dog weigh?

About 165 lb

3. Suppose you have 3 greyhounds for pets. They weigh 56 lb, 72 lb, and 63 lb. What is their combined weight?

191 lb

4. Suppose you want to buy some 40 lb bags of dog food at $33.00 per bag, including tax. If you had $100.00, could you buy 3 bags? Explain.

Yes; $33.00 + $33.00 + $33.00 = $99.00, which is less than $100.00.

5. Suppose you wanted to buy some dog toys and supplies. The total cost is $127.73. To find how much change you would get from $150.00, would it be best to use mental math, pencil and paper, or a calculator? Explain.

Sample answer: It would be best to use a calculator because you have to do many regroupings.

Name_____

PROBLEM-SOLVING APPLICATIONS   R 3-15

Small Countries

This chart shows the area of several small countries.

If Grenada's area was increased by 84 square kilometers, how many square kilometers would it be?

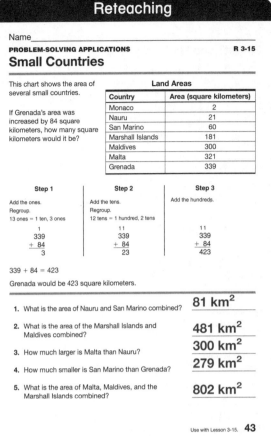

Land Areas	
Country	Area (square kilometers)
Monaco	2
Nauru	21
San Marino	60
Marshall Islands	181
Maldives	300
Malta	321
Grenada	339

Step 1
Add the ones.
Regroup.
13 ones = 1 ten, 3 ones
```
  1
 339
+ 84
   3
```

Step 2
Add the tens.
Regroup.
12 tens = 1 hundred, 2 tens
```
 11
 339
+ 84
  23
```

Step 3
Add the hundreds.
```
 11
 339
+ 84
 423
```

339 + 84 = 423

Grenada would be 423 square kilometers.

1. What is the area of Nauru and San Marino combined? **81 km^2**

2. What is the area of the Marshall Islands and Maldives combined? **481 km^2**

3. How much larger is Malta than Nauru? **300 km^2**

4. How much smaller is San Marino than Grenada? **279 km^2**

5. What is the area of Malta, Maldives, and the Marshall Islands combined? **802 km^2**

Name_____

Race to Victory!   E 3-15
REASONING

Six students entered this year's Fun Race.

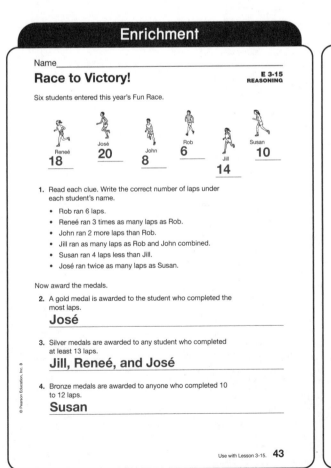

Renée **18**   José **20**   John **8**   Rob **6**   Jill **14**   Susan **10**

1. Read each clue. Write the correct number of laps under each student's name.

   • Rob ran 6 laps.
   • Renée ran 3 times as many laps as Rob.
   • John ran 2 more laps than Rob.
   • Jill ran as many laps as Rob and John combined.
   • Susan ran 4 laps less than Jill.
   • José ran twice as many laps as Susan.

Now award the medals.

2. A gold medal is awarded to the student who completed the most laps.

   José

3. Silver medals are awarded to any student who completed at least 13 laps.

   Jill, Renée, and José

4. Bronze medals are awarded to anyone who completed 10 to 12 laps.

   Susan

Name_____

PROBLEM-SOLVING APPLICATIONS   PS 3-15

Leaf Collection

Mikel spent $13.19 on supplies to display his leaf collection. He paid for the supplies with a $10.00 bill, a $5.00 bill, and a quarter. How much money did he have left?

Read and Understand

1. How much did Mikel spend? **$13.19**

2. How much did Mikel use to pay for the supplies? **$15.25**

3. What are you trying to find?

   How much money Mikel has left

Plan and Solve

4. Write a number sentence and solve the problem.

   $15.25 − $13.19 = $2.06

5. Write the answer in a complete sentence.

   Mikel has $2.06 left.

Look Back and Check

6. Explain how you can check your answer.

   Sample answer: Add $2.06 to $13.19 to see if it equals $15.25.

Solve Another Problem

7. Alaskan fur seals travel as far as 3,200 km south each autumn. Monarch butterflies travel to southern parts of North America, often traveling 1,600 km. How many more kilometers do fur seals travel than monarch butterflies?

   1,600 km more

Practice

Name_____

Time to the Half Hour and Quarter Hour

P 4-1

Sample answers for 1–2.

Write the time shown on each clock in two ways.

1. 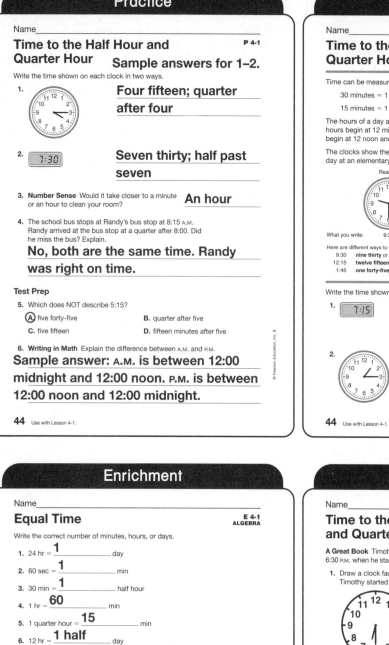 **Four fifteen; quarter after four**

2. `7:30`   **Seven thirty; half past seven**

3. **Number Sense** Would it take closer to a minute or an hour to clean your room? **An hour**

4. The school bus stops at Randy's bus stop at 8:15 A.M. Randy arrived at the bus stop at a quarter after 8:00. Did he miss the bus? Explain.

   No, both are the same time. Randy was right on time.

Test Prep

5. Which does NOT describe 5:15?
   Ⓐ five forty-five   B. quarter after five
   C. five fifteen   D. fifteen minutes after five

6. **Writing in Math** Explain the difference between A.M. and P.M.

   Sample answer: A.M. is between 12:00 midnight and 12:00 noon. P.M. is between 12:00 noon and 12:00 midnight.

© Pearson Education, Inc. 3

Reteaching

Name_____

Time to the Half Hour and Quarter Hour

R 4-1

Time can be measured in half hours and quarter hours.

    30 minutes = 1 half hour
    15 minutes = 1 quarter hour

The hours of a day are divided into A.M. and P.M. hours. A.M. hours begin at 12 midnight and end at 12 noon. P.M. hours begin at 12 noon and end at 12 midnight.

The clocks show the times of three events that happen every day at an elementary school.

Reading   Lunch   Recess

`1:45`

What you write: 9:30   12:15

Here are different ways to say each time.
 9:30   **nine thirty** or **half past nine**
12:15   **twelve fifteen** or **fifteen minutes after twelve** or **quarter after twelve**
 1:45   **one forty-five** or **fifteen minutes to two** or **quarter to two**

Write the time shown on each clock in two ways. **Sample answers:**

1. `7:15`   **Seven fifteen, a quarter past seven, or 15 minutes after seven**

2. **One fifteen, a quarter after one, or fifteen after one**

© Pearson Education, Inc. 3

Enrichment

Name_____

Equal Time

E 4-1
ALGEBRA

Write the correct number of minutes, hours, or days.

1. 24 hr = **1** _____ day
2. 60 sec = **1** _____ min
3. 30 min = **1** _____ half hour
4. 1 hr = **60** _____ min
5. 1 quarter hour = **15** _____ min
6. 12 hr = **1 half** _____ day
7. 45 min = **3** _____ quarter hours
8. 2 days = **48** _____ hr
9. four quarter hours = **60** _____ min
10. 1 hr = **2** _____ half hours
11. 1 half hour + 1 quarter hour = **45** _____ min
12. 4 quarter hours + 1 hr = **2** _____ hr
13. 1 hr = 15 min + **3** _____ quarter hours
14. 4 half hours − 2 half hours = **2** _____ half hours
15. 60 min − 1 half hour = **30** _____ min

© Pearson Education, Inc. 3

Problem Solving

Name_____

Time to the Half Hour and Quarter Hour

PS 4-1

A Great Book Timothy was reading a book about dinosaurs. It was 6:30 P.M. when he started reading. His bedtime was at 8:00 P.M.

1. Draw a clock face with the hands showing the time Timothy started reading.

2. Draw a clock face with the hands showing Timothy's bedtime.

3. Timothy finished reading chapter 9 at the time shown. Write the time in two ways.

   7:45; quarter to eight

4. **Writing in Math** Timothy wakes up for school at the time shown. Write the time Timothy wakes up in two different ways using words.   `7:15 A.M.`

   It is 7:15; so the time can be written as seven fifteen or as quarter after seven.

© Pearson Education, Inc. 3

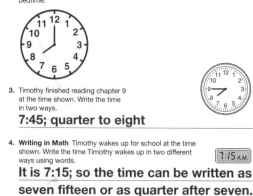

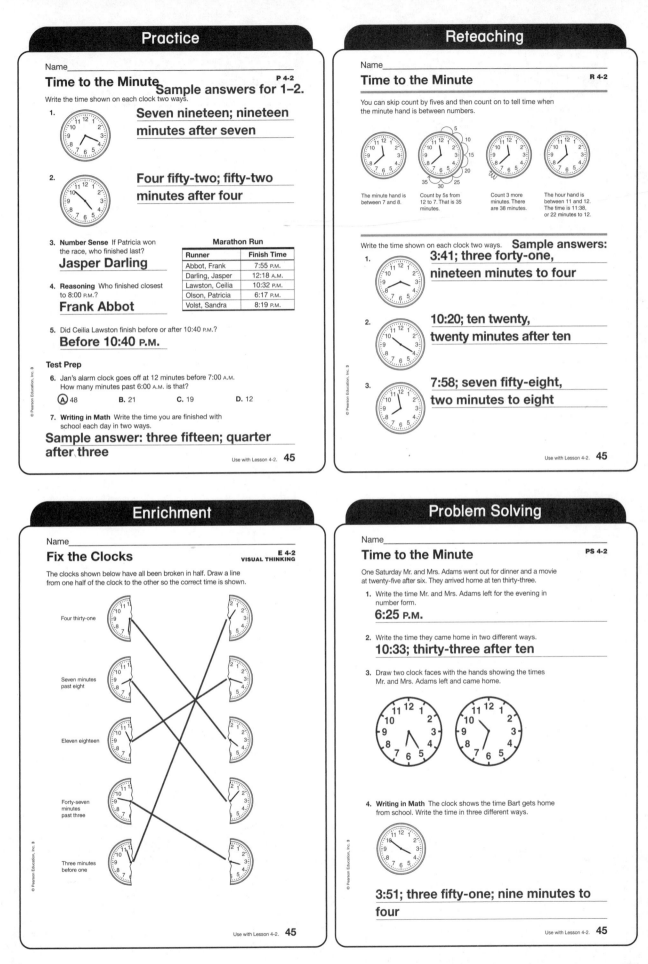

Practice

Name_____

Time to the Minute

Sample answers for 1–2.

P 4-2

Write the time shown on each clock two ways.

1. **Seven nineteen; nineteen minutes after seven**

2. **Four fifty-two; fifty-two minutes after four**

3. **Number Sense** If Patricia won the race, who finished last?
   Jasper Darling

4. **Reasoning** Who finished closest to 8:00 P.M.?
   Frank Abbot

Marathon Run	
Runner	Finish Time
Abbot, Frank	7:55 P.M.
Darling, Jasper	12:18 A.M.
Lawston, Ceilia	10:32 P.M.
Olson, Patricia	6:17 P.M.
Volst, Sandra	8:19 P.M.

5. Did Ceilia Lawston finish before or after 10:40 P.M.?
   Before 10:40 P.M.

Test Prep

6. Jan's alarm clock goes off at 12 minutes before 7:00 A.M. How many minutes past 6:00 A.M. is that?

   (A) 48   B. 21   C. 19   D. 12

7. **Writing in Math** Write the time you are finished with school each day in two ways.

   Sample answer: three fifteen; quarter after three

Use with Lesson 4-2. **45**

Reteaching

Name_____

Time to the Minute

R 4-2

You can skip count by fives and then count on to tell time when the minute hand is between numbers.

The minute hand is between 7 and 8.

Count by 5s from 12 to 7. That is 35 minutes.

Count 3 more minutes. There are 38 minutes.

The hour hand is between 11 and 12. The time is 11:38, or 22 minutes to 12.

Write the time shown on each clock two ways.   **Sample answers:**

1. **3:41; three forty-one, nineteen minutes to four**

2. **10:20; ten twenty, twenty minutes after ten**

3. **7:58; seven fifty-eight, two minutes to eight**

Use with Lesson 4-2. **45**

Enrichment

Name_____

Fix the Clocks

E 4-2
VISUAL THINKING

The clocks shown below have all been broken in half. Draw a line from one half of the clock to the other so the correct time is shown.

Four thirty-one

Seven minutes past eight

Eleven eighteen

Forty-seven minutes past three

Three minutes before one

Use with Lesson 4-2. **45**

Problem Solving

Name_____

Time to the Minute

PS 4-2

One Saturday Mr. and Mrs. Adams went out for dinner and a movie at twenty-five after six. They arrived home at ten thirty-three.

1. Write the time Mr. and Mrs. Adams left for the evening in number form.
   6:25 P.M.

2. Write the time they came home in two different ways.
   10:33; thirty-three after ten

3. Draw two clock faces with the hands showing the times Mr. and Mrs. Adams left and came home.

4. **Writing in Math** The clock shows the time Bart gets home from school. Write the time in three different ways.

   3:51; three fifty-one; nine minutes to four

Use with Lesson 4-2. **45**

Name_____

Elapsed Time

P 4-3

Find the elapsed time.

1. Start Time: 6:00 P.M.
   End Time: 7:15 P.M.
   1 hr 15 min

2. Start Time: 9:30 A.M.
   End Time: 11:55 A.M.
   2 hr 25 min

3. Start Time: 4:15 P.M.
   End Time: 7:22 P.M.
   3 hr 7 min

4. Start Time: 3:48 P.M.
   End Time: 8:11 P.M.
   4 hr 23 min

5. Tara's baby sister naps between 12:45 P.M. and 2:30 P.M. every day. How long is the baby's nap?
   1 hr 45 min

6. Write the beginning time and the ending time of your school day. What is the elapsed time of your school day?
   Sample answer: 8:15 A.M. to 3:00 P.M.; The school day is 6 hr 45 min.

Test Prep

7. Which is the elapsed time? Start Time: 1:01 P.M.
   End Time: 3:02 P.M.

   A. 3 hr 1 min
   B. 2 hr 12 min
   C. 2 hr 2 min
   D. 2 hr 1 min

8. **Writing in Math** Would you rather have your recess last from 10:30 A.M. to 10:45 A.M. or from 10:45 A.M. to 11:10 A.M.? Explain.

   Sample answer: I would rather have it last from 10:45 to 11:10 because that is 25 min. 10:30 to 10:45 is only 15 min.

Name_____

Elapsed Time

R 4-3

A children's museum is open from 1:00 P.M. to 6:35 P.M. every day. How long is the museum open?

Step 1	Step 2	Step 3
Find the starting time.	Count the hours.	Count the minutes.
Start at 1:00.	There are 5 hours from 1:00 P.M. to 6:00 P.M.	There are 35 minutes from 6:00 to 6:35. The time elapsed is 5:35.

Find the elapsed time.

1. **Start time:** 8:00 A.M.
   End time: 1:15 P.M.
   5 hr and 15 min

2. **Start time:** 3:25 A.M.
   End time: 5:40 A.M.
   2 hr and 15 min

3. **Start time:** 12:00 P.M.
   End time: 3:48 P.M.
   3 hr and 48 min

4. **Number Sense** A science class lasted from 1:15 until 2:05. Did the science class last more than or less than 1 hr?
   Less than 1 hr

Name_____

Field Trip

E 4-3
DECISION MAKING

Your class is planning a field trip to the zoo. You have been asked to make a schedule showing the beginning and ending time at each location. The length of time the class will be allowed to stay at each location is shown in the chart below. The trip will begin at 10:00. Leave 5 min between locations to give the class time to get from one place to another.

Location	Total Time Allowed
Birds	20 min
Dolphins and whales	35 min
Great apes	45 min
Reptiles	30 min
Small mammals	25 min
Fish	15 min
Lions	40 min
Bears	35 min
Lunchroom	55 min

Field Trip Schedule

Sample answers:

Location	Beginning Time	Ending Time
Great apes	10:00	**10:45**
Lions	**10:50**	**11:30**
Small mammals	**11:35**	**12:00**
Lunchroom	**12:05**	**1:00**
Bears	**1:05**	**1:40**
Birds	**1:45**	**2:05**
Reptiles	**2:10**	**2:40**
Fish	**2:45**	**3:00**
Dolphins and whales	**3:05**	**3:40**

What is the total elapsed time for the field trip to the zoo?
Total elapsed time = 5 hr 40 min

Name_____

Elapsed Time

PS 4-3

First Plane Trip Bob recently took his first airplane ride. He departed from New York City at 8:00 A.M. and arrived in Detroit, Michigan, at 9:50 A.M.

1. How long was the airplane ride?
   1 hr, 50 min

2. On the return flight a week later, Bob departed from Detroit at 7:10 A.M. and arrived in New York City 1 hr and 40 min later. What time did he arrive?
   8:50 A.M.

3. How much shorter was Bob's return trip?
   10 min

4. Susan flew from New York City all the way to Miami, Florida. The actual flying time was 3 hr and 15 min. If she left New York City on the 11:00 A.M. flight, what was her expected arrival time?
   2:15 P.M.

5. **Writing in Math** Juanita and Elizabeth have a softball game at 10:00 A.M. If it takes them 15 min to get home and the game lasts 1 hr 40 min, at what time will they get home? Explain.

   Sample answer: The game ended at 11:40 A.M. and the girls got home in 15 min, so they arrived home at 11:55 A.M.

Name_____

Using a Calendar

P 4-4

1. Write the ordinal number for the month of March. **3rd**

2. **Number Sense** How many months are in two years? **24 months**

Use the calendar for Exercises 3–7.

3. How many Sundays were in June? **5 Sundays**

June 2002

S	M	T	W	T	F	S
						1
2	3	4	5	6	7	8
9	10	11	12	13	14	15
16	17	18	19	20	21	22
23	24	25	26	27	28	29
30						

4. What day of the week was June 1? **Saturday**

5. Miguel left for vacation June 11. He returned home June 25. How many weeks was he gone? **2 weeks**

6. **Reasoning** On what day of the week was the Fourth of July celebrated? **Thursday**

7. Mr. Evans began to paint his house on June 14. It takes him nine days to finish the job. On what date did he finish painting the house? **June 22**

Test Prep

8. Macy's piano lessons begin the 1st of September. She has lessons for eight months. Which is the last month of her piano lessons?

A. March   **B.** April   C. June   D. July

9. **Writing in Math** Do some people live eight centuries or eight decades? Explain.

Sample answer: Some people live eight decades, which is 80 years. Eight centuries is 800 years. No one lives that long.

Use with Lesson 4-4. **47**

Name_____

Using a Calendar

R 4-4

You can use a calendar to find the days of the week and the months of a year.

Time	Order of the Months
1 week = 7 days	January
52 weeks = 1 year	February
	March
1 year = 12 months	April
	May
1 year = 365 days	June
	July
1 leap year = 366 days	August
	September
1 decade = 10 years	October
	November
1 century = 100 years	December

November

S	M	T	W	T	F	S
						1
2	3	4	5	6	7	8
9	10	11	12	13	14	15
16	17	18	19	20	21	22
23	24	25	26	27	28	29
30						

What is the ninth month of the year?
Count nine months starting with January. September is the ninth month of the year.

What date is the second Tuesday in November?
Locate the Tuesday column on the calendar. The 4th is the first Tuesday, and the 11th is the second Tuesday.

1. How many Mondays were there in November? **4 Mondays**

2. What date was the fourth Friday in November? **November 28**

3. How many Sundays were there in November? **5 Sundays**

4. What day of the week was November 12? **Wednesday**

5. **Number Sense** About how many days are there in two months? **Sample answer: About 60; Answers may range from 58 to 62.**

6. Write the ordinal number that represents the month of November when the months of the year are listed in order. **11th**

7. **Number Sense** How many weeks are in two years? **104 weeks**

Use with Lesson 4-4. **47**

Name_____

2010

E 4-4
DATA

The calendars below show 6 months from 2010. Find the date of each holiday on the calendars. Then write the first letter of the holiday on the calendar date, and write the holiday's date on the line.

June 2010

S	M	Tu	W	Th	F	S
		1	2	3	4	5
6	7	8	9	10	11	12
13	14	15	16	17	18	19
20	21	22	23	24	25	26
27	28	29	30			

July 2010

S	M	Tu	W	Th	F	S
				1	2	3
4	5	6	7	8	9	10
11	12	13	14	15	16	17
18	19	20	21	22	23	24
25	26	27	28	29	30	31

August 2010

S	M	Tu	W	Th	F	S
1	2	3	4	5	6	7
8	9	10	11	12	13	14
15	16	17	18	19	20	21
22	23	24	25	26	27	28
29	30	31				

September 2010

S	M	Tu	W	Th	F	S
			1	2	3	4
5	6	7	8	9	10	11
12	13	14	15	16	17	18
19	20	21	22	23	24	25
26	27	28	29	30		

October 2010

S	M	Tu	W	Th	F	S
					1	2
3	4	5	6	7	8	9
10	11	12	13	14	15	16
17	18	19	20	21	22	23
24	25	26	27	28	29	30
31						

November 2010

S	M	Tu	W	Th	F	S
	1	2	3	4	5	6
7	8	9	10	11	12	13
14	15	16	17	18	19	20
21	22	23	24	25	26	27
28	29	30				

1. Thanksgiving: the fourth Thursday in November **November 25**

2. Labor Day: the first Monday in September **September 6**

3. Independence Day: the first Sunday in July **July 4**

4. Flag Day: the second Monday in June **June 14**

5. Veteran's Day: the second Thursday in November **November 11**

6. Columbus Day: the second Monday in October **October 11**

Use with Lesson 4-4. **47**

Name_____

Using a Calendar

PS 4-4

A full Moon occurs once each month. In August the full Moon was seen on the 22nd.

August 2002

S	M	T	W	T	F	S
				1	2	3
4	5	6	7	8	9	10
11	12	13	14	15	16	17
18	19	20	21	22	23	24
25	26	27	28	29	30	31

September 2002

S	M	T	W	T	F	S
1	2	3	4	5	6	7
8	9	10	11	12	13	14
15	16	17	18	19	20	21
22	23	24	25	26	27	28
29	30					

1. What day of the week was the 22nd of August in the year 2002? **Thursday**

2. If the Moon was a crescent shape 1 week after the full Moon, on what day and date would that be? **Thursday, August 29, 2002**

3. Jamille started working on a school project on August 20, 2002. He finished 3 weeks and 5 days later. What day of the week and date did Jamille finish? **Sunday, September 15, 2002**

The Tosilito family went on vacation to San Francisco, California, on September 25, 2002. The family returned from vacation 6 days later.

4. **Writing in Math** Use the calendar to figure out the day and the date of the Tosilito family's return. Explain your answer.

Sample answer: The Tosilito family returned 6 days after September 25. The calendar for September ended on a Monday so the next day is Tuesday, October 1.

Use with Lesson 4-4. **47**

© Pearson Education, Inc. 3

Practice

Name_____

Using Tally Charts to Organize Data   P 4-5

Phillip took a survey to find out the age of each person in his class.

Ages of Classmates

Age	Tally	Number
8 years	ʬ I	6
9 years	ʬ ʬ II	12
10 years	III	3

1. How old are most of Phillip's classmates? **9 years old**

2. How many students are in Phillip's class? **21 students**

3. How many more students are 8 years old than 10 years old? **3 more students**

4. There are twice as many 9-year-olds than what age group? **8-year-olds**

5. Are there more or fewer students in Phillip's class than in your class?
Sample answer: More, there are only 20 students in my class.

Test Prep

6. Which shows the number for ʬ ʬ ʬ ʬ IIII?

   A. 14   **B** 24   C. 25   D. 44

7. **Writing in Math** Name five different topics that can be used to take a survey.
Sample answer: favorite class, favorite book, favorite TV show, favorite food, favorite sport

48 Use with Lesson 4-5.

© Pearson Education, Inc. 3

Reteaching

Name_____

Using Tally Charts to Organize Data   R 4-5

Students were asked, "What is your favorite subject at school?" You can use tally charts to help you organize data you collect from the survey.

Each subject that students chose as their favorite was listed, and a tally mark was recorded for each time that subject was given as an answer.

Period	Tally Marks	Number
Reading	ʬ II	7
Math	ʬ ʬ I	11
Science	IIII	4
Gym	ʬ I	6

1. What is the most popular subject in the survey? **Math**

2. How many students answered the survey altogether? **28 students**

3. In the survey, what is the least popular subject? **Science**

4. **Number Sense** What number is shown by ʬ ʬ IIII **14**

Use the data at the right for 5–7.

5. Make a tally chart to show the results.

Favorite Animal

Lion	Duck	Lion	Tiger
Bear	Tiger	Bear	Lion
Bear	Lion	Tiger	Tiger
Tiger	Lion	Duck	Bear

Animal	Tally Marks	Number
Lion	ʬ	5
Duck	II	2
Tiger	ʬ	5
Bear	IIII	4

6. How many people voted? **16 people**

7. Which animals got the same number of votes? **Lions and tigers**

48 Use with Lesson 4-5.

© Pearson Education, Inc. 3

Enrichment

Name_____

What Does the Survey Say?   E 4-5
NUMBER SENSE

The tally chart at the right shows the results of a class vote for favorite school day. Use the tally chart to find your way through the maze.

Favorite School Day

Day	Votes
Monday	ʬ
Tuesday	ʬ II
Wednesday	ʬ III
Thursday	IIII
Friday	ʬ ʬ II

Move to the square that has

1. the number of votes for Thursday.

2. one more than the votes for Monday.

3. two less than the votes for Friday.

4. twice the number of votes as Tuesday.

5. the votes for Monday and Tuesday combined.

6. three less than the votes for Wednesday.

7. the votes for Wednesday and Thursday combined.

8. three times the number of votes for Monday.

START	8	13	17	5
4	12	6	2	END
6	10	14	13	15
7	1	12	9	12

48 Use with Lesson 4-5.

© Pearson Education, Inc. 3

Problem Solving

Name_____

Using Tally Charts to Organize Data   PS 4-5

Favorite Subject Cheryl took a survey of third graders that asked, "What is your favorite subject in school?" She recorded the data using a tally chart.

Favorite Subject

Subject	Tally Marks	Number
Math	ʬ	5
Science	ʬ III	8
Art	ʬ I	6
Gym	IIII	4
Music	II	2
Spelling	III	3

1. How many third graders were surveyed?
28 third graders

2. How many more third graders voted for science than spelling?
5 third graders

3. What number is shown by ʬ ʬ ʬ? **15**

Salvatore kept track of how many times people said "please," "thank you," or "you're welcome" during lunch at the cafeteria counter.

> you're welcome, thank you, please, thank you, thank you, please, please, please, thank you, you're welcome, thank you, thank you, thank you, please, please, you're welcome, thank you, thank you, please

4. **Writing in Math** Use the data to complete the tally chart. Then tell which phrase was used most often. What was the total number of times it was used?

Salvatore's Survey

Polite Phrase	Tally	Number
Please	ʬ II	7
Thank you	ʬ IIII	9
You're welcome	III	3

Thank you; 9 times

48 Use with Lesson 4-5.

© Pearson Education, Inc. 3

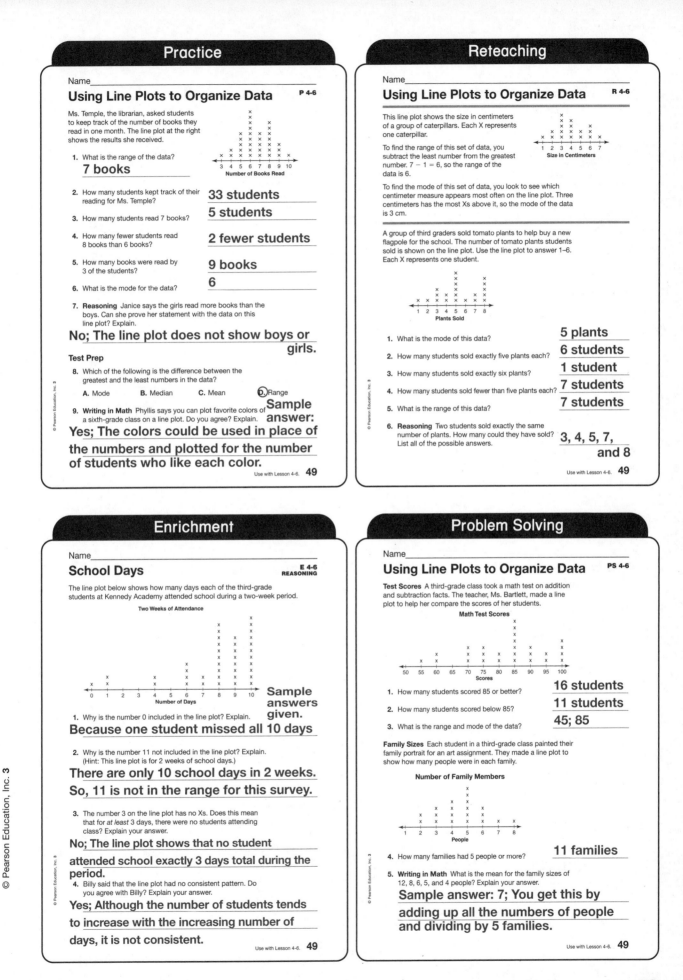

Practice

Name _____

Using Line Plots to Organize Data
P 4-6

Ms. Temple, the librarian, asked students to keep track of the number of books they read in one month. The line plot at the right shows the results she received.

Number of Books Read

1. What is the range of the data?

   7 books

2. How many students kept track of their reading for Ms. Temple?

   33 students

3. How many students read 7 books?

   5 students

4. How many fewer students read 8 books than 6 books?

   2 fewer students

5. How many books were read by 3 of the students?

   9 books

6. What is the mode for the data?

   6

7. **Reasoning** Janice says the girls read more books than the boys. Can she prove her statement with the data on this line plot? Explain.

   No; The line plot does not show boys or girls.

Test Prep

8. Which of the following is the difference between the greatest and the least numbers in the data?

   A. Mode   B. Median   C. Mean   **D.** Range

9. **Writing in Math** Phyllis says you can plot favorite colors of a sixth-grade class on a line plot. Do you agree? Explain. **Sample answer:**

   Yes; The colors could be used in place of the numbers and plotted for the number of students who like each color.

Use with Lesson 4-6. **49**

Reteaching

Name _____

Using Line Plots to Organize Data
R 4-6

This line plot shows the size in centimeters of a group of caterpillars. Each X represents one caterpillar.

Size in Centimeters

To find the range of this set of data, you subtract the least number from the greatest number. $7 - 1 = 6$, so the range of the data is 6.

To find the mode of this set of data, you look to see which centimeter measure appears most often on the line plot. Three centimeters has the most Xs above it, so the mode of the data is 3 cm.

A group of third graders sold tomato plants to help buy a new flagpole for the school. The number of tomato plants students sold is shown on the line plot. Use the line plot to answer 1–6. Each X represents one student.

Plants Sold

1. What is the mode of this data?

   5 plants

2. How many students sold exactly five plants each?

   6 students

3. How many students sold exactly six plants?

   1 student

4. How many students sold fewer than five plants each?

   7 students

5. What is the range of this data?

   7 students

6. **Reasoning** Two students sold exactly the same number of plants. How many could they have sold? List all of the possible answers.

   3, 4, 5, 7, and 8

Use with Lesson 4-6. **49**

Enrichment

Name _____

School Days
E 4-6
REASONING

The line plot below shows how many days each of the third-grade students at Kennedy Academy attended school during a two-week period.

Two Weeks of Attendance

Number of Days

Sample answers given.

1. Why is the number 0 included in the line plot? Explain.

   Because one student missed all 10 days

2. Why is the number 11 not included in the line plot? Explain. (Hint: This line plot is for 2 weeks of school days.)

   There are only 10 school days in 2 weeks. So, 11 is not in the range for this survey.

3. The number 3 on the line plot has no Xs. Does this mean that for *at least* 3 days, there were no students attending class? Explain your answer.

   No; The line plot shows that no student attended school exactly 3 days total during the period.

4. Billy said that the line plot had no consistent pattern. Do you agree with Billy? Explain your answer.

   Yes; Although the number of students tends to increase with the increasing number of days, it is not consistent.

Use with Lesson 4-6. **49**

Problem Solving

Name _____

Using Line Plots to Organize Data
PS 4-6

Test Scores A third-grade class took a math test on addition and subtraction facts. The teacher, Ms. Bartlett, made a line plot to help her compare the scores of her students.

Math Test Scores

Scores

1. How many students scored 85 or better?

   16 students

2. How many students scored below 85?

   11 students

3. What is the range and mode of the data?

   45; 85

Family Sizes Each student in a third-grade class painted their family portrait for an art assignment. They made a line plot to show how many people were in each family.

Number of Family Members

People

4. How many families had 5 people or more?

   11 families

5. **Writing in Math** What is the mean for the family sizes of 12, 8, 6, 5, and 4 people? Explain your answer.

   Sample answer: 7; You get this by adding up all the numbers of people and dividing by 5 families.

Use with Lesson 4-6. **49**

© Pearson Education, Inc. 3

Name_____

Reading Pictographs and Bar Graphs
P 4-7

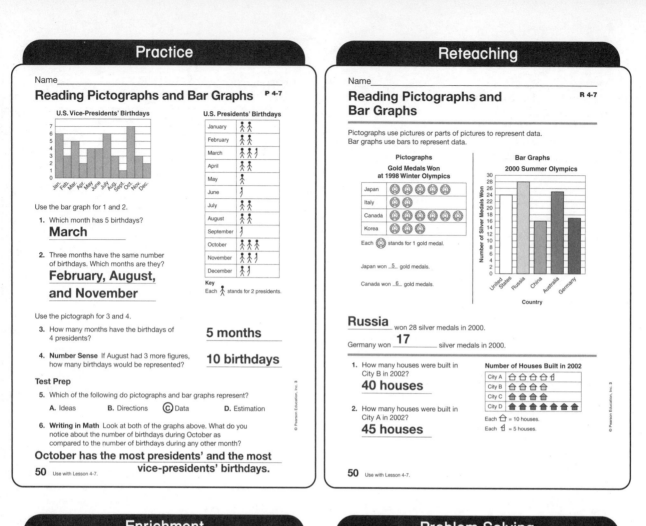

U.S. Vice-Presidents' Birthdays

U.S. Presidents' Birthdays

Use the bar graph for 1 and 2.

1. Which month has 5 birthdays?

   March

2. Three months have the same number of birthdays. Which months are they?

   February, August, and November

Use the pictograph for 3 and 4.

3. How many months have the birthdays of 4 presidents?

   5 months

4. **Number Sense** If August had 3 more figures, how many birthdays would be represented?

   10 birthdays

Test Prep

5. Which of the following do pictographs and bar graphs represent?

   A. Ideas   B. Directions   Ⓒ Data   D. Estimation

6. **Writing in Math** Look at both of the graphs above. What do you notice about the number of birthdays during October as compared to the number of birthdays during any other month?

   October has the most presidents' and the most vice-presidents' birthdays.

© Pearson Education, Inc. 3

Name_____

Reading Pictographs and Bar Graphs
R 4-7

Pictographs use pictures or parts of pictures to represent data.
Bar graphs use bars to represent data.

Pictographs

Gold Medals Won at 1998 Winter Olympics

Japan	
Italy	
Canada	
Korea	

Each stands for 1 gold medal.

Japan won __5__ gold medals.

Canada won __6__ gold medals.

Bar Graphs

2000 Summer Olympics

Russia won 28 silver medals in 2000.

Germany won __17__ silver medals in 2000.

1. How many houses were built in City B in 2002?

   40 houses

2. How many houses were built in City A in 2002?

   45 houses

Number of Houses Built in 2002

City A	
City B	
City C	
City D	

Each = 10 houses.
Each = 5 houses.

© Pearson Education, Inc. 3

Name_____

County Parks
E 4-7
DATA

The pictograph below shows the number of parks in four different counties. The sentences below are false. Use the data in the pictograph, and replace words in the sentences to make them true. The first one has been done for you.

Number of Parks

Franklin County	
Edison County	
Carver County	
Morse County	

Each = 2 parks.

1. Morse County has the ~~greatest~~ **least** number of parks.

2. Carver County has ~~more~~ **less** than twice the number of parks as Morse County.

   one park

3. Franklin County has ~~two more parks~~ **one park** than Edison County.

4. Carver County has the ~~least~~ **greatest** number of parks.

5. Edison County has ~~eight~~ **seven** parks.

6. The pictograph shows ~~25~~ **32** parks altogether.

7. If two more parks opened in Edison County, the pictograph would show four ~~whole~~ trees.

   and one-half

8. If four parks closed in Morse County, the pictograph would show one ~~and one-half~~ **whole tree**.

© Pearson Education, Inc. 3

Name_____

Reading Pictographs and Bar Graphs
PS 4-7

Today, there are many different types of phones for sale. The bar graph shows the number of different types of phones sold in one month at Abe's Communication Store.

Monthly Telephone Sales

1. How many phones were sold for the month?

   95 phones

2. How many more portable phones were sold than wall phones?

   30 phones

3. Of the novelty phones, 2 were shaped like cars and 6 were shaped like basketballs. The rest were shaped like an animal. How many phones were shaped like an animal?

   2 phones

4. **Writing in Math** Write a comparison problem that can be solved by using the graph and answer it.

   Check students' problems and answers.

© Pearson Education, Inc. 3

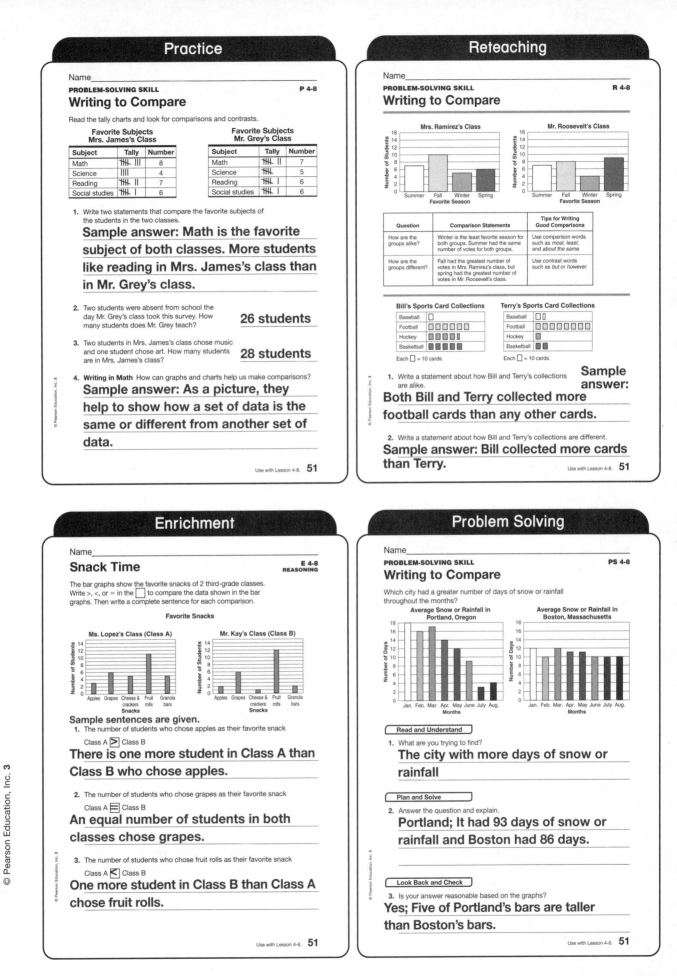

Practice

Name_____

PROBLEM-SOLVING SKILL   P 4-8
Writing to Compare

Read the tally charts and look for comparisons and contrasts.

Favorite Subjects
Mrs. James's Class

Subject	Tally	Number
Math	~~卌~~ III	8
Science	IIII	4
Reading	卌 II	7
Social studies	卌 I	6

Favorite Subjects
Mr. Grey's Class

Subject	Tally	Number
Math	卌 II	7
Science	卌	5
Reading	卌 I	6
Social studies	卌 I	6

1. Write two statements that compare the favorite subjects of the students in the two classes.

Sample answer: Math is the favorite subject of both classes. More students like reading in Mrs. James's class than in Mr. Grey's class.

2. Two students were absent from school the day Mr. Grey's class took this survey. How many students does Mr. Grey teach?

26 students

3. Two students in Mrs. James's class chose music and one student chose art. How many students are in Mrs. James's class?

28 students

4. **Writing in Math** How can graphs and charts help us make comparisons?

Sample answer: As a picture, they help to show how a set of data is the same or different from another set of data.

Use with Lesson 4-8. **51**

Reteaching

Name_____

PROBLEM-SOLVING SKILL   R 4-8
Writing to Compare

Mrs. Ramirez's Class — Number of Students (Summer, Fall, Winter, Spring) — Favorite Season

Mr. Roosevelt's Class — Number of Students (Summer, Fall, Winter, Spring) — Favorite Season

Question	Comparison Statements	Tips for Writing Good Comparisons
How are the groups alike?	Winter is the least favorite season for both groups. Summer had the same number of votes for both groups.	Use comparison words such as *most, least,* and *about the same.*
How are the groups different?	Fall had the greatest number of votes in Mrs. Ramirez's class, but spring had the greatest number of votes in Mr. Roosevelt's class.	Use contrast words such as *but* or *however.*

Bill's Sports Card Collections

Baseball	☐
Football	☐☐☐☐☐
Hockey	☐☐☐☐
Basketball	■■■■☐

Each ☐ = 10 cards.

Terry's Sports Card Collections

Baseball	☐☐
Football	☐☐☐☐☐☐☐
Hockey	
Basketball	■■

Each ☐ = 10 cards.

1. Write a statement about how Bill and Terry's collections are alike.

Sample answer:

Both Bill and Terry collected more football cards than any other cards.

2. Write a statement about how Bill and Terry's collections are different.

Sample answer: Bill collected more cards than Terry.

Use with Lesson 4-8. **51**

Enrichment

Name_____

Snack Time   E 4-8
                                                        REASONING

The bar graphs show the favorite snacks of 2 third-grade classes. Write >, <, or = in the ☐ to compare the data shown in the bar graphs. Then write a complete sentence for each comparison.

Favorite Snacks

Ms. Lopez's Class (Class A) — Number of Students (Apples, Grapes, Cheese & crackers, Fruit rolls, Granola bars) — Snacks

Mr. Kay's Class (Class B) — Number of Students (Apples, Grapes, Cheese & crackers, Fruit rolls, Granola bars) — Snacks

Sample sentences are given.

1. The number of students who chose apples as their favorite snack

Class A ▷ Class B

There is one more student in Class A than Class B who chose apples.

2. The number of students who chose grapes as their favorite snack

Class A = Class B

An equal number of students in both classes chose grapes.

3. The number of students who chose fruit rolls as their favorite snack

Class A ◁ Class B

One more student in Class B than Class A chose fruit rolls.

Use with Lesson 4-8. **51**

Problem Solving

Name_____

PROBLEM-SOLVING SKILL   PS 4-8
Writing to Compare

Which city had a greater number of days of snow or rainfall throughout the months?

Average Snow or Rainfall in Portland, Oregon — Number of Days (Jan. Feb. Mar. Apr. May June July Aug.) — Months

Average Snow or Rainfall in Boston, Massachusetts — Number of Days (Jan. Feb. Mar. Apr. May June July Aug.) — Months

Read and Understand

1. What are you trying to find?

The city with more days of snow or rainfall

Plan and Solve

2. Answer the question and explain.

Portland; It had 93 days of snow or rainfall and Boston had 86 days.

Look Back and Check

3. Is your answer reasonable based on the graphs?

Yes; Five of Portland's bars are taller than Boston's bars.

Use with Lesson 4-8. **51**

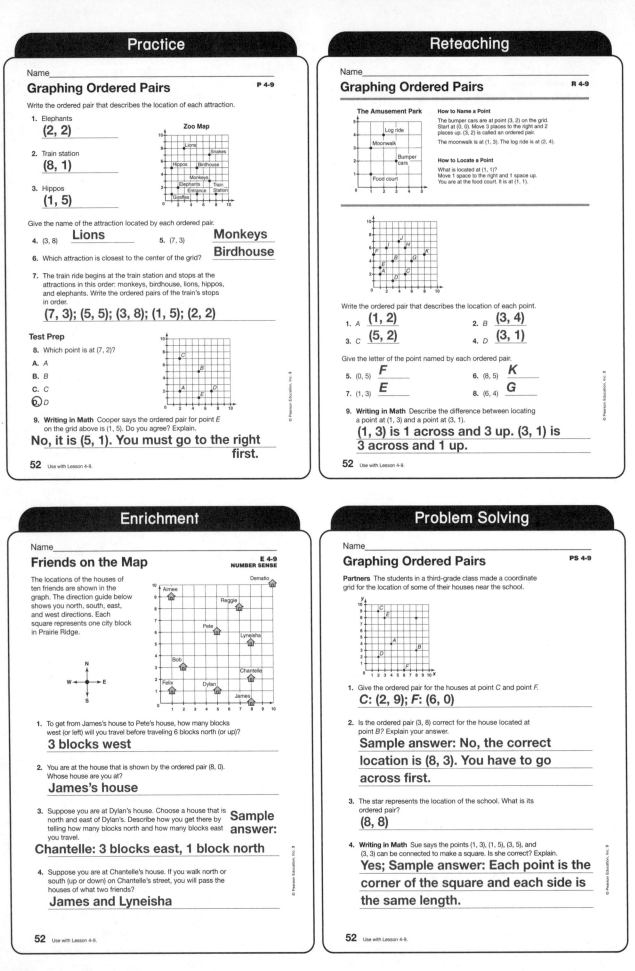

Practice

Graphing Ordered Pairs

P 4-9

Write the ordered pair that describes the location of each attraction.

Zoo Map

1. Elephants
(2, 2)

2. Train station
(8, 1)

3. Hippos
(1, 5)

Give the name of the attraction located by each ordered pair.

4. (3, 8) **Lions**

5. (7, 3) **Monkeys**

6. Which attraction is closest to the center of the grid? **Birdhouse**

7. The train ride begins at the train station and stops at the attractions in this order: monkeys, birdhouse, lions, hippos, and elephants. Write the ordered pairs of the train's stops in order.
(7, 3); (5, 5); (3, 8); (1, 5); (2, 2)

Test Prep

8. Which point is at (7, 2)?
A. A
B. B
C. C
D. D

9. **Writing in Math** Cooper says the ordered pair for point E on the grid above is (1, 5). Do you agree? Explain.
No, it is (5, 1). You must go to the right first.

Reteaching

Graphing Ordered Pairs

R 4-9

The Amusement Park

How to Name a Point
The bumper cars are at point (3, 2) on the grid. Start at (0, 0). Move 3 places to the right and 2 places up. (3, 2) is called an ordered pair.

The moonwalk is at (1, 3). The log ride is at (2, 4).

How to Locate a Point
What is located at (1, 1)?
Move 1 space to the right and 1 space up.
You are at the food court. It is at (1, 1).

Write the ordered pair that describes the location of each point.

1. A **(1, 2)**
2. B **(3, 4)**
3. C **(5, 2)**
4. D **(3, 1)**

Give the letter of the point named by each ordered pair.

5. (0, 5) **F**
6. (8, 5) **K**
7. (1, 3) **E**
8. (6, 4) **G**

9. **Writing in Math** Describe the difference between locating a point at (1, 3) and a point at (3, 1).
(1, 3) is 1 across and 3 up. (3, 1) is 3 across and 1 up.

Enrichment

Friends on the Map

E 4-9
NUMBER SENSE

The locations of the houses of ten friends are shown in the graph. The direction guide below shows you north, south, east, and west directions. Each square represents one city block in Prairie Ridge.

1. To get from James's house to Pete's house, how many blocks west (or left) will you travel before traveling 6 blocks north (or up)?
3 blocks west

2. You are at the house that is shown by the ordered pair (8, 0). Whose house are you at?
James's house

3. Suppose you are at Dylan's house. Choose a house that is north and east of Dylan's. Describe how you get there by telling how many blocks north and how many blocks east you travel.
Sample answer:
Chantelle: 3 blocks east, 1 block north

4. Suppose you are at Chantelle's house. If you walk north or south (up or down) on Chantelle's street, you will pass the houses of what two friends?
James and Lyneisha

Problem Solving

Graphing Ordered Pairs

PS 4-9

Partners The students in a third-grade class made a coordinate grid for the location of some of their houses near the school.

1. Give the ordered pair for the houses at point C and point F.
C: (2, 9); F: (6, 0)

2. Is the ordered pair (3, 8) correct for the house located at point B? Explain your answer.
Sample answer: No, the correct location is (8, 3). You have to go across first.

3. The star represents the location of the school. What is its ordered pair?
(8, 8)

4. **Writing in Math** Sue says the points (1, 3), (1, 5), (3, 5), and (3, 3) can be connected to make a square. Is she correct? Explain.
Yes; Sample answer: Each point is the corner of the square and each side is the same length.

© Pearson Education, Inc. 3

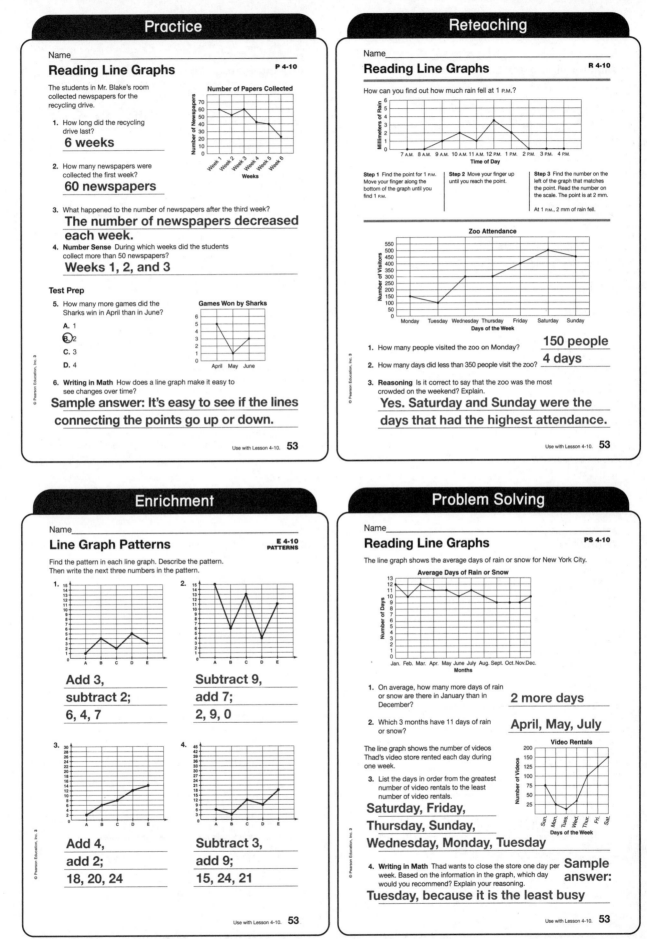

Practice

Name_____

Reading Line Graphs

P 4-10

The students in Mr. Blake's room collected newspapers for the recycling drive.

Number of Papers Collected

1. How long did the recycling drive last?

   6 weeks

2. How many newspapers were collected the first week?

   60 newspapers

3. What happened to the number of newspapers after the third week?

   The number of newspapers decreased each week.

4. **Number Sense** During which weeks did the students collect more than 50 newspapers?

   Weeks 1, 2, and 3

Test Prep

5. How many more games did the Sharks win in April than in June?

   Games Won by Sharks

   A. 1
   B. 2
   C. 3
   D. 4

6. **Writing in Math** How does a line graph make it easy to see changes over time?

   Sample answer: It's easy to see if the lines connecting the points go up or down.

Use with Lesson 4-10. **53**

Reteaching

Name_____

Reading Line Graphs

R 4-10

How can you find out how much rain fell at 1 P.M.?

Time of Day

Step 1 Find the point for 1 P.M. Move your finger along the bottom of the graph until you find 1 P.M.

Step 2 Move your finger up until you reach the point.

Step 3 Find the number on the left of the graph that matches the point. Read the number on the scale. The point is at 2 mm.

At 1 P.M., 2 mm of rain fell.

Zoo Attendance

1. How many people visited the zoo on Monday?

   150 people

2. How many days did less than 350 people visit the zoo?

   4 days

3. **Reasoning** Is it correct to say that the zoo was the most crowded on the weekend? Explain.

   Yes. Saturday and Sunday were the days that had the highest attendance.

Use with Lesson 4-10. **53**

Enrichment

Name_____

Line Graph Patterns

E 4-10
PATTERNS

Find the pattern in each line graph. Describe the pattern. Then write the next three numbers in the pattern.

1.

   Add 3, subtract 2;
   6, 4, 7

2.

   Subtract 9, add 7;
   2, 9, 0

3.

   Add 4, add 2;
   18, 20, 24

4.

   Subtract 3, add 9;
   15, 24, 21

Use with Lesson 4-10. **53**

Problem Solving

Name_____

Reading Line Graphs

PS 4-10

The line graph shows the average days of rain or snow for New York City.

Average Days of Rain or Snow

1. On average, how many more days of rain or snow are there in January than in December?

   2 more days

2. Which 3 months have 11 days of rain or snow?

   April, May, July

The line graph shows the number of videos Thad's video store rented each day during one week.

Video Rentals

3. List the days in order from the greatest number of video rentals to the least number of video rentals.

   Saturday, Friday, Thursday, Sunday, Wednesday, Monday, Tuesday

4. **Writing in Math** Thad wants to close the store one day per week. Based on the information in the graph, which day would you recommend? Explain your reasoning.

   Sample answer: Tuesday, because it is the least busy

Use with Lesson 4-10. **53**

© Pearson Education, Inc. 3

Practice

Name_____

Making Pictographs

P 4-11

Sanchez made an organized list of the marbles in his marble collection.

My Marbles	
Blue	16
Red	24
Green	28
Yellow	14
Metallic	4

1. Use Sanchez's list to complete the pictograph. **Sample answer:**

Sanchez's Marbles

Blue	OOOOOOOO
Red	OOOOOOOOOOOO
Green	OOOOOOOOOOOOOO
Yellow	OOOOOOO
Metallic	OO

Key Each **O** = **2** marbles.

2. Which type of marble would you say Sanchez would consider rare? Explain.

Metallic; Sanchez has fewer

metallic marbles than all the others.

Test Prep

3. Where can you look to find out what each symbol stands for on a pictograph?

A. Title   (B) Key   C. Data   D. Symbol

4. **Writing in Math** Pamela made a pictograph showing students' favorite drinks. Pamela drew 3 glasses to represent the 6 students who chose chocolate milk. Is her pictograph right? Explain.

Favorite Drinks

Drink	Number of Students
Chocolate milk	☐ ☐ ☐
Fruit juice	☐ ☐ ☐ ☐

Key Each ☐ = 2 students.

Sample answer: Yes, Pamela is correct

because each glass stands for 2 students.

54 Use with Lesson 4-11.

Reteaching

Name_____

Making Pictographs

R 4-11

A restaurant kept track of the number of items it sold in one hour. The tally table shows how many of each item was ordered. Use this data to make a pictograph.

Items Ordered

Food	Tally	Number
Pasta	卌 I	6
Salad	IIII	4
Casserole	卌 卌	10
Fish	卌 III	8

Pasta	
Salad	
Casserole	
Fish	

Sample answer: Each fork equals 2 meals.

Each ___ = ___ meals.

Step 1 Write a title to explain what the pictograph shows.

Step 2 Choose a symbol for the key. Because this pictograph is about food, a fork might be a good symbol. Add your symbol to the key. Decide how many votes each fork will stand for. Add this to the key.

Step 3 Decide how many symbols are needed for each food. Draw them.

Check students' work.

The data below show how Ms. Hashimoto's class voted on their favorite types of videos to rent.

Favorite Video	Tally	Number
Action	卌 III	**8**
Comedy	III	**3**
Drama	卌 I	**6**
Animated	卌 卌	**10**

Action	📼 📼 📼 📼
Comedy	📼 📼
Drama	📼 📼 📼
Animated	📼 📼 📼 📼 📼

Each 📼 = **2** votes.

1. Complete the table.

2. Complete the pictograph.

3. **Writing in Math** Write a title for the table and pictograph above.

Sample answer: Favorite Videos in Ms. Hashimoto's Class

54 Use with Lesson 4-11.

Enrichment

Name_____

E-mailing

E 4-11
DECISION MAKING

Kelly just learned how to use the e-mail program on her new computer. She recorded the number of e-mails she sent each week for three weeks on a tally chart. Circle choice A or B for each of the questions below. Then explain your choice.

Week	Tally	Number
1	卌 II	7
2	卌 IIII	9
3	卌 卌 IIII	14

1. Choose a title for your pictograph.
   A. Kelly's E-mails
   (B) E-mails Sent by Kelly Each Week

Sample answers are given.

Title B is more complete.

2. Choose a symbol to represent the data.
   A. a computer
   (B) a circle

The circle is easier to draw.

3. Choose the amount that each symbol will represent.
   (A) two e-mails
   B. three e-mails

It is easier to show one half of 2.

4. Complete the pictograph showing the number of e-mails Kelly sent each week. Use your choices above and the information from the tally chart. Remember to include a title.

E-mails Sent by Kelly Each Week

Week 1	OOOD
Week 2	OOOOD
Week 3	OOOOOOO

Each **O** = **2** e-mails.

54 Use with Lesson 4-11.

Problem Solving

Name_____

Making Pictographs

PS 4-11

Favorite Music A fifth-grade class was discussing what type of music was most popular. They could not agree, so they decided to take a survey.

1. Complete the tally chart.

Type of Music	Tally	Number
Rap	卌 I	**6**
Country	卌 卌	**10**
Pop	卌 卌 II	**12**
Rock	卌 II	**7**
R & B	卌 I	**6**

2. Use the data from the tally chart to complete the pictograph.

Favorite Music

Rap	♪♪♪
Country	♪♪♪♪♪
Pop	♪♪♪♪♪♪
Rock	♪♪♪.
R&B	♪♪♪

Each ♪ = 2 people.

. = 1 person

3. How many students were surveyed in all?

41 students

4. **Writing in Math** Explain how you know which type of music is the most popular.

Pop music is the most popular

because it has the most notes.

54 Use with Lesson 4-11.

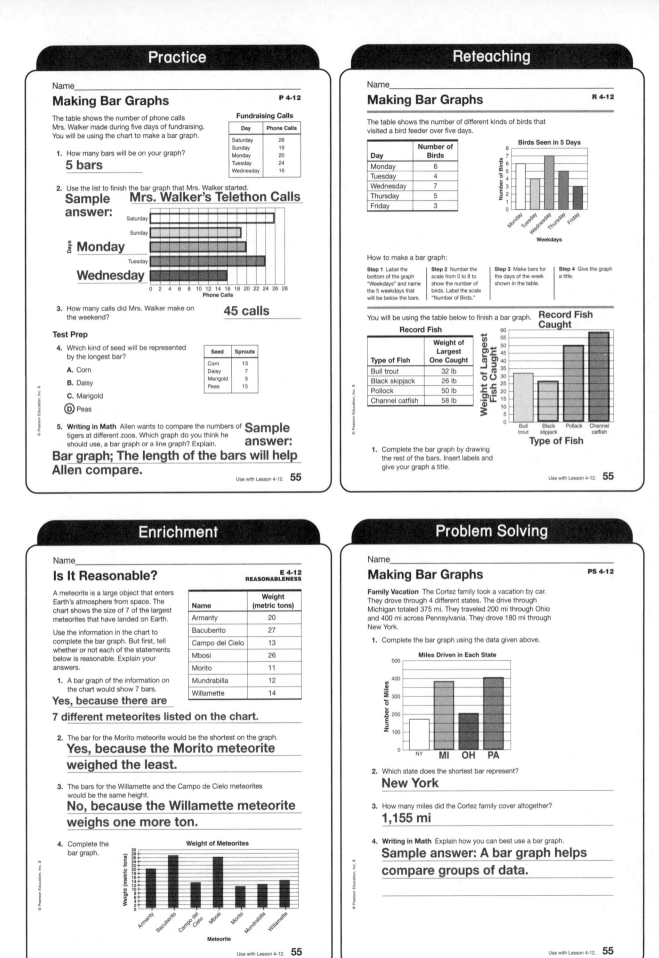

Practice

Name_____

Making Bar Graphs
P 4-12

The table shows the number of phone calls Mrs. Walker made during five days of fundraising. You will be using the chart to make a bar graph.

Fundraising Calls

Day	Phone Calls
Saturday	26
Sunday	19
Monday	20
Tuesday	24
Wednesday	16

1. How many bars will be on your graph?

5 bars

2. Use the list to finish the bar graph that Mrs. Walker started.

Sample answer:

Mrs. Walker's Telethon Calls

Saturday
Sunday
Monday
Tuesday
Wednesday

Days

Phone Calls
0 2 4 6 8 10 12 14 16 18 20 22 24 26 28

3. How many calls did Mrs. Walker make on the weekend?

45 calls

Test Prep

4. Which kind of seed will be represented by the longest bar?

Seed	Sprouts
Corn	13
Daisy	7
Marigold	5
Peas	15

A. Corn
B. Daisy
C. Marigold
(D) Peas

5. **Writing in Math** Allen wants to compare the numbers of tigers at different zoos. Which graph do you think he should use, a bar graph or a line graph? Explain. **Sample answer:**

Bar graph; The length of the bars will help Allen compare.

Reteaching

Name_____

Making Bar Graphs
R 4-12

The table shows the number of different kinds of birds that visited a bird feeder over five days.

Day	Number of Birds
Monday	6
Tuesday	4
Wednesday	7
Thursday	5
Friday	3

Birds Seen in 5 Days

Number of Birds
Weekdays: Monday, Tuesday, Wednesday, Thursday, Friday

How to make a bar graph:

Step 1 Label the bottom of the graph "Weekdays" and name the 5 weekdays that will be below the bars.

Step 2 Number the scale from 0 to 8 to show the number of birds. Label the scale "Number of Birds."

Step 3 Make bars for the days of the week shown in the table.

Step 4 Give the graph a title.

You will be using the table below to finish a bar graph.

Record Fish

Type of Fish	Weight of Largest One Caught
Bull trout	32 lb
Black skipjack	26 lb
Pollock	50 lb
Channel catfish	58 lb

Record Fish Caught

Weight of Largest Fish Caught
Type of Fish: Bull trout, Black slipjack, Pollack, Channel catfish

1. Complete the bar graph by drawing the rest of the bars. Insert labels and give your graph a title.

Enrichment

Name_____

Is It Reasonable?
E 4-12
REASONABLENESS

A meteorite is a large object that enters Earth's atmosphere from space. The chart shows the size of 7 of the largest meteorites that have landed on Earth.

Use the information in the chart to complete the bar graph. But first, tell whether or not each of the statements below is reasonable. Explain your answers.

Name	Weight (metric tons)
Armanty	20
Bacuberito	27
Campo del Cielo	13
Mbosi	26
Morito	11
Mundrabilla	12
Willamette	14

1. A bar graph of the information on the chart would show 7 bars.

Yes, because there are 7 different meteorites listed on the chart.

2. The bar for the Morito meteorite would be the shortest on the graph.

Yes, because the Morito meteorite weighed the least.

3. The bars for the Willamette and the Campo de Cielo meteorites would be the same height.

No, because the Willamette meteorite weighs one more ton.

4. Complete the bar graph.

Weight of Meteorites

Weight (metric tons)
Meteorite: Armanty, Bacuberito, Campo del Cielo, Mbosi, Morito, Mundrabilla, Willamette

---

Problem Solving

Name_____

Making Bar Graphs
PS 4-12

Family Vacation The Cortez family took a vacation by car. They drove through 4 different states. The drive through Michigan totaled 375 mi. They traveled 200 mi through Ohio and 400 mi across Pennsylvania. They drove 180 mi through New York.

1. Complete the bar graph using the data given above.

Miles Driven in Each State

Number of Miles
NY, MI, OH, PA

2. Which state does the shortest bar represent?

New York

3. How many miles did the Cortez family cover altogether?

1,155 mi

4. **Writing in Math** Explain how you can best use a bar graph.

Sample answer: A bar graph helps compare groups of data.

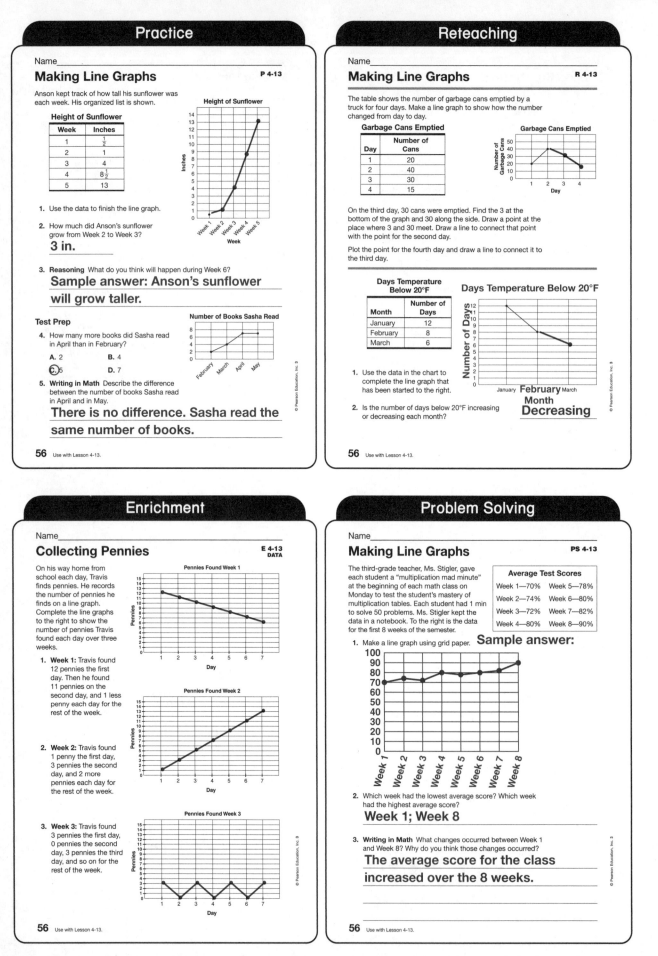

Name_____

Making Line Graphs

P 4-13

Anson kept track of how tall his sunflower was each week. His organized list is shown.

Height of Sunflower

Week	Inches
1	$\frac{1}{2}$
2	1
3	4
4	$8\frac{1}{2}$
5	13

Height of Sunflower

1. Use the data to finish the line graph.

2. How much did Anson's sunflower grow from Week 2 to Week 3?

   3 in.

3. **Reasoning** What do you think will happen during Week 6?

   Sample answer: Anson's sunflower will grow taller.

Test Prep

Number of Books Sasha Read

4. How many more books did Sasha read in April than in February?

   A. 2   B. 4
   C. 5   D. 7

5. **Writing in Math** Describe the difference between the number of books Sasha read in April and in May.

   There is no difference. Sasha read the same number of books.

Name_____

Making Line Graphs

R 4-13

The table shows the number of garbage cans emptied by a truck for four days. Make a line graph to show how the number changed from day to day.

Garbage Cans Emptied

Day	Number of Cans
1	20
2	40
3	30
4	15

Garbage Cans Emptied

On the third day, 30 cans were emptied. Find the 3 at the bottom of the graph and 30 along the side. Draw a point at the place where 3 and 30 meet. Draw a line to connect that point with the point for the second day.

Plot the point for the fourth day and draw a line to connect it to the third day.

Days Temperature Below 20°F

Month	Number of Days
January	12
February	8
March	6

Days Temperature Below 20°F

1. Use the data in the chart to complete the line graph that has been started to the right.

2. Is the number of days below 20°F increasing or decreasing each month?

   Decreasing

Name_____

Collecting Pennies

E 4-13
DATA

On his way home from school each day, Travis finds pennies. He records the number of pennies he finds on a line graph. Complete the line graphs to the right to show the number of pennies Travis found each day over three weeks.

Pennies Found Week 1

1. **Week 1:** Travis found 12 pennies the first day. Then he found 11 pennies on the second day, and 1 less penny each day for the rest of the week.

Pennies Found Week 2

2. **Week 2:** Travis found 1 penny the first day, 3 pennies the second day, and 2 more pennies each day for the rest of the week.

Pennies Found Week 3

3. **Week 3:** Travis found 3 pennies the first day, 0 pennies the second day, 3 pennies the third day, and so on for the rest of the week.

Name_____

Making Line Graphs

PS 4-13

The third-grade teacher, Ms. Stigler, gave each student a "multiplication mad minute" at the beginning of each math class on Monday to test the student's mastery of multiplication tables. Each student had 1 min to solve 50 problems. Ms. Stigler kept the data in a notebook. To the right is the data for the first 8 weeks of the semester.

Average Test Scores

Week 1—70%	Week 5—78%
Week 2—74%	Week 6—80%
Week 3—72%	Week 7—82%
Week 4—80%	Week 8—90%

1. Make a line graph using grid paper.

   Sample answer:

2. Which week had the lowest average score? Which week had the highest average score?

   Week 1; Week 8

3. **Writing in Math** What changes occurred between Week 1 and Week 8? Why do you think those changes occurred?

   The average score for the class increased over the 8 weeks.

© Pearson Education, Inc. 3

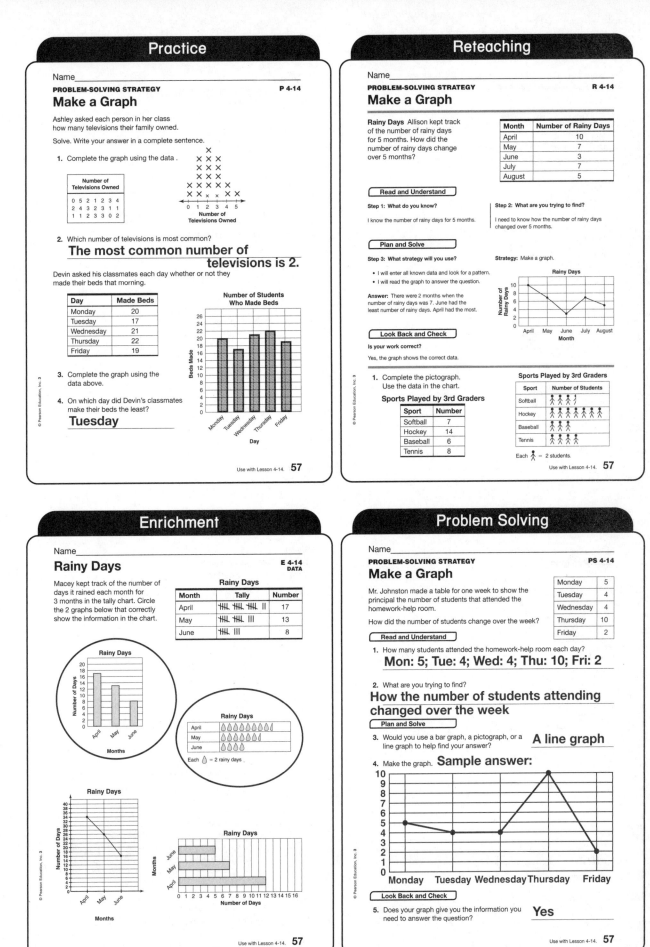

Practice

Name_____

PROBLEM-SOLVING STRATEGY   P 4-14

Make a Graph

Ashley asked each person in her class
how many televisions their family owned.

Solve. Write your answer in a complete sentence.

1. Complete the graph using the data.

Number of Televisions Owned						
0	5	2	1	2	3	4
2	4	3	2	3	1	1
1	1	2	3	3	0	2

```
                    ×
          ×   ×   ×
          ×   ×   ×
          ×   ×   ×
      ×   ×   ×   ×   ×
      ×   ×   ×   ×   ×
  ×   ×   ×   ×   ×   ×
  +---+---+---+---+---+---+
  0   1   2   3   4   5
         Number of
      Televisions Owned
```

2. Which number of televisions is most common?

   The most common number of
   televisions is 2.

Devin asked his classmates each day whether or not they
made their beds that morning.

Day	Made Beds
Monday	20
Tuesday	17
Wednesday	21
Thursday	22
Friday	19

Number of Students Who Made Beds

(bar graph: Monday, Tuesday, Wednesday, Thursday, Friday)

3. Complete the graph using the data above.

4. On which day did Devin's classmates make their beds the least?

   Tuesday

© Pearson Education, Inc. 3

Use with Lesson 4-14. **57**

Reteaching

Name_____

PROBLEM-SOLVING STRATEGY   R 4-14

Make a Graph

Rainy Days Allison kept track
of the number of rainy days
for 5 months. How did the
number of rainy days change
over 5 months?

Month	Number of Rainy Days
April	10
May	7
June	3
July	7
August	5

Read and Understand

Step 1: What do you know?

I know the number of rainy days for 5 months.

Step 2: What are you trying to find?

I need to know how the number of rainy days changed over 5 months.

Plan and Solve

Step 3: What strategy will you use?

- I will enter all known data and look for a pattern.
- I will read the graph to answer the question.

Answer: There were 2 months when the
number of rainy days was 7. June had the
least number of rainy days. April had the most.

Strategy: Make a graph.

Rainy Days (line graph: April, May, June, July, August)

Look Back and Check

Is your work correct?

Yes, the graph shows the correct data.

1. Complete the pictograph.
   Use the data in the chart.

Sports Played by 3rd Graders

Sport	Number
Softball	7
Hockey	14
Baseball	6
Tennis	8

Sports Played by 3rd Graders

Sport	Number of Students
Softball	人 人 人
Hockey	人 人 人 人 人 人 人
Baseball	人 人 人
Tennis	人 人 人 人

Each 人 = 2 students.

© Pearson Education, Inc. 3

Use with Lesson 4-14. **57**

Enrichment

Name_____

Rainy Days   E 4-14
                                                DATA

Macey kept track of the number of
days it rained each month for
3 months in the tally chart. Circle
the 2 graphs below that correctly
show the information in the chart.

Rainy Days

Month	Tally	Number
April	卌 卌 卌 II	17
May	卌 卌 III	13
June	卌 III	8

Rainy Days (bar graph: April, May, June)

Rainy Days (pictograph)

April	〇〇〇〇〇〇〇〇
May	〇〇〇〇〇〇〇
June	〇〇〇〇

Each 〇 = 2 rainy days.

Rainy Days (line graph: April, May, June)

Rainy Days (horizontal bar graph: June, May, April)

© Pearson Education, Inc. 3

Use with Lesson 4-14. **57**

Problem Solving

Name_____

PROBLEM-SOLVING STRATEGY   PS 4-14

Make a Graph

Mr. Johnston made a table for one week to show the
principal the number of students that attended the
homework-help room.

How did the number of students change over the week?

Monday	5
Tuesday	4
Wednesday	4
Thursday	10
Friday	2

Read and Understand

1. How many students attended the homework-help room each day?

   Mon: 5; Tue: 4; Wed: 4; Thu: 10; Fri: 2

2. What are you trying to find?

   How the number of students attending
   changed over the week

Plan and Solve

3. Would you use a bar graph, a pictograph, or a
   line graph to help find your answer?

   A line graph

4. Make the graph. **Sample answer:**

(line graph: Monday, Tuesday, Wednesday, Thursday, Friday — values 5, 4, 4, 10, 2)

Look Back and Check

5. Does your graph give you the information you
   need to answer the question?

   Yes

© Pearson Education, Inc. 3

Use with Lesson 4-14. **57**

Name_____

Car Wash

The third-grade class at Hawthorne Elementary School raised money to buy a new computer by having a car wash on the first Saturday of June.

Suppose the car wash began at 9:00 A.M. and ended at 1:00 P.M.

1. How many hours passed from the start to the finish of the car wash?   **4 hr**

2. The students took a break at 11:15 A.M. How much time passed from the start of the car wash until the break?
2 hr 15 min

The table shows how many cars were washed during each hour.

3. Use the table data to complete the bar graph for the number of cars washed each hour. The data for Hour 1 and Hour 3 are already completed.

Third-Grade Car Wash

Hour	Number of Cars
1	11
2	9
3	16
4	12

Third-Grade Car Wash

4. On which date in June did the car wash take place?
June 5

June						
S	M	T	W	T	F	S
				1	2	3
4	5					
6	7	8	9	10	11	12
13	14	15	16	17	18	19
20	21	22	23	24	25	26
27	28	29	30			

Name_____

Problem-Solving Applications

Students' Favorite Dogs

Dog	Number Counted
Beagle	
Collie	
Shepherd	
Poodle	
Dalmation	

Each 🐕 = 2 votes.

Students were asked to tell their favorite kind of dog. This pictograph shows how many students chose each kind of dog as their favorite. Use the pictograph to answer each exercise.

How many students chose a beagle? 6 students

Which dog had 5 votes? Shepherd

The chart below shows how many points a football team scored in each of a game's four quarters.

Quarter	Points Scored
1st	7
2nd	3
3rd	10
4th	6

Points Scored per Quarter

1. Complete the bar graph.

2. How many points were scored in the 3rd quarter?
10 points

3. How many points were scored in the entire game?
26 points

Name_____

Line Patterns

Find the pattern in each group of lines. Then draw the next three lines to continue the pattern.

1.

2.

3.

4.

5.

6.

Name_____

Lemonade Stand

Four children had lemonade stands. The lemonade at each stand cost $0.25 for each glass. The chart shows their sales for one week.

	Monday	Tuesday	Wednesday	Thursday	Friday
Kelly	$5	$4	$6	$7	$5
Antonio	$2	$3	$1	$1	$3
Bill	$6	$4	$6	$4	$10
Sue	$4	$1	$3	$2	$3

Use a graph to show who had the best total sales for the week.

Read and Understand

1. What are you trying to show?
Who had the best total sales in a week

Plan and Solve

2. First, find the total sales for each child.
Kelly $27, Antonio $10, Bill $30, Sue $13

3. Complete the graph.

Lemonade Sales

4. Who had the best total sales?
Bill

Look Back and Check

5. Did you make the best graph choice? How do you know?
Yes, bar graphs are used to compare information.

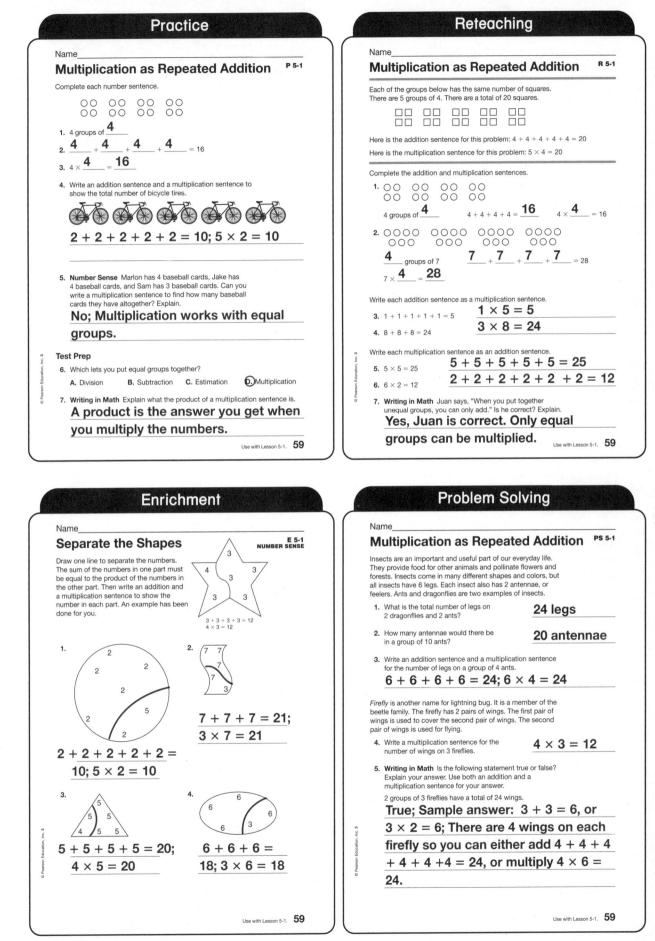

Practice

Name_____

Multiplication as Repeated Addition
P 5-1

Complete each number sentence.

○○ ○○ ○○ ○○
○○ ○○ ○○ ○○

1. 4 groups of **4**_____

2. **4** + **4** + **4** + **4** = 16

3. 4 × **4** = **16**

4. Write an addition sentence and a multiplication sentence to show the total number of bicycle tires.

$2 + 2 + 2 + 2 + 2 = 10; 5 \times 2 = 10$

5. **Number Sense** Marlon has 4 baseball cards, Jake has 4 baseball cards, and Sam has 3 baseball cards. Can you write a multiplication sentence to find how many baseball cards they have altogether? Explain.

No; Multiplication works with equal groups.

Test Prep

6. Which lets you put equal groups together?

A. Division   B. Subtraction   C. Estimation   (D.) Multiplication

7. **Writing in Math** Explain what the product of a multiplication sentence is.

A product is the answer you get when you multiply the numbers.

Reteaching

Name_____

Multiplication as Repeated Addition
R 5-1

Each of the groups below has the same number of squares.
There are 5 groups of 4. There are a total of 20 squares.

▢▢ ▢▢ ▢▢ ▢▢ ▢▢
▢▢ ▢▢ ▢▢ ▢▢ ▢▢

Here is the addition sentence for this problem: 4 + 4 + 4 + 4 + 4 = 20

Here is the multiplication sentence for this problem: 5 × 4 = 20

Complete the addition and multiplication sentences.

1. ○○ ○○ ○○ ○○
   ○○ ○○ ○○ ○○

   4 groups of **4**_____   4 + 4 + 4 + 4 = **16**   4 × **4** = 16

2. ○○○○ ○○○○ ○○○○ ○○○○
   ○○○   ○○○   ○○○   ○○○

   4____ groups of 7   **7** + **7** + **7** + **7** = 28

   7 × **4** = **28**

Write each addition sentence as a multiplication sentence.

3. 1 + 1 + 1 + 1 + 1 = 5   **$1 \times 5 = 5$**

4. 8 + 8 + 8 = 24   **$3 \times 8 = 24$**

Write each multiplication sentence as an addition sentence.

5. 5 × 5 = 25   **$5 + 5 + 5 + 5 + 5 = 25$**

6. 6 × 2 = 12   **$2 + 2 + 2 + 2 + 2 + 2 = 12$**

7. **Writing in Math** Juan says, "When you put together unequal groups, you can only add." Is he correct? Explain.

Yes, Juan is correct. Only equal groups can be multiplied.

Enrichment

Name_____

Separate the Shapes
E 5-1
NUMBER SENSE

Draw one line to separate the numbers. The sum of the numbers in one part must be equal to the product of the numbers in the other part. Then write an addition and a multiplication sentence to show the number in each part. An example has been done for you.

3
4   3   3
3   3

3 + 3 + 3 + 3 = 12
4 × 3 = 12

1.
2 2
2   2
2
2 5
2

$2 + 2 + 2 + 2 + 2 = 10; 5 \times 2 = 10$

2.
7 7
7
7
3

$7 + 7 + 7 = 21;$
$3 \times 7 = 21$

3.
5
5   5
4   5   5

$5 + 5 + 5 + 5 = 20;$
$4 \times 5 = 20$

4.
6
6   6
6   3
6

$6 + 6 + 6 = 18; 3 \times 6 = 18$

Problem Solving

Name_____

Multiplication as Repeated Addition
PS 5-1

Insects are an important and useful part of our everyday life. They provide food for other animals and pollinate flowers and forests. Insects come in many different shapes and colors, but all insects have 6 legs. Each insect also has 2 antennae, or feelers. Ants and dragonflies are two examples of insects.

1. What is the total number of legs on 2 dragonflies and 2 ants?   **24 legs**

2. How many antennae would there be in a group of 10 ants?   **20 antennae**

3. Write an addition sentence and a multiplication sentence for the number of legs on a group of 4 ants.

$6 + 6 + 6 + 6 = 24; 6 \times 4 = 24$

Firefly is another name for lightning bug. It is a member of the beetle family. The firefly has 2 pairs of wings. The first pair of wings is used to cover the second pair of wings. The second pair of wings is used for flying.

4. Write a multiplication sentence for the number of wings on 3 fireflies.   **$4 \times 3 = 12$**

5. **Writing in Math** Is the following statement true or false? Explain your answer. Use both an addition and a multiplication sentence for your answer.

2 groups of 3 fireflies have a total of 24 wings.

True; Sample answer: $3 + 3 = 6$, or $3 \times 2 = 6$; There are 4 wings on each firefly so you can either add 4 + 4 + 4 + 4 + 4 +4 = 24, or multiply 4 × 6 = 24.

© Pearson Education, Inc. 3

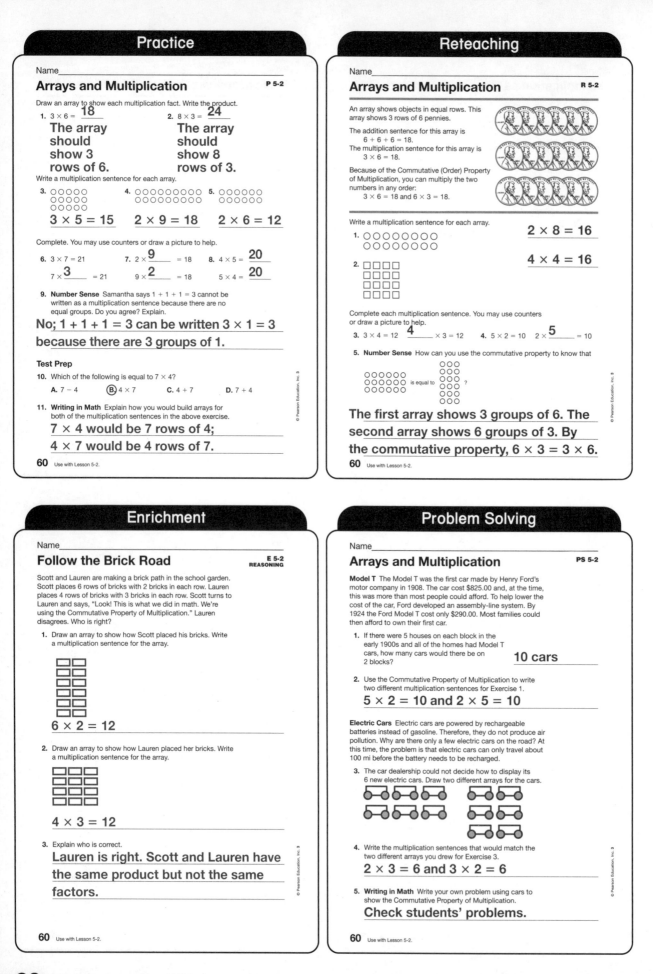

Practice

Name_____

Arrays and Multiplication

P 5-2

Draw an array to show each multiplication fact. Write the product.

1. $3 \times 6 =$ __18__ The array should show 3 rows of 6.

2. $8 \times 3 =$ __24__ The array should show 8 rows of 3.

Write a multiplication sentence for each array.

3. ○○○○○ ○○○○○ ○○○○○
$3 \times 5 = 15$

4. ○○○○○○○○○
$2 \times 9 = 18$

5. ○○○○○○ ○○○○○○
$2 \times 6 = 12$

Complete. You may use counters or draw a picture to help.

6. $3 \times 7 = 21$
$7 \times$ __3__ $= 21$

7. $2 \times$ __9__ $= 18$
$9 \times$ __2__ $= 18$

8. $4 \times 5 =$ __20__
$5 \times 4 =$ __20__

9. **Number Sense** Samantha says $1 + 1 + 1 = 3$ cannot be written as a multiplication sentence because there are no equal groups. Do you agree? Explain.

No; $1 + 1 + 1 = 3$ can be written $3 \times 1 = 3$ because there are 3 groups of 1.

Test Prep

10. Which of the following is equal to 7×4?

    A. $7 - 4$ **(B)** 4×7 **C.** $4 + 7$ **D.** $7 + 4$

11. **Writing in Math** Explain how you would build arrays for both of the multiplication sentences in the above exercise.

7×4 would be 7 rows of 4; 4×7 would be 4 rows of 7.

60 Use with Lesson 5-2.

Reteaching

Name_____

Arrays and Multiplication

R 5-2

An array shows objects in equal rows. This array shows 3 rows of 6 pennies.

The addition sentence for this array is
$6 + 6 + 6 = 18$.

The multiplication sentence for this array is
$3 \times 6 = 18$.

Because of the Commutative (Order) Property of Multiplication, you can multiply the two numbers in any order:
$3 \times 6 = 18$ and $6 \times 3 = 18$.

Write a multiplication sentence for each array.

1. ○○○○○○○○ ○○○○○○○○
$2 \times 8 = 16$

2. ▢▢▢▢ ▢▢▢▢ ▢▢▢▢ ▢▢▢▢
$4 \times 4 = 16$

Complete each multiplication sentence. You may use counters or draw a picture to help.

3. $3 \times 4 = 12$ __4__ $\times 3 = 12$

4. $5 \times 2 = 10$ $2 \times$ __5__ $= 10$

5. **Number Sense** How can you use the commutative property to know that

○○○○○○ ○○○○○○ ○○○○○○ is equal to ○○○ ○○○ ○○○ ○○○ ○○○ ○○○ ?

The first array shows 3 groups of 6. The second array shows 6 groups of 3. By the commutative property, $6 \times 3 = 3 \times 6$.

60 Use with Lesson 5-2.

Enrichment

Name_____

Follow the Brick Road

E 5-2
REASONING

Scott and Lauren are making a brick path in the school garden. Scott places 6 rows of bricks with 2 bricks in each row. Lauren places 4 rows of bricks with 3 bricks in each row. Scott turns to Lauren and says, "Look! This is what we did in math. We're using the Commutative Property of Multiplication." Lauren disagrees. Who is right?

1. Draw an array to show how Scott placed his bricks. Write a multiplication sentence for the array.

$6 \times 2 = 12$

2. Draw an array to show how Lauren placed her bricks. Write a multiplication sentence for the array.

$4 \times 3 = 12$

3. Explain who is correct.

Lauren is right. Scott and Lauren have the same product but not the same factors.

60 Use with Lesson 5-2.

Problem Solving

Name_____

Arrays and Multiplication

PS 5-2

Model T The Model T was the first car made by Henry Ford's motor company in 1908. The car cost $825.00 and, at the time, this was more than most people could afford. To help lower the cost of the car, Ford developed an assembly-line system. By 1924 the Ford Model T cost only $290.00. Most families could then afford to own their first car.

1. If there were 5 houses on each block in the early 1900s and all of the homes had Model T cars, how many cars would there be on 2 blocks?

    10 cars

2. Use the Commutative Property of Multiplication to write two different multiplication sentences for Exercise 1.

    $5 \times 2 = 10$ and $2 \times 5 = 10$

Electric Cars Electric cars are powered by rechargeable batteries instead of gasoline. Therefore, they do not produce air pollution. Why are there only a few electric cars on the road? At this time, the problem is that electric cars can only travel about 100 mi before the battery needs to be recharged.

3. The car dealership could not decide how to display its 6 new electric cars. Draw two different arrays for the cars.

4. Write the multiplication sentences that would match the two different arrays you drew for Exercise 3.

    $2 \times 3 = 6$ and $3 \times 2 = 6$

5. **Writing in Math** Write your own problem using cars to show the Commutative Property of Multiplication.

    Check students' problems.

60 Use with Lesson 5-2.

© Pearson Education, Inc. 3

Name_____

Writing Multiplication Stories

P 5-3

Write a multiplication story for each. Draw a picture to find each product.

1. 8×4

Multiplication stories and pictures will vary; $8 \times 4 = 32$

2. 9×3

Multiplication stories and pictures will vary; $9 \times 3 = 27$

3. Patrick works at the frozen-yogurt store after school. Yesterday he sold 4 double-scoop strawberry cones. How many scoops of strawberry frozen yogurt did he use?

8 scoops

4. Fiona has 3 pet rabbits. Each rabbit eats 3 carrots a day. How many carrots does Fiona need each day to feed her rabbits?

9 carrots

5. Algebra Sara has pet spiders. She keeps all of the spiders in the same tank. There are 24 spider legs in the tank. How many spiders does Sara have in the tank? (Hint: a spider has 8 legs.)

3 spiders

Test Prep

6. How many factors are in the multiplication sentence $9 \times 4 = 36$?

A. 1   **(B)** 2   **C.** 3   **D.** 4

7. Writing in Math Write a multiplication story with the factors 2 and 5.

Check students' stories.

Use with Lesson 5-3. **61**

Name_____

Writing Multiplication Stories

R 5-3

When you write a multiplication story you should:
- Always end the story with a question.
- Draw a picture to show the main idea.

Example:
Write a multiplication story for 5×9.

Josephine has 5 friends over for a snack. She gives each friend 9 grapes. How many grapes did Josephine give altogether?

Josephine gave 45 grapes altogether.

Write a multiplication story for each exercise. Draw a picture to find each product.

1. 4×3

Answers will vary. The product should be 12.

2. 5×2

Answers will vary. The product should be 10.

3. 1×6

Answers will vary. The product should be 6.

4. Number Sense Leshon mowed 7 lawns in his neighborhood. He made $5 for each lawn he mowed. Write a multiplication sentence to show how much money Leshon earned.

$7 \times \$5 = \$35$

Use with Lesson 5-3. **61**

Name_____

And Then What Happened?

E 5-3
NUMBER SENSE

Finish each word problem by writing a sentence that makes it into a multiplication problem. Write a multiplication sentence to solve the problem. Then write the answer in a complete sentence. The first one has been started for you.

Sample answers are given.

1. Caitlin has a puppy named Cubby Bear. Each day she brushes Cubby Bear for 5 min.

How many minutes does Caitlin brush Cubby Bear in 1 week?

Multiplication sentence: **$5 \times 7 = 35$**

Answer: **Caitlin brushes Cubby Bear for 35 min in 1 week.**

2. Alexis earns money by doing lawn work. Alexis is paid $4 for every lawn she mows.

Alexis mowed 4 lawns. How much money did she earn?

Multiplication sentence: **$4 \times \$4 = \$16$**

Answer: **Alexis earned $16 for mowing 4 lawns.**

3. John is having a party. He is going to give each person 2 party favors.

Six people are coming to John's party. How many party favors does he need?

Multiplication sentence: **$2 \times 6 = 12$**

Answer: **John needs 12 party favors.**

Use with Lesson 5-3. **61**

Name_____

Writing Multiplication Stories

PS 5-3

Brenna had a party for 5 friends. Her mom made a party favor bag for each friend. Each bag contained 4 pencils, 2 toys, and 3 stickers.

1. How many pencils did Brenna's mom need to buy to fill the 5 party-favor bags?

20 pencils

2. How many stickers and toys did Brenna's mom need to buy to fill the 5 party-favor bags?

15 stickers, 10 toys

3. How many party favors did Brenna's mom buy altogether? How do you know this is a multiplication story?

45 party favors; Sample answer: It involves putting together equal groups.

At Brenna's party, there was also a piñata filled with stamps in the shapes of animals. The animal shapes were a zebra, an elephant, a cow, and a horse.

4. Jillian broke the piñata. She found 3 stamps of each kind of animal. How many stamps did she find?

12 stamps

5. Writing in Math Write a multiplication story about Brenna's party. Draw a picture for your story. Solve the problem.

Check students' stories, pictures, and solutions.

Use with Lesson 5-3. **61**

Use with Chapter 5, Lesson 3 **61**

Name_____

PROBLEM-SOLVING STRATEGY   P 5-4

Make a Table

Complete the table to solve the problem. Write the answer in a complete sentence.

1. Each centerpiece for the community banquet has 4 flowers in a vase. There needs to be 7 centerpieces. How many flowers will be used to fill the vases?

Number of vases	1	2	3	4	5	6	7
Number of flowers	4	8	12	16	20	24	28

28 flowers are needed to fill 7 vases.

2. Mrs. King bought 18 grapefruit at the market. Her family eats 3 grapefruit each day. How many days will the grapefruit last?

Number of grapefruit	18	15	12	9	6	3
Number of days	1	2	3	4	5	6

The grapefruit will last for 6 days.

3. Edmond saves $5 each week. How much will he have in his savings account at the end of 5 weeks?

Number of weeks	1	2	3	4	5	6	7
Money saved	$5	$10	$15	$20	$25	$30	$35

Edmond will have $25 in his savings account at the end of 5 weeks.

4. **Reasoning** Will Edmond be able to buy a $36 skateboard at the end of 7 weeks? Explain.

No; At the end of 7 weeks he will only have $35.

© Pearson Education, Inc. 3

Name_____

PROBLEM-SOLVING STRATEGY   R 5-4

Make a Table

Planting For every flower Tonya plants, she will need to water it with 2 gal of water. How many gallons of water will she need for 6 plants?

Read and Understand

Step 1: What do you know?
You know how much water is needed for each plant.

Step 2: What are you trying to find?
You are trying to find how many gallons of water are needed for 6 plants.

Plan and Solve

What strategy will you use?
Strategy: Make a table.

First, set up your table with labels.

Number of flowers			
Gallons of water			

Enter the information you know.

Number of flowers	1	2	3
Gallons of water	2	4	6

Look for a pattern. Continue the table.

Find the answer in the table.

Number of flowers	1	2	3	4	5	6
Gallons of water	2	4	6	8	10	12

Tonya will need 12 gal of water to plant 6 flowers.

Complete the table to solve the problem. Write the answer in a complete sentence.

1. Mrs. Dolan's nursery school class uses crayons during coloring time. Each student gets 6 crayons. If there are 6 students, how many crayons are needed?

Number of students	1	2	3	4	5	6
Number of crayons	6	12	18	24	30	36

36 crayons are needed for 6 students.

© Pearson Education, Inc. 3

Name_____

Dot Patterns   E 5-4
                                    PATTERNS

Find the pattern. Then complete the pattern.

1.

2.

3.

4.

5.

© Pearson Education, Inc. 3

Name_____

PROBLEM-SOLVING STRATEGY   PS 5-4

Make a Table

Kathleen's aunt was having a cookout. Kathleen helped her set up the tables. She put a glass of water next to each plate. There were 6 plates at each table. There were 8 tables in the backyard. How many glasses of water did Kathleen need for the 8 tables?

Read and Understand

1. What are you trying to find?

Sample answer: How many glasses of water Kathleen needs for the 8 tables

Plan and Solve

2. How many glasses did she place at the first table? How many total glasses did she place after the second table?   **6; 12**

3. Finish the table to help solve the problem.

Number of Tables	1	2	3	4	5	6	7	8
Number of Glasses	6	12	18	24	30	36	42	48

4. Write your answer in a complete sentence.

Kathleen needs 48 glasses of water for the 8 tables.

Look Back and Check

5. Explain how the table helped you solve the problem.

Sample answer: The table helps you count the glasses at all 8 tables.

© Pearson Education, Inc. 3

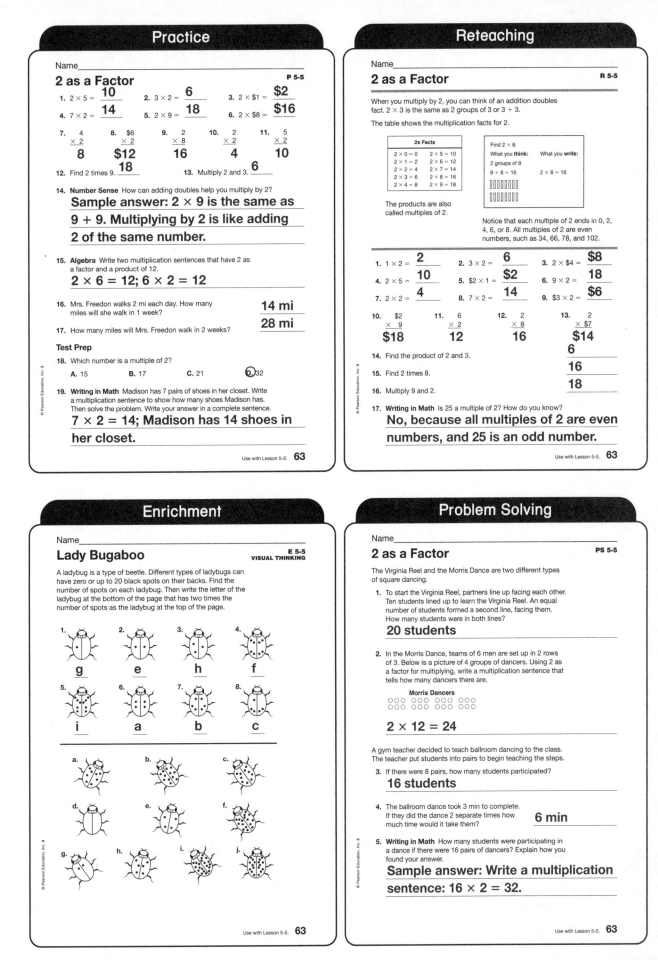

Practice

Name_____

2 as a Factor
P 5-5

1. 2 × 5 = __10__
2. 3 × 2 = __6__
3. 2 × $1 = __$2__
4. 7 × 2 = __14__
5. 2 × 9 = __18__
6. 2 × $8 = __$16__

7. 4
    × 2
    ___
    8

8. $6
    × 2
    ___
    $12

9. 2
    × 8
    ___
    16

10. 2
    × 2
    ___
    4

11. 5
    × 2
    ___
    10

12. Find 2 times 9. __18__
13. Multiply 2 and 3. __6__

14. **Number Sense** How can adding doubles help you multiply by 2?

Sample answer: 2 × 9 is the same as 9 + 9. Multiplying by 2 is like adding 2 of the same number.

15. **Algebra** Write two multiplication sentences that have 2 as a factor and a product of 12.

2 × 6 = 12; 6 × 2 = 12

16. Mrs. Freedon walks 2 mi each day. How many miles will she walk in 1 week? __14 mi__

17. How many miles will Mrs. Freedon walk in 2 weeks? __28 mi__

Test Prep

18. Which number is a multiple of 2?
    A. 15   B. 17   C. 21   D. 32

19. **Writing in Math** Madison has 7 pairs of shoes in her closet. Write a multiplication sentence to show how many shoes Madison has. Then solve the problem. Write your answer in a complete sentence.

7 × 2 = 14; Madison has 14 shoes in her closet.

© Pearson Education, Inc. 3

Reteaching

Name_____

2 as a Factor
R 5-5

When you multiply by 2, you can think of an addition doubles fact. 2 × 3 is the same as 2 groups of 3 or 3 + 3.

The table shows the multiplication facts for 2.

2s Facts	
2 × 0 = 0	2 × 5 = 10
2 × 1 = 2	2 × 6 = 12
2 × 2 = 4	2 × 7 = 14
2 × 3 = 6	2 × 8 = 16
2 × 4 = 8	2 × 9 = 18

The products are also called multiples of 2.

Find 2 × 8.
What you **think:**   What you **write:**
2 groups of 8
8 + 8 = 16   2 × 8 = 16

Notice that each multiple of 2 ends in 0, 2, 4, 6, or 8. All multiples of 2 are even numbers, such as 34, 66, 78, and 102.

1. 1 × 2 = __2__
2. 3 × 2 = __6__
3. 2 × $4 = __$8__
4. 2 × 5 = __10__
5. $2 × 1 = __$2__
6. 9 × 2 = __18__
7. 2 × 2 = __4__
8. 7 × 2 = __14__
9. $3 × 2 = __$6__

10. $2
    × 9
    ___
    $18

11. 6
    × 2
    ___
    12

12. 2
    × 8
    ___
    16

13. 2
    × $7
    ___
    $14

14. Find the product of 2 and 3. __6__
15. Find 2 times 8. __16__
16. Multiply 9 and 2. __18__

17. **Writing in Math** Is 25 a multiple of 2? How do you know?

No, because all multiples of 2 are even numbers, and 25 is an odd number.

© Pearson Education, Inc. 3

Enrichment

Name_____

Lady Bugaboo
E 5-5
VISUAL THINKING

A ladybug is a type of beetle. Different types of ladybugs can have zero or up to 20 black spots on their backs. Find the number of spots on each ladybug. Then write the letter of the ladybug at the bottom of the page that has two times the number of spots as the ladybug at the top of the page.

1. __g__   2. __e__   3. __h__   4. __f__

5. __i__   6. __a__   7. __b__   8. __c__

a.   b.   c.

d.   e.   f.

g.   h.   i.   j.

© Pearson Education, Inc. 3

Problem Solving

Name_____

2 as a Factor
PS 5-5

The Virginia Reel and the Morris Dance are two different types of square dancing.

1. To start the Virginia Reel, partners line up facing each other. Ten students lined up to learn the Virginia Reel. An equal number of students formed a second line, facing them. How many students were in both lines?

20 students

2. In the Morris Dance, teams of 6 men are set up in 2 rows of 3. Below is a picture of 4 groups of dancers. Using 2 as a factor for multiplying, write a multiplication sentence that tells how many dancers there are.

Morris Dancers
○○○ ○○○ ○○○ ○○○
○○○ ○○○ ○○○ ○○○

2 × 12 = 24

A gym teacher decided to teach ballroom dancing to the class. The teacher put students into pairs to begin teaching the steps.

3. If there were 8 pairs, how many students participated?

16 students

4. The ballroom dance took 3 min to complete. If they did the dance 2 separate times how much time would it take them? __6 min__

5. **Writing in Math** How many students were participating in a dance if there were 16 pairs of dancers? Explain how you found your answer.

Sample answer: Write a multiplication sentence: 16 × 2 = 32.

© Pearson Education, Inc. 3

5 as a Factor

P 5-6

1. $4 \times 5 =$ __20__ 2. $\$9 \times 5 =$ __$45__ 3. $5 \times 7 =$ __35__

4. $3 \times 5 =$ __15__ 5. $5 \times 2 =$ __10__ 6. $\$5 \times 5 =$ __$25__

7. $\begin{array}{r} 8 \\ \times\ \$5 \\ \hline \$40 \end{array}$ 8. $\begin{array}{r} 1 \\ \times\ 5 \\ \hline 5 \end{array}$ 9. $\begin{array}{r} 5 \\ \times\ 6 \\ \hline 30 \end{array}$ 10. $\begin{array}{r} 5 \\ \times\ 5 \\ \hline 25 \end{array}$ 11. $\begin{array}{r} 5 \\ \times\ 3 \\ \hline 15 \end{array}$

12. **Number Sense** What are two ways to skip count to find 2×5?
Count by 2s to 10; count by 5s to 10.

13. **Algebra** Write a number sentence to show that 5 is a factor of 35.
$5 \times 7 = 35$

14. There are 5 days in each school week. On how many days will you attend school over 9 weeks?
45 days

15. Seth has 45 pennies. Draw an array that shows how many nickels the pennies are worth.
The array should show 9 rows of 5.

Test Prep

16. Jay's favorite restaurant has 8 tables. Each table can seat 5 people. How many people can the restaurant seat?

A. 13 people   (B) 40 people   C. 45 people   D. 58 people

17. **Writing in Math** Is 115 a multiple of 5? Tell how you know.
Yes; Multiples of 5 end in 0 or 5.

---

5 as a Factor

R 5-6

You can use patterns and skip counting to multiply by 5.

Using skip counting to multiply by 5	Using patterns to multiply by 5
Find 5×7.	Find 5×8.

5s Facts

$5 \times 0 = 0$	$5 \times 5 = 25$
$5 \times 1 = 5$	$5 \times 6 = 30$
$5 \times 2 = 10$	$5 \times 7 = 35$
$5 \times 3 = 15$	$5 \times 8 = 40$
$5 \times 4 = 20$	$5 \times 9 = 45$

$5 + 5 + 5 + 5 + 5 + 5 + 5 = 35$

$5 \times 7 = 35$ $\begin{array}{r} 5 \\ \times\ 7 \\ \hline 35 \end{array}$

Each multiple of 5 ends in 0 or 5.
$5 \times 8 = 40$

1. $5 \times 2 =$ __10__ 2. $\$3 \times 5 =$ __$15__ 3. $5 \times 8 =$ __40__

4. $5 \times 6 =$ __30__ 5. $\$7 \times 5 =$ __$35__ 6. $9 \times 5 =$ __45__

7. $1 \times 5 =$ __5__ 8. $\$5 \times 5 =$ __$25__ 9. $4 \times 5 =$ __20__

10. $\begin{array}{r} 3 \\ \times\ 5 \\ \hline 15 \end{array}$ 11. $\begin{array}{r} \$5 \\ \times\ 4 \\ \hline \$20 \end{array}$ 12. $\begin{array}{r} 9 \\ \times\ 5 \\ \hline 45 \end{array}$

13. $\begin{array}{r} 5 \\ \times\ 7 \\ \hline 35 \end{array}$ 14. $\begin{array}{r} 2 \\ \times\ 8 \\ \hline 16 \end{array}$ 15. $\begin{array}{r} 5 \\ \times\ 5 \\ \hline 25 \end{array}$

16. Yolanda has 8 nickels in her pocket. How much money does she have?
Yolanda has $0.40, or 40 cents.

17. **Algebra** What factors could you multiply to get a product of 25?
$5 \times 5 = 25$

How Long Do They Live?

E 5-6
NUMBER SENSE

Different animals live to different ages. A mayfly lives 1 day while a turtle can live up to 100 years. Answer the questions to find out the average life span for each animal.

A garden dormouse lives for 5 years.

1. An American manatee lives about 6 times as long as a dormouse. About how long does an American manatee live?
About 30 years

2. A blue whale lives about 9 times as long as a dormouse. About how long does a blue whale live?
About 45 years

3. A Brazilian tapir lives about 7 times as long as a dormouse. About how long does a Brazilian tapir live?
About 35 years

4. A gray wolf lives about 4 times as long as a dormouse. About how long does a gray wolf live?
About 20 years

5. A hippopotamus lives about 8 times as long as a dormouse. About how long does a hippopotamus live?
About 40 years

6. A lion lives about 5 times as long as a dormouse. About how long does a lion live?
About 25 years

7. A slow loris lives about 2 times as long as a dormouse. About how long does a slow loris live?
About 10 years

8. Complete the table by writing the animal names above the correct life spans.

Animal	Slow loris	Gray wolf	Lion	Manatee	Tapir	Hippo	Blue whale
Lifespan	10 years	20 years	25 years	30 years	35 years	40 years	45 years

---

5 as a Factor

PS 5-6

Homework Kelsey was assigned math homework. He was given 8 word problems to solve. He estimated that it would take him 5 min to solve each problem.

1. How much time would it take Kelsey to complete his math homework?
40 min

2. Write a multiplication sentence for Exercise 1. Show skip counting as another way to solve the problem.
$8 \times 5 = 40$; 5, 10, 15, 20, 25, 30, 35, 40

3. What two factors would show how it could take Kelsey an hour to complete 12 problems at 5 min per problem?
$5 \times 12 = 60$

School Supplies The school store was having a clearance sale on supplies. Marge needed to buy more school supplies for the rest of the school year. She had $5.00 to spend.

Notebooks	$0.40
Pens	$0.30
Erasers	$0.10
Pencils	$0.20

SALE!

4. How much would it cost Marge to buy 5 pencils and 5 erasers? How much change would she get back from her $5.00 bill?
$1.50; $3.50

5. **Writing in Math** Could Marge buy 5 of each item on sale at the store? Explain.
Yes; Sample answer: The total for 5 notebooks, 5 pens, 5 erasers, and 5 pencils is exactly $5.00.

Name_____

10 as a Factor

P 5-7

1. $0 \times 10 =$ **0**   **2.** $10 \times 9 =$ **90**   **3.** $2 \times \$10 =$ **$20**

4. $6 \times 10 =$ **60**   **5.** $10 \times 1 =$ **10**   **6.** $10 \times \$3 =$ **$30**

7.	**8.**	**9.**	**10.**	**11.**
10 $\times \$8$	10 $\times 4$	10 $\times 7$	10 $\times 3$	10 $\times 2$
$80	**40**	**70**	**30**	**20**

12. Reasoning How can counting by 10s help you multiply by 10s?

Multiplying by 10 is the same as putting groups of 10 together. You can count by 10s, one 10 for each group.

13. Mary Ann earns $10 each week walking the neighborhood dogs. How much will she earn in 7 weeks?   **$70**

14. How long will it take Mary Ann to save $150?   **15 weeks**

15. Number Sense Draw 3 arrays to show that 20 is a multiple of 2, 5, and 10.

The arrays should show 2 rows of 10, 5 rows of 4, and 10 rows of 2.

Test Prep

16. Which is NOT a multiple of 10?

A. 30   B. 80   C. 100   **D.** 101

17. Writing in Math How can multiples of 10 also be multiples of 5?

There are two 5s in every 10.

Use with Lesson 5-7. **65**

© Pearson Education, Inc. 3

Name_____

10 as a Factor

R 5-7

The table shows the multiplication facts for 10.

10s Facts	
$10 \times 0 = 0$	$10 \times 5 = 50$
$10 \times 1 = 10$	$10 \times 6 = 60$
$10 \times 2 = 20$	$10 \times 7 = 70$
$10 \times 3 = 30$	$10 \times 8 = 80$
$10 \times 4 = 40$	$10 \times 9 = 90$

All multiples of 10 end with zero, such as 110; 2,350; and 467,000.

Find 10×5.

To find the answer, you can skip count or you can add a zero after the 5.

	Tens	Ones		Tens	Ones
		5	$\times 10 =$	5	0

$5 \times 10 = 50$

1. $10 \times 2 =$ **20**   **2.** $5 \times 10 =$ **50**   **3.** $10 \times 8 =$ **80**

4. $2 \times 8 =$ **16**   **5.** $\$10 \times 6 =$ **$60**   **6.** $7 \times 5 =$ **35**

7. $\$10 \times 4 =$ **$40**   **8.** $9 \times 2 =$ **18**   **9.** $8 \times 9 =$ **72**

10.	**11.**	**12.**
10 $\times 3$	$4 $\times 5$	2 $\times 2$
30	**$20**	**4**

13.	**14.**	**15.**
$10 $\times 6$	$8 $\times 5$	10 $\times 4$
$60	**$40**	**40**

16. Number Sense Is 49 a multiple of 10? Explain.

No; Multiples of 10 have a zero in the ones place.

Use with Lesson 5-7. **65**

© Pearson Education, Inc. 3

Name_____

Baseball Stats

E 5-7
DATA

The baseball team sold packs of baseball cards to earn money to buy new equipment. Its goal was to sell 500 packs of cards. Use the information from the pictograph to fill in the Baseball Card Stats Worksheet.

Packs of Cards Sold at $1.00 Each

Sunday	□□□□□□□□
Monday	□□□□□□□
Tuesday	□□□□□□
Wednesday	□□□□□
Thursday	□□□□□□□□□□
Friday	□□□□
Saturday	□□□

Each □ = 10 packs of baseball cards

Baseball Card Stats Worksheet

Day	Packs Sold	Money Earned
Sunday	80	$80.00
Monday	70	$70.00
Tuesday	60	$60.00
Wednesday	50	$50.00
Thursday	100	$100.00
Friday	40	$40.00
Saturday	30	$30.00

1. What was the total number of packs of baseball cards sold?

430 packs of baseball cards

2. What strategy did you use to find the total number of packs of baseball cards sold for the week?

I multiplied the number of squares in the pictograph by 10: $43 \times 10 = 430$

3. What was the total amount of money earned?   **$430.00**

4. Did the baseball team reach its goal? Explain.

No. The team was short by $70.00.

Use with Lesson 5-7. **65**

© Pearson Education, Inc. 3

Name_____

10 as a Factor

PS 5-7

Race Seth and Janice ran in a 10-km race. There were 7 other runners at the starting line with Seth and Janice. Seth usually ran a kilometer in 4 min, and Janice usually ran a kilometer in 5 min.

1. How many runners in total were at the starting line? If all of the runners finished the race, how many kilometers combined did they run?

9 runners; 90 km

2. If Janice ran in her usual time, how long would it take her to finish the race?   **50 min**

3. If both Seth and Janice run their usual times, who would finish the race first? Write two multiplication sentences you can use to answer the question.

Seth; $10 \times 5 = 50$ min, $10 \times 4 = 40$ min

Parade Day At the Independence Day Parade, Clarence the Clown had 10 each of 10 different colored buttons that said "smile." On every block that he marched in the parade, he gave out 10 buttons.

4. How many "smile" buttons did Clarence give out after marching 5 blocks in the parade?   **50 buttons**

5. Writing in Math Use the picture to write a multiplication story. Write a multiplication sentence and solve the problem.

Check students' multiplication stories and answers.

Use with Lesson 5-7. **65**

© Pearson Education, Inc. 3

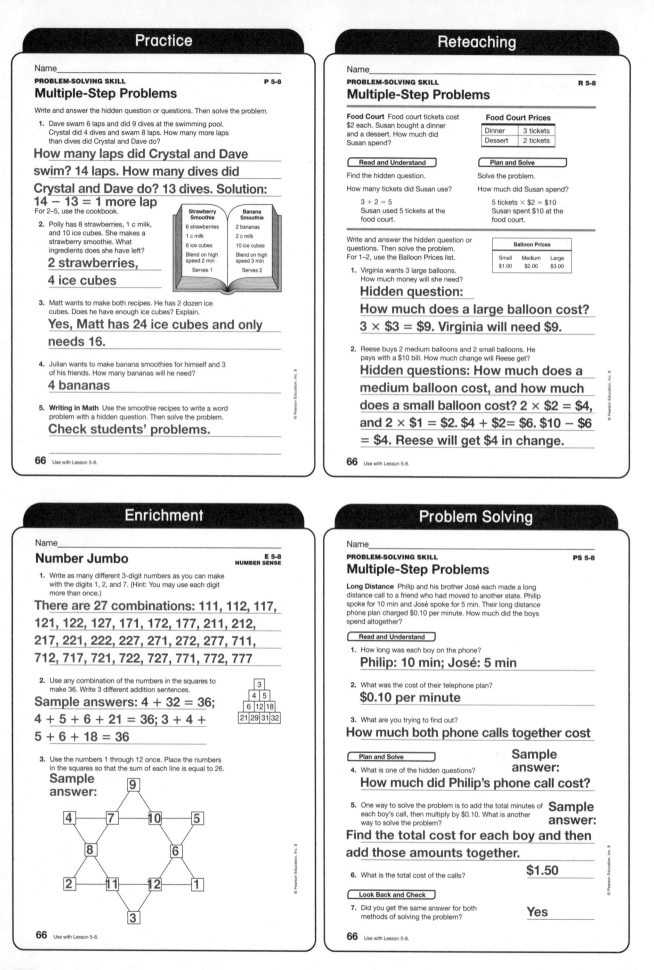

Practice

Multiple-Step Problems

Write and answer the hidden question or questions. Then solve the problem.

1. Dave swam 6 laps and did 9 dives at the swimming pool. Crystal did 4 dives and swam 8 laps. How many more laps than dives did Crystal and Dave do?

How many laps did Crystal and Dave swim? 14 laps. How many dives did Crystal and Dave do? 13 dives. Solution: 14 − 13 = 1 more lap

For 2–5, use the cookbook.

Strawberry Smoothie	Banana Smoothie
6 strawberries	2 bananas
1 c milk	2 c milk
6 ice cubes	10 ice cubes
Blend on high speed 2 min	Blend on high speed 3 min
Serves 1	Serves 2

2. Polly has 8 strawberries, 1 c milk, and 10 ice cubes. She makes a strawberry smoothie. What ingredients does she have left?

2 strawberries, 4 ice cubes

3. Matt wants to make both recipes. He has 2 dozen ice cubes. Does he have enough ice cubes? Explain.

Yes, Matt has 24 ice cubes and only needs 16.

4. Julian wants to make banana smoothies for himself and 3 of his friends. How many bananas will he need?

4 bananas

5. **Writing in Math** Use the smoothie recipes to write a word problem with a hidden question. Then solve the problem.

Check students' problems.

Reteaching

Multiple-Step Problems

Food Court Food court tickets cost $2 each. Susan bought a dinner and a dessert. How much did Susan spend?

Food Court Prices	
Dinner	3 tickets
Dessert	2 tickets

Read and Understand

Find the hidden question.

How many tickets did Susan use?

$3 + 2 = 5$
Susan used 5 tickets at the food court.

Plan and Solve

Solve the problem.

How much did Susan spend?

5 tickets × $2 = $10
Susan spent $10 at the food court.

Write and answer the hidden question or questions. Then solve the problem.
For 1–2, use the Balloon Prices list.

Balloon Prices		
Small	Medium	Large
$1.00	$2.00	$3.00

1. Virginia wants 3 large balloons. How much money will she need?

Hidden question: How much does a large balloon cost? 3 × $3 = $9. Virginia will need $9.

2. Reese buys 2 medium balloons and 2 small balloons. He pays with a $10 bill. How much change will Reese get?

Hidden questions: How much does a medium balloon cost, and how much does a small balloon cost? 2 × $2 = $4, and 2 × $1 = $2. $4 + $2= $6. $10 − $6 = $4. Reese will get $4 in change.

Enrichment

Number Jumbo

1. Write as many different 3-digit numbers as you can make with the digits 1, 2, and 7. (Hint: You may use each digit more than once.)

There are 27 combinations: 111, 112, 117, 121, 122, 127, 171, 172, 177, 211, 212, 217, 221, 222, 227, 271, 272, 277, 711, 712, 717, 721, 722, 727, 771, 772, 777

2. Use any combination of the numbers in the squares to make 36. Write 3 different addition sentences.

Sample answers: 4 + 32 = 36; 4 + 5 + 6 + 21 = 36; 3 + 4 + 5 + 6 + 18 = 36

	3		
	4	5	
6	12	18	
21	29	31	32

3. Use the numbers 1 through 12 once. Place the numbers in the squares so that the sum of each line is equal to 26.

Sample answer:

Problem Solving

Multiple-Step Problems

Long Distance Philip and his brother José each made a long distance call to a friend who had moved to another state. Philip spoke for 10 min and José spoke for 5 min. Their long distance phone plan charged $0.10 per minute. How much did the boys spend altogether?

Read and Understand

1. How long was each boy on the phone?

Philip: 10 min; José: 5 min

2. What was the cost of their telephone plan?

$0.10 per minute

3. What are you trying to find out?

How much both phone calls together cost

Plan and Solve

4. What is one of the hidden questions?

How much did Philip's phone call cost?

Sample answer:

5. One way to solve the problem is to add the total minutes of each boy's call, then multiply by $0.10. What is another way to solve the problem?

Find the total cost for each boy and then add those amounts together.

Sample answer:

6. What is the total cost of the calls?

$1.50

Look Back and Check

7. Did you get the same answer for both methods of solving the problem?

Yes

Name_____

Multiplying with 0 and 1

P 5-9

1. $1 \times 4 =$ **4**   2. $3 \times 0 =$ **0**   3. $\$9 \times 1 =$ **$9**

4. $0 \times 1 =$ **0**   5. $2 \times 0 =$ **0**   6. $0 \times 9 =$ **0**

7. $\begin{array}{r} 5 \\ \times\ 1 \\ \hline \mathbf{5} \end{array}$ 8. $\begin{array}{r} 1 \\ \times\ 7 \\ \hline \mathbf{7} \end{array}$ 9. $\begin{array}{r} 10 \\ \times\ 0 \\ \hline \mathbf{0} \end{array}$ 10. $\begin{array}{r} 6 \\ \times\ \$1 \\ \hline \mathbf{\$6} \end{array}$ 11. $\begin{array}{r} 1 \\ \times\ 8 \\ \hline \mathbf{8} \end{array}$

Compare. Write <, >, or = for each _____.

12. 1×5 **>** 7×0 13. 0×17 **=** 38×0

14. 1×97 **=** 97×1 15. 0×51 **<** 1×51

Write $\times$ or $+$ for each _____.

16. 1 **×** $7 = 7$ 17. 8 **+** $0 = 8$

18. 9 **+** $1 = 10$ 19. 3 **×** $0 = 0$

20. Sara keeps 4 boxes under her bed. Each box is for holding a different type of seashell. There are 0 shells in each box. Write a multiplication sentence to show how many seashells Sara has.

$4 \times 0 = 0$

Test Prep

21. Which is the product of 6×1?

A. 7   **B** 6   C. 5   D. 1

22. **Writing in Math** Angela says that the product of 0×0 is the same as the sum of $0 + 0$. Do you agree? Explain.

Yes; Zero groups of 0 is 0, and when you add 0 to 0 the answer is 0.

Use with Lesson 5-9. **67**

Name_____

Multiplying with 0 and 1

R 5-9

Zero and 1 have special multiplication properties.

The Identity (One) Property of Multiplication	The Zero Property of Multiplication
When you multiply a number and 1, the product is that number.	When you multiply a number and 0, the product is 0.
Examples:	Examples:
$4 \times 1 = 4$ $16 \times 1 = 16$	$5 \times 0 = 0$ $123 \times 0 = 0$
$1 \times 9 = 9$ $13 \times 1 = 13$	$17 \times 0 = 0$ $0 \times 58 = 0$
$251 \times 1 = 251$ $1 \times 48 = 48$	$0 \times 51 = 0$ $74 \times 0 = 0$

1. $1 \times 2 =$ **2**   2. $0 \times 3 =$ **0**   3. $4 \times 1 =$ **4**

4. $8 \times 0 =$ **0**   5. $\$6 \times 1 =$ **$6**   6. $1 \times 7 =$ **7**

7. $\begin{array}{r} \$1 \\ \times\ 7 \\ \hline \mathbf{\$7} \end{array}$ 8. $\begin{array}{r} 6 \\ \times\ 0 \\ \hline \mathbf{0} \end{array}$ 9. $\begin{array}{r} 8 \\ \times\ 1 \\ \hline \mathbf{8} \end{array}$

10. $\begin{array}{r} \$10 \\ \times\ 0 \\ \hline \mathbf{\$0} \end{array}$ 11. $\begin{array}{r} \$1 \\ \times\ 2 \\ \hline \mathbf{\$2} \end{array}$ 12. $\begin{array}{r} 0 \\ \times\ 9 \\ \hline \mathbf{0} \end{array}$

Complete each number sentence. Write <, >, or = for each $\bigcirc$.

13. 8×2 **(=)** 4×4 14. 19×1 **(>)** 37×0 15. 7×2 **(=)** $13 + 1$

Complete each number sentence. Write $\times$ or $+$ for each $\bigcirc$.

16. 5 **(+)** $0 = 5$ 17. 5 **(+)** $1 = 6$ 18. 1 **(×)** $5 = 5$

19. **Writing in Math** Write a multiplication sentence that shows the Zero Property of Multiplication. Explain why it shows this property.

Sample answer:

$81 \times 0 = 0$. Anytime you multiply a number by zero, the answer is zero.

Use with Lesson 5-9. **67**

Name_____

Nature Museum

E 5-9
DECISION MAKING

You are spending the afternoon at the nature museum. You have $15.00 to spend and $2\frac{1}{2}$ hr before the nature museum closes. Decide which exhibits you will see. Then record the time and the amount spent in the Nature Museum Log.

Nature Museum—Admission $5.00		
Exhibits	**Time**	**Price**
Butterflies	25 min	Free
Birds	30 min	Free
Frogs	15 min	Free
Backyard critters	25 min	$1.50
Flying insects	20 min	Free
Night creatures	45 min	$2.25
Guided nature hike	50 min	$4.00
Life in the trees	40 min	$3.50

Sample answer:

Nature Museum Log		
Exhibits Visited	**Time Used**	**Money Spent**
Admission	0 min	$5.00
Guided nature hike	**50 min**	**$4.00**
Life in the trees	**40 min**	**$3.50**
Night creatures	**45 min**	**$2.25**
Frogs	**15 min**	**Free**

Total time used: **150 min or $2\frac{1}{2}$ hour**

Total amount spent: **$14.75**

Use with Lesson 5-9. **67**

Name_____

Multiplying with 0 and 1

PS 5-9

The Cronin family would like to go to a circus that was in town, but they need to check out the ticket prices. A ticket for a child is $1.00, and a ticket for an adult is $5.00.

1. How much will it cost for the 4 Cronin children's tickets?

$4.00

2. A senior citizen's ticket costs the same as a child's ticket. How much will it cost for 7 senior citizens to attend the circus?

$7.00

3. It costs $1.00 for popcorn at the circus. If the circus sold 857 bags of popcorn, how much money did they make?

$857.00

Kate loves to garden. This year Kate planted the seeds for 4 tomato plants, 3 cucumber plants, and 2 green pepper plants. There was very little rain this summer. In August Kate found the tomato plant had only green tomatoes, the cucumber plant had flowers but no cucumbers, and there were no green peppers at all.

4. How many red ripe tomatoes was Kate able to harvest? Write a multiplication sentence for this problem.

$4 \times 0 = 0$; zero red ripe tomatoes

5. Write a number sentence for the total number of ripe vegetables Kate harvested in August.

$9 \times 0 = 0$; zero vegetables harvested

6. **Writing in Math** The product of two numbers is zero. One of the factors is zero. Explain why both 17 and 342 are correct answers for the other factor.

Sample answer: Since any number times zero equals zero, both numbers are correct.

Use with Lesson 5-9. **67**

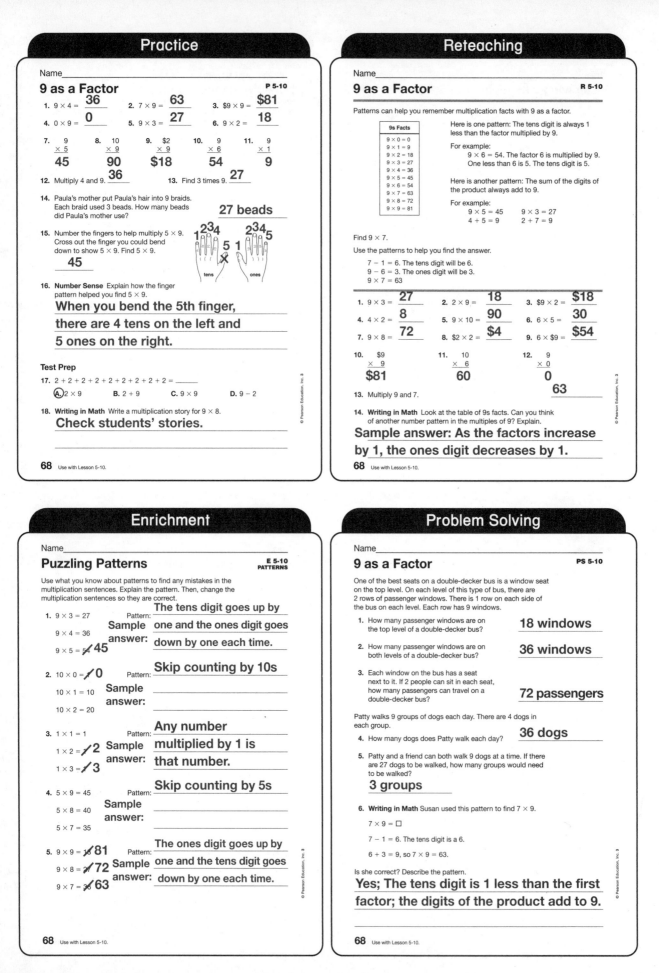

Practice

Name_____

9 as a Factor

1. $9 \times 4 =$ **36** 2. $7 \times 9 =$ **63** 3. $\$9 \times 9 =$ **$81**

4. $0 \times 9 =$ **0** 5. $9 \times 3 =$ **27** 6. $9 \times 2 =$ **18**

7. 9 8. 10 9. $2 10. 9 11. 9
   $\times 5$ $\times 9$ $\times 9$ $\times 6$ $\times 1$
   45 **90** **$18** **54** **9**

12. Multiply 4 and 9. **36**   13. Find 3 times 9. **27**

14. Paula's mother put Paula's hair into 9 braids. Each braid used 3 beads. How many beads did Paula's mother use?   **27 beads**

15. Number the fingers to help multiply 5×9. Cross out the finger you could bend down to show 5×9. Find 5×9.   **45**

16. **Number Sense** Explain how the finger pattern helped you find 5×9.
When you bend the 5th finger, there are 4 tens on the left and 5 ones on the right.

Test Prep

17. $2 + 2 + 2 + 2 + 2 + 2 + 2 + 2 + 2 =$ ____
    A. 2×9 **B.** $2 + 9$ **C.** 9×9 **D.** $9 - 2$

18. **Writing in Math** Write a multiplication story for 9×8.
Check students' stories.

Reteaching

Name_____

9 as a Factor

Patterns can help you remember multiplication facts with 9 as a factor.

9s Facts
$9 \times 0 = 0$
$9 \times 1 = 9$
$9 \times 2 = 18$
$9 \times 3 = 27$
$9 \times 4 = 36$
$9 \times 5 = 45$
$9 \times 6 = 54$
$9 \times 7 = 63$
$9 \times 8 = 72$
$9 \times 9 = 81$

Here is one pattern: The tens digit is always 1 less than the factor multiplied by 9.

For example:
$9 \times 6 = 54$. The factor 6 is multiplied by 9. One less than 6 is 5. The tens digit is 5.

Here is another pattern: The sum of the digits of the product always add to 9.

For example:
$9 \times 5 = 45$ $9 \times 3 = 27$
$4 + 5 = 9$ $2 + 7 = 9$

Find 9×7.

Use the patterns to help you find the answer.
$7 - 1 = 6$. The tens digit will be 6.
$9 - 6 = 3$. The ones digit will be 3.
$9 \times 7 = 63$

1. $9 \times 3 =$ **27** 2. $2 \times 9 =$ **18** 3. $\$9 \times 2 =$ **$18**

4. $4 \times 2 =$ **8** 5. $9 \times 10 =$ **90** 6. $6 \times 5 =$ **30**

7. $9 \times 8 =$ **72** 8. $\$2 \times 2 =$ **$4** 9. $6 \times \$9 =$ **$54**

10. $9 11. 10 12. 9
    $\times 9$ $\times 6$ $\times 0$
    $81 **60** **0**

13. Multiply 9 and 7.   **63**

14. **Writing in Math** Look at the table of 9s facts. Can you think of another number pattern in the multiples of 9? Explain.
Sample answer: As the factors increase by 1, the ones digit decreases by 1.

Enrichment

Name_____

Puzzling Patterns

Use what you know about patterns to find any mistakes in the multiplication sentences. Explain the pattern. Then, change the multiplication sentences so they are correct.

1. $9 \times 3 = 27$
   $9 \times 4 = 36$
   $9 \times 5 = 54$ **45**
   Pattern: **Sample answer:** **The tens digit goes up by one and the ones digit goes down by one each time.**

2. $10 \times 0 = 1$ **0**
   $10 \times 1 = 10$
   $10 \times 2 = 20$
   Pattern: **Skip counting by 10s**
   Sample answer:

3. $1 \times 1 = 1$
   $1 \times 2 = 1$ **2**
   $1 \times 3 = 1$ **3**
   Pattern: **Sample answer:** **Any number multiplied by 1 is that number.**

4. $5 \times 9 = 45$
   $5 \times 8 = 40$
   $5 \times 7 = 35$
   Pattern: **Skip counting by 5s**
   Sample answer:

5. $9 \times 9 = 18$ **81**
   $9 \times 8 = 27$ **72**
   $9 \times 7 = 36$ **63**
   Pattern: **Sample answer:** **The ones digit goes up by one and the tens digit goes down by one each time.**

Problem Solving

Name_____

9 as a Factor

One of the best seats on a double-decker bus is a window seat on the top level. On each level of this type of bus, there are 2 rows of passenger windows. There is 1 row on each side of the bus on each level. Each row has 9 windows.

1. How many passenger windows are on the top level of a double-decker bus?   **18 windows**

2. How many passenger windows are on both levels of a double-decker bus?   **36 windows**

3. Each window on the bus has a seat next to it. If 2 people can sit in each seat, how many passengers can travel on a double-decker bus?   **72 passengers**

Patty walks 9 groups of dogs each day. There are 4 dogs in each group.

4. How many dogs does Patty walk each day?   **36 dogs**

5. Patty and a friend can both walk 9 dogs at a time. If there are 27 dogs to be walked, how many groups would need to be walked?   **3 groups**

6. **Writing in Math** Susan used this pattern to find 7×9.

    $7 \times 9 = \square$

    $7 - 1 = 6$. The tens digit is a 6.

    $6 + 3 = 9$, so $7 \times 9 = 63$.

Is she correct? Describe the pattern.
Yes; The tens digit is 1 less than the first factor; the digits of the product add to 9.

© Pearson Education, Inc. 3

Name _____

Practicing Multiplication Facts
P 5-11

1. $9 \times 8 =$ __72__   2. $5 \times 4 =$ __20__   3. $1 \times 2 =$ __2__

4. $7 \times 0 =$ __0__   5. $8 \times 10 =$ __80__   6. $6 \times 2 =$ __12__

7. $\begin{array}{r} 5 \\ \times\, 6 \\ \hline 30 \end{array}$ 8. $\begin{array}{r} 3 \\ \times\, 5 \\ \hline 15 \end{array}$ 9. $\begin{array}{r} 9 \\ \times\, 4 \\ \hline 36 \end{array}$ 10. $\begin{array}{r} 1 \\ \times\, 1 \\ \hline 1 \end{array}$ 11. $\begin{array}{r} 2 \\ \times\, 7 \\ \hline 14 \end{array}$

Algebra Write the missing numbers.

12. $7 \times$ __0__ $= 0$ 13. __9__ $\times 4 = 36$

14. $2 \times$ __2__ $= 4$ 15. $8 \times$ __5__ $= 40$

16. **Number Sense** Is 30 a multiple of 5? How do you know?

Sample answers: Yes; It ends in 0. You can count by 5s to get to 30.

17. Seven friends went to the carnival. Each spent $0.20 on tickets. How much did they spend altogether on the tickets?   **$1.40**

Test Prep

18. Which is the product of 1×0?

A. 9×9 B. 0×9 C. 9×1 D. 1×9

19. **Writing in Math** Stacy multiplied 5×9 and said the answer was 44. What two patterns could you use to show that her answer is not correct?

Multiples of 5 must end in 5 or 0. The pattern of 9 shows that 4 should be in the tens and 5 should be in the ones. The answer is 45, not 44.

Name _____

Practicing Multiplication Facts
R 5-11

Here is how to make a set of flashcards.

- Write the first part of a multiplication fact on the front of the card.
- Write the product on the back.

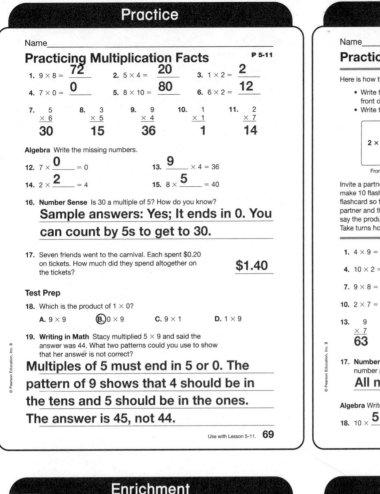

	Front		Back
	2×2		4

Invite a partner to make a set of 10 flashcards while you also make 10 flashcards. Use them to play a game together. Hold a flashcard so that the multiplication fact (the front) faces your partner and the product (the back) faces you. Have your partner say the product without looking at the back of the flashcard. Take turns holding the flashcards for each other.

1. $4 \times 9 =$ __36__   2. $2 \times 6 =$ __12__   3. $5 \times 4 =$ __20__

4. $10 \times 2 =$ __20__   5. $6 \times 1 =$ __6__   6. $2 \times 7 =$ __14__

7. $9 \times 8 =$ __72__   8. $7 \times 1 =$ __7__   9. $6 \times 1 =$ __6__

10. $2 \times 7 =$ __14__   11. $9 \times 8 =$ __72__   12. $7 \times 1 =$ __7__

13. $\begin{array}{r} 9 \\ \times\, 7 \\ \hline 63 \end{array}$ 14. $\begin{array}{r} 9 \\ \times\, 5 \\ \hline 25 \end{array}$ 15. $\begin{array}{r} 9 \\ \times\, 3 \\ \hline 27 \end{array}$ 16. $\begin{array}{r} 5 \\ \times\, 2 \\ \hline 10 \end{array}$

17. **Number Sense** Shawna thinks that $8 \times 2 = 17$. What number pattern shows that she is not correct?

All multiples of 2 are even numbers.

Algebra Write the missing number.

18. $10 \times$ __5__ $= 50$ 19. $9 \times$ __4__ $= 36$ 20. __9__ $\times 5 = 45$

Name _____

Mystery Products and Factors
E 5-11
NUMBER SENSE

Use the clues to find each factor or product.

1. The product is an even number less than 27.
One factor of the product is 3.
Another factor of the product is 8.
What is the product?   **24**

2. The product is greater than 4 but less than 40.
One factor of the product is 5.
The product can be described as an array of 5 groups of 5.
What is the product?   **25**

3. The factor is an odd number greater than 1 and less than 10.
This number is a factor of 30.
This number is a factor of 36.
What is the factor?   **3**

4. The product is greater than 36 and less than 80.
One factor of the product is 9.
The product is even.
Another factor of the product is 8.
What is the product?   **72**

5. The product is greater than 8 but less than 30.
One of the factors is 9.
The product is described as an array of 3 groups of 9.
What is the product?   **27**

6. The factor is less than 11.
This number is a factor of 24.
This number is a factor of 10.
The factor is even.
What is the factor?   **2**

Name _____

Practicing Multiplication Facts
PS 5-11

Library Day Once a week the students at North School visit the library. Each student in kindergarten and first grade checks out 1 book each week. Each student in second grade through fourth grade checks out 2 books each week. The fifth and sixth grade students each check out 3 books a week.

1. If 9 first-grade students, 2 fourth-grade students, and 4 fifth-grade students went to the library, how many books would they check out in all?   **25 books**

2. The librarian found that there were many books about caring for pets. There were 9 books each about dogs, cats, birds, fish, and rabbits. How many books were there about caring for pets altogether?   **45 books**

Zoo A class of third graders took a field trip to the zoo. On the bus, the students sat in groups of 4 with 1 adult chaperone. There were 6 groups in all.

3. How many students went to the zoo?   **24 students**

4. How many students and chaperones went to the zoo altogether?
30 students and chaperones altogether

5. **Writing in Math** Explain how knowing that $12 \times 10 = 120$ could help you find the product of 12×5.

Sample answer: You skip count by tens to get 12×10, so you can count by fives to get 60.

Name_____

Measure Your Lunch

Liquid and dry measurements use either customary units or metric units. If you go to a supermarket today or simply look in the kitchen, you will see that many of the products your family buys have both customary units and metric unit information.

1. A small can of soup weighs about 10 oz. Write an addition sentence and a multiplication sentence for about how many ounces of soup there are in 7 cans.

$$10 + 10 + 10 + 10 + 10 + 10 + 10 = 70;$$
$$7 \times 10 = 70$$

2. One serving of chicken-with-rice soup contains 8 g of carbohydrates. How many grams of carbohydrates are there in 5 servings of the soup?   **40 g**

3. One can of condensed chicken-with-rice soup contains 5 g of protein. Finish the table to find the total amount of protein in different numbers of cans.

Number of cans	1	2	3	4	5	6	7	8	9	10
Grams of protein	5	10	15	20	25	30	35	40	45	50

4. A small container of mixed-berry yogurt has 10 mg of cholesterol. How many milligrams of cholesterol are there in 4 small containers of mixed-berry yogurt?

40 mg of cholesterol

5. A small container of mixed-berry yogurt also has 9 g of protein. The recommended daily allowance of protein is about 45 grams. About how many small containers of mixed-berry yogurt do you have to eat to get the recommended daily amount of protein?

About 5 containers

Name_____

Dozens of Eggs!

At United States chicken farms, female chickens lay about 5 eggs per week. How many eggs would the chicken lay after 6 weeks?

You can make a table to solve this problem.

First, draw your table and enter the information you know.

Week	1	2	3	4	5	6
Eggs laid	5					

Then look for a pattern and continue the table.

Week	1	2	3	4	5	6
Eggs laid	5	10	15	20	25	30

After 6 weeks, the chicken will have laid about 30 eggs.

1. Tim collects eggs each morning on his family farm. If he collects 7 eggs each morning, how many eggs will he have after 7 days? Complete the table to solve this problem.

Day	1	2	3	4	5	6	7
Eggs collected	7	14	21	28	35	42	49

He will have 49 eggs.

2. Suppose there are 2 eggs in a carton. How many eggs will you have if you buy 3 cartons? 7 cartons? 9 cartons?

6 eggs; 14 eggs; 18 eggs

3. Suppose there are 5 eggs in a carton. How many eggs will you have if you buy 4 cartons? 8 cartons? 10 cartons?

20 eggs; 40 eggs; 50 eggs

4. Suppose there are 9 eggs in a carton. How many eggs will you have if you buy 5 cartons? 7 cartons? 9 cartons?

45 eggs; 63 eggs; 81 eggs

Name_____

Apples Are Appealing

Two thousand, five hundred different kinds of apples are grown in the United States. About 840 lb of apples can be harvested from one apple tree. This is enough to make about 420 qt of apple sauce.

> Applesauce Recipe
>
> 6 lb apples
> 2 c water
> 1 c raisins
> 3 tsp cinnamon
> 4 tsp vanilla

Find the amount of each ingredient you would need to make the number of recipes shown.

1. 2 times the recipe

Apples: **12 lb**
Water: **4 c**
Raisins: **2 c**
Cinnamon: **6 tsp**
Vanilla: **8 tsp**

2. 5 times the recipe

Apples: **30 lb**
Water: **10 c**
Raisins: **5 c**
Cinnamon: **15 tsp**
Vanilla: **20 tsp**

3. 9 times the recipe

Apples: **54 lb**
Water: **18 c**
Raisins: **9 c**
Cinnamon: **27 tsp**
Vanilla: **36 tsp**

4. 10 times the recipe

Apples: **60 lb**
Water: **20 c**
Raisins: **10 c**
Cinnamon: **30 tsp**
Vanilla: **40 tsp**

Name_____

Sidewalk Sale

A music store is having a sidewalk sale. All CDs are on sale at low prices for one day only. Any CDs that have a damaged case are on sale for $5. Any used CDs are on sale for $10. Lastly, all new CDs are on sale for $15. Calista has picked out 5 CDs with damaged cases, 1 new CD, and 1 used CD. How much will she pay altogether?

Read and Understand

1. How much does each type of CD cost?

Damaged: $5; used: $10; new: $15

2. How many of each type of CD did Calista pick out?

Damaged: 5; used: 1; new: 1

3. What are you trying to find?

How much Calista will pay

Plan and Solve

4. What operations will you use to solve the problem?

Multiplication and addition

5. Solve the problem and write the answer in a complete sentence.

Calista will spend $50.

Look Back and Check

6. Explain why you can use counting by 5s and 10s to check your answer.

Sample answer: Because the prices of all the CDs are 5 and 10 facts

Name_____

3 as a Factor

1. $1 \times 3 =$ **3** 2. $3 \times 7 =$ **21** 3. $\$6 \times 3 =$ **$18**

4. $8 \times 3 =$ **24** 5. $3 \times 8 =$ **24** 6. $3 \times 5 =$ **15**

7. $\begin{array}{r} 3 \\ \times 2 \\ \hline \mathbf{6} \end{array}$ 8. $\begin{array}{r} 4 \\ \times 3 \\ \hline \mathbf{12} \end{array}$ 9. $\begin{array}{r} 3 \\ \times 0 \\ \hline \mathbf{0} \end{array}$ 10. $\begin{array}{r} \$3 \\ \times 5 \\ \hline \mathbf{\$15} \end{array}$ 11. $\begin{array}{r} 3 \\ \times 9 \\ \hline \mathbf{27} \end{array}$

12. **Number Sense** What two multiplication facts can be added to find 3×7?

$2 \times 7 = 14$ and $1 \times 7 = 7$

13. There were 5 people who bought tickets to a football game. They each bought 3 tickets. How many tickets were bought altogether?

15 tickets

14. Marina has 3 colors of flowers. She has 3 of each color. How many flowers does she have altogether?

9 flowers

15. A group of 7 friends paid $3 each to get into a carnival. How much did they pay altogether?

$21

Test Prep

16. Tom gave each of his 5 friends 3 stickers. How many stickers did he give away?

A. 3 stickers   B. 5 stickers   C. 12 stickers   D. 15 stickers

17. **Writing in Math** Explain how you can break apart 3×9 to help you multiply.

You can break apart 3×9 into 1×9 and 2×9. $1 \times 9 = 9$, $2 \times 9 = 18$, and $9 + 18 = 27$, so $3 \times 9 = 27$.

Name_____

3 as a Factor

You can use an array to show multiplication. The number of rows is the first factor, and the number of columns is the second factor.

What You Show   **What You Think**

(1) $3 \times 1 = 3$
(3)

(2) $2 \times 2 = 4$
(2)

Complete the arrays.

$3 \times 5 =$ **15**

$2 \times$ **5** $=$ **10**

$1 \times$ **5** $=$ **5**

$3 \times$ **5** $= 15$

1. $3 \times 2 =$ **6** 2. $3 \times 4 =$ **12** 3. $3 \times 5 =$ **15**

4. $\begin{array}{r} 3 \\ \times 8 \\ \hline \mathbf{24} \end{array}$ 5. $\begin{array}{r} 3 \\ \times 9 \\ \hline \mathbf{27} \end{array}$ 6. $\begin{array}{r} 7 \\ \times 3 \\ \hline \mathbf{21} \end{array}$

7. **Number Sense** Each of 3 dogs has 6 puppies. How many puppies are there altogether?

18 puppies

Name_____

Flower Power

Alicia has 3 vases. She wants 9 flowers in each vase. She goes to the flower shop and buys enough flowers for 2 vases. For the 3rd vase, she cuts 9 flowers from her garden.

1. How many flowers are in all 3 vases? What is the multiplication sentence?

27 flowers; $3 \times 9 = 27$

2. Draw an array to show the multiplication fact.

3. How many flowers did she buy for 2 vases? Write the multiplication sentence.

18 flowers; $2 \times 9 = 18$

4. How many flowers did she cut from her garden for the last vase? Write the multiplication sentence.

9 flowers; $1 \times 9 = 9$

5. Explain how you can break apart arrays when you multiply by 3.

Sample answer: You can add a 2s fact and a 1s fact to find a 3s fact.

6. Show another strategy you can use to find the product 3×9.

Sample answer: Skip count by 3s; Use the Commutative Property of Multiplication so that $3 \times 9 = 9 \times 3$.

Name_____

3 as a Factor

Admission Jeni's family is going to the State Fair. Jeni and her 2 sisters will pay the child's price for admission, but her mom, dad, and 14-year-old brother will have to pay the adult's price.

Welcome to the STATE FAIR

Admissions	Price
Adult	$8.00
Child (Ages 4–12)	$5.00
Under Age 4	FREE!
"Ride-All-Day" wristbands	$12.00

1. How much will the family pay for Jeni and her 2 sisters?

$15.00

2. How much will the family pay for the 3 adult admissions?

$24.00

3. What will the family's total cost be for admission to the fair?

$39.00

4. No matter what a person's age, the price of a "Ride-All-Day" wristband is always the same. What is the cost of 3 wristbands?

$36.00

5. In 1998, 3 sets of triplets were born within 4 days at University Hospital in Cincinnati. How many babies were born?

9 babies

6. There are 3 ft in a yard. How many feet are there in 11 yd?

33 ft

7. **Writing in Math** Explain how you can solve Exercise 6 using two different arrays.

Sample answer: You can use a 3×11 array that is separated into a 2×11 array and a 1×11 array, which shows that $22 + 11 = 33$, or a 3×10 array and a 3×1 array, which shows $30 + 3 = 33$.

Name_____

4 as a Factor
P 6-2

1. $2 \times 4 = $ **8** 2. $4 \times 5 = $ **20** 3. $3 \times 4 = $ **12**

4. $4 \times 4 = $ **16** 5. $\$4 \times 8 = $ **$32** 6. $4 \times 6 = $ **24**

7. $\begin{array}{r} 1 \\ \times\ 4 \\ \hline \mathbf{4} \end{array}$ 8. $\begin{array}{r} 4 \\ \times\ 4 \\ \hline \mathbf{16} \end{array}$ 9. $\begin{array}{r} \$4 \\ \times\ 9 \\ \hline \mathbf{\$36} \end{array}$ 10. $\begin{array}{r} 0 \\ \times\ 4 \\ \hline \mathbf{0} \end{array}$ 11. $\begin{array}{r} 4 \\ \times\ 7 \\ \hline \mathbf{28} \end{array}$

12. **Number Sense** What multiplication fact can you double to find 4×7?

$2 \times 7 = 14$

13. Continue each pattern.

a. 20, 16, 12, **8** **4** **0**

b. 20, 24, 28, **32** **36** **40**

c. 8, 12, 16, **20** **24** **28**

14. There are 6 chairs around a table. Each chair has 4 legs. How many chair legs are around the table?

24 chair legs

15. Sally bought 4 movie tickets for herself and her friends. The tickets cost $8 each. How much money did Sally spend on the movie tickets?

$32

Test Prep

16. Aaron changed the tires on 5 cars. Each car had 4 tires. How many tires did Aaron change?

A. 12 tires B. 16 tires Ⓒ 20 tires D. 24 tires

17. **Writing in Math** Tessie multiplied 3×4, and then doubled it to find 6×8. Did she get the correct answer? Explain.

No; When $3 \times 4 = 12$ is doubled, it is $3 \times 8 = 24$.

Name_____

4 as a Factor
R 6-2

If you know a 2s multiplication fact, you can find a 4s multiplication fact.

When you double an array of 2×1, you get an array of 4×1.

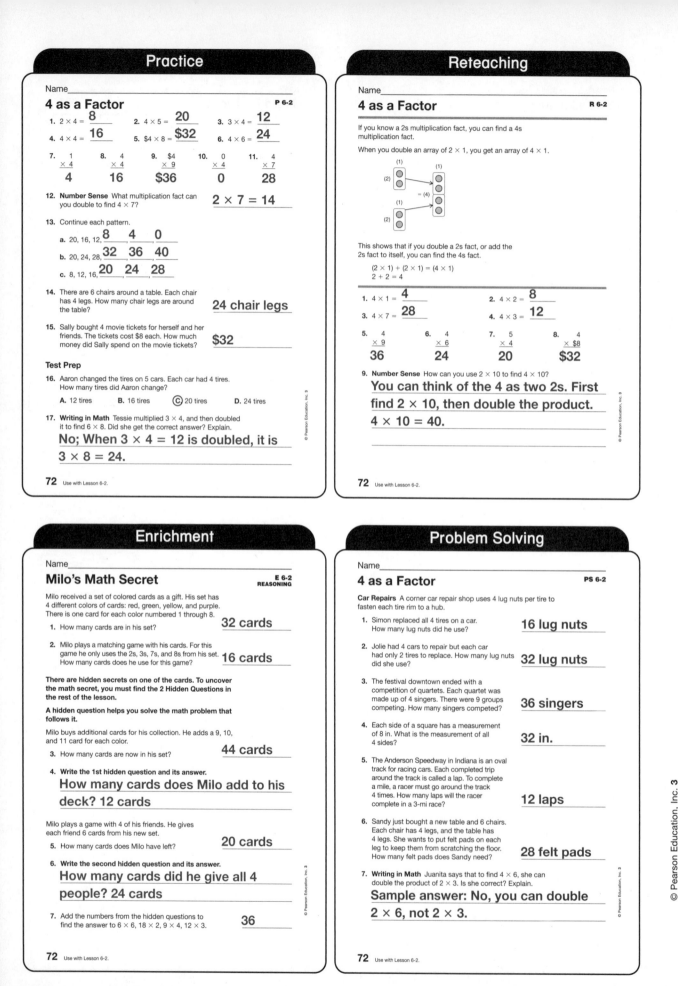

This shows that if you double a 2s fact, or add the 2s fact to itself, you can find the 4s fact.

$(2 \times 1) + (2 \times 1) = (4 \times 1)$
$2 + 2 = 4$

1. $4 \times 1 = $ **4** 2. $4 \times 2 = $ **8**

3. $4 \times 7 = $ **28** 4. $4 \times 3 = $ **12**

5. $\begin{array}{r} 4 \\ \times\ 9 \\ \hline \mathbf{36} \end{array}$ 6. $\begin{array}{r} 4 \\ \times\ 6 \\ \hline \mathbf{24} \end{array}$ 7. $\begin{array}{r} 5 \\ \times\ 4 \\ \hline \mathbf{20} \end{array}$ 8. $\begin{array}{r} 4 \\ \times\ \$8 \\ \hline \mathbf{\$32} \end{array}$

9. **Number Sense** How can you use 2×10 to find 4×10?

You can think of the 4 as two 2s. First find 2×10, then double the product. $4 \times 10 = 40$.

Name_____

Milo's Math Secret
E 6-2
REASONING

Milo received a set of colored cards as a gift. His set has 4 different colors of cards: red, green, yellow, and purple. There is one card for each color numbered 1 through 8.

1. How many cards are in his set?

32 cards

2. Milo plays a matching game with his cards. For this game he only uses the 2s, 3s, 7s, and 8s from his set. How many cards does he use for this game?

16 cards

There are hidden secrets on one of the cards. To uncover the math secret, you must find the 2 Hidden Questions in the rest of the lesson.

A hidden question helps you solve the math problem that follows it.

Milo buys additional cards for his collection. He adds a 9, 10, and 11 card for each color.

3. How many cards are now in his set?

44 cards

4. Write the 1st hidden question and its answer.

How many cards does Milo add to his deck? 12 cards

Milo plays a game with 4 of his friends. He gives each friend 6 cards from his new set.

5. How many cards does Milo have left?

20 cards

6. Write the second hidden question and its answer.

How many cards did he give all 4 people? 24 cards

7. Add the numbers from the hidden questions to find the answer to 6×6, 18×2, 9×4, 12×3.

36

Name_____

4 as a Factor
PS 6-2

Car Repairs A corner car repair shop uses 4 lug nuts per tire to fasten each tire rim to a hub.

1. Simon replaced all 4 tires on a car. How many lug nuts did he use?

16 lug nuts

2. Jolie had 4 cars to repair but each car had only 2 tires to replace. How many lug nuts did she use?

32 lug nuts

3. The festival downtown ended with a competition of quartets. Each quartet was made up of 4 singers. There were 9 groups competing. How many singers competed?

36 singers

4. Each side of a square has a measurement of 8 in. What is the measurement of all 4 sides?

32 in.

5. The Anderson Speedway in Indiana is an oval track for racing cars. Each completed trip around the track is called a lap. To complete a mile, a racer must go around the track 4 times. How many laps will the racer complete in a 3-mi race?

12 laps

6. Sandy just bought a new table and 6 chairs. Each chair has 4 legs, and the table has 4 legs. She wants to put felt pads on each leg to keep them from scratching the floor. How many felt pads does Sandy need?

28 felt pads

7. **Writing in Math** Juanita says that to find 4×6, she can double the product of 2×3. Is she correct? Explain.

Sample answer: No, you can double 2×6, not 2×3.

Practice

Name_____

P 6-3

6 and 7 as Factors

1. $5 \times 6 =$ **30**
2. $6 \times 3 =$ **18**
3. $6 \times 8 =$ **48**
4. $\$3 \times 7 =$ **$21**
5. $7 \times 10 =$ **70**
6. $7 \times 4 =$ **28**

7. $\begin{array}{r} \$4 \\ \times\ 6 \\ \hline \end{array}$ **$24**
8. $\begin{array}{r} 5 \\ \times\ 7 \\ \hline \end{array}$ **35**
9. $\begin{array}{r} 7 \\ \times\ 8 \\ \hline \end{array}$ **56**
10. $\begin{array}{r} 6 \\ \times\ 6 \\ \hline \end{array}$ **36**
11. $\begin{array}{r} 6 \\ \times\ 7 \\ \hline \end{array}$ **42**

12. Multiply 7 and 7. **49**

13. Multiply 1 and 6. **6**

14. Find the product of 6 and 9. **54**

15. Find 7 times 2. **14**

16. **Number Sense** What multiplication fact can be found by using the arrays for 2×9 and 5×9? **$7 \times 9 = 63$**

17. Raul's science class is hatching chicken eggs. If the eggs take 3 weeks to hatch, how many days until they hatch? **21 days**

18. Emily cut 7 apples into slices. There are 6 slices from each apple. How many apple slices did she cut in all? **42 slices**

Test Prep

19. Helen needs 6 more stuffed miniature bears to complete her collection. Each bear costs $9. How much will Helen have to spend to complete her collection?
   - A. $45
   - **Ⓑ $54**
   - C. $56
   - D. $63

20. **Writing in Math** Explain how you could use $5 \times 6 = 30$ to find the product of 6×6.

$5 \times 6 = 30$ is 5 groups of 6. Add one more group, and it becomes $30 + 6 = 36$, so $6 \times 6 = 36$.

Use with Lesson 6-3. **73**

© Pearson Education, Inc. 3

Reteaching

Name_____

R 6-3

6 and 7 as Factors

You can use multiplication facts that you already know to find multiplication facts you are unsure of.
You know the multiplication facts for 1s, 2s, and 5s.

Find 9×6.

Break apart an array for 9×6 into two separate arrays. Make one array for 5×6 in order to use your knowledge of 5s facts. Make the second array 4×6.

$5 \times 6 = 30$

$4 \times 6 = 24$

$30 + 24 = 54$, so $9 \times 6 = 54$

Find 7×8.

You can do the same thing to multiply by 7.
Break the array for 7×8 into two separate arrays: one for 5×8 and one for 2×8.

$5 \times 8 = 40$

$2 \times 8 = 16$

$40 + 16 = 56$, so $7 \times 8 = 56$

1. $2 \times 7 =$ **14**
2. $5 \times 7 =$ **35**
3. $7 \times 9 =$ **63**
4. $6 \times 4 =$ **24**
5. $6 \times 6 =$ **36**
6. $6 \times \$10 =$ **$60**

7. $\begin{array}{r} 4 \\ \times\ 7 \\ \hline \end{array}$ **28**
8. $\begin{array}{r} 8 \\ \times\ 6 \\ \hline \end{array}$ **48**
9. $\begin{array}{r} \$7 \\ \times\ 3 \\ \hline \end{array}$ **$21**
10. $\begin{array}{r} 5 \\ \times\ 9 \\ \hline \end{array}$ **45**

11. **Number Sense** Harold says "To find 6×8, I can use the facts for 5×4 and 1×4." Do you agree? Explain.

No. One factor stays the same, the other is separated. Use 5×8 and 1×8.

Use with Lesson 6-3. **73**

© Pearson Education, Inc. 3

Enrichment

Name_____

E 6-3
REASONING

Shelve That Idea

Janice wants to fill her shelves with books. Her bookcase has 5 shelves above her television and 2 shelves below the television. She needs 9 books to fill each shelf.

1. Fill in the shelves with the correct number of books.

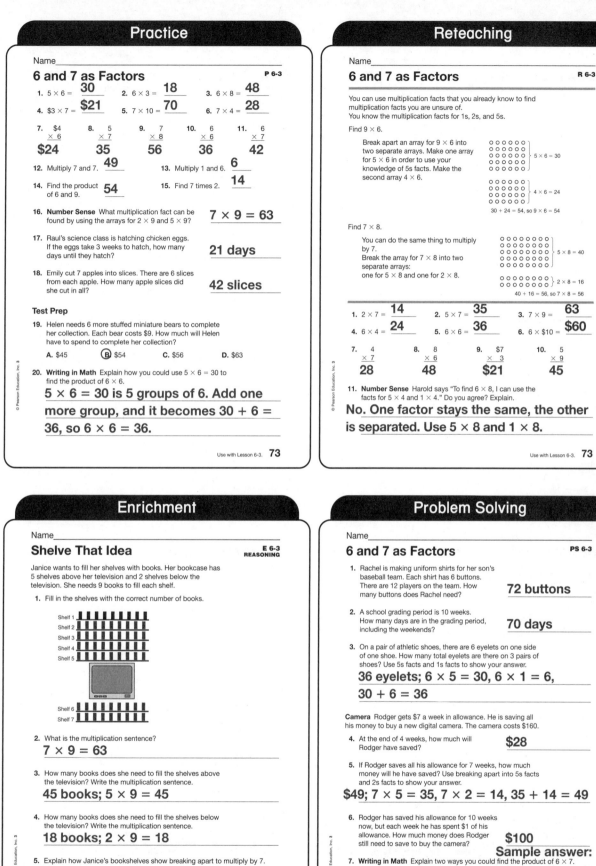

Shelf 1
Shelf 2
Shelf 3
Shelf 4
Shelf 5

Shelf 6
Shelf 7

2. What is the multiplication sentence? **$7 \times 9 = 63$**

3. How many books does she need to fill the shelves above the television? Write the multiplication sentence. **45 books; $5 \times 9 = 45$**

4. How many books does she need to fill the shelves below the television? Write the multiplication sentence. **18 books; $2 \times 9 = 18$**

5. Explain how Janice's bookshelves show breaking apart to multiply by 7.

You can use 5s and 2s facts to multiply by 7.

Use with Lesson 6-3. **73**

© Pearson Education, Inc. 3

Problem Solving

Name_____

PS 6-3

6 and 7 as Factors

1. Rachel is making uniform shirts for her son's baseball team. Each shirt has 6 buttons. There are 12 players on the team. How many buttons does Rachel need? **72 buttons**

2. A school grading period is 10 weeks. How many days are in the grading period, including the weekends? **70 days**

3. On a pair of athletic shoes, there are 6 eyelets on one side of one shoe. How many total eyelets are there on 3 pairs of shoes? Use 5s facts and 1s facts to show your answer.

36 eyelets; $6 \times 5 = 30$, $6 \times 1 = 6$, $30 + 6 = 36$

Camera Rodger gets $7 a week in allowance. He is saving all his money to buy a new digital camera. The camera costs $160.

4. At the end of 4 weeks, how much will Rodger have saved? **$28**

5. If Rodger saves all his allowance for 7 weeks, how much money will he have saved? Use breaking apart into 5s facts and 2s facts to show your answer. **$49; $7 \times 5 = 35$, $7 \times 2 = 14$, $35 + 14 = 49$**

6. Rodger has saved his allowance for 10 weeks now, but each week he has spent $1 of his allowance. How much money does Rodger still need to save to buy the camera? **$100**

Sample answer:

7. **Writing in Math** Explain two ways you could find the product of 6×7.

You could double the fact for $3 \times 7 = 21$, or you could first multiply $6 \times 5 = 30$ and $6 \times 2 = 12$, then add $30 + 12 = 42$.

Use with Lesson 6-3. **73**

© Pearson Education, Inc. 3

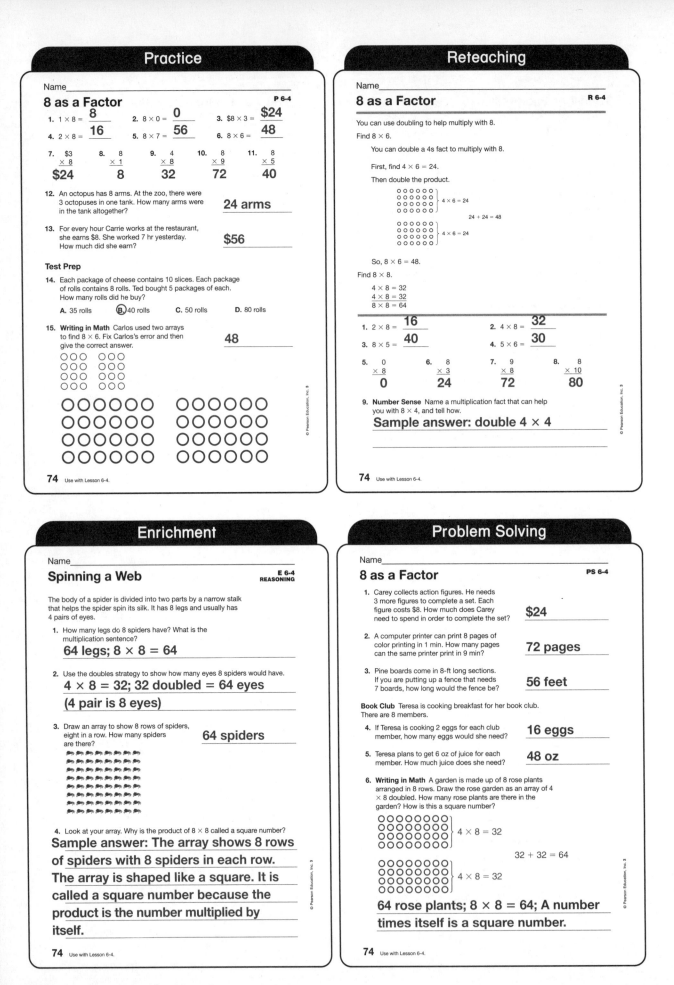

Practice

8 as a Factor

1. $1 \times 8 =$ **8**
2. $8 \times 0 =$ **0**
3. $$8 \times 3 =$ **$24**
4. $2 \times 8 =$ **16**
5. $8 \times 7 =$ **56**
6. $8 \times 6 =$ **48**

7.
$$3
$\times\ 8$
$24

8.
8
$\times\ 1$
8

9.
4
$\times\ 8$
32

10.
8
$\times\ 9$
72

11.
8
$\times\ 5$
40

12. An octopus has 8 arms. At the zoo, there were 3 octopuses in one tank. How many arms were in the tank altogether?   **24 arms**

13. For every hour Carrie works at the restaurant, she earns $8. She worked 7 hr yesterday. How much did she earn?   **$56**

Test Prep

14. Each package of cheese contains 10 slices. Each package of rolls contains 8 rolls. Ted bought 5 packages of each. How many rolls did he buy?

A. 35 rolls   (B.) 40 rolls   C. 50 rolls   D. 80 rolls

15. **Writing in Math** Carlos used two arrays to find 8×6. Fix Carlos's error and then give the correct answer.   **48**

○○○ ○○○
○○○ ○○○
○○○ ○○○
○○○ ○○○

○○○○○○   ○○○○○○
○○○○○○   ○○○○○○
○○○○○○   ○○○○○○
○○○○○○   ○○○○○○

© Pearson Education, Inc. 3

Reteaching

8 as a Factor

You can use doubling to help multiply with 8.

Find 8×6.

You can double a 4s fact to multiply with 8.

First, find $4 \times 6 = 24$.

Then double the product.

$4 \times 6 = 24$
$4 \times 6 = 24$
$24 + 24 = 48$

So, $8 \times 6 = 48$.

Find 8×8.

$4 \times 8 = 32$
$4 \times 8 = 32$
$8 \times 8 = 64$

1. $2 \times 8 =$ **16**
2. $4 \times 8 =$ **32**
3. $8 \times 5 =$ **40**
4. $5 \times 6 =$ **30**

5.
0
$\times\ 8$
0

6.
8
$\times\ 3$
24

7.
9
$\times\ 8$
72

8.
8
$\times\ 10$
80

9. **Number Sense** Name a multiplication fact that can help you with 8×4, and tell how.

Sample answer: double 4×4

© Pearson Education, Inc. 3

Enrichment

Spinning a Web

The body of a spider is divided into two parts by a narrow stalk that helps the spider spin its silk. It has 8 legs and usually has 4 pairs of eyes.

1. How many legs do 8 spiders have? What is the multiplication sentence?
64 legs; $8 \times 8 = 64$

2. Use the doubles strategy to show how many eyes 8 spiders would have.
$4 \times 8 = 32$; 32 doubled $= 64$ eyes
(4 pair is 8 eyes)

3. Draw an array to show 8 rows of spiders, eight in a row. How many spiders are there?   **64 spiders**

4. Look at your array. Why is the product of 8×8 called a square number?

Sample answer: The array shows 8 rows of spiders with 8 spiders in each row. The array is shaped like a square. It is called a square number because the product is the number multiplied by itself.

© Pearson Education, Inc. 3

Problem Solving

8 as a Factor

1. Carey collects action figures. He needs 3 more figures to complete a set. Each figure costs $8. How much does Carey need to spend in order to complete the set?   **$24**

2. A computer printer can print 8 pages of color printing in 1 min. How many pages can the same printer print in 9 min?   **72 pages**

3. Pine boards come in 8-ft long sections. If you are putting up a fence that needs 7 boards, how long would the fence be?   **56 feet**

Book Club Teresa is cooking breakfast for her book club. There are 8 members.

4. If Teresa is cooking 2 eggs for each club member, how many eggs would she need?   **16 eggs**

5. Teresa plans to get 6 oz of juice for each member. How much juice does she need?   **48 oz**

6. **Writing in Math** A garden is made up of 8 rose plants arranged in 8 rows. Draw the rose garden as an array of 4×8 doubled. How many rose plants are there in the garden? How is this a square number?

$4 \times 8 = 32$
$32 + 32 = 64$
$4 \times 8 = 32$

64 rose plants; $8 \times 8 = 64$; A number times itself is a square number.

© Pearson Education, Inc. 3

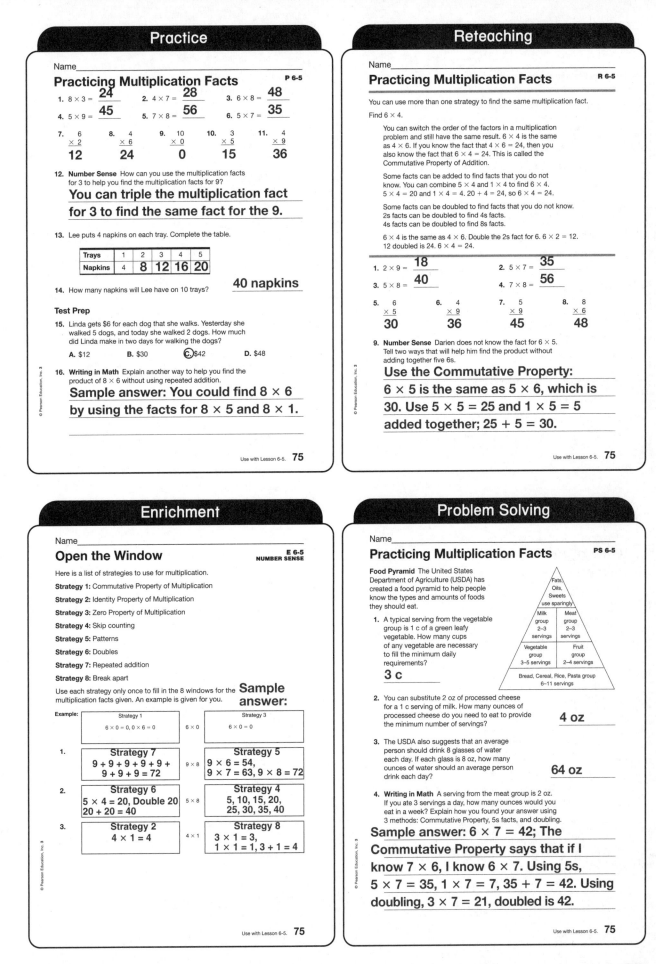

Name_____

Practicing Multiplication Facts

P 6-5

1. $8 \times 3 =$ __24__   2. $4 \times 7 =$ __28__   3. $6 \times 8 =$ __48__

4. $5 \times 9 =$ __45__   5. $7 \times 8 =$ __56__   6. $5 \times 7 =$ __35__

7. 6   8. 4   9. 10   10. 3   11. 4
  $\times 2$ $\times 6$ $\times 0$ $\times 5$ $\times 9$
  __12__   __24__   __0__   __15__   __36__

12. **Number Sense** How can you use the multiplication facts for 3 to help you find the multiplication facts for 9?

You can triple the multiplication fact for 3 to find the same fact for the 9.

13. Lee puts 4 napkins on each tray. Complete the table.

Trays	1	2	3	4	5
Napkins	4	8	12	16	20

14. How many napkins will Lee have on 10 trays?

40 napkins

Test Prep

15. Linda gets $6 for each dog that she walks. Yesterday she walked 5 dogs, and today she walked 2 dogs. How much did Linda make in two days for walking the dogs?
  A. $12   B. $30   C. $42   D. $48

16. **Writing in Math** Explain another way to help you find the product of 8×6 without using repeated addition.

Sample answer: You could find 8×6 by using the facts for 8×5 and 8×1.

Use with Lesson 6-5. **75**

Name_____

Practicing Multiplication Facts

R 6-5

You can use more than one strategy to find the same multiplication fact.

Find 6×4.

You can switch the order of the factors in a multiplication problem and still have the same result. 6×4 is the same as 4×6. If you know the fact that $4 \times 6 = 24$, then you also know the fact that $6 \times 4 = 24$. This is called the Commutative Property of Addition.

Some facts can be added to find facts that you do not know. You can combine 5×4 and 1×4 to find 6×4. $5 \times 4 = 20$ and $1 \times 4 = 4$. $20 + 4 = 24$, so $6 \times 4 = 24$.

Some facts can be doubled to find facts that you do not know. 2s facts can be doubled to find 4s facts. 4s facts can be doubled to find 8s facts.

6×4 is the same as 4×6. Double the 2s fact for 6. $6 \times 2 = 12$. 12 doubled is 24. $6 \times 4 = 24$.

1. $2 \times 9 =$ __18__   2. $5 \times 7 =$ __35__
3. $5 \times 8 =$ __40__   4. $7 \times 8 =$ __56__

5. 6   6. 4   7. 5   8. 8
  $\times 5$ $\times 9$ $\times 9$ $\times 6$
  __30__   __36__   __45__   __48__

9. **Number Sense** Darien does not know the fact for 6×5. Tell two ways that will help him find the product without adding together five 6s.

Use the Commutative Property: 6×5 is the same as 5×6, which is 30. Use $5 \times 5 = 25$ and $1 \times 5 = 5$ added together; $25 + 5 = 30$.

Use with Lesson 6-5. **75**

Name_____

Open the Window

E 6-5
NUMBER SENSE

Here is a list of strategies to use for multiplication.

Strategy 1: Commutative Property of Multiplication

Strategy 2: Identity Property of Multiplication

Strategy 3: Zero Property of Multiplication

Strategy 4: Skip counting

Strategy 5: Patterns

Strategy 6: Doubles

Strategy 7: Repeated addition

Strategy 8: Break apart

Use each strategy only once to fill in the 8 windows for the multiplication facts given. An example is given for you. **Sample answer:**

Example:	Strategy 1		Strategy 3
	$6 \times 0 = 0, 0 \times 6 = 0$	6×0	$6 \times 0 = 0$

1.	Strategy 7		Strategy 5
	$9 + 9 + 9 + 9 + 9 + 9 + 9 = 72$	9×8	$9 \times 6 = 54$, $9 \times 7 = 63$, $9 \times 8 = 72$

2.	Strategy 6		Strategy 4
	$5 \times 4 = 20$, Double 20 $20 + 20 = 40$	5×8	5, 10, 15, 20, 25, 30, 35, 40

3.	Strategy 2		Strategy 8
	$4 \times 1 = 4$	4×1	$3 \times 1 = 3$, $1 \times 1 = 1$, $3 + 1 = 4$

Use with Lesson 6-5. **75**

Name_____

Practicing Multiplication Facts

PS 6-5

Food Pyramid The United States Department of Agriculture (USDA) has created a food pyramid to help people know the types and amounts of foods they should eat.

Fats, Oils, Sweets use sparingly

Milk group 2–3 servings

Meat group 2–3 servings

Vegetable group 3–5 servings

Fruit group 2–4 servings

Bread, Cereal, Rice, Pasta group 6–11 servings

1. A typical serving from the vegetable group is 1 c of a green leafy vegetable. How many cups of any vegetable are necessary to fill the minimum daily requirements?

3 c

2. You can substitute 2 oz of processed cheese for a 1 c serving of milk. How many ounces of processed cheese do you need to eat to provide the minimum number of servings?

4 oz

3. The USDA also suggests that an average person should drink 8 glasses of water each day. If each glass is 8 oz, how many ounces of water should an average person drink each day?

64 oz

4. **Writing in Math** A serving from the meat group is 2 oz. If you ate 3 servings a day, how many ounces would you eat in a week? Explain how you found your answer using 3 methods: Commutative Property, 5s facts, and doubling.

Sample answer: $6 \times 7 = 42$; The Commutative Property says that if I know 7×6, I know 6×7. Using 5s, $5 \times 7 = 35$, $1 \times 7 = 7$, $35 + 7 = 42$. Using doubling, $3 \times 7 = 21$, doubled is 42.

Use with Lesson 6-5. **75**

© Pearson Education, Inc. 3

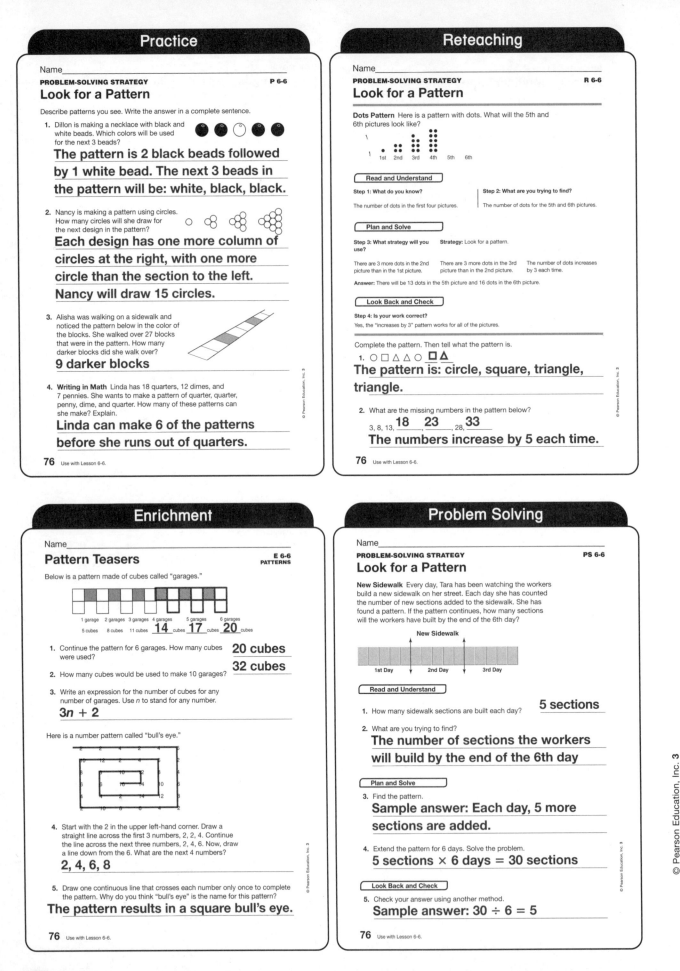

Practice

PROBLEM-SOLVING STRATEGY   P 6-6

Look for a Pattern

Describe patterns you see. Write the answer in a complete sentence.

1. Dillon is making a necklace with black and white beads. Which colors will be used for the next 3 beads?

The pattern is 2 black beads followed by 1 white bead. The next 3 beads in the pattern will be: white, black, black.

2. Nancy is making a pattern using circles. How many circles will she draw for the next design in the pattern?

Each design has one more column of circles at the right, with one more circle than the section to the left. Nancy will draw 15 circles.

3. Alisha was walking on a sidewalk and noticed the pattern below in the color of the blocks. She walked over 27 blocks that were in the pattern. How many darker blocks did she walk over?

9 darker blocks

4. **Writing in Math** Linda has 18 quarters, 12 dimes, and 7 pennies. She wants to make a pattern of quarter, quarter, penny, dime, and quarter. How many of these patterns can she make? Explain.

Linda can make 6 of the patterns before she runs out of quarters.

Reteaching

PROBLEM-SOLVING STRATEGY   R 6-6

Look for a Pattern

Dots Pattern Here is a pattern with dots. What will the 5th and 6th pictures look like?

1st 2nd 3rd 4th 5th 6th

Read and Understand

Step 1: What do you know?

The number of dots in the first four pictures.

Step 2: What are you trying to find?

The number of dots for the 5th and 6th pictures.

Plan and Solve

Step 3: What strategy will you use?

Strategy: Look for a pattern.

| There are 3 more dots in the 2nd picture than in the 1st picture. | There are 3 more dots in the 3rd picture than in the 2nd picture. | The number of dots increases by 3 each time. |

Answer: There will be 13 dots in the 5th picture and 16 dots in the 6th picture.

Look Back and Check

Step 4: Is your work correct?

Yes, the "increases by 3" pattern works for all of the pictures.

Complete the pattern. Then tell what the pattern is.

1. ○ □ △ △ ○ **□ △**

The pattern is: circle, square, triangle, triangle.

2. What are the missing numbers in the pattern below?

3, 8, 13, **18   23** , 28, **33**

The numbers increase by 5 each time.

Enrichment

Pattern Teasers

E 6-6
PATTERNS

Below is a pattern made of cubes called "garages."

1 garage   2 garages   3 garages   4 garages   5 garages   6 garages
5 cubes   8 cubes   11 cubes   **14** cubes **17** cubes **20** cubes

1. Continue the pattern for 6 garages. How many cubes were used?   **20 cubes**

2. How many cubes would be used to make 10 garages?   **32 cubes**

3. Write an expression for the number of cubes for any number of garages. Use *n* to stand for any number.

3n + 2

Here is a number pattern called "bull's eye."

4. Start with the 2 in the upper left-hand corner. Draw a straight line across the first 3 numbers, 2, 2, 4. Continue the line across the next three numbers, 2, 4, 6. Now, draw a line down from the 6. What are the next 4 numbers?

2, 4, 6, 8

5. Draw one continuous line that crosses each number only once to complete the pattern. Why do you think "bull's eye" is the name for this pattern?

The pattern results in a square bull's eye.

Problem Solving

PROBLEM-SOLVING STRATEGY   PS 6-6

Look for a Pattern

New Sidewalk Every day, Tara has been watching the workers build a new sidewalk on her street. Each day she has counted the number of new sections added to the sidewalk. She has found a pattern. If the pattern continues, how many sections will the workers have built by the end of the 6th day?

New Sidewalk

1st Day   2nd Day   3rd Day

Read and Understand

1. How many sidewalk sections are built each day?   **5 sections**

2. What are you trying to find?

The number of sections the workers will build by the end of the 6th day

Plan and Solve

3. Find the pattern.

Sample answer: Each day, 5 more sections are added.

4. Extend the pattern for 6 days. Solve the problem.

5 sections × 6 days = 30 sections

Look Back and Check

5. Check your answer using another method.

Sample answer: 30 ÷ 6 = 5

Name_____

Using Multiplication to Compare
P 6-7

1. Jim has lost 3 times as many teeth as his brother Justin. Justin has lost 3 teeth. How many teeth has Jim lost?

| Teeth Justin Lost | 3 |
| Teeth Jim Lost | **9** |

9 teeth

2. Sarah has 6 seashells. She has 7 times as many pieces of beach glass as she does seashells. How many pieces of beach glass does she have?

42 pieces of beach glass

3. The hardware store stocks 3 times as many gallons of white paint as they do gallons of gray paint. How many gallons of white paint are kept in stock at the hardware store?

18 gal of white paint

Painting Supplies

Item	Number
Large paintbrush	12
Small paintbrush	18
Black paint	3
Gray paint	6
Green paint	4
Red paint	6
White paint	**18**

4. **Number Sense** Tom has $8. Becky has 4 times as many dollars as Tom. How much money do they have altogether?

$40

Test Prep

5. Gina's house has 9 windows. Jonathan's house has twice as many windows as Gina's. How many windows are in Jonathan's house?

A. 9 windows B. 18 windows C. 21 windows D. 27 windows

6. **Writing in Math** Katie picked 7 times as many strawberries as Garrett. Garrett picked 6 quarts of strawberries. How many quarts did Katie pick? Which two multiplication facts can you use to help find the solution?

42 qt; Sample answer: 5 × 6 = 30 and 2 × 6 = 12, so 7 × 6 = 42.

© Pearson Education, Inc. 3

Name_____

Using Multiplication to Compare
R 6-7

The word *times* in a word problem means multiplication. If you have 3 times as many pencils as Joe does, it means that however many pencils Joe has, you have his pencils multiplied by 3.

| Pencil | Pencil | | | → Number of pencils |
| Pencil | Pencil | Pencil | Pencil | Pencil | Pencil → 3 times as many pencils |

The words *twice as many* or *2 times as many* mean to multiply by 2.

There are twice as many squares as there are circles.

1. Sara has twice as many ribbons as Harriet. Harriet has 6 ribbons. How many ribbons does Sarah have?

| 6 | → Harriet's ribbons |
| 6 | 6 | → Sara's ribbons |

12 ribbons

2. Luke is 6 years old. Danny is 3 times his age. How old is Danny?

18 years old

3. Paula has 3 rings. Kenya has 4 times as many rings. How many rings does Kenya have?

12 rings

4. **Number Sense** If Leroy has 9 sports cards, and Steve has 3 times as many, how many sports cards does Steve have?

27 sports cards

5. Jill invited 6 friends to her party. Mara invited twice as many to her sleepover. How many friends were invited to Mara's sleepover?

12 friends

© Pearson Education, Inc. 3

Name_____

At the Bakery
E 6-7
DATA

Julia, Pedro, and Michelle went to a local bakery to buy cookies for a class party. The owner of the bakery gave Julia, Pedro, and Michelle one free peanut butter cookie.

Cookies That Were Bought

	Oatmeal Cookies	Peanut Butter Cookies	Chocolate Chip Cookies
Julia	0	2	4
Pedro	24	8	8
Michelle	0	40	8

1. Fill in the chart with the correct number of cookies they each bought.
   - Julia bought 2 times as many chocolate chip cookies as peanut butter cookies.
   - Julia purchased 2 peanut butter cookies.
   - Julia did not buy any oatmeal cookies.

2. Write a number sentence for Julia's chocolate chip cookies.

   2 × 2 = 4 chocolate chip cookies

   - Pedro bought 1 times as many chocolate chip cookies as Michelle.
   - Pedro bought 4 times as many peanut butter cookies as Julia.
   - Pedro bought 3 times as many oatmeal cookies as peanut butter.

3. Write a number sentence for Pedro's oatmeal cookies.

   3 × 8 = 24 oatmeal cookies

   - Michelle bought 2 times as many chocolate chip cookies as Julia.
   - Michelle also purchased 5 times as many peanut butter cookies as Pedro.
   - Michelle bought 5 times as many oatmeal cookies as Pedro.

4. Write a number sentence for Michelle's peanut butter cookies.

   5 × 8 = 40 peanut butter cookies

© Pearson Education, Inc. 3

Name_____

Using Multiplication to Compare
PS 6-7

Buying in Bulk Jordan's mother likes to buy certain items in bulk. When she compares the number of items in a bulk package to those in a regular package, she always finds that she can save money by buying in bulk.

1. A regular-sized package of paper towels has 2 rolls of paper towels. The bulk package contains 6 times that many. How many rolls of paper towels are in the bulk package?

12 rolls

2. Health food bars are normally sold in a package of 4 bars. The bulk package has 8 times that amount. How many health food bars are in the bulk pack?

32 bars

3. A regular-sized package of boxes of facial tissue contains 3 boxes. The bulk size has 2 times as many. How many tissue boxes are in the bulk package?

6 boxes

Crayons Ben needs to buy crayons for the new school year. He can buy an 8-color package for $1.00, or a package with 3 times as many crayons for $1.99.

4. How many crayons are in the larger package?

24 crayons

5. How much would it cost to buy 3 of the crayon packages that contain 8 colors?

$3.00

6. **Writing in Math** Margaret has 8 red beads. Draw a picture to show she has 3 times as many white beads as red beads. Explain how the picture helps you use multiplication to compare.

| 8 | → Red Beads |
| 8 | 8 | 8 | → White Beads |

The picture makes it clear that 3 times as many is the same as 8 × 3 = 24.

© Pearson Education, Inc. 3

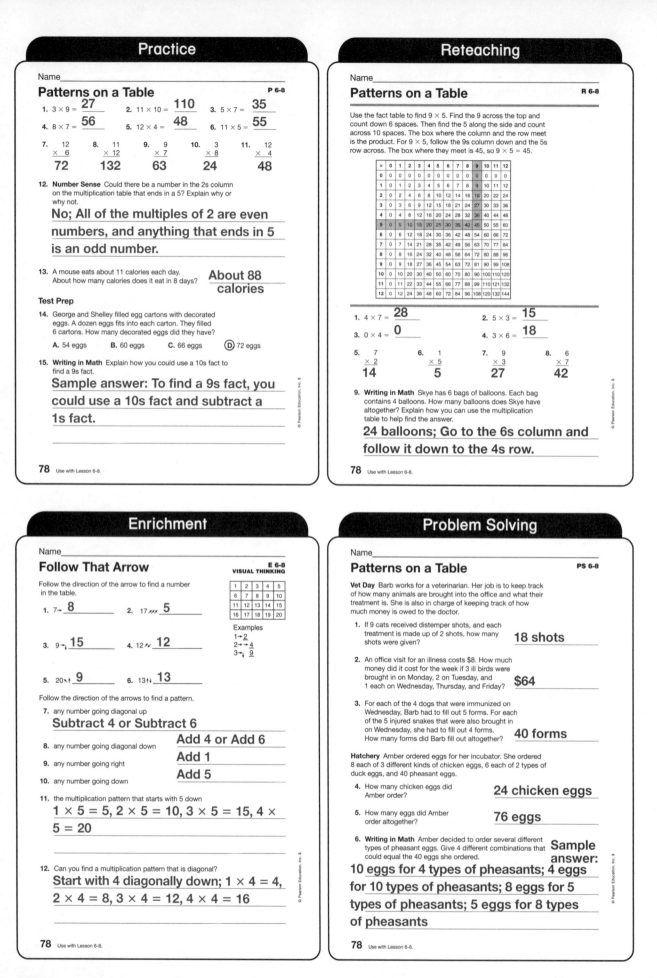

Practice

Name_____

Patterns on a Table
P 6-8

1. $3 \times 9 =$ __27__
2. $11 \times 10 =$ __110__
3. $5 \times 7 =$ __35__
4. $8 \times 7 =$ __56__
5. $12 \times 4 =$ __48__
6. $11 \times 5 =$ __55__

7. $\begin{array}{r} 12 \\ \times\ 6 \\ \hline 72 \end{array}$
8. $\begin{array}{r} 11 \\ \times\ 12 \\ \hline 132 \end{array}$
9. $\begin{array}{r} 9 \\ \times\ 7 \\ \hline 63 \end{array}$
10. $\begin{array}{r} 3 \\ \times\ 8 \\ \hline 24 \end{array}$
11. $\begin{array}{r} 12 \\ \times\ 4 \\ \hline 48 \end{array}$

12. **Number Sense** Could there be a number in the 2s column on the multiplication table that ends in a 5? Explain why or why not.

No; All of the multiples of 2 are even numbers, and anything that ends in 5 is an odd number.

13. A mouse eats about 11 calories each day. About how many calories does it eat in 8 days?   **About 88 calories**

Test Prep

14. George and Shelley filled egg cartons with decorated eggs. A dozen eggs fits into each carton. They filled 6 cartons. How many decorated eggs did they have?

   A. 54 eggs   **B.** 60 eggs   **C.** 66 eggs   **D** 72 eggs

15. **Writing in Math** Explain how you could use a 10s fact to find a 9s fact.

   Sample answer: To find a 9s fact, you could use a 10s fact and subtract a 1s fact.

Reteaching

Name_____

Patterns on a Table
R 6-8

Use the fact table to find 9×5. Find the 9 across the top and count down 6 spaces. Then find the 5 along the side and count across 10 spaces. The box where the column and the row meet is the product. For 9×5, follow the 9s column down and the 5s row across. The box where they meet is 45, so $9 \times 5 = 45$.

×	0	1	2	3	4	5	6	7	8	9	10	11	12
0	0	0	0	0	0	0	0	0	0	0	0	0	0
1	0	1	2	3	4	5	6	7	8	9	10	11	12
2	0	2	4	6	8	10	12	14	16	18	20	22	24
3	0	3	6	9	12	15	18	21	24	27	30	33	36
4	0	4	8	12	16	20	24	28	32	36	40	44	48
5	0	5	10	15	20	25	30	35	40	45	50	55	60
6	0	6	12	18	24	30	36	42	48	54	60	66	72
7	0	7	14	21	28	35	42	49	56	63	70	77	84
8	0	8	16	24	32	40	48	56	64	72	80	88	96
9	0	9	18	27	36	45	54	63	72	81	90	99	108
10	0	10	20	30	40	50	60	70	80	90	100	110	120
11	0	11	22	33	44	55	66	77	88	99	110	121	132
12	0	12	24	36	48	60	72	84	96	108	120	132	144

1. $4 \times 7 =$ __28__
2. $5 \times 3 =$ __15__
3. $0 \times 4 =$ __0__
4. $3 \times 6 =$ __18__

5. $\begin{array}{r} 7 \\ \times\ 2 \\ \hline 14 \end{array}$
6. $\begin{array}{r} 1 \\ \times\ 5 \\ \hline 5 \end{array}$
7. $\begin{array}{r} 9 \\ \times\ 3 \\ \hline 27 \end{array}$
8. $\begin{array}{r} 6 \\ \times\ 7 \\ \hline 42 \end{array}$

9. **Writing in Math** Skye has 6 bags of balloons. Each bag contains 4 balloons. How many balloons does Skye have altogether? Explain how you can use the multiplication table to help find the answer.

   24 balloons; Go to the 6s column and follow it down to the 4s row.

Enrichment

Name_____

Follow That Arrow
E 6-8
VISUAL THINKING

Follow the direction of the arrow to find a number in the table.

1	2	3	4	5
6	7	8	9	10
11	12	13	14	15
16	17	18	19	20

1. $7 \rightarrow$ __8__
2. $17 \nearrow$ __5__

Examples
$1 \rightarrow \underline{2}$
$2 \rightarrow \underline{4}$
$3 \rightarrow \underline{9}$

3. $9 \nwarrow$ __15__
4. $12 \nearrow$ __12__

5. $20 \nwarrow$ __9__
6. $13 \downarrow$ __13__

Follow the direction of the arrows to find a pattern.

7. any number going diagonal up
   Subtract 4 or Subtract 6

8. any number going diagonal down
   Add 4 or Add 6

9. any number going right
   Add 1

10. any number going down
    Add 5

11. the multiplication pattern that starts with 5 down
    $1 \times 5 = 5, 2 \times 5 = 10, 3 \times 5 = 15, 4 \times 5 = 20$

12. Can you find a multiplication pattern that is diagonal?
    Start with 4 diagonally down; $1 \times 4 = 4$, $2 \times 4 = 8$, $3 \times 4 = 12$, $4 \times 4 = 16$

Problem Solving

Name_____

Patterns on a Table
PS 6-8

Vet Day Barb works for a veterinarian. Her job is to keep track of how many animals are brought into the office and what their treatment is. She is also in charge of keeping track of how much money is owed to the doctor.

1. If 9 cats received distemper shots, and each treatment is made up of 2 shots, how many shots were given?   **18 shots**

2. An office visit for an illness costs $8. How much money did it cost for the week if 3 ill birds were brought in on Monday, 2 on Tuesday, and 1 each on Wednesday, Thursday, and Friday?   **$64**

3. For each of the 4 dogs that were immunized on Wednesday, Barb had to fill out 5 forms. For each of the 5 injured snakes that were also brought in on Wednesday, she had to fill out 4 forms. How many forms did Barb fill out altogether?   **40 forms**

Hatchery Amber ordered eggs for her incubator. She ordered 8 each of 3 different kinds of chicken eggs, 6 each of 2 types of duck eggs, and 40 pheasant eggs.

4. How many chicken eggs did Amber order?   **24 chicken eggs**

5. How many eggs did Amber order altogether?   **76 eggs**

6. **Writing in Math** Amber decided to order several different types of pheasant eggs. Give 4 different combinations that could equal the 40 eggs she ordered.   **Sample answer: 10 eggs for 4 types of pheasants; 4 eggs for 10 types of pheasants; 8 eggs for 5 types of pheasants; 5 eggs for 8 types of pheasants**

Name_____

Multiplying with Three Factors

P 6-9

1. $1 \times 2 \times 3 =$ **6**   2. $2 \times 2 \times 4 =$ **16**   3. $8 \times 2 \times 2 =$ **32**

4. $6 \times 2 \times 1 =$ **12**   5. $5 \times 5 \times 2 =$ **50**   6. $3 \times 3 \times 3 =$ **27**

7. $1 \times 7 \times 8 =$ **56**   8. $0 \times 9 \times 8 =$ **0**   9. $6 \times 2 \times 5 =$ **60**

10. **Number Sense** Harvey says $9 \times 8 \times$ (any other number) will always be greater than the product of $2 \times 9 \times 4$. Do you agree? Explain.

No; $2 \times 9 \times 4 = 72$ and $8 \times 9 = 72$. If the third number is a 0 or a 1, the product will not be greater. $8 \times 9 \times 0 = 0$; $8 \times 9 \times 1 = 72$

11. Write three ways to find $3 \times 2 \times 4$.

6×4; 3×8; 12×2

12. Sarah and Amanda each have 2 bags with 4 marbles in each. How many marbles do they have altogether?

16 marbles

13. Jesse bought 2 sheets of stamps. On each sheet there are 5 rows of stamps with 6 stamps in each row. How many stamps did Jesse buy?

60 stamps

Test Prep

14. Which is the product of $2 \times 3 \times 2$?

A. 6   B. 7   C. 10   (D.) 12

15. **Writing in Math** A classroom has 6 tables. The teacher puts 2 pencils, 1 eraser, and 1 sheet of stickers into each bag, and puts 4 bags on each table. How many pencils did the teacher put in the bags altogether? Write a multiplication sentence and solve the problem.

48 pencils; $6 \times 2 \times 4 = 48$

© Pearson Education, Inc. 3

Name_____

Multiplying with Three Factors

R 6-9

When more than two factors are being multiplied, you can multiply them in any order and the product will be the same. This is called the Associative (grouping) Property of Multiplication.

Here are three different ways to multiply $6 \times 5 \times 4$.

Multiply the 6 and 5 first.	Multiply the 5 and 4 first.	Multiply the 6 and 4 first.
$(6 \times 5) \times 4$	$6 \times (5 \times 4)$	$(6 \times 4) \times 5$
$30 \times 4 = 120$	$6 \times 20 = 120$	$24 \times 5 = 120$

In each example, the product is the same. This means that you can find the easiest way to multiply more than two numbers.

1. $3 \times 2 \times 1 =$ **6**   2. $2 \times 3 \times 5 =$ **30**

3. $3 \times 3 \times 2 =$ **18**   4. $7 \times 2 \times 1 =$ **14**

5. $4 \times 7 \times 2 =$ **56**   6. $5 \times 1 \times 2 =$ **10**

7. $5 \times 2 \times 4 =$ **40**   8. $4 \times 0 \times 3 =$ **0**

9. $1 \times 0 \times 4 =$ **0**   10. $3 \times 4 \times 5 =$ **60**

11. $1 \times 4 \times 6 =$ **24**   12. $2 \times 2 \times 6 =$ **24**

13. $4 \times 1 \times 7 =$ **28**   14. $8 \times 2 \times 1 =$ **16**

15. **Number Sense** How do you know that $4 \times 2 \times 2$ is the same as 4×4? Explain.

$4 \times 2 \times 2$ is the same as 4×4 because $2 \times 2 = 4$.

© Pearson Education, Inc. 3

Name_____

Welcome to Camp

E 6-9
DECISION MAKING

You are going camping for 3 days. Here is a list of what you packed.

1 leaky tent	Eating utensils & dishes
1 sleeping bag	Toothpaste
Soap	Clothing & swimwear

Weather Forecast

Thunderstorms—Friday A.M. through P.M.

Hot and buggy—Saturday

Cool front—Saturday evening

Sunny—Sunday

- You plan to arrive at the campsite on Friday morning and leave Sunday afternoon. The weather report has been posted.
- You have $90.00 to spend on food and supplies.
- A food bag has 1 meal. You must buy a drink for each food bag that you buy.
- You must have at least $5.00 left to buy a bus pass for the 6 hr ride home.

1. The General Store sells everything you might need. Write the number of each item you would buy on the list.

2. How much did you spend altogether?

$74.70

3. How much do you have left?

$15.30

Sample answer:

General Store	
$2.95 Mosquito spray	**1**
$5.00 Rainproof poncho	**1**
$3.00 Firewood—1 night	**1**
$5.00 Food bag	**9**
$0.75 Bottled water	**9**
$1.25 Toothbrush	**1**
$6.95 Waterproofing for tent	**1**
$1.45 Box of matches	**1**
$1.50 Flashlight with batteries	**1**
$0.85 Shampoo	**1**

© Pearson Education, Inc. 3

Name_____

Multiplying with Three Factors

PS 6-9

1. If a bookseller in Chicago wraps every 2 books together in bubble wrap, then packages them into small boxes that contain 2 bubble-wrap packs each, and then into cartons that will hold 6 small boxes, how many books will the bookseller send out in each carton?

24 books

2. A parking lot is arranged in rows with 2 cars back to back and 5 cars across. If there are 4 rows, how many cars can park in the lot?

40 cars

3. There are 2 c in a pint, 2 pt in a quart, and 4 qt in a gallon. How many cups are there in a gallon?

16 c

4. Kathy multiplied $3 \times 4 \times 5$ this way. Using the Associative Property of Multiplication, show another way Kathy could have multiplied $3 \times 4 \times 5$.

$3 \times 5 = 15$, $15 \times 4 = 60$

Kathy's Solution

$3 \times 4 \times 5 =$
$12 \times 5 =$
60

Sample answer:

5. **Writing in Math** An orange grower packages his premium oranges in crates of 3 layers. Each layer is 3 oranges wide and 2 oranges long. How many oranges are sent out in a crate? Draw a picture that represents a crate and write a multiplication sentence that answers the question.

Layer 1

Layer 2 $2 \times 3 \times 3 = 18$

Layer 3

2 oranges $\times$ 3 oranges $\times$ 3 layers = 18 oranges

© Pearson Education, Inc. 3

Name_____

Find a Rule

P 6-10

Write a rule for each table. Complete the table.

1.

Number of boxes	1	2	3	4	5
Number of grapefruits	4	8	12	16	20

Multiply by 4.

2.

Number of people	1	2	3	4	5
Number of fingers	10	20	30	40	50

Multiply by 10.

3.

In	6	2	7	1	4
Out	18	6	21	3	12

Multiply by 3.

4. Number Sense Caleb filled baskets with flowers. He filled 5 baskets with the same number of roses in each basket. He used 35 roses. How many roses went into each basket?

7 roses

Test Prep

5. The rule for a table is *Multiply by 5*. If a 3 is the **In** number, what is the **Out** number?

(A) 15   **B.** 10   **C.** 5   **D.** 3

6. Writing in Math What is the multiplication rule for this table? Why doesn't the rule *Add 6* work? Complete the table.

In	6	7	8	9	10
Out	12	14	16	18	20

Multiply by 2; Sample answer: When the In value is 10, the Out value is 20, and 10 + 6 = 16, not 20.

© Pearson Education, Inc. 3

Name_____

Find a Rule

R 6-10

David is cooking pancakes. He makes 3 pancakes for each person in his family. Today he needs to make pancakes for 9 people. He isn't sure how many he needs to make. If David used a table, he would see a rule for a pattern between the number of pancakes and the number of people eating those pancakes.

Number of people	1	2	3
Number of pancakes	3	6	

The rule for the pattern is multiply by 3. To make pancakes for 9 people, he takes the number of people, 9, and follows the rule, multiply by 3, to find that he needs to make 27 pancakes.

Write a rule for each table. Complete the table.

1.

Number of tents	1	2	3	4	5
Number of hikers	4	8	12	16	20

Multiply by 4

2.

In	3	4	1	2	7
Out	15	20	5	10	35

Multiply by 5

3.

In	2	4	6	8	10
Out	14	28	42	56	70

Multiply by 7

4. Number Sense Chris can sand 7 planks in 1 hour. How many planks can he sand in 3 hours?

21 planks

© Pearson Education, Inc. 3

Name_____

Right Answer, Write Rule

E 6-10
ALGEBRA

1. Ashley has a recipe that calls for 5 tbsp of olive oil. She only has a teaspoon. If 1 tbsp is equal to 3 tsp, how many teaspoons does she need?

15 tsp

Complete the table.

Number of Tablespoons	1	2	3	4	5
Number of Teaspoons	3	6	9	12	15

Write the rule.

Sample answer: For every tablespoon, multiply by 3 to find the teaspoons.

2. What number comes next?

2, 3, 6, 7, 14, **15**

Write the rule.

Sample answer: Add 1 and then multiply that number by 2.

3. José and his dad went to an aquarium and saw a tank with 5 octopi. José counted 8 tentacles on 1 octopus. Tentacles are like long arms. How many tentacles do 5 octopi have? Write the rule.

40 tentacles

Sample answer: Multiply the number of octopi by 8 to find the number of tentacles.

© Pearson Education, Inc. 3

Name_____

Find a Rule

PS 6-10

Speed Different types of helicopters fly at different speeds. A traffic helicopter might stay in one place for long periods of time, while a transport helicopter will move quickly. The average speed of a helicopter is shown in the table.

Minutes	1	2	3	4	5
Distance in Miles	2	4	6		

1. How many miles will a helicopter travel in 1 min? In 2 min?

2 mi; 4 mi

2. Write a multiplication rule that will work for the helicopter-speed table.

Multiply by 2

3. How many miles will the helicopter travel in 5 min?

10 mi

4. How many miles will it travel in 9 min?

18 mi

5. Every week Dion spends $3 on dog treats for his collie, Mambo. By the 4th week he has spent $12 on Mambo's treats. In what week will he have spent $21 total?

7th week

6. Writing in Math Explain a different pattern for Mambo's treats where Dion spends $21.

Sample answer: Dion could have spent $7 a week. In the 3rd week he would have spent $21.

© Pearson Education, Inc. 3

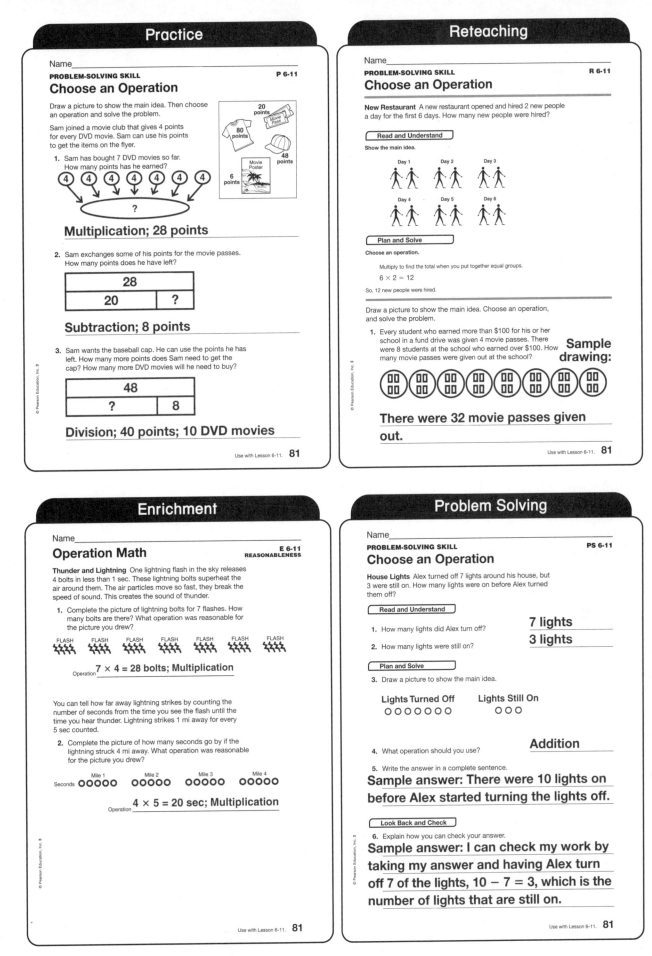

Practice

PROBLEM-SOLVING SKILL   P 6-11

Choose an Operation

Draw a picture to show the main idea. Then choose an operation and solve the problem.

Sam joined a movie club that gives 4 points for every DVD movie. Sam can use his points to get the items on the flyer.

1. Sam has bought 7 DVD movies so far. How many points has he earned?

Multiplication; 28 points

2. Sam exchanges some of his points for the movie passes. How many points does he have left?

28	
20	?

Subtraction; 8 points

3. Sam wants the baseball cap. He can use the points he has left. How many more points does Sam need to get the cap? How many more DVD movies will he need to buy?

48	
?	8

Division; 40 points; 10 DVD movies

Use with Lesson 6-11. **81**

Reteaching

PROBLEM-SOLVING SKILL   R 6-11

Choose an Operation

New Restaurant A new restaurant opened and hired 2 new people a day for the first 6 days. How many new people were hired?

Read and Understand

Show the main idea.

Day 1   Day 2   Day 3

Day 4   Day 5   Day 6

Plan and Solve

Choose an operation.

Multiply to find the total when you put together equal groups.

$6 \times 2 = 12$

So, 12 new people were hired.

Draw a picture to show the main idea. Choose an operation, and solve the problem.

1. Every student who earned more than $100 for his or her school in a fund drive was given 4 movie passes. There were 8 students at the school who earned over $100. How many movie passes were given out at the school?

Sample drawing:

There were 32 movie passes given out.

Use with Lesson 6-11. **81**

Enrichment

Operation Math

E 6-11
REASONABLENESS

Thunder and Lightning One lightning flash in the sky releases 4 bolts in less than 1 sec. These lightning bolts superheat the air around them. The air particles move so fast, they break the speed of sound. This creates the sound of thunder.

1. Complete the picture of lightning bolts for 7 flashes. How many bolts are there? What operation was reasonable for the picture you drew?

FLASH   FLASH   FLASH   FLASH   FLASH   FLASH   FLASH

Operation **$7 \times 4 = 28$ bolts; Multiplication**

You can tell how far away lightning strikes by counting the number of seconds from the time you see the flash until the time you hear thunder. Lightning strikes 1 mi away for every 5 sec counted.

2. Complete the picture of how many seconds go by if the lightning struck 4 mi away. What operation was reasonable for the picture you drew?

Mile 1   Mile 2   Mile 3   Mile 4

Seconds ooooo   ooooo   ooooo   ooooo

Operation **$4 \times 5 = 20$ sec; Multiplication**

Use with Lesson 6-11. **81**

Problem Solving

PROBLEM-SOLVING SKILL   PS 6-11

Choose an Operation

House Lights Alex turned off 7 lights around his house, but 3 were still on. How many lights were on before Alex turned them off?

Read and Understand

1. How many lights did Alex turn off?   **7 lights**

2. How many lights were still on?   **3 lights**

Plan and Solve

3. Draw a picture to show the main idea.

Lights Turned Off   Lights Still On

o o o o o o o   o o o

4. What operation should you use?   **Addition**

5. Write the answer in a complete sentence.

Sample answer: There were 10 lights on before Alex started turning the lights off.

Look Back and Check

6. Explain how you can check your answer.

Sample answer: I can check my work by taking my answer and having Alex turn off 7 of the lights, $10 - 7 = 3$, which is the number of lights that are still on.

Use with Lesson 6-11. **81**

© Pearson Education, Inc. 3

Name_____

PROBLEM-SOLVING APPLICATIONS   P 6-12

Television

In 2002, there were 10 national and international stations. There were also 56 national cable-program channels. A newspaper lists the TV-programming schedule each day for evening viewing from 8:00 P.M. until 12:30 A.M.

1. During that time period, 8 cable stations will show 2 movies each. How many movies will be shown then?

16 movies

2. During that same period, 6 other cable stations will show 3 movies each. How many movies will be shown by those 6 cable stations?

18 movies

3. From 8:00 P.M. to 12:30 A.M., 6 of the network channels will each have a total of 5 programs. How many programs will be shown by those channels?

30 programs

4. There are 4 cable channels that will show nine 30-minute programs during this period. How many programs will be shown by those 4 cable channels?

36 programs

5. Between 8:00 P.M. and 12:30 A.M., Network A shows 7 programs, Network B shows 6 programs, Network C shows 5 programs, and Network D shows 9 programs. Which networks show more programs altogether, Networks A and B, or Networks C and D? Explain.

Networks C and D; 7 + 6 = 13 and 5 + 9 = 14; 14 > 13

A newspaper costs $0.50 an issue. Suppose you bought the newspaper using only one type of coin, either dimes, nickels, or pennies.

6. How many dimes would you need to buy a newspaper?

5 dimes

7. How many nickels would you need?

10 nickels

8. How many pennies would you need?

50 pennies

© Pearson Education, Inc. 3

Name_____

PROBLEM-SOLVING APPLICATIONS   R 6-12

Terms

The word *term* means how long a person will perform an elected duty. The chart below shows how long a term is for the president, senators, and representatives of the United States government.

Elected Position	Term
President	4 years
Senator	6 years
U.S. representative	2 years

A president can only serve 2 terms. How many years is that?

You would use multiplication to solve this problem. If 1 term equals 4 years, then 2 terms equal 8 years.

4 years		⟶ 1 term
4 years	4 years	⟶ 2 × 4 = 8 years

1. For how many years would a representative serve if he or she served 3 terms?

6 years

2. If a representative served 5 terms, how many years would it be?

10 years

3. In 1991, the state of Colorado passed a law stating that a U.S. representative from that state could serve a maximum of 6 terms. How many years equal 6 terms?

12 years

4. If a senator serves 7 terms, how many years would it be?

42 years

5. **Number Sense** Which is longer, 2 terms as senator or 7 terms as a representative? How do you know?

7 terms as a representative, because it equals 14 years. 2 terms as a senator only equals 12 years.

© Pearson Education, Inc. 3

Name_____

Pizza by the Numbers

E 6-12
NUMBER SENSE

Each man, woman, and child in the United States eats about 46 slices of pizza a year. That adds up to 23 lb of pizza a year, because 2 slices of pizza equal about 1 lb of pizza.

1. If 4 friends each ate 2 lb of pizza, how many slices of pizza did they eat?

16 slices; 4 people × 2 × 2 slices (which equals 1 lb) = 16 slices

In Italy in 1830, the first pizzeria in the world was opened. Modern pizza was born in 1889 when Don Raffaele Esposito prepared a special dish in honor of the Italian queen's visit. In 1905, Gennaro Lombardi opened the first licensed American pizzeria.

2. How many years after the first pizzeria in the world was opened was the modern pizza created?

59 years

3. How many years after the first pizzeria was opened in Italy was a pizzeria opened in America?

75 years

When you cut a pizza down the middle, or in half, you get 2 big slices. If you cut the pizza in half again, you get 4 slices.

4. How many slices of pizza will you get if you cut the pizza a third time?

6 slices

5. Draw a picture of how many slices of pizza you will get if you cut it a fourth time. How many slices will you get?

8 slices

8 slices

© Pearson Education, Inc. 3

Name_____

PROBLEM-SOLVING APPLICATIONS   PS 6-12

Paper Weights

Tomas purchases computer paper in boxes that contain 2,500 sheets of paper. Each box weighs 20 lb. The cart Tomas uses says, "Do not load this cart with more than 100 lb." How many boxes of paper can Tomas put on his cart?

Read and Understand

1. What extra information is given?

There are 2,500 sheets of paper in a box.

2. How much does each box of paper weigh?

20 lb

3. What are you trying to find?

The number of boxes Tomas can put on the cart without going over 100 lb

Plan and Solve

4. Complete the table.

Number of Boxes	1	2	3	4	5
Weight in Pounds	20	40	60	80	100

5. Write the answer in a complete sentence.

Tomas can put 5 boxes of paper on his cart.

Look Back and Check

6. Explain how you can check your answer. **Sample answer: I could subtract 20 lb from 100 until I reached 0. The number of times I subtracted 20 would be the number of boxes, 5.**

© Pearson Education, Inc. 3

Name_____

Division as Sharing

P 7-1

Use counters or draw a picture to solve.

1. 3 bicycles   6 wheels

   How many wheels are on each bicycle?

   2 wheels

2. 12 tennis balls   4 canisters

   How many tennis balls are in each canister?

   3 tennis balls

3. 16 bananas   4 bunches

   How many bananas are in each bunch?

   4 bananas

4. **Number Sense** One box contains 12 granola bars. Two bars are in each package. How many packages are in each box of granola bars?

   6 packages

5. Isabella and her 5 friends went to a concert at the school. They spent a total of $42 for the tickets. Each ticket was the same price. How much was each ticket?

   $7

6. In a yearbook club, a teacher gave out 3 new folders to each student. The teacher gave out 27 folders in all. How many students are in the yearbook club?

   9 students

Test Prep

7. Which is the quotient of $20 \div 5$?

   A. 2   B. 3   C. 4   D. 5

8. **Writing in Math** Tanya and her family went out for frozen yogurt. They ordered 10 scoops of frozen yogurt. Every person received 2 scoops. Explain how to find the number of people in Tanya's family. Then write the answer.

Sample answer: $10 \div 2 = 5$. There are 5 people in Tanya's family.

© Pearson Education, Inc. 3

Use with Lesson 7-1. **83**

Name_____

Division as Sharing

R 7-1

You can use counters to show division problems:

There are 6 shirts and 3 boxes. How many shirts fit in each box?

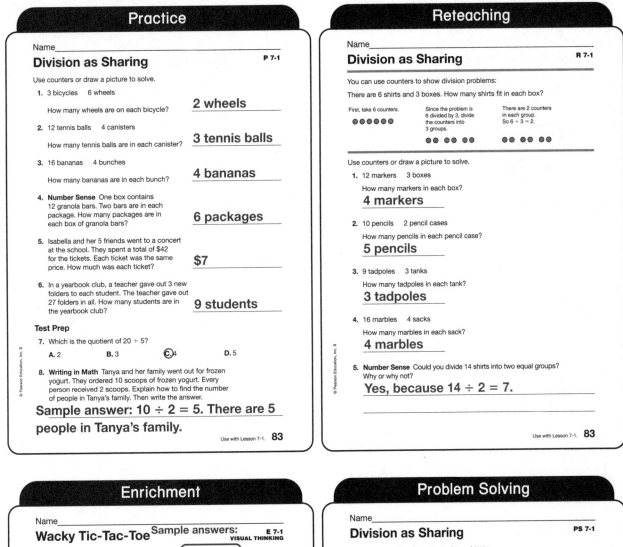

First, take 6 counters.

Since the problem is 6 divided by 3, divide the counters into 3 groups.

There are 2 counters in each group. So $6 \div 3 = 2$.

Use counters or draw a picture to solve.

1. 12 markers   3 boxes

   How many markers in each box?

   4 markers

2. 10 pencils   2 pencil cases

   How many pencils in each pencil case?

   5 pencils

3. 9 tadpoles   3 tanks

   How many tadpoles in each tank?

   3 tadpoles

4. 16 marbles   4 sacks

   How many marbles in each sack?

   4 marbles

5. **Number Sense** Could you divide 14 shirts into two equal groups? Why or why not?

   Yes, because $14 \div 2 = 7$.

© Pearson Education, Inc. 3

Use with Lesson 7-1. **83**

Name_____

Wacky Tic-Tac-Toe

Sample answers:

E 7-1
VISUAL THINKING

1. Circle to show 3 Xs in 3 equal groups. Then complete the division sentence.

   $\underline{9} \div 3 = 3$

2. Circle to show 4 Os in 4 equal groups. Then write a division sentence.

   $\underline{16} \div \underline{4} = \underline{4}$

3. Circle to show 2 Xs in 6 equal groups. Then write a division sentence.

   $\underline{12} \div \underline{6} = \underline{2}$

4. Circle to show 5 Os in 3 equal groups. Then write a division sentence.

   $\underline{15} \div \underline{3} = \underline{5}$

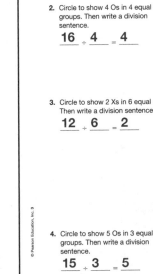

© Pearson Education, Inc. 3

Use with Lesson 7-1. **83**

Name_____

Division as Sharing

PS 7-1

1. Suppose a female cat had a litter of 6 kittens. The owners wanted 2 of their friends to share the kittens equally. How many kittens did each friend receive?

   3 kittens

2. The Johnson's family cat had a litter of 8 kittens. They kept 2 kittens and gave the others equally to 3 different people. How many kittens did each of the 3 people receive?

   2 kittens

3. Susan raises 3 different types of cats: tabbies, angoras, and calicos. Currently she has 9 cats. There are equal numbers of each type. How many of each type does she have? Draw a picture that shows how you solved the problem.

   Tabbies   Angoras   Calicos

   3 of each type

4. Dr. Raymond treats cats in her 3 veterinary clinics. She has 24 cats in the clinics. If there are an equal number of cats in each clinic, how many cats are in each one?

   8 cats

5. **Writing in Math** If Dr. Raymond opens a 4th clinic and brings an equal number of cats to each one, how many cats will there be in each clinic now? Explain your answer.

   6 cats; Sample answer: The number of cats is still 24, but there are now 4 clinics. So, $24 \div 4 = 6$.

© Pearson Education, Inc. 3

Use with Lesson 7-1. **83**

Use with Chapter 7, Lesson 1   **83**

Name_____

Division as Repeated Subtraction

P 7-2

Use counters or draw a picture to solve.

1. 35 stickers

   5 stickers on each sheet

   How many sheets?
   7 sheets

2. 40 leaves

   4 leaves painted on each vase

   How many vases?
   10 vases

On Mackinac Island in Michigan, people rent bicycles because no cars are allowed on the island. The table shows the number of people who rode tandem bicycles each month. Two people ride on each tandem bicycle. How many bicycles were rented each month?

People Renting Tandem Bicycles	
Month	People
May	8
June	24
July	16
August	22
September	14

3. May   **4 bicycles**

4. June   **12 bicycles**

5. July   **8 bicycles**

6. August   **11 bicycles**

7. How many bicycles were rented in all?   **42 bicycles**

Test Prep

8. Keisha has to carry 24 boxes to her room. She can carry 3 boxes on each trip. How many trips will she take?

   A. 7 trips   (B) 8 trips   C. 9 trips   D. 10 trips

9. **Writing in Math** Tamara says that $15 \div 3 = 5$. Is she correct? Explain how you know.

   Yes; Sample answer: You can subtract 3 from 15 five times. So, $15 \div 3 = 5$.

© Pearson Education, Inc. 3

Name_____

Division as Repeated Subtraction

R 7-2

You can also think of division as repeated subtraction. Here is an example:

Joe has 15 sweaters. He is packing them into boxes. Each box holds 3 sweaters. How many boxes does Joe need?

Start with 15 sweaters. Subtract 3 at a time until there are no sweaters left. Then count the subtractions.

$15 - 3 = 12$
$12 - 3 = 9$
$9 - 3 = 6$
$6 - 3 = 3$
$3 - 3 = 0$

I can subtract three 5 times. Then there are zero sweaters left over.

You can also use division.
$15 \div 3 = 5$
Fifteen divided by 3 equals 5.
Joe needs 5 boxes.

Use counters or draw a picture to solve.

1. 10 markers   5 markers in each box

   How many boxes? **2 boxes**

2. 20 books   5 books on each shelf

   How many shelves? **4 shelves**

3. 8 hamsters   2 hamsters in each cage

   How many cages? **4 cages**

4. **Writing in Math** Show how you can use repeated subtraction to find how many groups of 3 are in 18. Then write the division sentence for the problem.

   Sample answer: $18 - 3 = 15$; $15 - 3 = 12$; $12 - 3 = 9$; $9 - 3 = 6$; $6 - 3 = 3$; $3 - 3 = 0$. $18 \div 3 = 6$

© Pearson Education, Inc. 3

Name_____

Number Riddle

E 7-2
REASONING

Start with the number 24 for each. Write the answer. Then write the letter for the number in the blank below to solve the riddle.

1. Subtract 12. Subtract 12.   **0** E

2. Divide by 2.   **12** U

3. Subtract 8.   **16** T

4. Divide by 3.   **8** C

5. Subtract 6. Subtract 6. Subtract 6.   **6** A

6. Subtract 4.   **20** R

7. Subtract 2. Subtract 2. Subtract 2.   **18** D

8. Divide by 8.   **3** B

9. Divide by 6.   **4** N

10. Divide by 12.   **2** O

A division sentence and a subtraction sentence were in a race. The division sentence was called the winner. What was the subtraction sentence called?

D E F E A T E D
18 0 0 6 16 0 18

S U B T R A C T I O N
12 3 16 20 6 8 16 2 4

© Pearson Education, Inc. 3

Name_____

Division as Repeated Subtraction

PS 7-2

1. Bobby has a box of 24 crayons. He wants to share his crayons equally among as many of his classmates as possible. He decides he will give out 4 crayons to each classmate. Using repeated subtraction, find out how many classmates will each receive 4 crayons.

   $24 - 4 = 20$, $20 - 4 = 16$, $16 - 4 = 12$, $12 - 4 = 8$, $8 - 4 = 4$, $4 - 4 = 0$; 6 classmates

2. If Bobby decided to give 3 crayons to each classmate, how many students would receive crayons?

   8 classmates, $24 \div 3 = 8$

3. If Bobby's art class had 12 students, could each student receive crayons from the box of 24? How many would each student receive?

   Yes; 2 crayons each

4. Four students want to share a total of 16 crayons. They decide to subtract 2 crayons each time to see how many groups of 2 they will make. How many groups of 2 will they make?

   8 groups of 2

5. How many crayons will each of the 4 students get?

   4 crayons

6. **Writing in Math** Brenda and Linda have 12 crayons to share equally. To find out how many crayons each person should get, Brenda decided to make as many groups of 7 crayons as she can. Will Brenda's method work? Explain.

   Sample answer: No, Brenda will get 1 group of 7 and 1 group of 5. She should start with a smaller number, or count out one for each until they are all gone. Each should get 6 crayons.

© Pearson Education, Inc. 3

Name_____

Writing Division Stories

P 7-3

Write a division story for each number sentence.
Then use counters or draw a picture to solve.

Check students' stories for 1 and 2.

1. $54 \div 6 = \square$

2. $36 \div 9 = x$

_____

_____

_____

_____

In Colonial times, people held quilting bees. During a quilting bee, people would get together and work to make quilts. Suppose each person brought the same number of pieces of cloth to make the quilt.

	Size of Quilt		
	Twin	Full	Queen
Pieces of Cloth	50	77	108

3. If 10 people come to the quilting bee, how many pieces would each person need to bring to make a twin-size quilt?

5 pieces

4. What size quilt can the people make if 9 people each bring 12 pieces of cloth?

Queen size

Test Prep

5. If you have 21 ice cubes, and 7 ice cubes are in each cup of juice, how many cups do you need?

A. 2 cups   B. 3 cups   C. 4 cups   D. 5 cups

6. **Writing in Math** Copy and finish the story shown for $22 \div 2$. Use counters or draw a picture to find the answer. Then write your own division story for $22 \div 2$.

> Justin has 22 ▓. He wants to put 2 ▓ in each group. How many groups will there be?

Sample answer: Justin has 22 balloons. He puts 2 balloons in each group. There will be 11 groups.

Name_____

Writing Division Stories

R 7-3

How to write a division story:

First, look at the number sentence given. Think of a situation in which the larger number is divided by the smaller number. For example, with the number sentence $20 \div 2 = n$, you might think of 20 dollars divided between 2 friends. Here is a division story for $20 \div 2 = n$:

Sample answers for 1–3.

> Dan's father gave him $20 for cutting the grass and doing other chores around the house. Since Dan's friend Steve helped him, Dan decided to divide the money by 2. How much did each boy receive?

Write a division story for each. Then use counters or draw a picture to solve.

1. $15 \div 3 = n$

Fred has 15 fish. If he places 3 fish in each bowl, how many bowls will he need? 5

2. $12 \div 2 = n$

There are 12 cats. The cats are placed in 2 separate rooms. How many cats are in each room? 6

3. **Number Sense** Sheila wrote a story problem. In her story, she asked how many equal groups 16 flowers could be put in. What does she need to tell about the groups?

Sheila needs to tell the number of groups, or the size of the groups.

Name_____

Find the Pairs

E 7-3 REASONING

The number box contains 15 pairs of numbers. Match each pair to the correct description below.

Number Box				
7, 1	5, 5	10, 3	2, 1	9, 3
16, 4	8, 4	3, 3	12, 2	1, 8
11, 2	12, 6	15, 5	3, 4	18, 9

1. Difference is 6, quotient is 2 — **12, 6**

2. Sum is 6, product is 9 — **3, 3**

3. Difference is 7, product is 30 — **10, 3**

4. Sum is 9, product is 8 — **1, 8**

5. Difference is 6, quotient is 3 — **9, 3**

6. Sum is 3, product is 2 — **2, 1**

7. Difference is 0, product is 25 — **5, 5**

8. Difference is 4, quotient is 2 — **8, 4**

9. Sum is 20, quotient is 4 — **16, 4**

10. Difference is 9, product is 22 — **11, 2**

11. Sum is 7, product is 12 — **3, 4**

12. Sum is 14, quotient is 6 — **12, 2**

13. Sum is 20, quotient is 3 — **15, 5**

14. Difference is 9, quotient is 2 — **18, 9**

15. Sum is 8, product is 7 — **7, 1**

Name_____

Writing Division Stories

PS 7-3

1. Henry has 20 apples and wants to put the same number of apples in each of 5 baskets. Draw a picture of his story and write the division sentence. How many apples will he put in each basket?

$20 \div 5 = 4$

Henry's Apples

$20 \div 5 = 4$ apples

2. Bananas are sold 6 to a bunch for small ones and 3 to a bunch for large ones. Robin is buying bananas for her class picnic. There are 24 students in Robin's class. How many bunches of large bananas would she need? How many bunches of small bananas would she need? Write a division sentence for each problem.

$24 \div 3 = 8$ bunches of large bananas, $24 \div 6 = 4$ bunches of small bananas

3. Darlene and Frank find that a carton of oranges is on sale. Each layer of the carton has 6 oranges and there are 3 layers. If they divided the oranges equally among their 2 brothers and 2 sisters, how many oranges would each receive? Would there be any left over for Darlene and Frank?

4 oranges; yes, one for each of them

4. **Writing in Math** Write your own division story about the number sentence $20 \div 2 = \blacksquare$.

Check students' stories.

Practice

Name_____

PROBLEM-SOLVING STRATEGY   P 7-4

Try, Check, and Revise

Solve. Write each answer in a sentence.

1. Olivia has 16 slices of bread and 2 rolls. How many
   sandwiches can she make?

Olivia can make 10 sandwiches.

2. Benjamin has 18 video games and 4 board games. He
   buys two new video games. How many games does he
   have in all?

Benjamin has 24 games.

3. Savannah is making a flower arrangement. She can choose
   12 roses. She can choose equal amounts of 4 different
   colors. How many of each color can she choose?

Savannah can choose 3 roses of each color.

4. Christian went fishing today for 2 hr. He caught 3 fish in the
   first hour he was fishing. He caught the same number of
   fish the second hour. He caught 2 more fish yesterday than
   he caught today. How many fish did he catch yesterday?

Christian caught 8 fish yesterday.

5. Four lines are drawn on a piece of paper. The third line is
   blue. The line above the blue line is red. The fourth line is
   orange. The first line is yellow. What color is the second line?

The second line is red.

6. **Writing in Math** Ms. Ricardo has 21 students in her class.
   She has 5 tables in the classroom. If all of the students sit
   at the tables, will there be an equal number of students at
   each table? Explain.

No; Sample answer: 21 does not divide
equally by 5.

86   Use with Lesson 7-4.

© Pearson Education, Inc. 3

Reteaching

Name_____

PROBLEM-SOLVING STRATEGY   R 7-4

Try, Check, and Revise

New Pencils Stephanie needs 15 pencils for school. Pencils
come in packs of 4, 5, or 6. If she wants to buy 3 equal-sized
packs of pencils, what size pack of pencils should she buy?

> **Read and Understand**

Step 1: What do you know? She needs 15 pencils. Pencils come in packs of 4, 5, or 6.

Step 2: What are you trying to find? Find what size pack she needs to buy to have 3 equal-sized
packs.

> **Plan and Solve**

Step 3: What strategy will you use? Try, check, and revise

Try: packs of 4

Check: $4 + 4 + 4 = 12$ Too low

Revise: packs of 5

Check: $5 + 5 + 5 = 15$ That's it!

> **Look Back and Check**

Step 4: Is your answer reasonable? Yes, 3 packs of 5 pencils equal 15 pencils.

Solve. Write each answer in a sentence.

1. There are 12 fish in Zack's aquarium. He has 2 kinds of
   fish: guppies and tetras. He has 4 more guppies than
   tetras. How many of each kind of fish does he have?

He has 8 guppies and 4 tetras.

2. The sum of two numbers is 33. Both numbers are less than
   20. The numbers are 3 apart. What are the numbers?

The numbers are 15 and 18.

86   Use with Lesson 7-4.

© Pearson Education, Inc. 3

Enrichment

Name_____

Crossing Town   E 7-4
                                         MENTAL MATH

Complete the route to each friend's house by writing the correct
number on each block. Then use the completed route map to
answer the questions below.

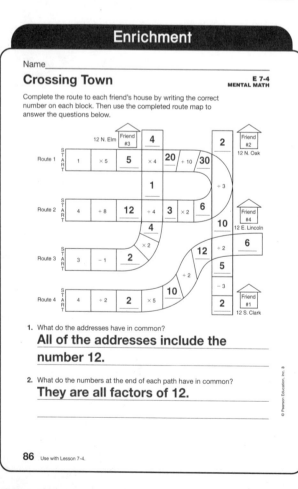

1. What do the addresses have in common?

All of the addresses include the
number 12.

2. What do the numbers at the end of each path have in common?

They are all factors of 12.

86   Use with Lesson 7-4.

© Pearson Education, Inc. 3

Problem Solving

Name_____

PROBLEM-SOLVING STRATEGY   PS 7-4

Try, Check, and Revise

In basketball, it is possible to score 1, 2, or 3 points with 1 shot.
A regular basket is worth 2 points. A free throw is worth 1 point.
A basket from behind the 3-point line is worth 3 points. Hillary
scored a total of 10 points in a game. What are two different
possibilities for Hillary's scoring if she scored at least two kinds
of baskets?

> **Read and Understand**

1. What are the three possible score choices?

1: free throw, 2: basket, 3: basket

2. What are you trying to find?

Two different ways Hillary could score 10 points

> **Plan and Solve**

3. Choose one score to try. Divide Hillary's total points by that score.

Sample answer: 3, $10 ÷ 3 = 3$, 3-point shots

4. Add another score type, if needed.

Add 1 free throw, three 3-point shots = 10 points

5. Solve the problem in a different way.

$10 ÷ 2 = (4 × 2) + 1 + 1$, 4 regular
baskets and 2 free throws

> **Look Back and Check**

6. Check that both answers equal the same number of points.

$9 + 1 = 10$ and $8 + 2 = 10$

86   Use with Lesson 7-4.

© Pearson Education, Inc. 3

86   Use with Chapter 7, Lesson 4

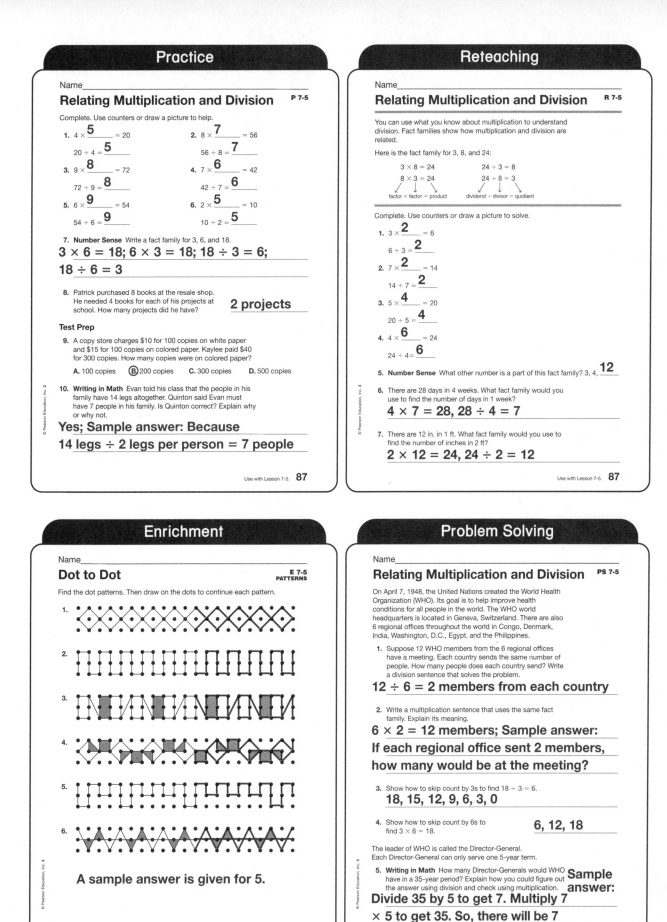

Practice

Name_____

Relating Multiplication and Division   P 7-5

Complete. Use counters or draw a picture to help.

1. $4 \times \underline{5} = 20$
   $20 \div 4 = \underline{5}$

2. $8 \times \underline{7} = 56$
   $56 \div 8 = \underline{7}$

3. $9 \times \underline{8} = 72$
   $72 \div 9 = \underline{8}$

4. $7 \times \underline{6} = 42$
   $42 \div 7 = \underline{6}$

5. $6 \times \underline{9} = 54$
   $54 \div 6 = \underline{9}$

6. $2 \times \underline{5} = 10$
   $10 \div 2 = \underline{5}$

7. **Number Sense** Write a fact family for 3, 6, and 18.

$3 \times 6 = 18; 6 \times 3 = 18; 18 \div 3 = 6;$
$18 \div 6 = 3$

8. Patrick purchased 8 books at the resale shop. He needed 4 books for each of his projects at school. How many projects did he have?

2 projects

Test Prep

9. A copy store charges $10 for 100 copies on white paper and $15 for 100 copies on colored paper. Kaylee paid $40 for 300 copies. How many copies were on colored paper?

   A. 100 copies   (B) 200 copies   C. 300 copies   D. 500 copies

10. **Writing in Math** Evan told his class that the people in his family have 14 legs altogether. Quinton said Evan must have 7 people in his family. Is Quinton correct? Explain why or why not.

Yes; Sample answer: Because
14 legs ÷ 2 legs per person = 7 people

Use with Lesson 7-5. **87**

Reteaching

Name_____

Relating Multiplication and Division   R 7-5

You can use what you know about multiplication to understand division. Fact families show how multiplication and division are related.

Here is the fact family for 3, 8, and 24:

$3 \times 8 = 24$ $24 \div 3 = 8$
$8 \times 3 = 24$ $24 \div 8 = 3$

factor × factor = product   dividend ÷ divisor = quotient

Complete. Use counters or draw a picture to solve.

1. $3 \times \underline{2} = 6$
   $6 \div 3 = \underline{2}$

2. $7 \times \underline{2} = 14$
   $14 \div 7 = \underline{2}$

3. $5 \times \underline{4} = 20$
   $20 \div 5 = \underline{4}$

4. $4 \times \underline{6} = 24$
   $24 \div 4 = \underline{6}$

5. **Number Sense** What other number is a part of this fact family? 3, 4, **12**

6. There are 28 days in 4 weeks. What fact family would you use to find the number of days in 1 week?

$4 \times 7 = 28, 28 \div 4 = 7$

7. There are 12 in. in 1 ft. What fact family would you use to find the number of inches in 2 ft?

$2 \times 12 = 24, 24 \div 2 = 12$

Use with Lesson 7-5. **87**

Enrichment

Name_____

Dot to Dot   E 7-5 PATTERNS

Find the dot patterns. Then draw on the dots to continue each pattern.

1.
2.
3.
4.
5.
6.

A sample answer is given for 5.

Use with Lesson 7-5. **87**

Problem Solving

Name_____

Relating Multiplication and Division   PS 7-5

On April 7, 1948, the United Nations created the World Health Organization (WHO). Its goal is to help improve health conditions for all people in the world. The WHO world headquarters is located in Geneva, Switzerland. There are also 6 regional offices throughout the world in Congo, Denmark, India, Washington, D.C., Egypt, and the Philippines.

1. Suppose 12 WHO members from the 6 regional offices have a meeting. Each country sends the same number of people. How many people does each country send? Write a division sentence that solves the problem.

$12 \div 6 = 2$ **members from each country**

2. Write a multiplication sentence that uses the same fact family. Explain its meaning.

$6 \times 2 = 12$ **members; Sample answer:**
If each regional office sent 2 members,
how many would be at the meeting?

3. Show how to skip count by 3s to find $18 \div 3 = 6$.

18, 15, 12, 9, 6, 3, 0

4. Show how to skip count by 6s to find $3 \times 6 = 18$.

6, 12, 18

The leader of WHO is called the Director-General. Each Director-General can only serve one 5-year term.

5. **Writing in Math** How many Director-Generals would WHO have in a 35-year period? Explain how you could figure out the answer using division and check using multiplication. **Sample answer:**
Divide 35 by 5 to get 7. Multiply 7
× 5 to get 35. So, there will be 7
Director-Generals in 35 years.

Use with Lesson 7-5. **87**

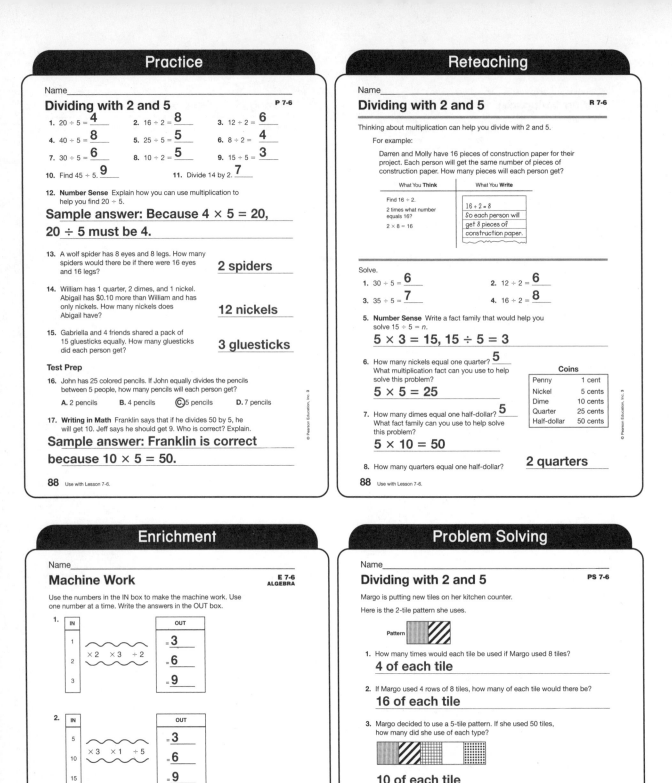

Name_____

Dividing with 2 and 5
P 7-6

1. $20 \div 5 = $ __4__
2. $16 \div 2 = $ __8__
3. $12 \div 2 = $ __6__
4. $40 \div 5 = $ __8__
5. $25 \div 5 = $ __5__
6. $8 \div 2 = $ __4__
7. $30 \div 5 = $ __6__
8. $10 \div 2 = $ __5__
9. $15 \div 5 = $ __3__
10. Find $45 \div 5$. __9__
11. Divide 14 by 2. __7__

12. **Number Sense** Explain how you can use multiplication to help you find $20 \div 5$.

Sample answer: Because 4 × 5 = 20, 20 ÷ 5 must be 4.

13. A wolf spider has 8 eyes and 8 legs. How many spiders would there be if there were 16 eyes and 16 legs?

2 spiders

14. William has 1 quarter, 2 dimes, and 1 nickel. Abigail has $0.10 more than William and has only nickels. How many nickels does Abigail have?

12 nickels

15. Gabriella and 4 friends shared a pack of 15 gluesticks equally. How many gluesticks did each person get?

3 gluesticks

Test Prep

16. John has 25 colored pencils. If John equally divides the pencils between 5 people, how many pencils will each person get?

A. 2 pencils   B. 4 pencils   C. 5 pencils   D. 7 pencils

17. **Writing in Math** Franklin says that if he divides 50 by 5, he will get 10. Jeff says he should get 9. Who is correct? Explain.

Sample answer: Franklin is correct because 10 × 5 = 50.

Name_____

Dividing with 2 and 5
R 7-6

Thinking about multiplication can help you divide with 2 and 5.

For example:

Darren and Molly have 16 pieces of construction paper for their project. Each person will get the same number of pieces of construction paper. How many pieces will each person get?

What You Think	What You Write
Find $16 \div 2$. 2 times what number equals 16? $2 \times 8 = 16$	$16 \div 2 = 8$ So each person will get 8 pieces of construction paper.

Solve.

1. $30 \div 5 = $ __6__
2. $12 \div 2 = $ __6__
3. $35 \div 5 = $ __7__
4. $16 \div 2 = $ __8__

5. **Number Sense** Write a fact family that would help you solve $15 \div 5 = n$.

5 × 3 = 15, 15 ÷ 5 = 3

6. How many nickels equal one quarter? __5__ What multiplication fact can you use to help solve this problem?

5 × 5 = 25

7. How many dimes equal one half-dollar? __5__ What fact family can you use to help solve this problem?

5 × 10 = 50

Coins	
Penny	1 cent
Nickel	5 cents
Dime	10 cents
Quarter	25 cents
Half-dollar	50 cents

8. How many quarters equal one half-dollar?

2 quarters

Name_____

Machine Work
E 7-6
ALGEBRA

Use the numbers in the IN box to make the machine work. Use one number at a time. Write the answers in the OUT box.

1.

IN		OUT
1	$\times 2 \quad \times 3 \quad \div 2$	= __3__
2		= __6__
3		= __9__

2.

IN		OUT
5	$\times 3 \quad \times 1 \quad \div 5$	= __3__
10		= __6__
15		= __9__

3.

IN		OUT
2	$\times 10 \quad \div 2 \quad \div 5$	= __2__
3		= __3__
4		= __4__

Name_____

Dividing with 2 and 5
PS 7-6

Margo is putting new tiles on her kitchen counter.

Here is the 2-tile pattern she uses.

Pattern

1. How many times would each tile be used if Margo used 8 tiles?

4 of each tile

2. If Margo used 4 rows of 8 tiles, how many of each tile would there be?

16 of each tile

3. Margo decided to use a 5-tile pattern. If she used 50 tiles, how many did she use of each type?

10 of each tile

4. Write the division sentence you used for Exercise 3.

50 ÷ 5 = 10

5. **Writing in Math** During 10 months, a writer wrote 5 children's books. If each book took the same amount of time to write, how long did the writer take to write each book? Explain.

2 months; Sample answer: 10 months ÷ 5 books = 2 months per book

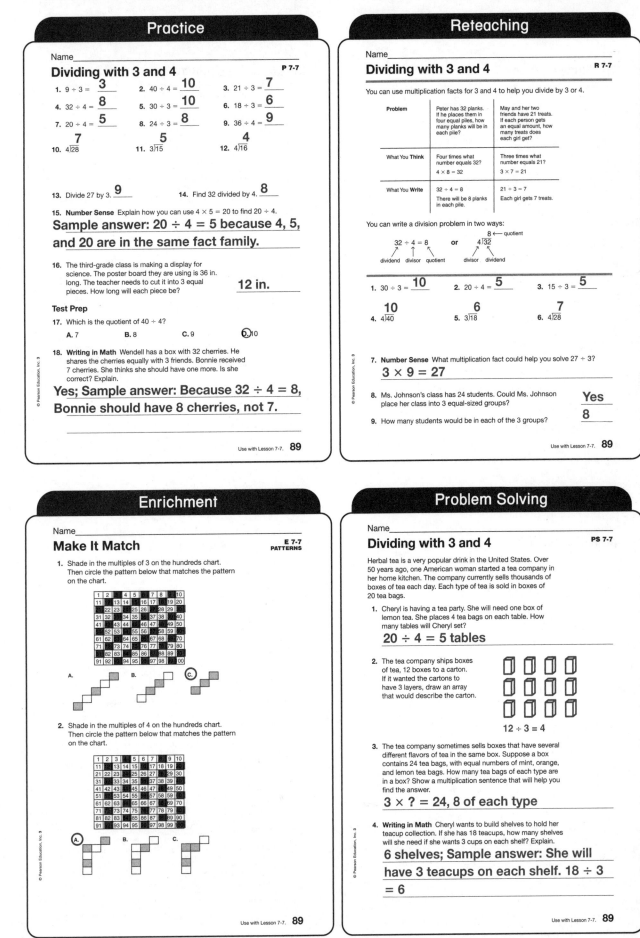

Practice

Name_____

Dividing with 3 and 4 — P 7-7

1. $9 \div 3 = $ **3**   2. $40 \div 4 = $ **10**   3. $21 \div 3 = $ **7**

4. $32 \div 4 = $ **8**   5. $30 \div 3 = $ **10**   6. $18 \div 3 = $ **6**

7. $20 \div 4 = $ **5**   8. $24 \div 3 = $ **8**   9. $36 \div 4 = $ **9**

10. **7** $4\overline{)28}$ 11. **5** $3\overline{)15}$ 12. **4** $4\overline{)16}$

13. Divide 27 by 3. **9**   14. Find 32 divided by 4. **8**

15. **Number Sense** Explain how you can use $4 \times 5 = 20$ to find $20 \div 4$.

Sample answer: $20 \div 4 = 5$ because 4, 5, and 20 are in the same fact family.

16. The third-grade class is making a display for science. The poster board they are using is 36 in. long. The teacher needs to cut it into 3 equal pieces. How long will each piece be?

12 in.

Test Prep

17. Which is the quotient of $40 \div 4$?

A. 7   B. 8   C. 9   D. 10

18. **Writing in Math** Wendell has a box with 32 cherries. He shares the cherries equally with 3 friends. Bonnie received 7 cherries. She thinks she should have one more. Is she correct? Explain.

Yes; Sample answer: Because $32 \div 4 = 8$, Bonnie should have 8 cherries, not 7.

© Pearson Education, Inc. 3

Use with Lesson 7-7. **89**

Reteaching

Name_____

Dividing with 3 and 4 — R 7-7

You can use multiplication facts for 3 and 4 to help you divide by 3 or 4.

Problem	Peter has 32 planks. If he places them in four equal piles, how many planks will be in each pile?	May and her two friends have 21 treats. If each person gets an equal amount, how many treats does each girl get?
What You **Think**	Four times what number equals 32? $4 \times 8 = 32$	Three times what number equals 21? $3 \times 7 = 21$
What You **Write**	$32 \div 4 = 8$ There will be 8 planks in each pile.	$21 \div 3 = 7$ Each girl gets 7 treats.

You can write a division problem in two ways:

$32 \div 4 = 8$ or $4\overline{)32}$ ← quotient

dividend divisor quotient   divisor dividend

1. $30 \div 3 = $ **10**   2. $20 \div 4 = $ **5**   3. $15 \div 3 = $ **5**

4. **10** $4\overline{)40}$ 5. **6** $3\overline{)18}$ 6. **7** $4\overline{)28}$

7. **Number Sense** What multiplication fact could help you solve $27 \div 3$?

$3 \times 9 = 27$

8. Ms. Johnson's class has 24 students. Could Ms. Johnson place her class into 3 equal-sized groups?

Yes

9. How many students would be in each of the 3 groups?

8

© Pearson Education, Inc. 3

Use with Lesson 7-7. **89**

Enrichment

Name_____

Make It Match — E 7-7 PATTERNS

1. Shade in the multiples of 3 on the hundreds chart. Then circle the pattern below that matches the pattern on the chart.

A.   B.   **C.**

2. Shade in the multiples of 4 on the hundreds chart. Then circle the pattern below that matches the pattern on the chart.

A.   B.   C.

© Pearson Education, Inc. 3

Use with Lesson 7-7. **89**

Problem Solving

Name_____

Dividing with 3 and 4 — PS 7-7

Herbal tea is a very popular drink in the United States. Over 50 years ago, one American woman started a tea company in her home kitchen. The company currently sells thousands of boxes of tea each day. Each type of tea is sold in boxes of 20 tea bags.

1. Cheryl is having a tea party. She will need one box of lemon tea. She places 4 tea bags on each table. How many tables will Cheryl set?

$20 \div 4 = 5$ tables

2. The tea company ships boxes of tea, 12 boxes to a carton. If it wanted the cartons to have 3 layers, draw an array that would describe the carton.

$12 \div 3 = 4$

3. The tea company sometimes sells boxes that have several different flavors of tea in the same box. Suppose a box contains 24 tea bags, with equal numbers of mint, orange, and lemon tea bags. How many tea bags of each type are in a box? Show a multiplication sentence that will help you find the answer.

$3 \times ? = 24$, 8 of each type

4. **Writing in Math** Cheryl wants to build shelves to hold her teacup collection. If she has 18 teacups, how many shelves will she need if she wants 3 cups on each shelf? Explain.

6 shelves; Sample answer: She will have 3 teacups on each shelf. $18 \div 3 = 6$

© Pearson Education, Inc. 3

Use with Lesson 7-7. **89**

© Pearson Education, Inc. 3

Name_____

Dividing with 6 and 7

P 7-8

1. $36 \div 6 =$ __6__   2. $42 \div 6 =$ __7__   3. $70 \div 7 =$ __10__

4. $60 \div 6 =$ __10__   5. $56 \div 7 =$ __8__   6. $49 \div 7 =$ __7__

7. $6 \div 6 =$ __1__   8. $28 \div 7 =$ __4__   9. $18 \div 6 =$ __3__

10. $6\overline{)24}$ __4__   11. $7\overline{)35}$ __5__   12. $6\overline{)30}$ __5__

13. Divide 12 by 6. __2__   14. Find 42 divided by 7. __6__

15. **Number Sense** How many groups of 6 are there in 36? Explain how you know.

__6; Sample answer: I can multiply to check:__
__$6 \times 6 = 36$.__

16. Connor has 48 apples. He separated the apples equally into 6 crates. How many apples are there in each crate?   __8 apples__

17. Sierra's karate class lasts 56 days. How many weeks does the class last?   __8 weeks__

Test Prep

18. Jada's third-grade class is leaving on a field trip. There are 32 people going on the field trip. The group will ride in vans that each hold 8 people. How many vans will the class need?

Ⓐ 4 vans   **B.** 5 vans   **C.** 6 vans   **D.** 7 vans

19. **Writing in Math** Kyle says there are exactly 4 weeks in February. Is he right? Explain.

__Yes; Sample answer: There are 28 days__
__in February, so $28 \div 7 = 4$ weeks.__

90 Use with Lesson 7-8.

Name_____

Dividing with 6 and 7

R 7-8

When you divide, you separate things into equal groups.

For example:

Find $35 \div 7$.

| There are 35 circles. | Divide them into 7 equal groups. | There are 5 circles in each group. So $35 \div 7 = 5$ |

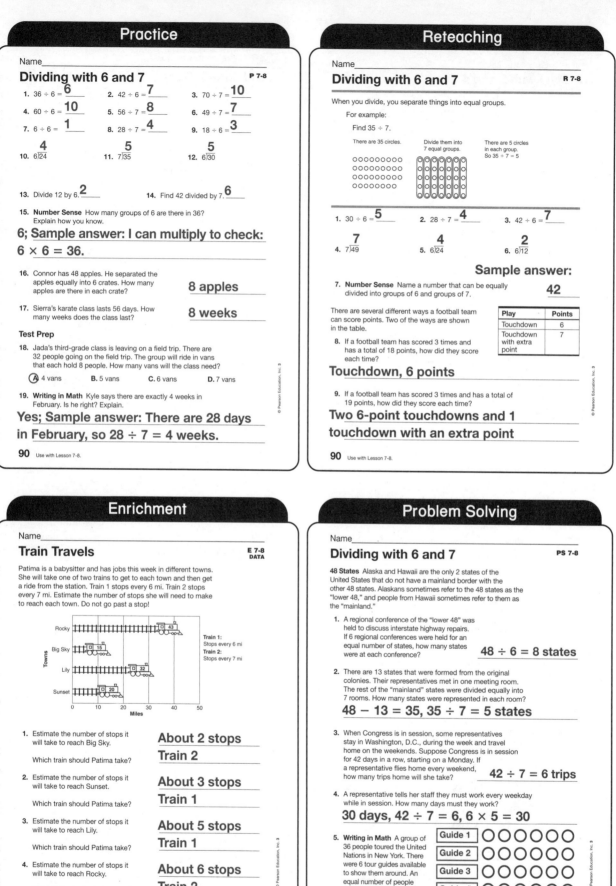

1. $30 \div 6 =$ __5__   2. $28 \div 7 =$ __4__   3. $42 \div 6 =$ __7__

4. $7\overline{)49}$ __7__   5. $6\overline{)24}$ __4__   6. $6\overline{)12}$ __2__

7. **Number Sense** Name a number that can be equally divided into groups of 6 and groups of 7.

Sample answer: __42__

There are several different ways a football team can score points. Two of the ways are shown in the table.

Play	Points
Touchdown	6
Touchdown with extra point	7

8. If a football team has scored 3 times and has a total of 18 points, how did they score each time?

__Touchdown, 6 points__

9. If a football team has scored 3 times and has a total of 19 points, how did they score each time?

__Two 6-point touchdowns and 1__
__touchdown with an extra point__

90 Use with Lesson 7-8.

Name_____

Train Travels

E 7-8
DATA

Patima is a babysitter and has jobs this week in different towns. She will take one of two trains to get to each town and then get a ride from the station. Train 1 stops every 6 mi. Train 2 stops every 7 mi. Estimate the number of stops she will need to make to reach each town. Do not go past a stop!

Train 1:
Stops every 6 mi
Train 2:
Stops every 7 mi

1. Estimate the number of stops it will take to reach Big Sky.

Which train should Patima take?

__About 2 stops__
__Train 2__

2. Estimate the number of stops it will take to reach Sunset.

Which train should Patima take?

__About 3 stops__
__Train 1__

3. Estimate the number of stops it will take to reach Lily.

Which train should Patima take?

__About 5 stops__
__Train 1__

4. Estimate the number of stops it will take to reach Rocky.

Which train should Patima take?

__About 6 stops__
__Train 2__

90 Use with Lesson 7-8.

Name_____

Dividing with 6 and 7

PS 7-8

48 States Alaska and Hawaii are the only 2 states of the United States that do not have a mainland border with the other 48 states. Alaskans sometimes refer to the 48 states as the "lower 48," and people from Hawaii sometimes refer to them as the "mainland."

1. A regional conference of the "lower 48" was held to discuss interstate highway repairs. If 6 regional conferences were held for an equal number of states, how many states were at each conference?   __$48 \div 6 = 8$ states__

2. There are 13 states that were formed from the original colonies. Their representatives met in one meeting room. The rest of the "mainland" states were divided equally into 7 rooms. How many states were represented in each room?

__$48 - 13 = 35$, $35 \div 7 = 5$ states__

3. When Congress is in session, some representatives stay in Washington, D.C., during the week and travel home on the weekends. Suppose Congress is in session for 42 days in a row, starting on a Monday. If a representative flies home every weekend, how many trips home will she take?   __$42 \div 7 = 6$ trips__

4. A representative tells her staff they must work every weekday while in session. How many days must they work?

__30 days, $42 \div 7 = 6$, $6 \times 5 = 30$__

5. **Writing in Math** A group of 36 people toured the United Nations in New York. There were 6 tour guides available to show them around. An equal number of people went into each group. Draw a picture to show how many people were with each tour guide.

Guide 1	○ ○ ○ ○ ○ ○
Guide 2	○ ○ ○ ○ ○ ○
Guide 3	○ ○ ○ ○ ○ ○
Guide 4	○ ○ ○ ○ ○ ○
Guide 5	○ ○ ○ ○ ○ ○
Guide 6	○ ○ ○ ○ ○ ○

90 Use with Lesson 7-8.

© Pearson Education, Inc. 3

Name_____

Dividing with 8 and 9
P 7-9

1. $27 \div 9 = $ **3**   2. $45 \div 9 = $ **5**   3. $72 \div 8 = $ **9**

4. $81 \div 9 = $ **9**   5. $24 \div 8 = $ **3**   6. $63 \div 9 = $ **7**

7. $64 \div 8 = $ **8**   8. $36 \div 9 = $ **4**   9. $48 \div 8 = $ **6**

10. **2** $9\overline{)18}$ 11. **5** $8\overline{)40}$ 12. **8** $9\overline{)72}$

13. Find 16 divided by 8. **2**   14. Divide 90 by 9. **10**

15. **Number Sense** What multiplication fact can help you find $32 \div 8$?

Sample answer: The fact $8 \times 4 = 32$ helps to find that $32 \div 8 = 4$.

16. Nicholas scored 16 runs in the first 8 baseball games he played. If he scored the same number of times in each game, how many runs did he score in each game?   **2 runs**

Test Prep

17. Mr. Carlos brought 32 pencils to school. He shared them equally among the 8 students in the math group. How many pencils did each student get?

A. 2 pencils   B. 3 pencils   Ⓒ 4 pencils   D. 5 pencils

18. **Writing in Math** Adam made 19 paper cranes on Monday and 8 on Tuesday. He gave 9 of his friends an equal number of cranes. How many did each friend receive? Explain how you found your answer.

3 paper cranes; Sample answer: Because $19 + 8 = 27$ and $27 \div 9 = 3$

© Pearson Education, Inc. 3

Name_____

Dividing with 8 and 9
R 7-9

Remembering multiplication facts can help you divide by 8 and 9.

What multiplication fact can help you solve $24 \div 8$?

$8 \times 1 = 8$ $8 \times 6 = 48$
$8 \times 2 = 16$ $8 \times 7 = 56$
$(8 \times 3 = 24)$ $8 \times 8 = 64$
$8 \times 4 = 32$ $8 \times 9 = 72$
$8 \times 5 = 40$ $8 \times 10 = 80$

If $8 \times 3 = 24$, then $24 \div 8 = 3$.

What multiplication fact can help you solve $27 \div 9$?

$9 \times 1 = 9$ $9 \times 6 = 54$
$9 \times 2 = 18$ $9 \times 7 = 63$
$(9 \times 3 = 27)$ $9 \times 8 = 72$
$9 \times 4 = 36$ $9 \times 9 = 81$
$9 \times 5 = 45$ $9 \times 10 = 90$

If $9 \times 3 = 27$, then $27 \div 9 = 3$.

1. $32 \div 8 = $ **4**   2. $54 \div 9 = $ **6**   3. $48 \div 8 = $ **6**

4. **8** $9\overline{)72}$ 5. **7** $9\overline{)63}$ 6. **7** $8\overline{)56}$

7. **Number Sense** What multiplication problem would you solve to find a number that can be divided equally by 8 and by 9?   **$8 \times 9 = 72$**

8. From 1912 until the beginning of 1959, the United States had 48 states. The flag at that time had 48 stars, one for each state. The 48 stars on the flag were arranged in 6 equal rows. How many stars were in each row?   **8 stars**

© Pearson Education, Inc. 3

Name_____

Follow the Rules
E 7-9
REASONING

1. Read the rule in each column and row. Then write a number in each box that fits the rules in its column and row. Do not use any number more than once.

Sample answers are given.

	has 6 as a factor	is less than 100	has 8 as a factor
has 4 as a factor	24	80	40
has the digit 3 in it	36	35	32
has 4 in the tens place	48	41	48
is an even number	60	2	88
has 6 in the ones place	66	56	16

2. Now make your own chart like the one above. When you are finished, give it to a classmate to fill in. Make sure your chart does not ask for a number that cannot be made, such as "an odd number that has 2 as a factor."

Check students' charts.

© Pearson Education, Inc. 3

Name_____

Dividing with 8 and 9
PS 7-9

An array of 64 small squares are arranged to form one large square.

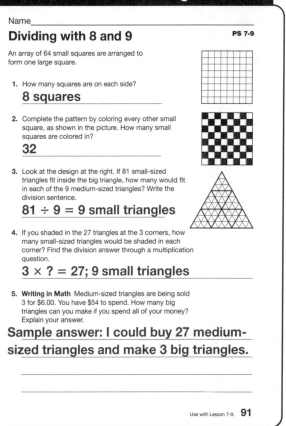

1. How many squares are on each side?

8 squares

2. Complete the pattern by coloring every other small square, as shown in the picture. How many small squares are colored in?

32

3. Look at the design at the right. If 81 small-sized triangles fit inside the big triangle, how many would fit in each of the 9 medium-sized triangles? Write the division sentence.

$81 \div 9 = 9$ small triangles

4. If you shaded in the 27 triangles at the 3 corners, how many small-sized triangles would be shaded in each corner? Find the division answer through a multiplication question.

$3 \times ? = 27$; 9 small triangles

5. **Writing in Math** Medium-sized triangles are being sold 3 for $6.00. You have $54 to spend. How many big triangles can you make if you spend all of your money? Explain your answer.

Sample answer: I could buy 27 medium-sized triangles and make 3 big triangles.

© Pearson Education, Inc. 3

Name_____

Dividing with 0 and 1

1. $9 \div 1 = $ **9**   **2.** $0 \div 8 = $ **0**   **3.** $7 \div 7 = $ **1**

4. $0 \div 9 = $ **0**   **5.** $3 \div 3 = $ **1**   **6.** $6 \div 1 = $ **6**

7. **3** $1\overline{)3}$ **8.** **1** $4\overline{)4}$ **9.** **0** $8\overline{)0}$

10. Divide 0 by 2. **0**_____   **11.** Divide 7 by 1. **7**_____

12. Number Sense Explain how you know that $45 \div 0$ cannot be done.

Sample answer: No number multiplied
by 0 will equal 45.

Compare. Use <, >, or =.

13. $6 \div 6 \; \boxed{=} \; 4 \div 4$ **14.** $0 \div 5 \; \boxed{<} \; 5 \div 5$ **15.** $10 \div 1 \; \boxed{>} \; 7 \div 1$

Test Prep

16. Which is the quotient of $0 \div 9$?

   A. 9   **B.** 5
   C. 1   **(D.)** 0

17. Writing in Math Explain why $10 - 0 = 10$ but $0 \div 10 = 0$.

Sample answer: Taking 0 away from 10
will leave 10. Zero times 10 equals 0, so
0 divided by 10 equals 0.

Name_____

Dividing with 0 and 1

There are special rules to follow when dividing by 1 or 0.

Rule	Example	What You Think	What You Write
When any number is divided by 1, the quotient is that number.	$7 \div 1 = ?$	1 times what number = 7? $1 \times 7 = 7$ So, $7 \div 1 = 7$	$7 \div 1 = 7$ or $1\overline{)7}$
When any number (except 0) is divided by itself, the quotient is 1.	$8 \div 8 = ?$	8 times what number = 8? $8 \times 1 = 8$ So, $8 \div 8 = 1$	$8 \div 8 = 1$ or $8\overline{)8}$
When zero is divided by a number (except 0), the quotient is 0.	$0 \div 5 = ?$	5 times what number = 0? $5 \times 0 = 0$ So, $0 \div 5 = 0$	$0 \div 5 = 0$ or $5\overline{)0}$
You cannot divide a number by 0.	$9 \div 0 = ?$	0 times what number = 9? There is no number that works, so $9 \div 0$ cannot be done.	$9 \div 0$ cannot be done

1. $25 \div 1 = $ **25**   **2.** $9 \div 9 = $ **1**   **3.** $0 \div 8 = $ **0**

4. **7** $1\overline{)7}$ **5.** **1** $12\overline{)12}$ **6. Cannot be done** $0\overline{)17}$

Compare. Use <, >, or =.

7. $15 \div 1 \; \boxed{>} \; 15 \div 15$ **8.** $0 \div 12 \; \boxed{<} \; 12 \div 12$

9. $8 \div 1 \; \boxed{=} \; 8 \div 1$ **10.** $1 \div 1 \; \boxed{>} \; 0 \div 1$

Name_____

Dinner Is Served

Cherry School has a winter fair every December. The students help to prepare and serve the food. Some foods need to be heated up in a microwave. Other foods are cold and do not need to be heated. Look at the chart. Then answer the questions.

Food	Minutes to Heat Up
Bowl of pasta	1
Sandwich	0
Chicken wrap	1
Salad	0
Bowl of chili	1

1. The fourth-grade class is serving sandwiches. How many minutes will this class need to heat 45 sandwiches?   **0 min**

2. The sixth-grade class is serving pasta. How many minutes will this class need to heat 30 bowls of pasta?   **30 min**

3. The second-grade class is serving chicken wraps. How many minutes will this class need to heat 25 wraps?   **25 min**

4. The seventh-grade class is serving chili. How many minutes will this class need to heat 20 bowls of chili?   **20 min**

5. The first-grade class is serving salad. How many minutes will this class need to heat 35 plates of salad?   **0 min**

Name_____

Dividing with 0 and 1

Lorne, Todd, and Scott worked for a delivery service. Every weekday they picked up packages from location A and took them across town to location B. Here was the work schedule for last week.

Monday	8 packages
Tuesday	4 packages
Wednesday	6 packages
Thursday	3 packages
Friday	0 packages

1. On Monday, Todd and Scott were the drivers on duty. If each one took an equal amount of packages, how many would each deliver to location B?

4 packages

2. On Tuesday, Lorne was the only driver. Show a division sentence that explains how many packages Lorne delivered to location B.

$4 \div 1 = 4$ packages

3. On Thursday, all the packages went to the same person, so they were packed in a single carton. Write a division sentence that shows how many packages were in the 1 carton.

$3 \div 1 = 3$ packages

4. Write a division sentence to show how many cartons were packed on Thursday if 3 packages fit into each carton.

$3 \div 3 = 1$ carton

5. Writing in Math Todd, Lorne, and Scott showed up for work on Friday. Each person was going to deliver the same number of packages. But there had been a terrible snowstorm that day, so there were no packages to deliver. Write a division sentence to show how many packages each one delivered. Explain your answer.

$0 \div 3 = 0$; Sample answer: Since there
were no packages, the rule that zero
divided by any number is zero is used.

Name_____

P 7-11

Remainders

Use counters or draw a picture to find each quotient and remainder.

1. 39 ÷ 6 = **6 R3**   2. 20 ÷ 3 = **6 R2**   3. 11 ÷ 3 = **3 R2**

4. 9 ÷ 2 = **4 R1**   5. 7 ÷ 3 = **2 R1**   6. 13 ÷ 6 = **2 R1**

7. 36 ÷ 3 = **12**   8. 25 ÷ 4 = **6 R1**   9. 45 ÷ 6 = **7 R3**

10. Holly bought a box of 65 souvenir magnets on her vacation. She wants to share them equally with her 9 friends. How many magnets will each friend get? How many magnets will be left over?

7 magnets; 2 leftover magnets

11. Sebastian and Caitlin have 11 thank-you cards to send. They agreed that if each of them sends 5 they will be finished. Do you agree? Explain.

No, there will still be 1 thank-you card left.

Test Prep

12. Yvonne can carry 7 books at one time, and she wants to carry 25 books to her room. How many books will she carry on her fourth trip?

A. 1 book   B. 2 books   C. 3 books   **D.** 4 books

13. **Writing in Math** Anna has 30 fruit snacks that she wants to share with her class. Because there are 25 people in her class, Anna used 30 ÷ 25 to find the number of snacks she will have left over. Will she find the correct answer? Explain.

Yes; Sample answer: Anna will find that she will have 5 fruit snacks left over because 30 ÷ 25 = 1 R5.

Name_____

R 7-11

Remainders

Keith has 21 sports cards. Each plastic sleeve holds 6 cards. How many sleeves will be filled? Will there be any cards left over?

Find 21 ÷ 6.

What You **Do**	What You **Write**
Draw a picture to show the main idea of the problem.	21 ÷ 6 = 3 R3
	3 R3 is read "three remainder three."
	Keith filled 3 sleeves. He has 3 cards left over.

There are 3 groups of 6 with 3 left over. The remainder is 3.

Use counters or draw a picture to find each quotient and remainder.

1. 16 ÷ 5 = **3 R1**   2. 14 ÷ 3 = **4 R2**   3. 19 ÷ 8 = **2 R3**

4. 17 ÷ 4 = **4 R1**   5. 8 ÷ 3 = **2 R2**   6. 11 ÷ 7 = **1 R4**

7. **Number Sense** Jamal divided 16 by 5. His answer was 2 R6. Is his answer correct? If not, what is the correct answer?

No, his answer should be 3 R1.

There are 50 states in the United States. Mr. Hernandez's students are going to study each state.

8. Mr. Hernandez has assigned a group of 8 students to write paragraphs about the states. If the group of 8 students needs to write a paragraph about each of the 50 states, can the work be divided evenly among the students in the group?

No

If not, how many states are left over?

2 left over

Name_____

E 7-11
NUMBER SENSE

Happy Trails

The Happy Trails travel company takes people on hiking trips. Each person on the trip carries a backpack. The weight of the total supplies is divided equally among the members of the group and the guides. The remainder is the extra weight.

Complete the chart. Then answer the questions.

Trip	Total Weight of Gear	Number of People	Weight Each Person Carries	Extra Weight
1	58 lb	6	**9 lb**	**4 lb**
2	70 lb	8	**8 lb**	**6 lb**
3	83 lb	9	**9 lb**	**2 lb**

1. The guides on each trip carry the extra weight. There are two guides on each trip. How much extra weight does each guide carry on each trip?

Trip 1: **2 lb**   Trip 2: **3 lb**   Trip 3: **1 lb**

2. How much total weight does each guide carry on each trip?

Trip 1: **11 lb**   Trip 2: **11 lb**   Trip 3: **10 lb**

3. Each guide is paid $5 extra for each extra pound. How much extra will each guide be paid for each trip?

Trip 1: **$10**   Trip 2: **$15**   Trip 3: **$5**

4. If the weight of the gear is changed to 72 lb for all trips, will the guides earn any extra money? Explain.

No; Sample answer: There is no remainder or extra weight.

Name_____

PS 7-11

Remainders

Ms. Leonard has organized her math class so that she completes a unit every 7 days, including homework for weekends. In months that are longer than 28 days, the extra days are for math activities, such as math games, math puzzles, and reading about famous people in math history.

1. This is a leap year, so February has 29 days. How many units will she complete? How many days will be left for math activities?

4 units; 1 day

2. September has 30 days but the first 2 days of the month are during summer vacation. Will the students have time for math activities in September?

No

3. November has 31 days. How many days will the students have for math activities?

3 days

Students are making bows to decorate the school assembly. Mr. Carson's class has designed a small bow that will take 5 in. of ribbon to make and a large bow that will take 9 in. of ribbon to make. Ribbon is on sale for 3 yd for $1. (Hint: There are 36 in. in a yard.)

4. How many small bows can they make from 1 yd of ribbon?

7 small bows

5. How much ribbon will be left over?

1 in. of ribbon

6. Mr. Carson told them that they must make at least 2 large bows. How many small bows can they make? How much ribbon will be left over? Explain how you solved the problem.

3 small bows and 3 in. left over; Sample answer: 2 large bows take 18 in., which leaves 15 in. for 3 bows with 3 in. left over.

Name_____

Division Patterns with 10, 11, and 12   P 7-12

Find each quotient. You may use a multiplication table,
counters, or draw a picture to help.

1. $121 \div 11 =$ **11**   2. $70 \div 7 =$ **10**   3. $132 \div 11 =$ **12**

4. $72 \div 12 =$ **6**   5. $66 \div 6 =$ **11**   6. $40 \div 4 =$ **10**

7. $300 \div 30 =$ **10**   8. $22 \div 2 =$ **11**   9. $200 \div 10 =$ **20**

10. $8\overline{)88}$ **11**   11. $9\overline{)36}$ **4**   12. $10\overline{)110}$ **11**

13. **Number Sense** Adrian said that any 2-digit number with
2 identical digits is divisible by 11. Do you agree? Explain.

Yes; Sample answer: For example,
$44 \div 11 = 4$ and $55 \div 11 = 5$

14. Madeline purchased 10 sweaters for $100.
How much did she spend for each sweater?   **$10**

Test Prep

15. Henry bought 4 dozen eggs. How many eggs did he buy?

Ⓐ 48 eggs   **B.** 60 eggs   **C.** 72 eggs   **D.** 84 eggs

16. **Writing in Math** Explain how you can find the quotient of $400 \div 10$.

Sample answer: There are ten 10s in 100.
So, there must be forty 10s in 400: 100 +
100 + 100 + 100 = 400.

© Pearson Education, Inc. 3

Name_____

Division Patterns with 10, 11, and 12   R 7-12

A number is divisible by another number when it can be divided
by that number and the remainder is 0. For example, $80 \div 10 =$
8. You can also say that 80 is a **multiple** of 10. The chart below
shows the multiples of 10, 11, and 12.

×	0	1	2	3	4	5	6	7	8	9	10	11	12
0	0	0	0	0	0	0	0	0	0	0	0	0	0
1	0	1	2	3	4	5	6	7	8	9	10	11	12
2	0	2	4	6	8	10	12	14	16	18	20	22	24
3	0	3	6	9	12	15	18	21	24	27	30	33	36
4	0	4	8	12	16	20	24	28	32	36	40	44	48
5	0	5	10	15	20	25	30	35	40	45	50	55	60
6	0	6	12	18	24	30	36	42	48	54	60	66	72
7	0	7	14	21	28	35	42	49	56	63	70	77	84
8	0	8	16	24	32	40	48	56	64	72	80	88	96
9	0	9	18	27	36	45	54	63	72	81	90	99	108
10	0	10	20	30	40	50	60	70	80	90	100	110	120
11	0	11	22	33	44	55	66	77	88	99	110	121	132
12	0	12	24	36	48	60	72	84	96	108	120	132	144

- The numbers 0, 10, 20, ... 120 are all multiples of 10. Each of these numbers is divisible by 10. For example, $30 \div 10 = 3$.
- The numbers 0, 11, 22, ... 132 are all multiples of 11. Each of these numbers is divisible by 11. For example, $99 \div 11 = 9$.
- The numbers 0, 12, 24, ... 144 are all multiples of 12. Each of these numbers is divisible by 12. For example, $108 \div 12 = 9$.

Find each quotient. You may use a multiplication table,
counters, or draw a picture to help.

1. $48 \div 12 =$ **4**   2. $50 \div 10 =$ **5**   3. $44 \div 11 =$ **4**

4. $11\overline{)66}$ **6**   5. $10\overline{)20}$ **2**   6. $12\overline{)48}$ **4**

7. **Writing in Math** Explain how you can use skip counting to find $70 \div 10$.

Sample answer: I can count up by 10s
and see that there are 7 tens in 70.

© Pearson Education, Inc. 3

Name_____

Name the Numbers   E 7-12
REASONING

As you can see, there are missing numbers in the diagrams
below. Any number that is above two other numbers is the
product of those numbers. Use multiplication and division to
find the missing numbers.

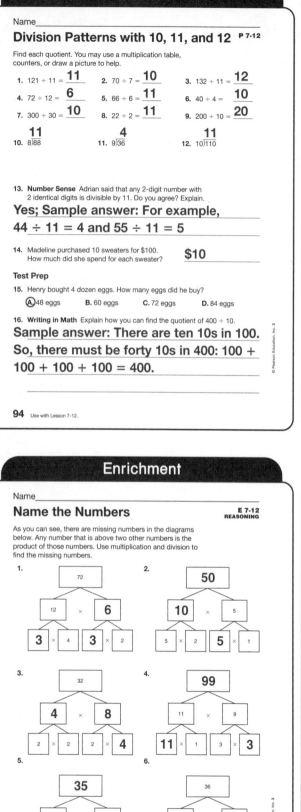

© Pearson Education, Inc. 3

Name_____

Division Patterns with 10, 11, 12   PS 7-12

A decade is 10 years long. In 1817, James Monroe became the
5th president of the United States, and 40 years later, James
Buchanan became the 15th president of the United States.

1. How many decades passed between Monroe
and Buchanan?

4 decades

2. President Theodore Roosevelt was 60 years old
at the time of his death. How many decades did
Theodore Roosevelt live?

6 decades

3. John Quincy Adams, the 2nd president,
lived for 90 years. For how many decades
did John Quincy Adams live?

9 decades

4. Andrew planted a tree in his backyard. The tree
grew 11 in. each year. If the tree is now 66 in. tall,
how many years ago did Andrew plant it?

6 years

5. **Writing in Math** Esther needed 72 eggs for the football
team breakfast. How many dozen eggs does she need?
Explain.

6 dozen; Sample answer: There are 12
eggs in 1 dozen, so $72 \div 12 = 6$.

© Pearson Education, Inc. 3

Name_____

P 7-13

Translating Words to Expressions

Write a numerical expression for each word phrase.

1. 42 minus 10 baseballs

$42 - 10$

2. four times as many crayons as 4 colored pencils

4×4

3. $9 less than $25

$\$25 - \$9$

4. 15 toys given out equally to 5 students

$15 \div 5$

5. 12 times as long as 2 in.

12×2

6. 4 people sharing 8 rolls equally

$8 \div 4$

There are 12 cups in one package. Write a numerical expression for how many there will be when there are

7. 2 fewer cups.

$12 - 2$

8. 8 more cups.

$12 + 8$

9. 6 times as many cups.

12×6

10. half the number of cups.

$12 \div 2$

Choose the numerical expression that matches the situation.

11. Karl eats all 5 of his carrots.
   A. $5 + 5$
   B. $5 - 5$

12. Both cats receive 10 oz of food.
   A. $10 \div 2$
   B. 10×2

13. **Writing in Math** Write two situations that would use the numerical expression $27 \div 9$.

Sample answer: The third-grade class of 27 separated into 9 equal groups; Mr. Simon gave the 27 pencils to 9 students.

Use with Lesson 7-13. **95**

Name_____

R 7-13

Translating Words to Expressions

Family Kay has 5 fewer aunts than cousins. She has 15 cousins. Write a numerical expression that shows how many aunts and cousins Kay has total.

The words in the problem give you clues about the operation.

Word or Phrase	Use
Total	+
Difference of	−
Times	×
Half; placed into equal groups	÷

Since Kay has 15 cousins, and 5 fewer aunts than cousins, she must have 10 aunts. The numerical expression that shows the total number of aunts and cousins she has is 10 + 15.

Write the numerical expression for each word phrase.

1. 14 baseball cards placed into 2 equal groups

$14 \div 2$

2. 12 more than 85

$85 + 12$

3. 6 times as long as 7

6×7

4. 3 times as old as 5

3×5

5. the total of 4 cats and 15 dogs

$4 + 15$

6. $14 less than $44

$\$44 - \$14$

7. **Writing in Math** Write a word phrase for this numerical expression: 8×5.

Sample answer: 8 times 5

Use with Lesson 7-13. **95**

Name_____

Whose Bike Is That?

E 7-13
REASONING

Laura, Daniel, John, Linda, Susan, and Samuel went bike riding. They parked their bikes in a row at the beach. Below are five clues that will help you find the order in which the six bike riders parked their bikes. Write the name of each person on the correct line.

- Daniel is parked to the right of John.

- Laura is parked on the end, but her bike is not farthest to the left.

- John is not parked on the end.

- Linda's bike is parked next to Laura's.

- Samuel is parked next to Linda.

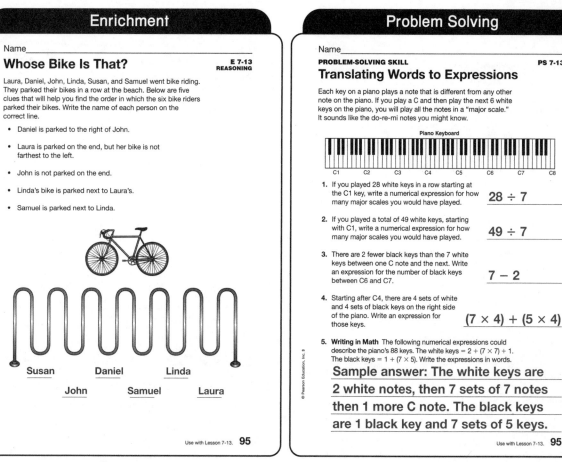

Susan   Daniel   Linda

John   Samuel   Laura

Use with Lesson 7-13. **95**

Name_____

PS 7-13

Translating Words to Expressions

Each key on a piano plays a note that is different from any other note on the piano. If you play a C and then play the next 6 white keys on the piano, you will play all the notes in a "major scale." It sounds like the do-re-mi notes you might know.

Piano Keyboard

C1   C2   C3   C4   C5   C6   C7   C8

1. If you played 28 white keys in a row starting at the C1 key, write a numerical expression for how many major scales you would have played.

$28 \div 7$

2. If you played a total of 49 white keys, starting with C1, write a numerical expression for how many major scales you would have played.

$49 \div 7$

3. There are 2 fewer black keys than the 7 white keys between one C note and the next. Write an expression for the number of black keys between C6 and C7.

$7 - 2$

4. Starting after C4, there are 4 sets of white and 4 sets of black keys on the right side of the piano. Write an expression for those keys.

$(7 \times 4) + (5 \times 4)$

5. **Writing in Math** The following numerical expressions could describe the piano's 88 keys. The white keys = 2 + (7 × 7) + 1. The black keys = 1 + (7 × 5). Write the expressions in words.

Sample answer: The white keys are 2 white notes, then 7 sets of 7 notes then 1 more C note. The black keys are 1 black key and 7 sets of 5 keys.

Use with Lesson 7-13. **95**

Name_____

The Dividing Life

Solve. Write your answer in a complete sentence.

1. Bailey is collecting dimes. She has 4 quarters. If Bailey changes her quarters for dimes at the bank, how many dimes will she get?

Bailey will get 10 dimes for 4 quarters.

2. At the zoo, there are 8 elephants and 2 trainers. How many elephants does each trainer work with if they both work with the same number of elephants?

Each trainer works with 4 elephants.

3. There are 16 oz in a pound of butter. While making bread, Andre read that he needs half that amount for the recipe. How many ounces does Andre need?

Andre needs 8 oz of butter.

4. Thomas has 3 boxes for toys in his room. He has 33 toys. If he divides the toys equally, how many toys will Thomas put into each box?

Thomas will put 11 toys in each box.

5. Makayla has 32 books. She let each of her 4 friends borrow the same number of books. They borrowed all of Makayla's books. How many books did each friend borrow?

Each friend borrowed 8 books.

6. Ms. Lucas has 19 paintbrushes for art class and 4 tables. If she puts an equal number of brushes on each table, how many brushes will be on each table? How many brushes will be left over?

Ms. Lucas put 4 brushes on each table.
There will be 3 brushes left over.

Name_____

The Student Musicians

The fifth- and sixth-grade string music students at Highland Elementary gave a concert. Several different groups of student musicians played songs. One of the groups had 4 members. Their instruments had a total of 20 strings. What instruments could these group members be playing?

String Instruments	
Instrument	Number of Strings
Violin	4
Viola	4
Cello	4
Bass	4
Guitar	6

Try: First, try 1 guitar and 3 violins.

Check: 3 violins × 4 strings each = 12 strings, plus 6 guitar strings equals 18 strings. This answer is too low by 2 strings.

Revise: I'll try 2 violins and 2 guitars. This should give me 20 strings. 4 × 2 = 8, 6 × 2 = 12, 12 + 8 = 20.

This answer works. I have 4 string players and 20 strings.

1. There are a total of 32 string players in the fifth and sixth grades. There are 6 more fifth graders than sixth graders. How many string players are in each grade?

19 fifth graders, 13 sixth graders

2. The 32 string players often play in groups of 4 players. How many groups of 4 players could they form?

8 groups

3. If the string players are divided into groups of 6 players, are there any students left over? **Yes** If so, how many? **2 left over**

4. The string players played a concert that included 5 songs. The songs were all the same length. The concert lasted 30 min. How long was each song?

6 min

Name_____

Foot and Wing Race

The graph below shows the top speeds at which certain animals and insects can travel. These speeds are measured over short distances. Imagine that the animals and insects could run or fly at these speeds for many hours and over longer distances.

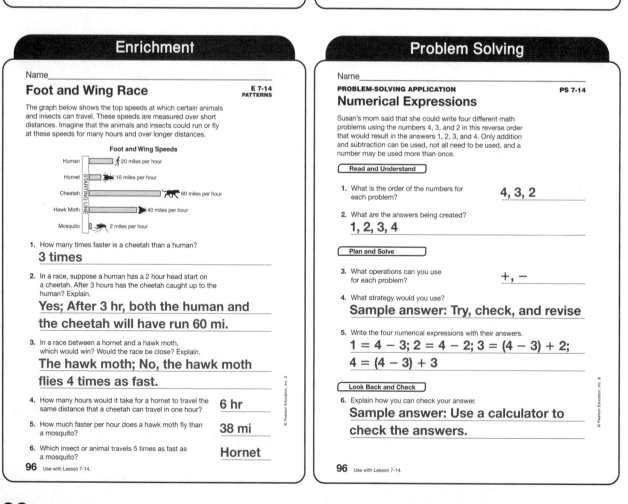

Foot and Wing Speeds

Human	20 miles per hour
Hornet	10 miles per hour
Cheetah	60 miles per hour
Hawk Moth	40 miles per hour
Mosquito	2 miles per hour

1. How many times faster is a cheetah than a human?

3 times

2. In a race, suppose a human has a 2 hour head start on a cheetah. After 3 hours has the cheetah caught up to the human? Explain.

Yes; After 3 hr, both the human and the cheetah will have run 60 mi.

3. In a race between a hornet and a hawk moth, which would win? Would the race be close? Explain.

The hawk moth; No, the hawk moth flies 4 times as fast.

4. How many hours would it take for a hornet to travel the same distance that a cheetah can travel in one hour? **6 hr**

5. How much faster per hour does a hawk moth fly than a mosquito? **38 mi**

6. Which insect or animal travels 5 times as fast as a mosquito? **Hornet**

Name_____

Numerical Expressions

Susan's mom said that she could write four different math problems using the numbers 4, 3, and 2 in this reverse order that would result in the answers 1, 2, 3, and 4. Only addition and subtraction can be used, not all need to be used, and a number may be used more than once.

Read and Understand

1. What is the order of the numbers for each problem?

4, 3, 2

2. What are the answers being created?

1, 2, 3, 4

Plan and Solve

3. What operations can you use for each problem?

+, −

4. What strategy would you use?

Sample answer: Try, check, and revise

5. Write the four numerical expressions with their answers.

$1 = 4 - 3; 2 = 4 - 2; 3 = (4 - 3) + 2;$
$4 = (4 - 3) + 3$

Look Back and Check

6. Explain how you can check your answer.

Sample answer: Use a calculator to check the answers.

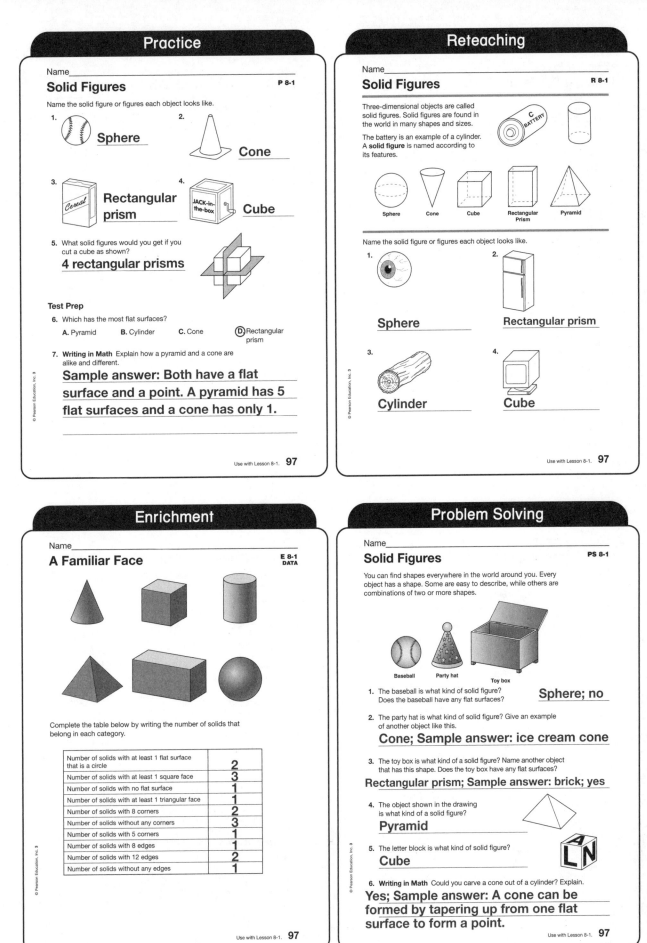

Practice

Name the solid figure or figures each object looks like.

1. **Sphere**

2. **Cone**

3. **Rectangular prism**

4. **Cube**

5. What solid figures would you get if you cut a cube as shown?

4 rectangular prisms

Test Prep

6. Which has the most flat surfaces?

A. Pyramid   B. Cylinder   C. Cone   (D) Rectangular prism

7. **Writing in Math** Explain how a pyramid and a cone are alike and different.

Sample answer: Both have a flat surface and a point. A pyramid has 5 flat surfaces and a cone has only 1.

© Pearson Education, Inc. 3

Use with Lesson 8-1. **97**

Reteaching

Three-dimensional objects are called solid figures. Solid figures are found in the world in many shapes and sizes.

The battery is an example of a cylinder. A **solid figure** is named according to its features.

Sphere   Cone   Cube   Rectangular Prism   Pyramid

Name the solid figure or figures each object looks like.

1. **Sphere**

2. **Rectangular prism**

3. **Cylinder**

4. **Cube**

© Pearson Education, Inc. 3

Use with Lesson 8-1. **97**

Enrichment

Complete the table below by writing the number of solids that belong in each category.

Number of solids with at least 1 flat surface that is a circle	2
Number of solids with at least 1 square face	3
Number of solids with no flat surface	1
Number of solids with at least 1 triangular face	1
Number of solids with 8 corners	2
Number of solids without any corners	3
Number of solids with 5 corners	1
Number of solids with 8 edges	1
Number of solids with 12 edges	2
Number of solids without any edges	1

© Pearson Education, Inc. 3

Use with Lesson 8-1. **97**

Problem Solving

You can find shapes everywhere in the world around you. Every object has a shape. Some are easy to describe, while others are combinations of two or more shapes.

Baseball   Party hat   Toy box

1. The baseball is what kind of solid figure? Does the baseball have any flat surfaces?

Sphere; no

2. The party hat is what kind of solid figure? Give an example of another object like this.

Cone; Sample answer: ice cream cone

3. The toy box is what kind of a solid figure? Name another object that has this shape. Does the toy box have any flat surfaces?

Rectangular prism; Sample answer: brick; yes

4. The object shown in the drawing is what kind of a solid figure?

Pyramid

5. The letter block is what kind of solid figure?

Cube

6. **Writing in Math** Could you carve a cone out of a cylinder? Explain.

Yes; Sample answer: A cone can be formed by tapering up from one flat surface to form a point.

© Pearson Education, Inc. 3

Use with Lesson 8-1. **97**

Name_____

Relating Solids and Shapes

P 8-2

Complete the table.

Solid Figure	Faces	Edges	Corners
1. Cube	6	12	8
2. Pyramid	5	8	5
3. Rectangular prism	6	12	8

4. How many flat surfaces does this coffee can have?

2

Jane is making a building for her math project. How many corners does each combination of figures have?

5. 2 rectangular prisms   **16 corners**

6. 2 pyramids   **10 corners**

7. 2 cubes and 1 cylinder   **16 corners**

Test Prep

8. Which figure is NOT part of this object?

Ⓐ Sphere   **B.** Cylinder

C. Cone   **D.** Cube

9. **Writing in Math** How could you describe a cylinder to someone who has never seen one?

Sample answer: A cylinder is a rounded figure with a flat circle at each end.

98   Use with Lesson 8-2.

© Pearson Education, Inc. 3

Name_____

Relating Solids and Shapes

R 8-2

In a drawing of a solid figure, it is not always easy to find the number of faces, edges, or corners. Sometimes it helps to imagine that the solid figure is transparent.

By using a transparent cube, you can count each face. Remember that each flat surface is called a **face.**

There are 6 faces on a cube.

Use the transparent cube to count the number of edges. Remember that an **edge** is a line segment where two faces meet. There are 12 edges on a cube.

Can you use the transparent cube to find the number of corners on a cube? Remember a **corner** is the point where 2 or more edges meet. There are 8 corners on a cube.

1. How many faces does a rectangular prism have?   **6 faces**

2. How many edges does a pyramid have?   **8 edges**

3. How many corners does a rectangular prism have?   **8 corners**

4. **Reasoning** How are a cube and a rectangular prism alike? How are they different?

Sample answer: The cube and rectangular prism have the same number of faces, edges, and corners. The cube has all of the edge lengths the same, and a rectangular prism does not.

98   Use with Lesson 8-2.

© Pearson Education, Inc. 3

Name_____

Solid Comparisons

E 8-2
NUMBER SENSE

Write <, >, or = in each ◯ to compare the solid figures.

1. number of corners on a 🧊 ⟨**>**⟩ number of corners on a 🔺

2. number of faces on a 🔺 ⟨**<**⟩ number of faces on a ▱

3. number of edges on a 🔺 ⟨**<**⟩ number of edges on a ▱

4. number of corners on a 🧊 ⟨**=**⟩ number of corners on a ▱

Write each in order from greatest to least.

5. The number of faces, edges, and corners on a ▱

Edges (12); corners (8); faces (6)

6. The number of corners on a 🔺, a 🔺, and a ▱

Rectangular prism (8); pyramid (5); cone (0)

7. The number of flat surfaces on a 🧊, a 🔺, a ⚪, and a 🛢️

Cube (6); cylinder (2); cone (1); sphere (0)

8. The number of edges on a ⚪, a ▱, and a 🔺

Rectangular prism (12); pyramid (8); sphere (0)

98   Use with Lesson 8-2.

© Pearson Education, Inc. 3

Name_____

Relating Solids and Shapes

PS 8-2

Many buildings and homes use smokestacks. A smokestack is especially important for a home fireplace. Some ashes float away from the fire and are moved outside through the chimney.

1. What kind of solid figure is the smokestack?

Cylinder

2. How many edges does it have?   **0 edges**

3. How many corners does it have?   **0 corners**

Sometimes people build buildings with unusual shapes. The drawing shows a building in the shape of a wedge.

4. How many corners does it have?

6 corners

5. Find a rectangular face. How many corners does the rectangular face have?   **4 corners**

6. How many edges are on each rectangular face?   **4 edges**

7. **Writing in Math** Explain why a cube has the same number of corners as a rectangular prism.

Sample answer: A cube is a rectangular prism with equal sides, so a cube has the same number of corners as a rectangular prism.

98   Use with Lesson 8-2.

© Pearson Education, Inc. 3

---

98   Use with Chapter 8, Lesson 2

© Pearson Education, Inc. 3

Name_____

PROBLEM-SOLVING STRATEGY   P 8-3

Act It Out

Solve each problem by acting it out. Write the answer in a complete sentence.

Kate built the 3 houses below with her building blocks. How many blocks did she use for each house?

1.   Kate used 6 blocks.

2.   Kate used 9 blocks.

3.   Kate used 12 blocks.

Jamie and Peter are playing a rhythm game. Every time Jamie claps his hands, Peter stomps his feet twice.

4. After Jamie has clapped his hands 8 times, how many times has Peter stomped his feet?

Peter stomped his feet 16 times.

5. If Peter stomps his feet 12 times, how many times does Jamie clap his hands?

Jamie claps his hands 6 times.

6. If pencils were sold 4 to a pack, how many would be in 6 packs?

There would be 24 pencils in 6 packs.

7. **Decision Making** You are going to buy twice as many pencils as someone who has 8 pencils. How many packs of pencils will you buy?

I will buy 4 packs of pencils.

© Pearson Education, Inc. 3

Use with Lesson 8-3.   **99**

Name_____

PROBLEM-SOLVING STRATEGY   R 8-3

Act It Out

Bricks Jacob wants to know how many bricks there are in the stack, and he knows the stack is completely filled. How many bricks are in the stack?

Read and Understand

Step 1: What do you know? The bottom layer of bricks is 3 bricks wide and 3 bricks long. The middle layer of bricks is 2 bricks wide and 2 bricks long. There is one brick on the top.

Step 2: What are you trying to find? The total number of bricks in the stack

Plan and Solve

Step 3: What strategy will you use?   **Strategy:** Act it out

Bottom: 9   Middle: 4   Top: 1

$9 + 4 + 1 = 14$ Answer: There are a total of 14 bricks in the stack.

Look Back and Check

Step 4: Is your answer reasonable? Yes. The bottom layer has 9, the middle layer has 4, and the top layer has 1 brick.

1. When the wall has been built up to the fifth layer, how many cylinder-shaped blocks will have been used?

7 cylinder-shaped blocks

© Pearson Education, Inc. 3

Use with Lesson 8-3.   **99**

Name_____

Town Square   E 8-3
                               DECISION MAKING

In the Geotown Square, there are several shops and entertainment areas. The signs on the buildings show the prices of items you can purchase and the entertainment you can choose. For each exercise, write how you would spend your money and tell how much money you have left. Make sure you do not spend more than you have!

Sample answers for 1–4.

1. You have one $5 bill, three $1 bills, 6 quarters, 3 dimes.

Play 12 video games; $0.80 left

2. You have one $10 bill, 4 nickels, and 7 pennies.

Buy 2 hardcover books and a sketch pad; $1.47 left

3. You have two $5 bills, two $1 bills, 3 quarters, 1 dime, and 3 nickels.

See 1 movie and play 10 video games; $1.50 left

4. You have fifteen $1 bills, 16 quarters, and 10 dimes.

Buy a box of crayons, a sketch pad, and a paint set; $16.55 left

© Pearson Education, Inc. 3

Use with Lesson 8-3.   **99**

Name_____

PROBLEM-SOLVING STRATEGY   PS 8-3

Act It Out

Gifts A gift store had a special sale. If you bought 3 gifts, you would get 1 for free. If Sarah bought 9 gifts, how many gifts did she get for free?

Read and Understand

1. How many gifts do you have to buy to get 1 for free?   **3 gifts**

2. How many gifts did Sarah buy?   **9 gifts**

3. What are you trying to find?

How many gifts Sarah got for free

Plan and Solve

4. What strategy will you use?   **Act it out**
   Sample answer:
5. What objects do you need to act it out?   **Counters**

6. Solve the problem, and write your answer in a complete sentence.

Sarah got 3 gifts for free.

Look Back and Check

7. Is your answer reasonable?

Yes. 9 divided by 3 is 3, so it checks.

Solve Another Problem

8. Billy plays baseball. For every 5 hits he gets he strikes out 1 time. If Billy strikes out 5 times, how many hits does he get?   **25 hits**

© Pearson Education, Inc. 3

Use with Lesson 8-3.   **99**

Use with Chapter 8, Lesson 3   **99**

Practice

Lines and Line Segments   P 8-4

Write the name for each.

1. **Line**

2. **Ray**

3. **Intersecting lines**

4. Draw a set of parallel lines.

Use the map. Tell if the trails are parallel or intersecting.

Treetop Trail
Nature Center
Wildflower Trail
Sand Dune Trail

5. Treetop and Sand Dune
   Parallel

6. Sand Dune and Wildflower
   Intersecting

Test Prep

7. How many times does a pair of intersecting lines cross?

   A. Never   B. 1 time   C. 2 times   D. 3 times

8. **Writing in Math** Explain how you can tell the difference between a ray and a line.

   Sample answer: Rays are endless in one direction. Lines are endless in both.

100   Use with Lesson 8-4.

© Pearson Education, Inc. 3

Reteaching

Lines and Line Segments   R 8-4

You can find lines and parts of lines in shapes and objects.

| A **line** is a set of points that is endless in both directions. Lines have arrows on each end. | A **line segment** is part of a line. It has an endpoint on each end. | A **ray** is part of a line that is endless in one direction. A ray has an endpoint on one end and an arrow on the other. | **Parallel lines** never cross. They also stay the same distance apart from one another. | **Intersecting lines** cross at one point. Any lines that are not parallel are intersecting. |

Write the name for each.

1. **Parallel lines**   2. **Ray**

3. **Intersecting lines**   4. **Line segment**

5. **Intersecting lines**   6. **Line**

7. **Reasoning** Is it possible for two rays to be parallel to each other?   **Yes**

100   Use with Lesson 8-4.

© Pearson Education, Inc. 3

Enrichment

Follow the Points   E 8-4
                                         VISUAL THINKING

B
1 2 3 4 5
C
6 7 8 9 10   F
      G
11 12 13 14 15
D
16 17 18 19 20   A
E
21 22 23 24 25

Sample answers for 1, 7, and 8.

1. Draw a line passing through point 25. Label it A.

2. Draw a ray from point 1 to point 2. Label it B.

3. Draw line segments from point 6 to point 10 (Label this one C) and from point 16 to point 20 (Label this one D).

4. What is the name for a pair of line segments such as C and D?
   Parallel line segments

5. Draw a line segment from point 21 to point 13. Label it E.

6. What is the name for a pair of line segments such as D and E?
   Intersecting line segments

7. Draw a line that will never intersect E. Label it F.

8. Draw a line segment that intersects both D and F at exactly one point. Label it G.

100   Use with Lesson 8-4.

© Pearson Education, Inc. 3

Problem Solving

Lines and Line Segments   PS 8-4

1. What is an exact position called?
   A point

2. What is a set of points that is endless in both directions called?
   A line

3. What is part of a line called?
   A line segment

4. What is part of a line that is endless in one direction called?
   A ray

5. How could you change a line into a line segment?
   By adding two points that mark the ends of the line segment

6. How could you change a line segment into a ray?
   By adding an arrow to one end

7. Are the lines shown intersecting lines or parallel lines?
   Intersecting lines

8. **Writing in Math** Draw two rays that are not parallel to each other and never intersect. Explain.
   Sample answer: If the rays are pointing away from each other, they will never intersect.

100   Use with Lesson 8-4.

© Pearson Education, Inc. 3

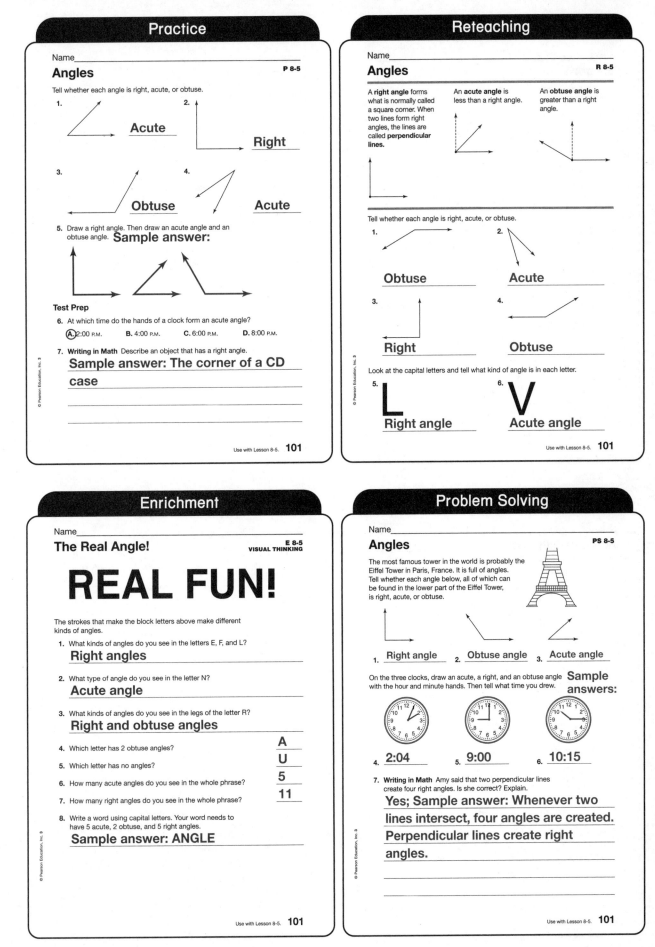

Practice

Name_____

Angles   P 8-5

Tell whether each angle is right, acute, or obtuse.

1. **Acute**

2. **Right**

3. **Obtuse**

4. **Acute**

5. Draw a right angle. Then draw an acute angle and an obtuse angle. **Sample answer:**

Test Prep

6. At which time do the hands of a clock form an acute angle?
    A. 2:00 P.M.   **B.** 4:00 P.M.   **C.** 6:00 P.M.   **D.** 8:00 P.M.

7. **Writing in Math** Describe an object that has a right angle.
    Sample answer: The corner of a CD case

© Pearson Education, Inc. 3

Use with Lesson 8-5. **101**

Reteaching

Name_____

Angles   R 8-5

A **right angle** forms what is normally called a square corner. When two lines form right angles, the lines are called **perpendicular lines.**

An **acute angle** is less than a right angle.

An **obtuse angle** is greater than a right angle.

Tell whether each angle is right, acute, or obtuse.

1. **Obtuse**

2. **Acute**

3. **Right**

4. **Obtuse**

Look at the capital letters and tell what kind of angle is in each letter.

5. **L** **Right angle**

6. **V** **Acute angle**

© Pearson Education, Inc. 3

Use with Lesson 8-5. **101**

Enrichment

Name_____

The Real Angle!   E 8-5
                                           VISUAL THINKING

REAL FUN!

The strokes that make the block letters above make different kinds of angles.

1. What kinds of angles do you see in the letters E, F, and L?
    Right angles

2. What type of angle do you see in the letter N?
    Acute angle

3. What kinds of angles do you see in the legs of the letter R?
    Right and obtuse angles

4. Which letter has 2 obtuse angles?   **A**

5. Which letter has no angles?   **U**

6. How many acute angles do you see in the whole phrase? **5**

7. How many right angles do you see in the whole phrase? **11**

8. Write a word using capital letters. Your word needs to have 5 acute, 2 obtuse, and 5 right angles.
    Sample answer: ANGLE

© Pearson Education, Inc. 3

Use with Lesson 8-5. **101**

Problem Solving

Name_____

Angles   PS 8-5

The most famous tower in the world is probably the Eiffel Tower in Paris, France. It is full of angles. Tell whether each angle below, all of which can be found in the lower part of the Eiffel Tower, is right, acute, or obtuse.

1. **Right angle**
2. **Obtuse angle**
3. **Acute angle**

On the three clocks, draw an acute, a right, and an obtuse angle with the hour and minute hands. Then tell what time you drew. **Sample answers:**

4. **2:04**
5. **9:00**
6. **10:15**

7. **Writing in Math** Amy said that two perpendicular lines create four right angles. Is she correct? Explain.
    Yes; Sample answer: Whenever two lines intersect, four angles are created. Perpendicular lines create right angles.

© Pearson Education, Inc. 3

Use with Lesson 8-5. **101**

© Pearson Education, Inc. 3

Name

Polygons

P 8-6

Is each figure below a polygon? If it is a polygon, give its name.
If not, explain why.

1.

No; The figure is not closed.

2.

Yes; pentagon

Which polygon has

3. 6 sides?   **Hexagon**

4. 8 sides?   **Octagon**

5. Reasoning Explain how you know the next polygon in the pattern.

Square; Sample answer: There is always a square after the two triangles.

Test Prep

6. Which is NOT a polygon?

   A. Triangle   **B.** Pentagon   **C.** Circle   **D.** Hexagon

7. Writing in Math Explain why the shape of a football is not a polygon.

Sample answer: The shape of a football has no straight lines.

© Pearson Education, Inc. 3

Name

Polygons

R 8-6

Polygons are closed figures that are made up of straight line segments.

Not a polygon
Not a closed figure

Not a polygon
Not all straight lines

Polygon
Closed figure
All straight lines

The number of sides in a polygon gives the polygon its name.

Triangle	Quadrilateral	Pentagon	Hexagon	Octagon
3 sides	4 sides	5 sides	6 sides	8 sides

Is each figure a polygon? If it is a polygon, give its name. If not, explain why.

1.

2.

Not a polygon; one side is curved, not straight.

Quadrilateral

3.

4.

Hexagon

Not a polygon; not a closed figure

© Pearson Education, Inc. 3

Name

Alphabet Polygons

E 8-6
VISUAL THINKING

A	B	C	D	E	F	G	H	I
J	K	L	M	N	O	P	Q	R
S	T	U	V	W	X	Y	Z	

Sample answers for 1–5.

Use the letters in the alphabet to answer the questions below.
Use each letter only one time.

1. You can make polygons of some of the letters by drawing just one more line segment. Which letters are they?

E, L, V, A

2. With which letters can you make exactly 2 polygons by drawing 2 more line segments?

F, H, K, M, N, T, W, Z

3. By drawing 3 more line segments, with what letters can you make 3 polygons?

Y, M, W, X

4. Can you make 4 polygons by drawing 4 line segments with a letter? If yes, which letter?

Yes; I, X

5. Why can you not make polygons with the remaining letters?

They all have curved lines.

Name

Polygons

PS 8-6

You can draw lines connecting the angles of a polygon to make new polygons. Follow the directions for 1–5.

Sample answers:

1. Draw a line connecting two angles of the hexagon to make a triangle and a pentagon.

2. Draw a line connecting two angles of the hexagon to make two quadrilaterals.

3. Draw two lines connecting angles of the hexagon to make a quadrilateral and two triangles.

4. Draw two lines connecting angles of the hexagon to make four quadrilaterals.

5. Draw three lines connecting angles of the hexagon to make six triangles.

6. Writing in Math A hexagon has one more side than a pentagon. Does that mean you could not draw a hexagon inside a pentagon? Explain.

No; Sample answer: You can draw a hexagon inside a pentagon as long as it is smaller in size.

© Pearson Education, Inc. 3

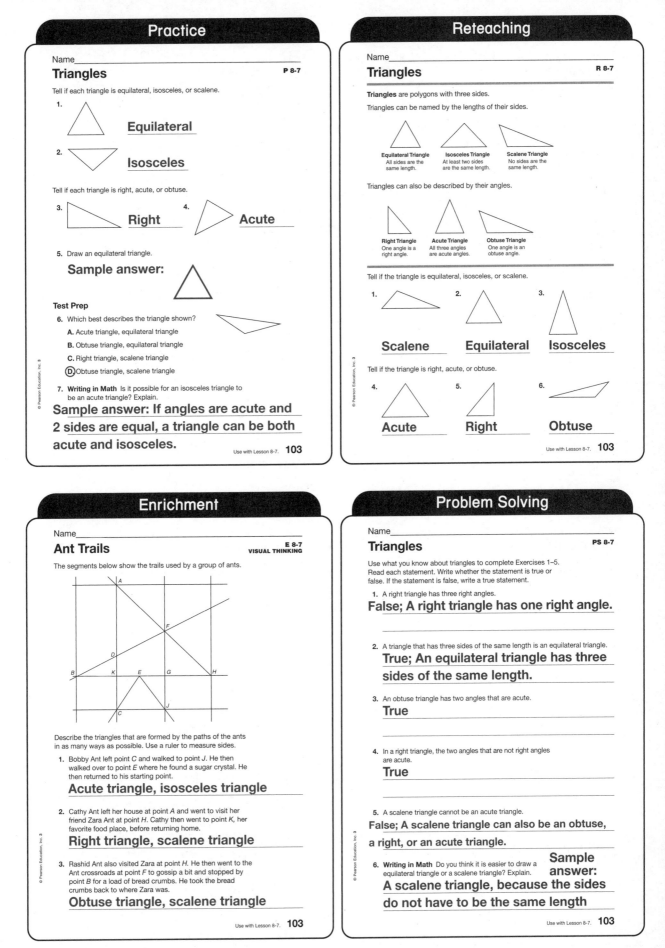

Practice

Name_____

Triangles   P 8-7

Tell if each triangle is equilateral, isosceles, or scalene.

1. **Equilateral**

2. **Isosceles**

Tell if each triangle is right, acute, or obtuse.

3. **Right**   4. **Acute**

5. Draw an equilateral triangle.

Sample answer:

Test Prep

6. Which best describes the triangle shown?
    A. Acute triangle, equilateral triangle
    B. Obtuse triangle, equilateral triangle
    C. Right triangle, scalene triangle
    D. Obtuse triangle, scalene triangle

7. **Writing in Math** Is it possible for an isosceles triangle to be an acute triangle? Explain.

Sample answer: If angles are acute and 2 sides are equal, a triangle can be both acute and isosceles.

Use with Lesson 8-7. **103**

© Pearson Education, Inc. 3

Reteaching

Name_____

Triangles   R 8-7

Triangles are polygons with three sides.

Triangles can be named by the lengths of their sides.

Equilateral Triangle   **Isosceles Triangle**   **Scalene Triangle**
All sides are the   At least two sides   No sides are the
same length.   are the same length.   same length.

Triangles can also be described by their angles.

Right Triangle   **Acute Triangle**   **Obtuse Triangle**
One angle is a   All three angles   One angle is an
right angle.   are acute angles.   obtuse angle.

Tell if the triangle is equilateral, isosceles, or scalene.

1. **Scalene**   2. **Equilateral**   3. **Isosceles**

Tell if the triangle is right, acute, or obtuse.

4. **Acute**   5. **Right**   6. **Obtuse**

Use with Lesson 8-7. **103**

© Pearson Education, Inc. 3

Enrichment

Name_____

Ant Trails   E 8-7
                                  VISUAL THINKING

The segments below show the trails used by a group of ants.

Describe the triangles that are formed by the paths of the ants in as many ways as possible. Use a ruler to measure sides.

1. Bobby Ant left point C and walked to point J. He then walked over to point E where he found a sugar crystal. He then returned to his starting point.

    Acute triangle, isosceles triangle

2. Cathy Ant left her house at point A and went to visit her friend Zara Ant at point H. Cathy then went to point K, her favorite food place, before returning home.

    Right triangle, scalene triangle

3. Rashid Ant also visited Zara at point H. He then went to the Ant crossroads at point F to gossip a bit and stopped by point B for a load of bread crumbs. He took the bread crumbs back to where Zara was.

    Obtuse triangle, scalene triangle

Use with Lesson 8-7. **103**

© Pearson Education, Inc. 3

Problem Solving

Name_____

Triangles   PS 8-7

Use what you know about triangles to complete Exercises 1–5. Read each statement. Write whether the statement is true or false. If the statement is false, write a true statement.

1. A right triangle has three right angles.

    False; A right triangle has one right angle.

2. A triangle that has three sides of the same length is an equilateral triangle.

    True; An equilateral triangle has three sides of the same length.

3. An obtuse triangle has two angles that are acute.

    True

4. In a right triangle, the two angles that are not right angles are acute.

    True

5. A scalene triangle cannot be an acute triangle.

    False; A scalene triangle can also be an obtuse, a right, or an acute triangle.

6. **Writing in Math** Do you think it is easier to draw a equilateral triangle or a scalene triangle? Explain.

    Sample answer: A scalene triangle, because the sides do not have to be the same length

Use with Lesson 8-7. **103**

© Pearson Education, Inc. 3

Name

Quadrilaterals

P 8-8

Write the name of each quadrilateral.

1. Rectangle

2. Parallelogram

3. Square

4. Reasoning Explain why a triangle is not a quadrilateral.

Sample answer: Quadrilaterals have 4 sides and triangles only have 3.

5. Draw a quadrilateral with four equal sides, but no right angles. What is its name?

Rhombus

Test Prep

6. Which of the following correctly names the figure?

A. Rhombus   B. Trapezoid

C. Parallelogram   D. Rectangle

7. Writing in Math If you turn a rhombus upside down, will it still be a rhombus? Explain.

Yes; Sample answer: Turning a rhombus does not change its shape or sides.

104 Use with Lesson 8-8.

© Pearson Education, Inc. 3

Name

Quadrilaterals

R 8-8

Special quadrilaterals can be separated into groups. The chart shows how they are defined.

Write the name of each quadrilateral.

1. Trapezoid

2. Rectangle

3. Parallelogram

4. Square

5. Rhombus

6. Trapezoid

104 Use with Lesson 8-8.

© Pearson Education, Inc. 3

Name

Four-sided Fun

E 8-8
VISUAL THINKING

Write the names of the two quadrilaterals that make up each figure below. Then draw the two quadrilaterals.

1. rectangle / square

2. square / rhombus

3. parallelogram / rectangle

Sample answer:

4. rectangle / rectangle

5. trapezoid / parallelogram

104 Use with Lesson 8-8.

© Pearson Education, Inc. 3

Name

Quadrilaterals

PS 8-8

Write the name of the quadrilateral that is being described. Be careful! Some may have more than one correct answer. If this is so, write all correct answers.

1. I have four sides and all of my sides have the same length. What am I?

Square or rhombus

2. I have four sides. My opposite sides are parallel and equal in length. Each angle is a right angle. What am I?

Rectangle or square

3. I have four sides. My opposite sides are parallel and equal in length. My four sides are not all equal in length. What am I?

Rectangle or parallelogram

4. I have only one pair of parallel sides. What am I?

Trapezoid

5. You can make my shape by using exactly two triangles. What am I?

Rectangle, square, parallelogram, rhombus, or trapezoid

6. Writing in Math Amanda said that a square and a rhombus are the same, except that a square has all right angles. Is she correct? Explain.

Yes; Both a square and a rhombus have opposite sides that are parallel and all the sides are the same length.

104 Use with Lesson 8-8.

© Pearson Education, Inc. 3

© Pearson Education, Inc. 3

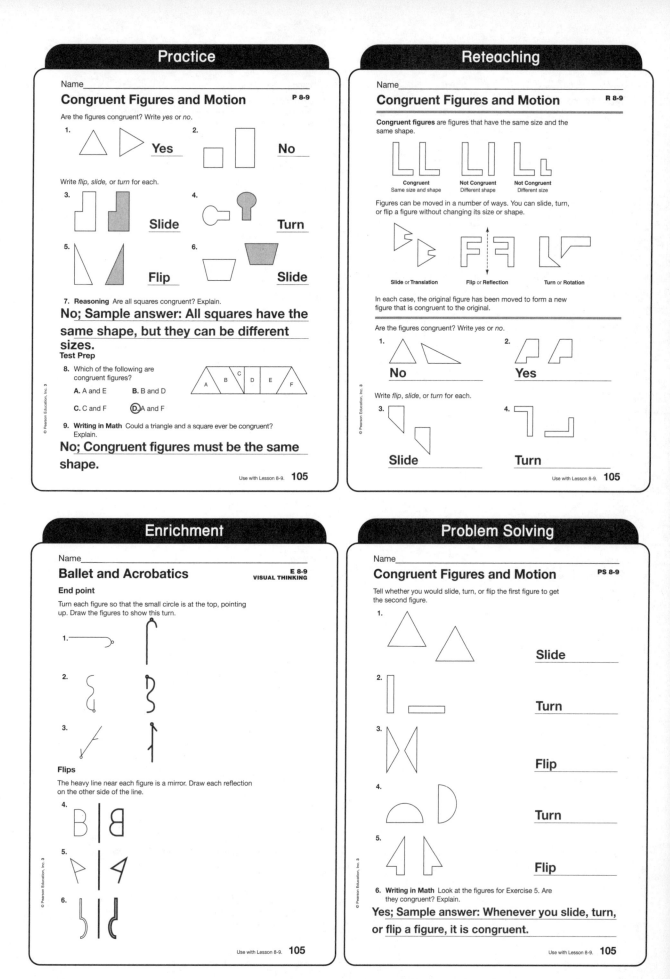

Practice

Name_____

Congruent Figures and Motion
P 8-9

Are the figures congruent? Write *yes* or *no*.

1. **Yes**

2. **No**

Write *flip*, *slide*, or *turn* for each.

3. **Slide**

4. **Turn**

5. **Flip**

6. **Slide**

7. **Reasoning** Are all squares congruent? Explain.

No; Sample answer: All squares have the same shape, but they can be different sizes.

Test Prep

8. Which of the following are congruent figures?

   A. A and E   **B.** B and D

   C. C and F   **(D.)** A and F

9. **Writing in Math** Could a triangle and a square ever be congruent? Explain.

No; Congruent figures must be the same shape.

Use with Lesson 8-9. **105**

Reteaching

Name_____

Congruent Figures and Motion
R 8-9

Congruent figures are figures that have the same size and the same shape.

Congruent
Same size and shape

Not Congruent
Different shape

Not Congruent
Different size

Figures can be moved in a number of ways. You can slide, turn, or flip a figure without changing its size or shape.

Slide or **Translation**

Flip or **Reflection**

Turn or **Rotation**

In each case, the original figure has been moved to form a new figure that is congruent to the original.

Are the figures congruent? Write *yes* or *no*.

1. **No**

2. **Yes**

Write *flip*, *slide*, or *turn* for each.

3. **Slide**

4. **Turn**

Use with Lesson 8-9. **105**

Enrichment

Name_____

Ballet and Acrobatics
E 8-9
VISUAL THINKING

End point

Turn each figure so that the small circle is at the top, pointing up. Draw the figures to show this turn.

1.

2.

3.

Flips

The heavy line near each figure is a mirror. Draw each reflection on the other side of the line.

4.

5.

6.

Use with Lesson 8-9. **105**

Problem Solving

Name_____

Congruent Figures and Motion
PS 8-9

Tell whether you would slide, turn, or flip the first figure to get the second figure.

1. **Slide**

2. **Turn**

3. **Flip**

4. **Turn**

5. **Flip**

6. **Writing in Math** Look at the figures for Exercise 5. Are they congruent? Explain.

Yes; Sample answer: Whenever you slide, turn, or flip a figure, it is congruent.

Use with Lesson 8-9. **105**

Name_____

Symmetry

P 8-10

Tell whether each figure is symmetric. Write *yes* or *no*.

1. **No**

2. **Yes**

3. **No**

4. **Yes**

5. **Reasoning** Does the triangle in Exercise 2 have more than 1 line of symmetry? How can you tell?

Yes; Sample answer: It can be cut in half equally from each of its 3 corners.

6. Tell how many lines of symmetry the figure at the right has. Draw the lines of symmetry.

4 lines of symmetry

Test Prep

7. Which figure has the most lines of symmetry?

A. Square B. Circle C. Triangle D. Hexagon

8. **Writing in Math** Can a chair be symmetric? Explain.

Sample answer: Yes; A chair can be symmetric from the front.

106 Use with Lesson 8-10.

© Pearson Education, Inc. 3

Name_____

Symmetry

R 8-10

Figures are **symmetric** if you can divide them in half and both halves are congruent.

The figure is symmetric. The halves match.

The figure is not symmetric. The halves do not match.

The figure is symmetric. The halves match.

A line which divides a symmetric figure is called a **line of symmetry.** Some figures have more than one line of symmetry.

The figure has two lines of symmetry.

The figure has one line of symmetry.

The figure has three lines of symmetry.

Tell whether each figure is symmetric. Write *yes* or *no*.

1. **No**

2. **Yes**

3. **No**

4. **Yes**

5. **Yes**

6. **Yes**

106 Use with Lesson 8-10.

© Pearson Education, Inc. 3

Name_____

Playing Around with Symmetry

E 8-10
NUMBER SENSE

Five students are playing a game with a spinner. When the spinner lands on a shape, the player marks his or her score card with that shape. There is also a "lose 1 turn" space on the spinner. The points earned depend on the shape and the symmetry of the shape. See the point chart for the number of points for each shape. The results of the game for each player are shown on the score cards.

Shapes Point Chart

Triangle—3 points
Pentagon—2 points
Trapezoid—1 point

*Double the points for symmetrical figures.

1. Who had the greatest number of shapes?

Leigh

2. Which player scored the most points?

Sylvia

3. Did the person with the fewest shapes have the least score?

No

4. Which player had the most symmetrical shapes?

Sylvia

5. Which player had the fewest shapes?

Marisa

6. Who had the least score?

Kathy

Kathy

Sylvia

Geno

Marisa

Leigh

106 Use with Lesson 8-10.

© Pearson Education, Inc. 3

Name_____

Symmetry

PS 8-10

1. Is the guitar symmetric? If it is, how many lines of symmetry does it have?

Yes; One line of symmetry

2. Is the baseball bat symmetric? If it is, how many lines of symmetry does it have?

Yes; One line of symmetry

3. Is the fork symmetric? If it is, how many lines of symmetry does it have?

Yes; One line of symmetry

4. Does a circle have more than one line of symmetry? Explain.

Yes; Any line drawn from one point through the center to a point opposite it is a line of symmetry.

5. **Writing in Math** Which numeral from 5 to 9 is symmetric? Explain your answer.

8 has two lines of symmetry, one horizontal line and one vertical line through the number.

106 Use with Lesson 8-10.

© Pearson Education, Inc. 3

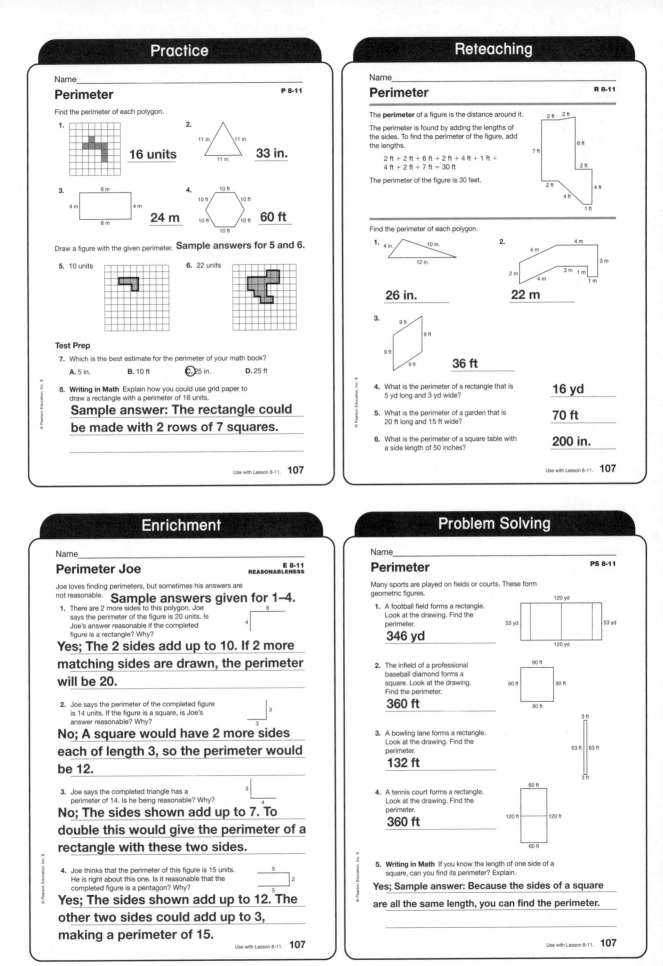

Name_____

Perimeter   P 8-11

Find the perimeter of each polygon.

1.
16 units

2.
11 in.   11 in.
11 in.
33 in.

3.
8 m
4 m   4 m
8 m
24 m

4.
10 ft   10 ft
10 ft   10 ft
10 ft   10 ft
60 ft

Draw a figure with the given perimeter. **Sample answers for 5 and 6.**

5. 10 units

6. 22 units

Test Prep

7. Which is the best estimate for the perimeter of your math book?

   A. 5 in.   **B.** 10 ft   **C.** 25 in.   **D.** 25 ft

8. **Writing in Math** Explain how you could use grid paper to draw a rectangle with a perimeter of 18 units.

Sample answer: The rectangle could be made with 2 rows of 7 squares.

© Pearson Education, Inc. 3

Name_____

Perimeter   R 8-11

The **perimeter** of a figure is the distance around it.

The perimeter is found by adding the lengths of the sides. To find the perimeter of the figure, add the lengths.

2 ft + 2 ft + 6 ft + 2 ft + 4 ft + 1 ft + 4 ft + 2 ft + 7 ft = 30 ft

The perimeter of the figure is 30 feet.

2 ft   2 ft
7 ft   6 ft
2 ft
2 ft   4 ft
4 ft
1 ft

Find the perimeter of each polygon.

1.
4 in.   10 in.
12 in.
26 in.

2.
4 m
4 m   3 m
2 m   4 m   3 m 1 m
1 m
22 m

3.
9 ft
9 ft
9 ft
9 ft
36 ft

4. What is the perimeter of a rectangle that is 5 yd long and 3 yd wide?

16 yd

5. What is the perimeter of a garden that is 20 ft long and 15 ft wide?

70 ft

6. What is the perimeter of a square table with a side length of 50 inches?

200 in.

© Pearson Education, Inc. 3

Name_____

Perimeter Joe   E 8-11
                                   REASONABLENESS

Joe loves finding perimeters, but sometimes his answers are not reasonable. **Sample answers given for 1–4.**

1. There are 2 more sides to this polygon. Joe says the perimeter of the figure is 20 units. Is Joe's answer reasonable if the completed figure is a rectangle? Why?

                                      6
                                 4

Yes; The 2 sides add up to 10. If 2 more matching sides are drawn, the perimeter will be 20.

2. Joe says the perimeter of the completed figure is 14 units. If the figure is a square, is Joe's answer reasonable? Why?

                                    3
                           3

No; A square would have 2 more sides each of length 3, so the perimeter would be 12.

3. Joe says the completed triangle has a perimeter of 14. Is he being reasonable? Why?

                                    3
                             4

No; The sides shown add up to 7. To double this would give the perimeter of a rectangle with these two sides.

4. Joe thinks that the perimeter of this figure is 15 units. He is right about this one. Is it reasonable that the completed figure is a pentagon? Why?

                                    5
                             2
                             5

Yes; The sides shown add up to 12. The other two sides could add up to 3, making a perimeter of 15.

© Pearson Education, Inc. 3

Name_____

Perimeter   PS 8-11

Many sports are played on fields or courts. These form geometric figures.

1. A football field forms a rectangle. Look at the drawing. Find the perimeter.

                                120 yd
                53 yd   53 yd
                                  120 yd

346 yd

2. The infield of a professional baseball diamond forms a square. Look at the drawing. Find the perimeter.

                                90 ft
               90 ft   90 ft
                              90 ft

360 ft

3. A bowling lane forms a rectangle. Look at the drawing. Find the perimeter.

                                3 ft
               63 ft 63 ft
                                3 ft

132 ft

4. A tennis court forms a rectangle. Look at the drawing. Find the perimeter.

                                60 ft
              120 ft   120 ft
                              60 ft

360 ft

5. **Writing in Math** If you know the length of one side of a square, can you find its perimeter? Explain.

Yes; Sample answer: Because the sides of a square are all the same length, you can find the perimeter.

© Pearson Education, Inc. 3

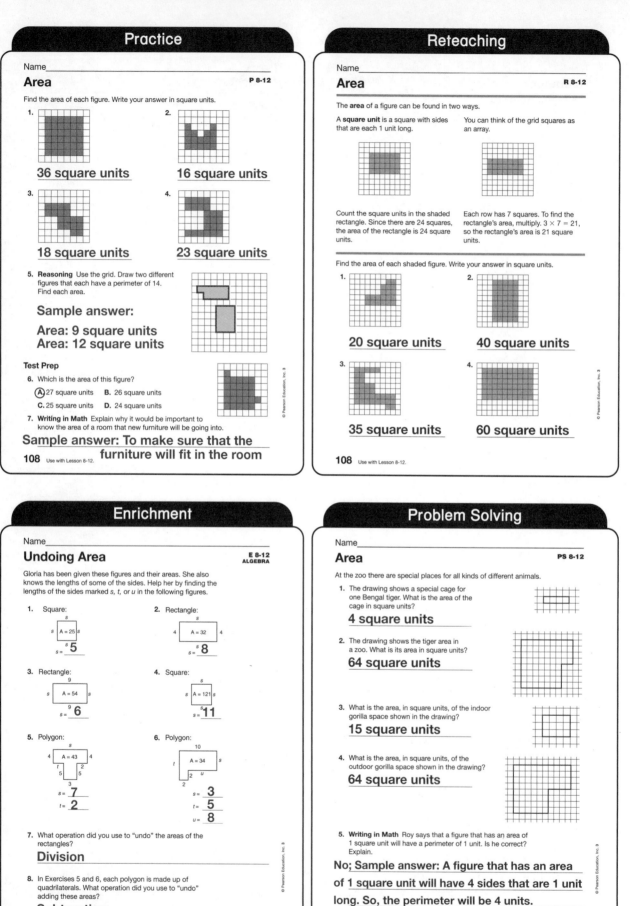

Practice

Name_____

Area
P 8-12

Find the area of each figure. Write your answer in square units.

1.

36 square units

2.

16 square units

3.

18 square units

4.

23 square units

5. **Reasoning** Use the grid. Draw two different figures that each have a perimeter of 14. Find each area.

Sample answer:

Area: 9 square units
Area: 12 square units

Test Prep

6. Which is the area of this figure?

(A) 27 square units   **B.** 26 square units

C. 25 square units   **D.** 24 square units

7. **Writing in Math** Explain why it would be important to know the area of a room that new furniture will be going into.

Sample answer: To make sure that the furniture will fit in the room

---

Reteaching

Name_____

Area
R 8-12

The **area** of a figure can be found in two ways.

A **square unit** is a square with sides that are each 1 unit long.

You can think of the grid squares as an array.

Count the square units in the shaded rectangle. Since there are 24 squares, the area of the rectangle is 24 square units.

Each row has 7 squares. To find the rectangle's area, multiply. $3 \times 7 = 21$, so the rectangle's area is 21 square units.

Find the area of each shaded figure. Write your answer in square units.

1.

20 square units

2.

40 square units

3.

35 square units

4.

60 square units

Enrichment

Name_____

Undoing Area
E 8-12
ALGEBRA

Gloria has been given these figures and their areas. She also knows the lengths of some of the sides. Help her by finding the lengths of the sides marked s, t, or u in the following figures.

1. Square:

s | A = 25 | s
$s =$ **5**

2. Rectangle:

4 | A = 32 | 4
$s =$ **8**

3. Rectangle:

9
s | A = 54 | s
$s =$ **6**

4. Square:

s
s | A = 121 | s
$s =$ **11**

5. Polygon:

s
4 | A = 43 | 4
t 2
5   5
3
$s =$ **7**
$t =$ **2**

6. Polygon:

10
| A = 34 | s
t
u
2
$s =$ **3**
$t =$ **5**
$u =$ **8**

7. What operation did you use to "undo" the areas of the rectangles?

Division

8. In Exercises 5 and 6, each polygon is made up of quadrilaterals. What operation did you use to "undo" adding these areas?

Subtraction

Problem Solving

Name_____

Area
PS 8-12

At the zoo there are special places for all kinds of different animals.

1. The drawing shows a special cage for one Bengal tiger. What is the area of the cage in square units?

4 square units

2. The drawing shows the tiger area in a zoo. What is its area in square units?

64 square units

3. What is the area, in square units, of the indoor gorilla space shown in the drawing?

15 square units

4. What is the area, in square units, of the outdoor gorilla space shown in the drawing?

64 square units

5. **Writing in Math** Roy says that a figure that has an area of 1 square unit will have a perimeter of 1 unit. Is he correct? Explain.

No; Sample answer: A figure that has an area of 1 square unit will have 4 sides that are 1 unit long. So, the perimeter will be 4 units.

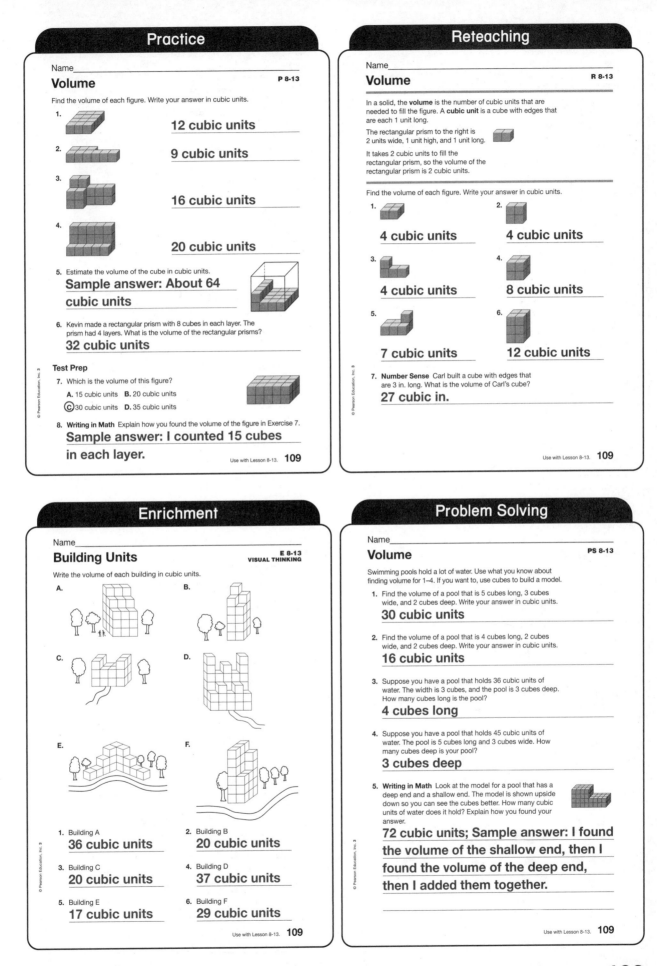

Practice

Name_____

Volume

P 8-13

Find the volume of each figure. Write your answer in cubic units.

1. **12 cubic units**

2. **9 cubic units**

3. **16 cubic units**

4. **20 cubic units**

5. Estimate the volume of the cube in cubic units.
Sample answer: About 64 cubic units

6. Kevin made a rectangular prism with 8 cubes in each layer. The prism had 4 layers. What is the volume of the rectangular prisms?
32 cubic units

Test Prep

7. Which is the volume of this figure?
   A. 15 cubic units   B. 20 cubic units
   C. 30 cubic units   D. 35 cubic units

8. **Writing in Math** Explain how you found the volume of the figure in Exercise 7.
Sample answer: I counted 15 cubes in each layer.

Use with Lesson 8-13. **109**

Reteaching

Name_____

Volume

R 8-13

In a solid, the **volume** is the number of cubic units that are needed to fill the figure. A **cubic unit** is a cube with edges that are each 1 unit long.

The rectangular prism to the right is 2 units wide, 1 unit high, and 1 unit long.

It takes 2 cubic units to fill the rectangular prism, so the volume of the rectangular prism is 2 cubic units.

Find the volume of each figure. Write your answer in cubic units.

1. **4 cubic units**
2. **4 cubic units**
3. **4 cubic units**
4. **8 cubic units**
5. **7 cubic units**
6. **12 cubic units**

7. **Number Sense** Carl built a cube with edges that are 3 in. long. What is the volume of Carl's cube?
27 cubic in.

Use with Lesson 8-13. **109**

Enrichment

Name_____

Building Units

E 8-13
VISUAL THINKING

Write the volume of each building in cubic units.

A.

B.

C.

D.

E.

F.

1. Building A **36 cubic units**
2. Building B **20 cubic units**
3. Building C **20 cubic units**
4. Building D **37 cubic units**
5. Building E **17 cubic units**
6. Building F **29 cubic units**

Use with Lesson 8-13. **109**

Problem Solving

Name_____

Volume

PS 8-13

Swimming pools hold a lot of water. Use what you know about finding volume for 1–4. If you want to, use cubes to build a model.

1. Find the volume of a pool that is 5 cubes long, 3 cubes wide, and 2 cubes deep. Write your answer in cubic units.
30 cubic units

2. Find the volume of a pool that is 4 cubes long, 2 cubes wide, and 2 cubes deep. Write your answer in cubic units.
16 cubic units

3. Suppose you have a pool that holds 36 cubic units of water. The width is 3 cubes, and the pool is 3 cubes deep. How many cubes long is the pool?
4 cubes long

4. Suppose you have a pool that holds 45 cubic units of water. The pool is 5 cubes long and 3 cubes wide. How many cubes deep is your pool?
3 cubes deep

5. **Writing in Math** Look at the model for a pool that has a deep end and a shallow end. The model is shown upside down so you can see the cubes better. How many cubic units of water does it hold? Explain how you found your answer.

72 cubic units; Sample answer: I found the volume of the shallow end, then I found the volume of the deep end, then I added them together.

Use with Lesson 8-13. **109**

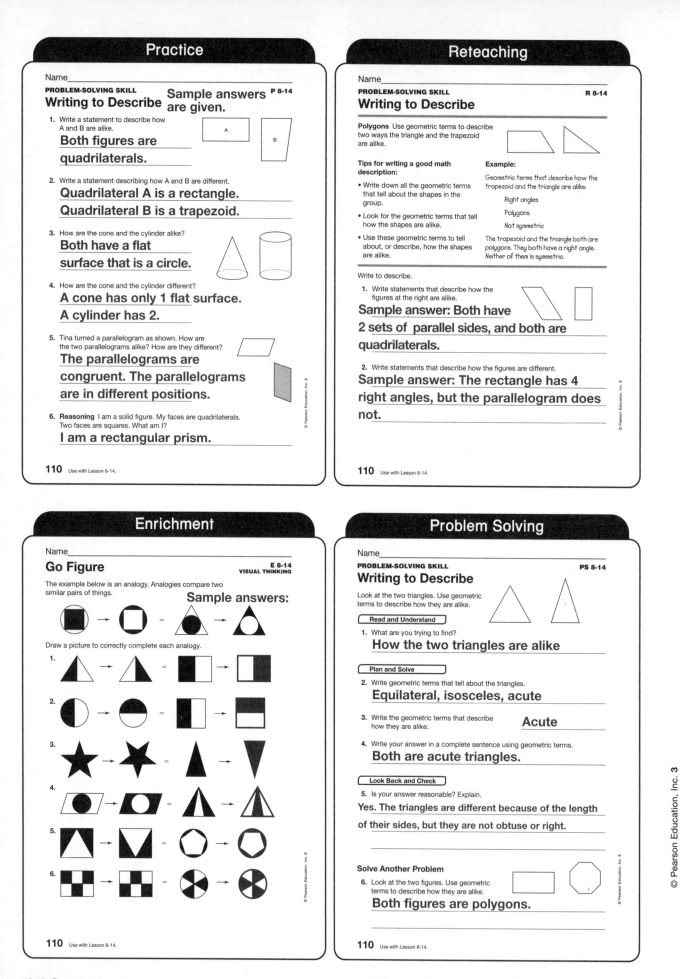

Practice

PROBLEM-SOLVING SKILL Sample answers P 8-14
Writing to Describe are given.

1. Write a statement to describe how A and B are alike.

Both figures are quadrilaterals.

2. Write a statement describing how A and B are different.

Quadrilateral A is a rectangle. Quadrilateral B is a trapezoid.

3. How are the cone and the cylinder alike?

Both have a flat surface that is a circle.

4. How are the cone and the cylinder different?

A cone has only 1 flat surface. A cylinder has 2.

5. Tina turned a parallelogram as shown. How are the two parallelograms alike? How are they different?

The parallelograms are congruent. The parallelograms are in different positions.

6. **Reasoning** I am a solid figure. My faces are quadrilaterals. Two faces are squares. What am I?

I am a rectangular prism.

110 Use with Lesson 8-14.

Reteaching

PROBLEM-SOLVING SKILL R 8-14
Writing to Describe

Polygons Use geometric terms to describe two ways the triangle and the trapezoid are alike.

Tips for writing a good math description:

• Write down all the geometric terms that tell about the shapes in the group.

• Look for the geometric terms that tell how the shapes are alike.

• Use these geometric terms to tell about, or describe, how the shapes are alike.

Example:

Geometric terms that describe how the trapezoid and the triangle are alike:

 Right angles
 Polygons
 Not symmetric

The trapezoid and the triangle both are polygons. They both have a right angle. Neither of them is symmetric.

Write to describe.

1. Write statements that describe how the figures at the right are alike.

Sample answer: Both have 2 sets of parallel sides, and both are quadrilaterals.

2. Write statements that describe how the figures are different.

Sample answer: The rectangle has 4 right angles, but the parallelogram does not.

110 Use with Lesson 8-14.

Enrichment

Go Figure E 8-14
VISUAL THINKING

The example below is an analogy. Analogies compare two similar pairs of things.

Sample answers:

Draw a picture to correctly complete each analogy.

1.
2.
3.
4.
5.
6.

110 Use with Lesson 8-14.

Problem Solving

PROBLEM-SOLVING SKILL PS 8-14
Writing to Describe

Look at the two triangles. Use geometric terms to describe how they are alike.

Read and Understand

1. What are you trying to find?

How the two triangles are alike

Plan and Solve

2. Write geometric terms that tell about the triangles.

Equilateral, isosceles, acute

3. Write the geometric terms that describe how they are alike.

Acute

4. Write your answer in a complete sentence using geometric terms.

Both are acute triangles.

Look Back and Check

5. Is your answer reasonable? Explain.

Yes. The triangles are different because of the length of their sides, but they are not obtuse or right.

Solve Another Problem

6. Look at the two figures. Use geometric terms to describe how they are alike.

Both figures are polygons.

110 Use with Lesson 8-14.

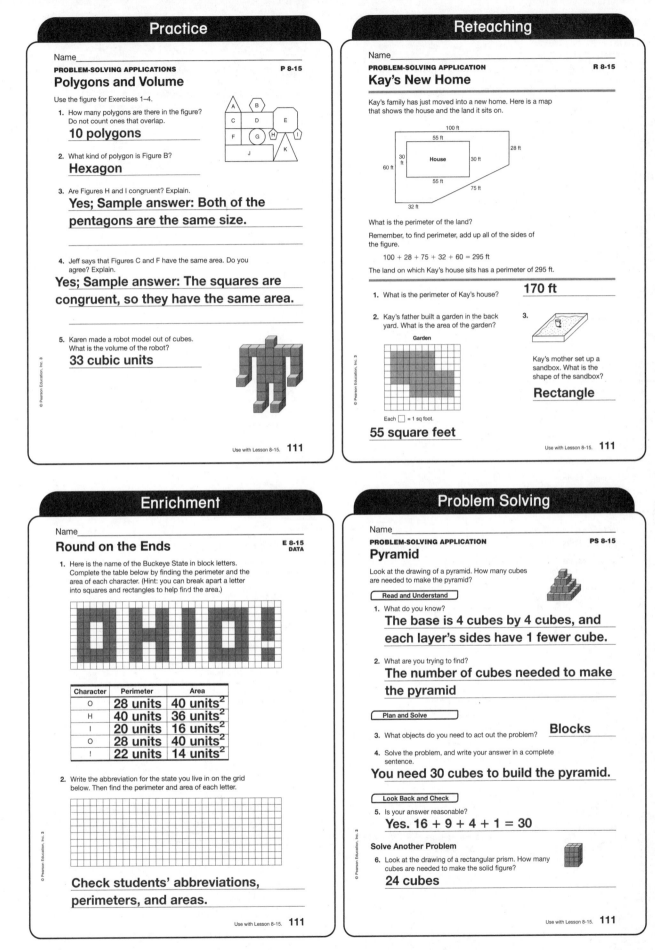

Practice

Name_____

PROBLEM-SOLVING APPLICATIONS   P 8-15

Polygons and Volume

Use the figure for Exercises 1–4.

1. How many polygons are there in the figure? Do not count ones that overlap.

10 polygons

2. What kind of polygon is Figure B?

Hexagon

3. Are Figures H and I congruent? Explain.

Yes; Sample answer: Both of the pentagons are the same size.

4. Jeff says that Figures C and F have the same area. Do you agree? Explain.

Yes; Sample answer: The squares are congruent, so they have the same area.

5. Karen made a robot model out of cubes. What is the volume of the robot?

33 cubic units

Use with Lesson 8-15. **111**

Reteaching

Name_____

PROBLEM-SOLVING APPLICATION   R 8-15

Kay's New Home

Kay's family has just moved into a new home. Here is a map that shows the house and the land it sits on.

What is the perimeter of the land?

Remember, to find perimeter, add up all of the sides of the figure.

100 + 28 + 75 + 32 + 60 = 295 ft

The land on which Kay's house sits has a perimeter of 295 ft.

1. What is the perimeter of Kay's house?   **170 ft**

2. Kay's father built a garden in the back yard. What is the area of the garden?

Garden

3.

Kay's mother set up a sandbox. What is the shape of the sandbox?

Rectangle

Each ▢ = 1 sq foot.

55 square feet

Use with Lesson 8-15. **111**

Enrichment

Name_____

Round on the Ends   E 8-15 DATA

1. Here is the name of the Buckeye State in block letters. Complete the table below by finding the perimeter and the area of each character. (Hint: you can break apart a letter into squares and rectangles to help find the area.)

Character	Perimeter	Area
O	28 units	40 units^2
H	40 units	36 units^2
I	20 units	16 units^2
O	28 units	40 units^2
!	22 units	14 units^2

2. Write the abbreviation for the state you live in on the grid below. Then find the perimeter and area of each letter.

Check students' abbreviations, perimeters, and areas.

Use with Lesson 8-15. **111**

Problem Solving

Name_____

PROBLEM-SOLVING APPLICATION   PS 8-15

Pyramid

Look at the drawing of a pyramid. How many cubes are needed to make the pyramid?

Read and Understand

1. What do you know?

The base is 4 cubes by 4 cubes, and each layer's sides have 1 fewer cube.

2. What are you trying to find?

The number of cubes needed to make the pyramid

Plan and Solve

3. What objects do you need to act out the problem?   **Blocks**

4. Solve the problem, and write your answer in a complete sentence.

You need 30 cubes to build the pyramid.

Look Back and Check

5. Is your answer reasonable?

Yes. 16 + 9 + 4 + 1 = 30

Solve Another Problem

6. Look at the drawing of a rectangular prism. How many cubes are needed to make the solid figure?

24 cubes

Use with Lesson 8-15. **111**

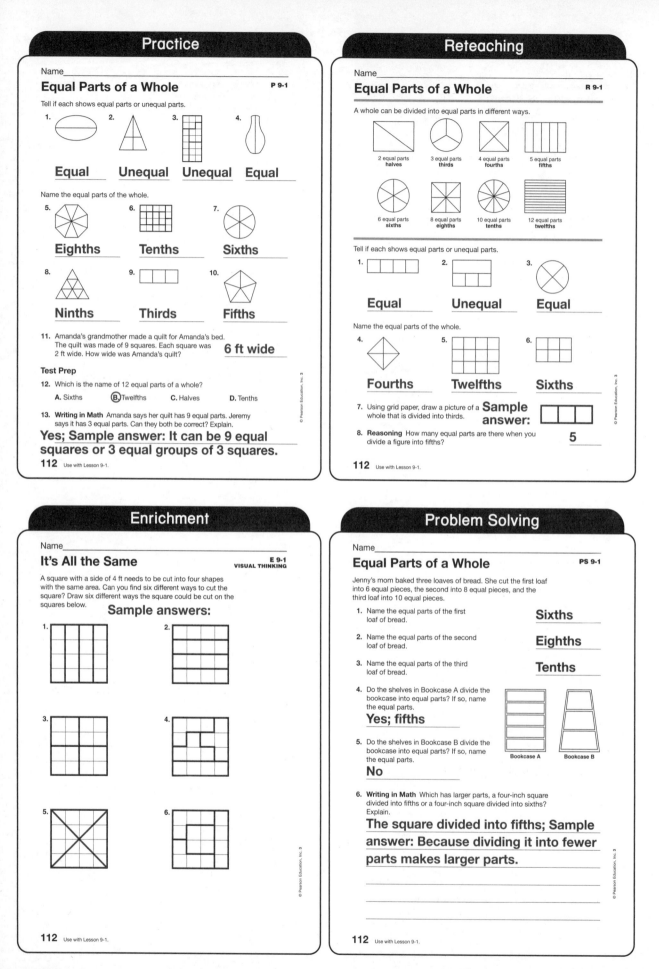

Name_____

Equal Parts of a Whole
P 9-1

Tell if each shows equal parts or unequal parts.

1. **Equal** 2. **Unequal** 3. **Unequal** 4. **Equal**

Name the equal parts of the whole.

5. **Eighths** 6. **Tenths** 7. **Sixths**

8. **Ninths** 9. **Thirds** 10. **Fifths**

11. Amanda's grandmother made a quilt for Amanda's bed. The quilt was made of 9 squares. Each square was 2 ft wide. How wide was Amanda's quilt?

6 ft wide

Test Prep

12. Which is the name of 12 equal parts of a whole?

A. Sixths (B.) Twelfths C. Halves D. Tenths

13. **Writing in Math** Amanda says her quilt has 9 equal parts. Jeremy says it has 3 equal parts. Can they both be correct? Explain.

Yes; Sample answer: It can be 9 equal squares or 3 equal groups of 3 squares.

112 Use with Lesson 9-1.

© Pearson Education, Inc. 3

Name_____

Equal Parts of a Whole
R 9-1

A whole can be divided into equal parts in different ways.

2 equal parts halves | 3 equal parts thirds | 4 equal parts fourths | 5 equal parts fifths

6 equal parts sixths | 8 equal parts eighths | 10 equal parts tenths | 12 equal parts twelfths

Tell if each shows equal parts or unequal parts.

1. **Equal** 2. **Unequal** 3. **Equal**

Name the equal parts of the whole.

4. **Fourths** 5. **Twelfths** 6. **Sixths**

7. Using grid paper, draw a picture of a whole that is divided into thirds. **Sample answer:**

8. **Reasoning** How many equal parts are there when you divide a figure into fifths? **5**

112 Use with Lesson 9-1.

© Pearson Education, Inc. 3

Name_____

It's All the Same
E 9-1
VISUAL THINKING

A square with a side of 4 ft needs to be cut into four shapes with the same area. Can you find six different ways to cut the square? Draw six different ways the square could be cut on the squares below.

Sample answers:

1. 2.

3. 4.

5. 6.

112 Use with Lesson 9-1.

© Pearson Education, Inc. 3

Name_____

Equal Parts of a Whole
PS 9-1

Jenny's mom baked three loaves of bread. She cut the first loaf into 6 equal pieces, the second into 8 equal pieces, and the third loaf into 10 equal pieces.

1. Name the equal parts of the first loaf of bread. **Sixths**

2. Name the equal parts of the second loaf of bread. **Eighths**

3. Name the equal parts of the third loaf of bread. **Tenths**

4. Do the shelves in Bookcase A divide the bookcase into equal parts? If so, name the equal parts.

Yes; fifths

5. Do the shelves in Bookcase B divide the bookcase into equal parts? If so, name the equal parts.

No

Bookcase A   Bookcase B

6. **Writing in Math** Which has larger parts, a four-inch square divided into fifths or a four-inch square divided into sixths? Explain.

The square divided into fifths; Sample answer: Because dividing it into fewer parts makes larger parts.

112 Use with Lesson 9-1.

© Pearson Education, Inc. 3

© Pearson Education, Inc. 3

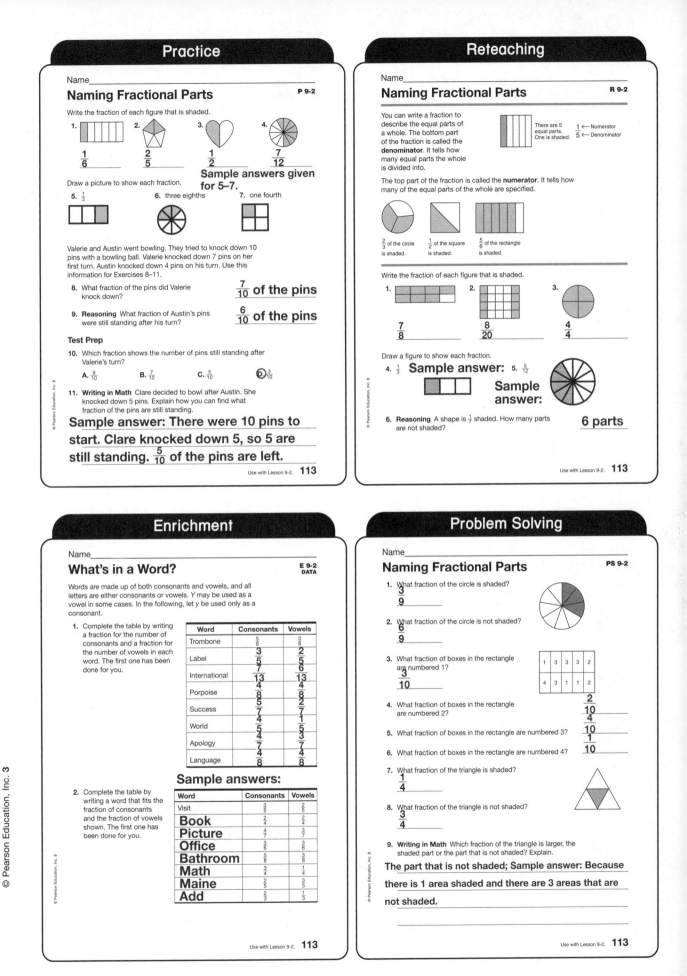

Practice

Name_____

Naming Fractional Parts
P 9-2

Write the fraction of each figure that is shaded.

1. $\frac{1}{6}$ 2. $\frac{2}{5}$ 3. $\frac{1}{2}$ 4. $\frac{7}{12}$

Sample answers given for 5–7.

Draw a picture to show each fraction.

5. $\frac{1}{3}$ 6. three eighths   7. one fourth

Valerie and Austin went bowling. They tried to knock down 10 pins with a bowling ball. Valerie knocked down 7 pins on her first turn. Austin knocked down 4 pins on his turn. Use this information for Exercises 8–11.

8. What fraction of the pins did Valerie knock down? $\frac{7}{10}$ **of the pins**

9. **Reasoning** What fraction of Austin's pins were still standing after his turn? $\frac{6}{10}$ **of the pins**

Test Prep

10. Which fraction shows the number of pins still standing after Valerie's turn?

A. $\frac{9}{10}$ B. $\frac{7}{10}$ C. $\frac{5}{10}$ D. $\frac{3}{10}$

11. **Writing in Math** Clare decided to bowl after Austin. She knocked down 5 pins. Explain how you can find what fraction of the pins are still standing.

Sample answer: There were 10 pins to start. Clare knocked down 5, so 5 are still standing. $\frac{5}{10}$ of the pins are left.

Use with Lesson 9-2. **113**

Reteaching

Name_____

Naming Fractional Parts
R 9-2

You can write a fraction to describe the equal parts of a whole. The bottom part of the fraction is called the **denominator**. It tells how many equal parts the whole is divided into.

There are 5 equal parts. One is shaded. $\frac{1}{5}$ ← Numerator ← Denominator

The top part of the fraction is called the **numerator**. It tells how many of the equal parts of the whole are specified.

$\frac{2}{3}$ of the circle is shaded. $\frac{1}{2}$ of the square is shaded. $\frac{5}{6}$ of the rectangle is shaded.

Write the fraction of each figure that is shaded.

1. $\frac{7}{8}$ 2. $\frac{8}{20}$ 3. $\frac{4}{4}$

Draw a figure to show each fraction.

4. $\frac{1}{3}$ **Sample answer:**   5. $\frac{5}{12}$ **Sample answer:**

6. **Reasoning** A shape is $\frac{1}{7}$ shaded. How many parts are not shaded?   **6 parts**

Use with Lesson 9-2. **113**

Enrichment

Name_____

What's in a Word?
E 9-2 DATA

Words are made up of both consonants and vowels, and all letters are either consonants or vowels. *Y* may be used as a vowel in some cases. In the following, let *y* be used only as a consonant.

1. Complete the table by writing a fraction for the number of consonants and a fraction for the number of vowels in each word. The first one has been done for you.

Word	Consonants	Vowels
Trombone	$\frac{5}{8}$	$\frac{3}{8}$
Label	$\frac{3}{5}$	$\frac{2}{5}$
International	$\frac{7}{13}$	$\frac{6}{13}$
Porpoise	$\frac{4}{8}$	$\frac{4}{8}$
Success	$\frac{5}{7}$	$\frac{2}{7}$
World	$\frac{4}{5}$	$\frac{1}{5}$
Apology	$\frac{4}{7}$	$\frac{3}{7}$
Language	$\frac{4}{8}$	$\frac{4}{8}$

2. Complete the table by writing a word that fits the fraction of consonants and the fraction of vowels shown. The first one has been done for you.

Sample answers:

Word	Consonants	Vowels
Visit	$\frac{3}{5}$	$\frac{2}{5}$
Book	$\frac{2}{4}$	$\frac{2}{4}$
Picture	$\frac{4}{7}$	$\frac{3}{7}$
Office	$\frac{3}{6}$	$\frac{3}{6}$
Bathroom	$\frac{5}{8}$	$\frac{3}{8}$
Math	$\frac{3}{4}$	$\frac{1}{4}$
Maine	$\frac{2}{5}$	$\frac{3}{5}$
Add	$\frac{2}{3}$	$\frac{1}{3}$

Use with Lesson 9-2. **113**

Problem Solving

Name_____

Naming Fractional Parts
PS 9-2

1. What fraction of the circle is shaded? $\frac{3}{9}$

2. What fraction of the circle is not shaded? $\frac{6}{9}$

3. What fraction of boxes in the rectangle are numbered 1? $\frac{3}{10}$

1	3	3	3	2
4	3	1	1	2

4. What fraction of boxes in the rectangle are numbered 2? $\frac{2}{10}$

5. What fraction of boxes in the rectangle are numbered 3? $\frac{4}{10}$

6. What fraction of boxes in the rectangle are numbered 4? $\frac{1}{10}$

7. What fraction of the triangle is shaded? $\frac{1}{4}$

8. What fraction of the triangle is not shaded? $\frac{3}{4}$

9. **Writing in Math** Which fraction of the triangle is larger, the shaded part or the part that is not shaded? Explain.

The part that is not shaded; Sample answer: Because there is 1 area shaded and there are 3 areas that are not shaded.

Use with Lesson 9-2. **113**

© Pearson Education, Inc. 3

Name_____

Equivalent Fractions

P 9-3

Complete each number sentence.

1.

| 1 |

| $\frac{1}{2}$ |

| $\frac{1}{10}$ | $\frac{1}{10}$ | $\frac{1}{10}$ | $\frac{1}{10}$ | $\frac{1}{10}$ |

$\frac{1}{2} = \frac{5}{10}$

2.

| 1 |

| $\frac{1}{3}$ | $\frac{1}{3}$ |

| $\frac{1}{6}$ | $\frac{1}{6}$ | $\frac{1}{6}$ | $\frac{1}{6}$ |

$\frac{2}{3} = \frac{4}{6}$

3.

$\frac{1}{2} = \frac{6}{12}$

4. **Reasoning** Samuel has read $\frac{5}{6}$ of his assignment. Judy has read $\frac{10}{12}$ of her assignment. Who has read more? Explain.

Sample answer: They have both read the same amount. $\frac{5}{6} = \frac{10}{12}$

5. One half of the square is shaded. Draw three more ways to show $\frac{1}{2}$.

Sample answer:

Test Prep

6. Which completes the pattern? $\frac{2}{3} = \frac{4}{6} = \frac{6}{9} = \frac{8}{12} = \frac{10}{\blacksquare}$

   A. 4   B. 8   C. 12   (D) 15

7. **Writing in Math** Amy finished $\frac{6}{12}$ of the problems on her timed test. Jackson finished $\frac{4}{6}$ of the problems on the timed test. Did they finish the same fraction of the problems? Explain.

No; Sample answer: An equivalent fraction for $\frac{4}{6}$ is $\frac{8}{12}$, which is not $\frac{6}{12}$.

114   Use with Lesson 9-3.

© Pearson Education, Inc. 3

Name_____

Equivalent Fractions

R 9-3

Figure A has 1 out of 2 parts shaded. The fraction which is shaded is $\frac{1}{2}$.

Figure B has 2 out of 4 parts shaded. The fraction which is shaded is $\frac{2}{4}$.

Figure A   Figure B

Both figures have the same amount shaded. This means that the fractions $\frac{1}{2}$ and $\frac{2}{4}$ are equivalent. They both state that half of the figure is shaded.

So, $\frac{2}{4} = \frac{1}{2}$.

Complete each number sentence.

1.

$\frac{4}{6} = \frac{8}{12}$

2.

$\frac{4}{5} = \frac{8}{10}$

Continue each pattern.

3. $\frac{1}{3} = \frac{2}{6} = \frac{3}{9} = \frac{4}{12}$

4. $\frac{1}{5} = \frac{2}{10} = \frac{3}{15} = \frac{4}{20} = \frac{5}{25}$

5. **Reasoning** Mary and Bill are each reading the same book. Mary read $\frac{1}{4}$ of the book. Bill says that since he read $\frac{2}{8}$ of the book, he read more. Is Bill correct? Explain.

No, because $\frac{1}{4} = \frac{2}{8}$.

114   Use with Lesson 9-3.

© Pearson Education, Inc. 3

Name_____

Match Maker

E 9-3
VISUAL THINKING

Write the letter of the shape on the right that shows the same fractional amount as the shape on the left. The shapes can be different sizes, but must show equivalent fractions.

1.   B

2.   E

3.   D

4.   F

5.   C

6.   A

A.

B.

C.

D.

E.

F.

114   Use with Lesson 9-3.

© Pearson Education, Inc. 3

Name_____

Equivalent Fractions

PS 9-3

Continue each pattern.

1. $\frac{1}{4} = \frac{2}{8} = \frac{3}{12} = \frac{4}{16} = \frac{5}{20} = \frac{6}{24}$

2. $\frac{2}{5} = \frac{4}{10} = \frac{6}{15} = \frac{8}{20} = \frac{10}{25} = \frac{12}{30}$

3. $\frac{1}{3} = \frac{2}{6} = \frac{3}{9} = \frac{4}{12} = \frac{5}{15} = \frac{6}{18}$

4. Shade each picture to match the number sentence.

   $\frac{1}{2} = \frac{4}{8}$

5. Angie gave away 2 pieces of her orange. How many pieces would Gary need to give away to equal the pieces of orange Angie gave away?

   4 pieces

6. **Writing in Math** Can a fraction with a 2 in the numerator equal $\frac{1}{2}$? Explain. You may use fraction strips to help.

Yes; Sample answer: $\frac{2}{4}$ equals $\frac{1}{2}$.

114   Use with Lesson 9-3.

© Pearson Education, Inc. 3

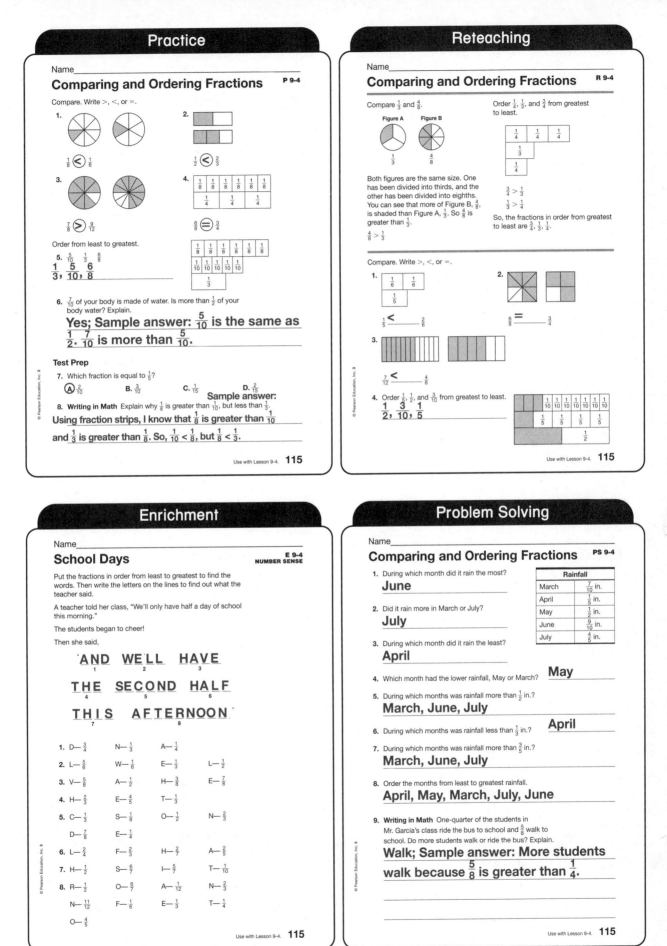

Practice

Name_____

Comparing and Ordering Fractions   P 9-4

Compare. Write >, <, or =.

1. $\frac{1}{8}$ < $\frac{1}{6}$

2. $\frac{1}{2}$ < $\frac{2}{3}$

3. $\frac{7}{8}$ > $\frac{9}{12}$

4. $\frac{6}{8}$ = $\frac{3}{4}$

Order from least to greatest.

5. $\frac{5}{10}$, $\frac{1}{3}$, $\frac{6}{8}$

$\frac{1}{3}$, $\frac{5}{10}$, $\frac{6}{8}$

6. $\frac{7}{10}$ of your body is made of water. Is more than $\frac{1}{2}$ of your body water? Explain.

Yes; Sample answer: $\frac{5}{10}$ is the same as $\frac{1}{2}$. $\frac{7}{10}$ is more than $\frac{5}{10}$.

Test Prep

7. Which fraction is equal to $\frac{1}{5}$?

Ⓐ $\frac{2}{10}$ B. $\frac{3}{10}$ C. $\frac{1}{15}$ D. $\frac{2}{15}$

8. **Writing in Math** Explain why $\frac{1}{8}$ is greater than $\frac{1}{10}$, but less than $\frac{1}{3}$.

Sample answer: Using fraction strips, I know that $\frac{1}{8}$ is greater than $\frac{1}{10}$ and $\frac{1}{3}$ is greater than $\frac{1}{8}$. So, $\frac{1}{10} < \frac{1}{8}$, but $\frac{1}{8} < \frac{1}{3}$.

Use with Lesson 9-4. **115**

© Pearson Education, Inc. 3

Reteaching

Name_____

Comparing and Ordering Fractions   R 9-4

Compare $\frac{1}{3}$ and $\frac{4}{8}$.

Figure A   Figure B

$\frac{1}{3}$ $\frac{4}{8}$

Both figures are the same size. One has been divided into thirds, and the other has been divided into eighths. You can see that more of Figure B, $\frac{4}{8}$, is shaded than Figure A, $\frac{1}{3}$. So $\frac{4}{8}$ is greater than $\frac{1}{3}$.

$\frac{4}{8} > \frac{1}{3}$

Order $\frac{1}{4}$, $\frac{1}{3}$, and $\frac{3}{4}$ from greatest to least.

$\frac{3}{4} > \frac{1}{3}$

$\frac{1}{3} > \frac{1}{4}$

So, the fractions in order from greatest to least are $\frac{3}{4}$, $\frac{1}{3}$, $\frac{1}{4}$.

Compare. Write >, <, or =.

1. $\frac{1}{5}$ < $\frac{2}{6}$

2. $\frac{6}{8}$ = $\frac{3}{4}$

3. $\frac{7}{12}$ < $\frac{4}{6}$

4. Order $\frac{1}{5}$, $\frac{1}{2}$, and $\frac{3}{10}$ from greatest to least.

$\frac{1}{2}$, $\frac{3}{10}$, $\frac{1}{5}$

Use with Lesson 9-4. **115**

© Pearson Education, Inc. 3

Enrichment

Name_____

School Days   E 9-4   NUMBER SENSE

Put the fractions in order from least to greatest to find the words. Then write the letters on the lines to find out what the teacher said.

A teacher told her class, "We'll only have half a day of school this morning."

The students began to cheer!

Then she said,

"AND WE'LL HAVE
  1   2   3

THE SECOND HALF
 4   5   6

THIS AFTERNOON"
 7   8

1. D—$\frac{3}{4}$ N—$\frac{1}{3}$ A—$\frac{1}{4}$

2. L—$\frac{5}{6}$ W—$\frac{1}{8}$ E—$\frac{1}{3}$ L—$\frac{1}{2}$

3. V—$\frac{5}{6}$ A—$\frac{1}{2}$ H—$\frac{3}{8}$ E—$\frac{7}{8}$

4. H—$\frac{2}{3}$ E—$\frac{4}{5}$ T—$\frac{1}{3}$

5. C—$\frac{1}{3}$ S—$\frac{1}{8}$ O—$\frac{1}{2}$ N—$\frac{2}{3}$

   D—$\frac{7}{8}$ E—$\frac{1}{4}$

6. L—$\frac{2}{4}$ F—$\frac{2}{3}$ H—$\frac{2}{7}$ A—$\frac{2}{5}$

7. H—$\frac{1}{2}$ S—$\frac{6}{7}$ I—$\frac{5}{7}$ T—$\frac{1}{10}$

8. R—$\frac{1}{2}$ O—$\frac{6}{7}$ A—$\frac{1}{12}$ N—$\frac{2}{3}$

   N—$\frac{11}{12}$ F—$\frac{1}{6}$ E—$\frac{1}{3}$ T—$\frac{1}{4}$

   O—$\frac{4}{5}$

Use with Lesson 9-4. **115**

© Pearson Education, Inc. 3

Problem Solving

Name_____

Comparing and Ordering Fractions   PS 9-4

Rainfall	
March	$\frac{7}{10}$ in.
April	$\frac{1}{5}$ in.
May	$\frac{1}{2}$ in.
June	$\frac{9}{10}$ in.
July	$\frac{4}{5}$ in.

1. During which month did it rain the most?

June

2. Did it rain more in March or July?

July

3. During which month did it rain the least?

April

4. Which month had the lower rainfall, May or March? **May**

5. During which months was rainfall more than $\frac{1}{2}$ in.?

March, June, July

6. During which months was rainfall less than $\frac{1}{3}$ in.? **April**

7. During which months was rainfall more than $\frac{3}{5}$ in.?

March, June, July

8. Order the months from least to greatest rainfall.

April, May, March, July, June

9. **Writing in Math** One-quarter of the students in Mr. Garcia's class ride the bus to school and $\frac{5}{8}$ walk to school. Do more students walk or ride the bus? Explain.

Walk; Sample answer: More students walk because $\frac{5}{8}$ is greater than $\frac{1}{4}$.

Use with Lesson 9-4. **115**

© Pearson Education, Inc. 3

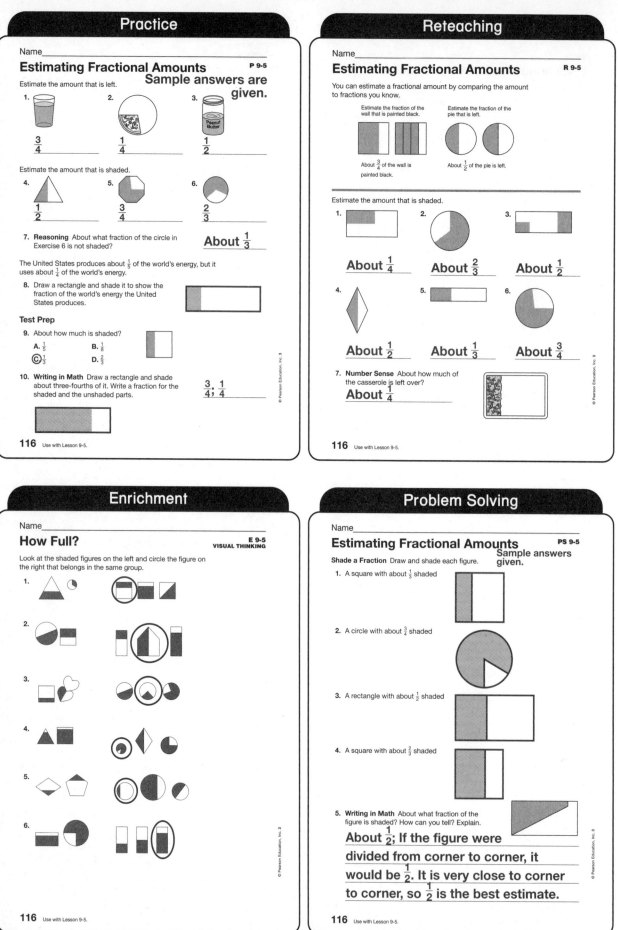

Practice

Name_____

Estimating Fractional Amounts   P 9-5

Sample answers are
given.
Estimate the amount that is left.

1. $\frac{3}{4}$

2. $\frac{1}{4}$

3. $\frac{1}{2}$

Estimate the amount that is shaded.

4. $\frac{1}{2}$

5. $\frac{3}{4}$

6. $\frac{2}{3}$

7. **Reasoning** About what fraction of the circle in
    Exercise 6 is not shaded?

    About $\frac{1}{3}$

The United States produces about $\frac{1}{5}$ of the world's energy, but it
uses about $\frac{1}{4}$ of the world's energy.

8. Draw a rectangle and shade it to show the
    fraction of the world's energy the United
    States produces.

Test Prep

9. About how much is shaded?

    A. $\frac{1}{5}$ B. $\frac{1}{8}$

    C. $\frac{1}{3}$ D. $\frac{2}{3}$

10. **Writing in Math** Draw a rectangle and shade
    about three-fourths of it. Write a fraction for the
    shaded and the unshaded parts.

    $\frac{3}{4}$; $\frac{1}{4}$

Reteaching

Name_____

Estimating Fractional Amounts   R 9-5

You can estimate a fractional amount by comparing the amount
to fractions you know.

Estimate the fraction of the
wall that is painted black.

About $\frac{3}{4}$ of the wall is
painted black.

Estimate the fraction of the
pie that is left.

About $\frac{1}{2}$ of the pie is left.

Estimate the amount that is shaded.

1. About $\frac{1}{4}$

2. About $\frac{2}{3}$

3. About $\frac{1}{2}$

4. About $\frac{1}{2}$

5. About $\frac{1}{3}$

6. About $\frac{3}{4}$

7. **Number Sense** About how much of
    the casserole is left over?

    About $\frac{1}{4}$

Enrichment

Name_____

How Full?   E 9-5
VISUAL THINKING

Look at the shaded figures on the left and circle the figure on
the right that belongs in the same group.

1.

2.

3.

4.

5.

6.

Problem Solving

Name_____

Estimating Fractional Amounts   PS 9-5

Shade a Fraction Draw and shade each figure.

Sample answers
given.

1. A square with about $\frac{1}{3}$ shaded

2. A circle with about $\frac{3}{4}$ shaded

3. A rectangle with about $\frac{1}{2}$ shaded

4. A square with about $\frac{2}{3}$ shaded

5. **Writing in Math** About what fraction of the
    figure is shaded? How can you tell? Explain.

    About $\frac{1}{2}$; If the figure were
    divided from corner to corner, it
    would be $\frac{1}{2}$. It is very close to corner
    to corner, so $\frac{1}{2}$ is the best estimate.

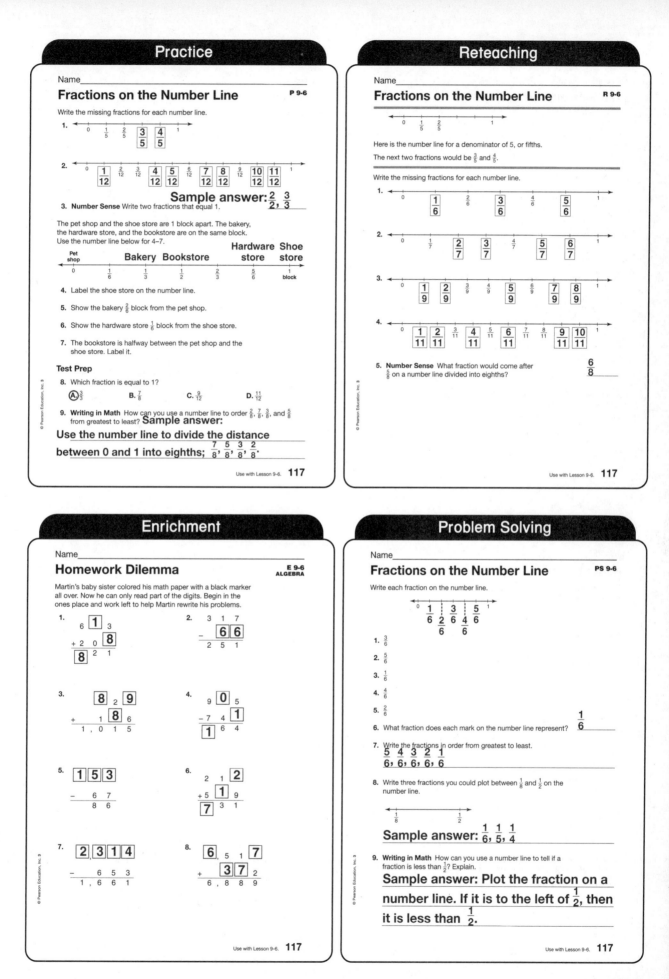

Name_____

Fractions on the Number Line

P 9-6

Write the missing fractions for each number line.

1. 0, 1/5, 2/5, [3/5], [4/5], 1

2. 0, [1/12], 2/12, 3/12, [4/12], [5/12], 6/12, [7/12], [8/12], 9/12, [10/12], [11/12], 1

Sample answer: 2/3, 3/3

3. **Number Sense** Write two fractions that equal 1.

The pet shop and the shoe store are 1 block apart. The bakery, the hardware store, and the bookstore are on the same block. Use the number line below for 4–7.

Pet shop 0 — Bakery 1/6 — 1/3 — Bookstore 1/2 — 2/3 — Hardware store 5/6 — Shoe store 1 block

4. Label the shoe store on the number line.

5. Show the bakery 2/6 block from the pet shop.

6. Show the hardware store 1/6 block from the shoe store.

7. The bookstore is halfway between the pet shop and the shoe store. Label it.

Test Prep

8. Which fraction is equal to 1?

Ⓐ 3/3   B. 7/8   C. 9/12   D. 11/12

9. **Writing in Math** How can you use a number line to order 2/8, 7/8, 3/8, and 5/8 from greatest to least? **Sample answer:**

Use the number line to divide the distance between 0 and 1 into eighths; 7/8, 5/8, 3/8, 2/8.

Use with Lesson 9-6. **117**

© Pearson Education, Inc. 3

Name_____

Fractions on the Number Line

R 9-6

0, 1/5, 2/5, 1

Here is the number line for a denominator of 5, or fifths. The next two fractions would be 3/5 and 4/5.

Write the missing fractions for each number line.

1. 0, [1/6], 2/6, [3/6], 4/6, [5/6], 1

2. 0, 1/7, [2/7], [3/7], 4/7, [5/7], [6/7], 1

3. 0, [1/9], [2/9], 3/9, 4/9, [5/9], 6/9, [7/9], [8/9], 1

4. 0, [1/11], [2/11], 3/11, [4/11], 5/11, [6/11], 7/11, 8/11, [9/11], [10/11], 1

5. **Number Sense** What fraction would come after 5/8 on a number line divided into eighths? — 6/8

Use with Lesson 9-6. **117**

© Pearson Education, Inc. 3

Name_____

Homework Dilemma

E 9-6
ALGEBRA

Martin's baby sister colored his math paper with a black marker all over. Now he can only read part of the digits. Begin in the ones place and work left to help Martin rewrite his problems.

1. 6 [1] 3
   + 2 0 [8]
   [8] 2 1

2. 3 1 7
   − [6 6]
   2 5 1

3. [8] 2 [9]
   +   1 [8] 6
   1, 0 1 5

4. 9 [0] 5
   − 7 4 [1]
   [1] 6 4

5. [1 5 3]
   −   6 7
   8 6

6. 2 1 [2]
   + 5 [1] 9
   [7] 3 1

7. [2 3 1 4]
   −   6 5 3
   1, 6 6 1

8. [6], 5 1 [7]
   +   [3 7] 2
   6, 8 8 9

Use with Lesson 9-6. **117**

© Pearson Education, Inc. 3

Name_____

Fractions on the Number Line

PS 9-6

Write each fraction on the number line.

0, 1/6, 2/6, 3/6, 4/6, 5/6, 1

1. 3/6

2. 5/6

3. 1/6

4. 4/6

5. 2/6

6. What fraction does each mark on the number line represent? — 1/6

7. Write the fractions in order from greatest to least.
   5/6, 4/6, 3/6, 2/6, 1/6

8. Write three fractions you could plot between 1/8 and 1/2 on the number line.

   1/8 — 1/2

   Sample answer: 1/6, 1/5, 1/4

9. **Writing in Math** How can you use a number line to tell if a fraction is less than 1/2? Explain.

   Sample answer: Plot the fraction on a number line. If it is to the left of 1/2, then it is less than 1/2.

Use with Lesson 9-6. **117**

© Pearson Education, Inc. 3

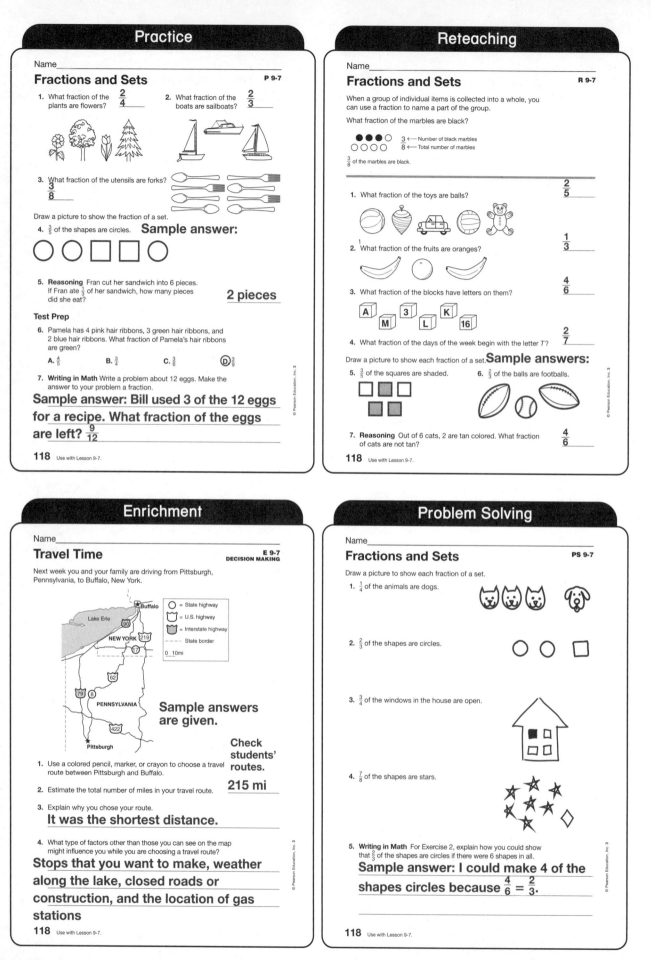

Practice

Fractions and Sets
P 9-7

1. What fraction of the plants are flowers? $\frac{2}{4}$

2. What fraction of the boats are sailboats? $\frac{2}{3}$

3. What fraction of the utensils are forks? $\frac{3}{8}$

Draw a picture to show the fraction of a set.

4. $\frac{3}{5}$ of the shapes are circles. **Sample answer:**

5. **Reasoning** Fran cut her sandwich into 6 pieces. If Fran ate $\frac{1}{3}$ of her sandwich, how many pieces did she eat?   **2 pieces**

Test Prep

6. Pamela has 4 pink hair ribbons, 3 green hair ribbons, and 2 blue hair ribbons. What fraction of Pamela's hair ribbons are green?

   A. $\frac{4}{5}$ B. $\frac{3}{4}$ C. $\frac{3}{6}$ (D) $\frac{3}{9}$

7. **Writing in Math** Write a problem about 12 eggs. Make the answer to your problem a fraction.

Sample answer: Bill used 3 of the 12 eggs for a recipe. What fraction of the eggs are left? $\frac{9}{12}$

118 Use with Lesson 9-7.

Reteaching

Fractions and Sets
R 9-7

When a group of individual items is collected into a whole, you can use a fraction to name a part of the group.

What fraction of the marbles are black?

● ● ● ○ $\frac{3}{8}$ ← Number of black marbles
○ ○ ○ ○   ← Total number of marbles

$\frac{3}{8}$ of the marbles are black.

1. What fraction of the toys are balls? $\frac{2}{5}$

2. What fraction of the fruits are oranges? $\frac{1}{3}$

3. What fraction of the blocks have letters on them? $\frac{4}{6}$

4. What fraction of the days of the week begin with the letter *T*? $\frac{2}{7}$

Draw a picture to show each fraction of a set. **Sample answers:**

5. $\frac{3}{5}$ of the squares are shaded.

6. $\frac{2}{3}$ of the balls are footballs.

7. **Reasoning** Out of 6 cats, 2 are tan colored. What fraction of cats are not tan? $\frac{4}{6}$

118 Use with Lesson 9-7.

Enrichment

Travel Time
E 9-7
DECISION MAKING

Next week you and your family are driving from Pittsburgh, Pennsylvania, to Buffalo, New York.

○ = State highway
⬡ = U.S. highway
⬟ = Interstate highway
--- = State border
0   10mi

Sample answers are given.

Check students' routes.

215 mi

1. Use a colored pencil, marker, or crayon to choose a travel route between Pittsburgh and Buffalo.

2. Estimate the total number of miles in your travel route.

3. Explain why you chose your route.
   It was the shortest distance.

4. What type of factors other than those you can see on the map might influence you while you are choosing a travel route?
   Stops that you want to make, weather along the lake, closed roads or construction, and the location of gas stations

118 Use with Lesson 9-7.

Problem Solving

Fractions and Sets
PS 9-7

Draw a picture to show each fraction of a set.

1. $\frac{1}{4}$ of the animals are dogs.

2. $\frac{2}{3}$ of the shapes are circles.

3. $\frac{3}{4}$ of the windows in the house are open.

4. $\frac{7}{8}$ of the shapes are stars.

5. **Writing in Math** For Exercise 2, explain how you could show that $\frac{2}{3}$ of the shapes are circles if there were 6 shapes in all.

Sample answer: I could make 4 of the shapes circles because $\frac{4}{6} = \frac{2}{3}$.

118 Use with Lesson 9-7.

© Pearson Education, Inc. 3

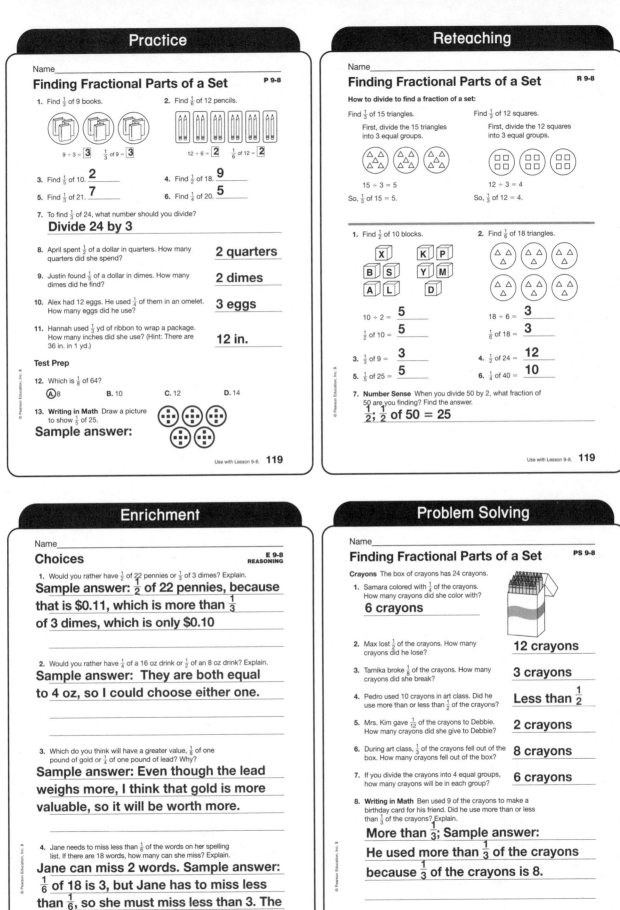

Practice

Name_____

Finding Fractional Parts of a Set

P 9-8

1. Find $\frac{1}{3}$ of 9 books.

$9 \div 3 =$ **3** $\frac{1}{3}$ of 9 = **3**

2. Find $\frac{1}{6}$ of 12 pencils.

$12 \div 6 =$ **2** $\frac{1}{6}$ of 12 = **2**

3. Find $\frac{1}{5}$ of 10. **2**

4. Find $\frac{1}{2}$ of 18. **9**

5. Find $\frac{1}{3}$ of 21. **7**

6. Find $\frac{1}{4}$ of 20. **5**

7. To find $\frac{1}{3}$ of 24, what number should you divide?

Divide 24 by 3

8. April spent $\frac{1}{2}$ of a dollar in quarters. How many quarters did she spend?

2 quarters

9. Justin found $\frac{1}{5}$ of a dollar in dimes. How many dimes did he find?

2 dimes

10. Alex had 12 eggs. He used $\frac{1}{4}$ of them in an omelet. How many eggs did he use?

3 eggs

11. Hannah used $\frac{1}{3}$ yd of ribbon to wrap a package. How many inches did she use? (Hint: There are 36 in. in 1 yd.)

12 in.

Test Prep

12. Which is $\frac{1}{8}$ of 64?

(A) 8   B. 10   C. 12   D. 14

13. **Writing in Math** Draw a picture to show $\frac{1}{5}$ of 25.

Sample answer:

Use with Lesson 9-8. **119**

Reteaching

Name_____

Finding Fractional Parts of a Set

R 9-8

How to divide to find a fraction of a set:

Find $\frac{1}{3}$ of 15 triangles.

First, divide the 15 triangles into 3 equal groups.

$15 \div 3 = 5$

So, $\frac{1}{3}$ of 15 = 5.

Find $\frac{1}{3}$ of 12 squares.

First, divide the 12 squares into 3 equal groups.

$12 \div 3 = 4$

So, $\frac{1}{3}$ of 12 = 4.

1. Find $\frac{1}{2}$ of 10 blocks.

$10 \div 2 =$ **5**

$\frac{1}{2}$ of 10 = **5**

2. Find $\frac{1}{6}$ of 18 triangles.

$18 \div 6 =$ **3**

$\frac{1}{6}$ of 18 = **3**

3. $\frac{1}{3}$ of 9 = **3**

4. $\frac{1}{2}$ of 24 = **12**

5. $\frac{1}{5}$ of 25 = **5**

6. $\frac{1}{4}$ of 40 = **10**

7. **Number Sense** When you divide 50 by 2, what fraction of 50 are you finding? Find the answer.

$\frac{1}{2}$; $\frac{1}{2}$ of 50 = 25

Use with Lesson 9-8. **119**

Enrichment

Name_____

Choices

E 9-8
REASONING

1. Would you rather have $\frac{1}{2}$ of 22 pennies or $\frac{1}{3}$ of 3 dimes? Explain.

Sample answer: $\frac{1}{2}$ of 22 pennies, because that is $0.11, which is more than $\frac{1}{3}$ of 3 dimes, which is only $0.10

2. Would you rather have $\frac{1}{4}$ of a 16 oz drink or $\frac{1}{2}$ of an 8 oz drink? Explain.

Sample answer: They are both equal to 4 oz, so I could choose either one.

3. Which do you think will have a greater value, $\frac{1}{8}$ of one pound of gold or $\frac{1}{4}$ of one pound of lead? Why?

Sample answer: Even though the lead weighs more, I think that gold is more valuable, so it will be worth more.

4. Jane needs to miss less than $\frac{1}{6}$ of the words on her spelling list. If there are 18 words, how many can she miss? Explain.

Jane can miss 2 words. Sample answer: $\frac{1}{6}$ of 18 is 3, but Jane has to miss less than $\frac{1}{6}$, so she must miss less than 3. The highest number that is less than 3 is 2.

Use with Lesson 9-8. **119**

Problem Solving

Name_____

Finding Fractional Parts of a Set

PS 9-8

Crayons The box of crayons has 24 crayons.

1. Samara colored with $\frac{1}{4}$ of the crayons. How many crayons did she color with?

6 crayons

2. Max lost $\frac{1}{2}$ of the crayons. How many crayons did he lose?

12 crayons

3. Tamika broke $\frac{1}{8}$ of the crayons. How many crayons did she break?

3 crayons

4. Pedro used 10 crayons in art class. Did he use more than or less than $\frac{1}{2}$ of the crayons?

Less than $\frac{1}{2}$

5. Mrs. Kim gave $\frac{1}{12}$ of the crayons to Debbie. How many crayons did she give to Debbie?

2 crayons

6. During art class, $\frac{1}{3}$ of the crayons fell out of the box. How many crayons fell out of the box?

8 crayons

7. If you divide the crayons into 4 equal groups, how many crayons will be in each group?

6 crayons

8. **Writing in Math** Ben used 9 of the crayons to make a birthday card for his friend. Did he use more than or less than $\frac{1}{3}$ of the crayons? Explain.

More than $\frac{1}{3}$; Sample answer: He used more than $\frac{1}{3}$ of the crayons because $\frac{1}{3}$ of the crayons is 8.

Use with Lesson 9-8. **119**

Name_____

Adding and Subtracting Fractions   P 9-9

Add or subtract. You may use fraction strips or draw a picture to help.

1. $\frac{3}{8} + \frac{2}{8} = \frac{5}{8}$ _____

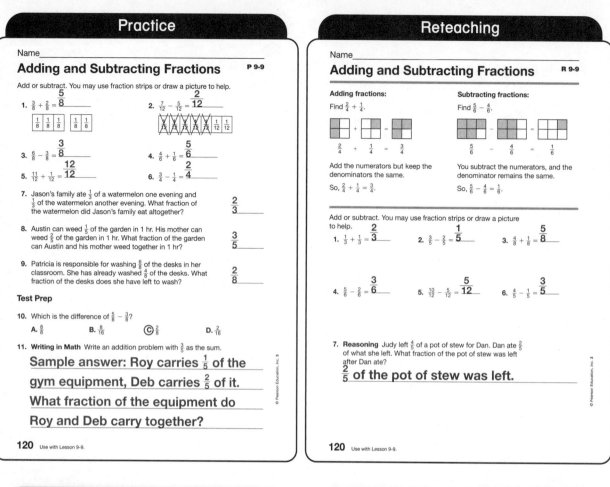

2. $\frac{7}{12} - \frac{5}{12} = \frac{2}{12}$ _____

3. $\frac{6}{8} - \frac{3}{8} = \frac{3}{8}$ _____

4. $\frac{4}{6} + \frac{1}{6} = \frac{5}{6}$ _____

5. $\frac{11}{12} + \frac{1}{12} = \frac{12}{12}$ _____

6. $\frac{3}{4} - \frac{1}{4} = \frac{2}{4}$ _____

7. Jason's family ate $\frac{1}{3}$ of a watermelon one evening and $\frac{1}{3}$ of the watermelon another evening. What fraction of the watermelon did Jason's family eat altogether? $\frac{2}{3}$

8. Austin can weed $\frac{1}{5}$ of the garden in 1 hr. His mother can weed $\frac{2}{5}$ of the garden in 1 hr. What fraction of the garden can Austin and his mother weed together in 1 hr? $\frac{3}{5}$

9. Patricia is responsible for washing $\frac{6}{8}$ of the desks in her classroom. She has already washed $\frac{4}{8}$ of the desks. What fraction of the desks does she have left to wash? $\frac{2}{8}$

Test Prep

10. Which is the difference of $\frac{5}{8} - \frac{3}{8}$?

A. $\frac{8}{8}$ B. $\frac{8}{16}$ C $\frac{2}{8}$ D. $\frac{2}{16}$

11. **Writing in Math** Write an addition problem with $\frac{3}{5}$ as the sum.

Sample answer: Roy carries $\frac{1}{5}$ of the gym equipment, Deb carries $\frac{2}{5}$ of it. What fraction of the equipment do Roy and Deb carry together?

120   Use with Lesson 9-9.

© Pearson Education, Inc. 3

Name_____

Adding and Subtracting Fractions   R 9-9

Adding fractions:

Find $\frac{2}{4} + \frac{1}{4}$.

$\frac{2}{4}$ + $\frac{1}{4}$ = $\frac{3}{4}$

Add the numerators but keep the denominators the same.

So, $\frac{2}{4} + \frac{1}{4} = \frac{3}{4}$.

Subtracting fractions:

Find $\frac{5}{6} - \frac{4}{6}$.

$\frac{5}{6}$ − $\frac{4}{6}$ = $\frac{1}{6}$

You subtract the numerators, and the denominator remains the same.

So, $\frac{5}{6} - \frac{4}{6} = \frac{1}{6}$.

Add or subtract. You may use fraction strips or draw a picture to help.

1. $\frac{1}{3} + \frac{1}{3} = \frac{2}{3}$ _____

2. $\frac{3}{5} - \frac{2}{5} = \frac{1}{5}$ _____

3. $\frac{4}{8} + \frac{1}{8} = \frac{5}{8}$ _____

4. $\frac{5}{6} - \frac{2}{6} = \frac{3}{6}$ _____

5. $\frac{10}{12} - \frac{5}{12} = \frac{5}{12}$ _____

6. $\frac{4}{5} - \frac{1}{5} = \frac{3}{5}$ _____

7. **Reasoning** Judy left $\frac{4}{5}$ of a pot of stew for Dan. Dan ate $\frac{2}{5}$ of what she left. What fraction of the pot of stew was left after Dan ate?

$\frac{2}{5}$ of the pot of stew was left.

120   Use with Lesson 9-9.

© Pearson Education, Inc. 3

Name_____

Make It Whole   E 9-9
VISUAL THINKING

Circle the shaded figure on the right that you need to add to the figure on the left to make a whole shaded figure. An example is shown below.

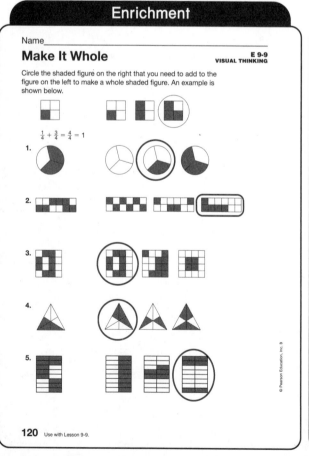

$\frac{1}{4} + \frac{3}{4} = \frac{4}{4} = 1$

1.

2.

3.

4.

5.

120   Use with Lesson 9-9.

© Pearson Education, Inc. 3

Name_____

Adding and Subtracting Fractions   PS 9-9

Jim's Neighborhood The chart shows the distances between some places in Jim's neighborhood.

From	To	Distance
Jim's house	Library	$\frac{2}{8}$ miles
Library	Bank	$\frac{5}{8}$ miles
Jim's house	School	$\frac{4}{8}$ miles
School	Library	$\frac{1}{8}$ miles
Jim's house	Grocery store	$\frac{3}{8}$ miles
Grocery store	Bank	$\frac{3}{8}$ miles

1. Jim walked from his house to school. After school, he walked to the library. How far did he walk? $\frac{5}{8}$ mi

2. From Jim's house, how much farther is it to the grocery store than to the library? $\frac{1}{8}$ mi

3. Jim walked from his house to the library. Then he walked from the library to the bank. How far did he walk? $\frac{7}{8}$ mi

4. From Jim's house, how much farther is it to the school than to the library? $\frac{2}{8}$ mi

5. Jim rode his bike from his house to the grocery store. Then he rode to the bank. How far did he ride? $\frac{6}{8}$ mi

6. From Jim's house, how much farther is it to the school than to the grocery store? $\frac{1}{8}$ mi

7. **Writing in Math** On Friday, Jim walked to the library and back home. On Saturday, he walked to the grocery store and back home. On which day did he walk farther? Explain.

Saturday; Sample answer: He walked $\frac{4}{8}$ mi on Friday and $\frac{6}{8}$ mi on Saturday. He walked farther on Saturday.

120   Use with Lesson 9-9.

© Pearson Education, Inc. 3

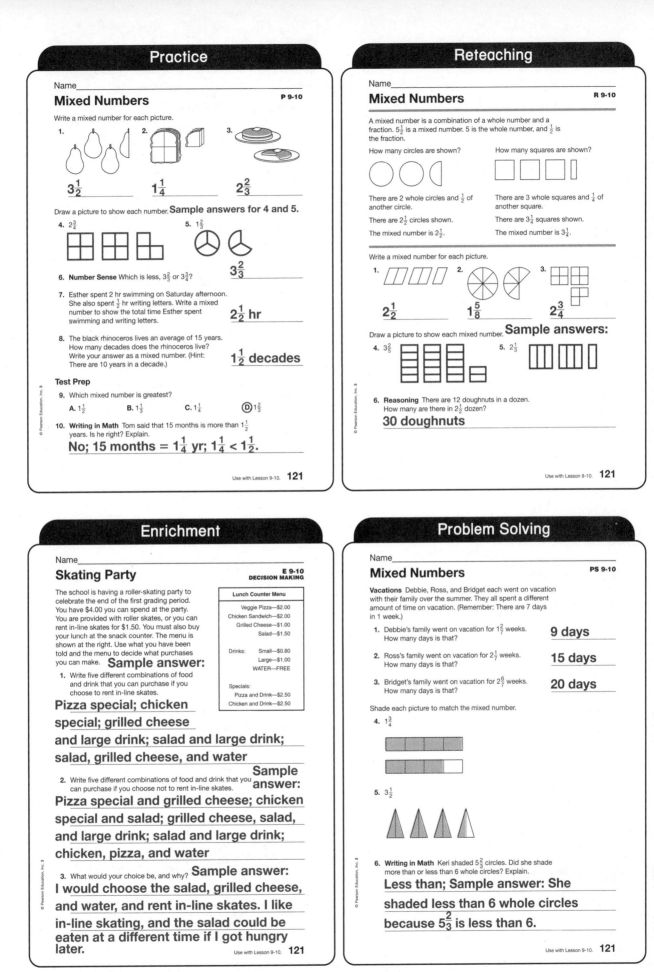

Practice

Name_____

Mixed Numbers
P 9-10

Write a mixed number for each picture.

1.

$3\frac{1}{2}$

2.

$1\frac{1}{4}$

3.

$2\frac{2}{3}$

Draw a picture to show each number. **Sample answers for 4 and 5.**

4. $2\frac{3}{4}$

5. $1\frac{2}{3}$

$3\frac{2}{3}$

6. **Number Sense** Which is less, $3\frac{2}{3}$ or $3\frac{3}{4}$?

7. Esther spent 2 hr swimming on Saturday afternoon. She also spent $\frac{1}{2}$ hr writing letters. Write a mixed number to show the total time Esther spent swimming and writing letters.

$2\frac{1}{2}$ hr

8. The black rhinoceros lives an average of 15 years. How many decades does the rhinoceros live? Write your answer as a mixed number. (Hint: There are 10 years in a decade.)

$1\frac{1}{2}$ decades

Test Prep

9. Which mixed number is greatest?

A. $1\frac{1}{2}$ B. $1\frac{1}{3}$ C. $1\frac{1}{4}$ (D) $1\frac{2}{3}$

10. **Writing in Math** Tom said that 15 months is more than $1\frac{1}{2}$ years. Is he right? Explain.

No; 15 months = $1\frac{1}{4}$ yr; $1\frac{1}{4} < 1\frac{1}{2}$.

Reteaching

Name_____

Mixed Numbers
R 9-10

A mixed number is a combination of a whole number and a fraction. $5\frac{1}{2}$ is a mixed number. 5 is the whole number, and $\frac{1}{2}$ is the fraction.

How many circles are shown?

There are 2 whole circles and $\frac{1}{2}$ of another circle.

There are $2\frac{1}{2}$ circles shown.

The mixed number is $2\frac{1}{2}$.

How many squares are shown?

There are 3 whole squares and $\frac{1}{4}$ of another square.

There are $3\frac{1}{4}$ squares shown.

The mixed number is $3\frac{1}{4}$.

Write a mixed number for each picture.

1.

$2\frac{1}{2}$

2.

$1\frac{5}{8}$

3.

$2\frac{3}{4}$

Draw a picture to show each mixed number. **Sample answers:**

4. $3\frac{2}{5}$

5. $2\frac{1}{3}$

6. **Reasoning** There are 12 doughnuts in a dozen. How many are there in $2\frac{1}{2}$ dozen?

30 doughnuts

Enrichment

Name_____

Skating Party
E 9-10
DECISION MAKING

The school is having a roller-skating party to celebrate the end of the first grading period. You have $4.00 you can spend at the party. You are provided with roller skates, or you can rent in-line skates for $1.50. You must also buy your lunch at the snack counter. The menu is shown at the right. Use what you have been told and the menu to decide what purchases you can make. **Sample answer:**

Lunch Counter Menu
Veggie Pizza—$2.00
Chicken Sandwich—$2.00
Grilled Cheese—$1.00
Salad—$1.50
Drinks: Small—$0.80
Large—$1.00
WATER—FREE
Specials:
Pizza and Drink—$2.50
Chicken and Drink—$2.50

1. Write five different combinations of food and drink that you can purchase if you choose to rent in-line skates.

Pizza special; chicken special; grilled cheese and large drink; salad and large drink; salad, grilled cheese, and water

2. Write five different combinations of food and drink that you can purchase if you choose not to rent in-line skates. **Sample answer:**

Pizza special and grilled cheese; chicken special and salad; grilled cheese, salad, and large drink; salad and large drink; chicken, pizza, and water

3. What would your choice be, and why? **Sample answer:**

I would choose the salad, grilled cheese, and water, and rent in-line skates. I like in-line skating, and the salad could be eaten at a different time if I got hungry later.

Problem Solving

Name_____

Mixed Numbers
PS 9-10

Vacations Debbie, Ross, and Bridget each went on vacation with their family over the summer. They all spent a different amount of time on vacation. (Remember: There are 7 days in 1 week.)

1. Debbie's family went on vacation for $1\frac{2}{7}$ weeks. How many days is that?

9 days

2. Ross's family went on vacation for $2\frac{1}{7}$ weeks. How many days is that?

15 days

3. Bridget's family went on vacation for $2\frac{6}{7}$ weeks. How many days is that?

20 days

Shade each picture to match the mixed number.

4. $1\frac{3}{4}$

5. $3\frac{1}{2}$

6. **Writing in Math** Keri shaded $5\frac{2}{3}$ circles. Did she shade more or less than 6 whole circles? Explain.

Less than; Sample answer: She shaded less than 6 whole circles because $5\frac{2}{3}$ is less than 6.

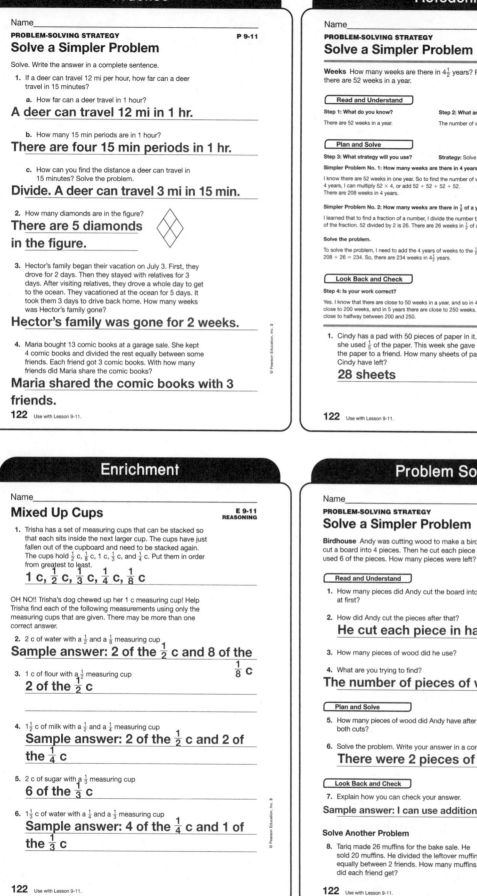

Name_____

PROBLEM-SOLVING STRATEGY   P 9-11
Solve a Simpler Problem

Solve. Write the answer in a complete sentence.

1. If a deer can travel 12 mi per hour, how far can a deer travel in 15 minutes?

   a. How far can a deer travel in 1 hour?

A deer can travel 12 mi in 1 hr.

   b. How many 15 min periods are in 1 hour?

There are four 15 min periods in 1 hr.

   c. How can you find the distance a deer can travel in 15 minutes? Solve the problem.

Divide. A deer can travel 3 mi in 15 min.

2. How many diamonds are in the figure?

There are 5 diamonds
in the figure.

3. Hector's family began their vacation on July 3. First, they drove for 2 days. Then they stayed with relatives for 3 days. After visiting relatives, they drove a whole day to get to the ocean. They vacationed at the ocean for 5 days. It took them 3 days to drive back home. How many weeks was Hector's family gone?

Hector's family was gone for 2 weeks.

4. Maria bought 13 comic books at a garage sale. She kept 4 comic books and divided the rest equally between some friends. Each friend got 3 comic books. With how many friends did Maria share the comic books?

Maria shared the comic books with 3
friends.

122 Use with Lesson 9-11.

© Pearson Education, Inc. 3

Name_____

PROBLEM-SOLVING STRATEGY   R 9-11
Solve a Simpler Problem

Weeks How many weeks are there in $4\frac{1}{2}$ years? Remember, there are 52 weeks in a year.

[Read and Understand]

Step 1: What do you know?   Step 2: What are you trying to find?
There are 52 weeks in a year.   The number of weeks in $4\frac{1}{2}$ years

[Plan and Solve]

Step 3: What strategy will you use?   Strategy: Solve a simpler problem

Simpler Problem No. 1: How many weeks are there in 4 years?

I know there are 52 weeks in one year. So to find the number of weeks in 4 years, I can multiply 52×4, or add $52 + 52 + 52 + 52$. There are 208 weeks in 4 years.

Simpler Problem No. 2: How many weeks are there in $\frac{1}{2}$ of a year?

I learned that to find a fraction of a number, I divide the number by the denominator of the fraction. 52 divided by 2 is 26. There are 26 weeks in $\frac{1}{2}$ of a year.

Solve the problem.

To solve the problem, I need to add the 4 years of weeks to the $\frac{1}{2}$ year of weeks. $208 + 26 = 234$. So, there are 234 weeks in $4\frac{1}{2}$ years.

[Look Back and Check]

Step 4: Is your work correct?

Yes. I know that there are close to 50 weeks in a year, and so in 4 years there are close to 200 weeks, and in 5 years there are close to 250 weeks. 234 weeks is close to halfway between 200 and 250.

1. Cindy has a pad with 50 pieces of paper in it. Last week she used $\frac{1}{5}$ of the paper. This week she gave 12 sheets of the paper to a friend. How many sheets of paper does Cindy have left?

28 sheets

122 Use with Lesson 9-11.

© Pearson Education, Inc. 3

Name_____

Mixed Up Cups   E 9-11
                                                   REASONING

1. Trisha has a set of measuring cups that can be stacked so that each sits inside the next larger cup. The cups have just fallen out of the cupboard and need to be stacked again. The cups hold $\frac{1}{2}$ c, $\frac{1}{8}$ c, 1 c, $\frac{1}{3}$ c, and $\frac{1}{4}$ c. Put them in order from greatest to least.

1 c, $\frac{1}{2}$ c, $\frac{1}{3}$ c, $\frac{1}{4}$ c, $\frac{1}{8}$ c

OH NO!! Trisha's dog chewed up her 1 c measuring cup! Help Trisha find each of the following measurements using only the measuring cups that are given. There may be more than one correct answer.

2. 2 c of water with a $\frac{1}{2}$ and a $\frac{1}{8}$ measuring cup

Sample answer: 2 of the $\frac{1}{2}$ c and 8 of the $\frac{1}{8}$ c

3. 1 c of flour with a $\frac{1}{2}$ measuring cup

2 of the $\frac{1}{2}$ c

4. $1\frac{1}{2}$ c of milk with a $\frac{1}{2}$ and a $\frac{1}{4}$ measuring cup

Sample answer: 2 of the $\frac{1}{2}$ c and 2 of the $\frac{1}{4}$ c

5. 2 c of sugar with a $\frac{1}{3}$ measuring cup

6 of the $\frac{1}{3}$ c

6. $1\frac{1}{3}$ c of water with a $\frac{1}{4}$ and a $\frac{1}{3}$ measuring cup

Sample answer: 4 of the $\frac{1}{4}$ c and 1 of the $\frac{1}{3}$ c

122 Use with Lesson 9-11.

© Pearson Education, Inc. 3

Name_____

PROBLEM-SOLVING STRATEGY   PS 9-11
Solve a Simpler Problem

Birdhouse Andy was cutting wood to make a birdhouse. He cut a board into 4 pieces. Then he cut each piece in half. He used 6 of the pieces. How many pieces were left?

[Read and Understand]

1. How many pieces did Andy cut the board into at first?   **4 pieces**

2. How did Andy cut the pieces after that?

He cut each piece in half.

3. How many pieces of wood did he use?   **6 pieces**

4. What are you trying to find?

The number of pieces of wood left over

[Plan and Solve]

5. How many pieces of wood did Andy have after both cuts?   **8 pieces**

6. Solve the problem. Write your answer in a complete sentence.

There were 2 pieces of wood left.

[Look Back and Check]

7. Explain how you can check your answer.

Sample answer: I can use addition to check: $2 + 6 = 8$.

Solve Another Problem

8. Tariq made 26 muffins for the bake sale. He sold 20 muffins. He divided the leftover muffins equally between 2 friends. How many muffins did each friend get?   **3 muffins**

122 Use with Lesson 9-11.

© Pearson Education, Inc. 3

---

122   Use with Chapter 9, Lesson 11

Name_____

Length Check students' estimates.

P 9-12

Estimate each length. Then measure to the nearest inch.

1.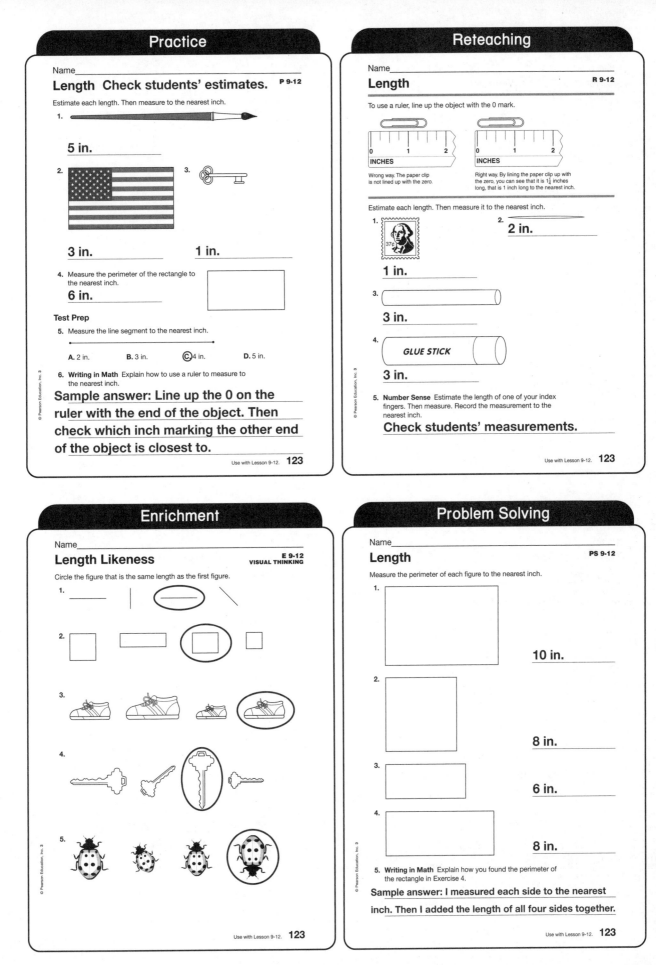

5 in.

2.

3 in.

3.

1 in.

4. Measure the perimeter of the rectangle to the nearest inch.

6 in.

Test Prep

5. Measure the line segment to the nearest inch.

A. 2 in.   **B.** 3 in.   (C) 4 in.   **D.** 5 in.

6. **Writing in Math** Explain how to use a ruler to measure to the nearest inch.

Sample answer: Line up the 0 on the ruler with the end of the object. Then check which inch marking the other end of the object is closest to.

© Pearson Education, Inc. 3

Name_____

Length

R 9-12

To use a ruler, line up the object with the 0 mark.

Wrong way. The paper clip is not lined up with the zero.

Right way. By lining the paper clip up with the zero, you can see that it is 1¼ inches long, that is 1 inch long to the nearest inch.

Estimate each length. Then measure it to the nearest inch.

1.

2.

2 in.

1 in.

3.

3 in.

4. GLUE STICK

3 in.

5. **Number Sense** Estimate the length of one of your index fingers. Then measure. Record the measurement to the nearest inch.

Check students' measurements.

© Pearson Education, Inc. 3

Name_____

Length Likeness

E 9-12
VISUAL THINKING

Circle the figure that is the same length as the first figure.

1.

2.

3.

4.

5.

© Pearson Education, Inc. 3

Name_____

Length

PS 9-12

Measure the perimeter of each figure to the nearest inch.

1.

10 in.

2.

8 in.

3.

6 in.

4.

8 in.

5. **Writing in Math** Explain how you found the perimeter of the rectangle in Exercise 4.

Sample answer: I measured each side to the nearest inch. Then I added the length of all four sides together.

© Pearson Education, Inc. 3

Name_____

Measuring to the Nearest $\frac{1}{2}$ and $\frac{1}{4}$ Inch

P 9-13

Measure the length of each object to the nearest $\frac{1}{2}$ and $\frac{1}{4}$ inch.

1.

1 in.; 1 in.

2.

2 in.; $2\frac{1}{4}$ in.

3.

$4\frac{1}{2}$ in.; $4\frac{1}{2}$ in.

4. Draw a line segment that is $3\frac{3}{4}$ in. long. **Sample answer:**

5. **Estimation** Estimate the length of the pencil you are using to the nearest $\frac{1}{4}$ inch. Then measure to check. Record your estimate and measurement.

Check students' estimates and measurements.

Test Prep

6. Which can NOT be a length to the nearest $\frac{1}{4}$ inch?

A. $\frac{1}{4}$ in.　　B. $\frac{1}{2}$ in.　　C. $\frac{3}{8}$ in.　　D. 1 in.

7. **Writing in Math** Eric and Madison both measured the same trading card. Eric says the card is 3 in. long. Madison says it is $2\frac{3}{4}$ in. long. Their teacher says they are both correct. How is this possible?

Sample answer: Eric measured to the nearest $\frac{1}{2}$ inch, and Madison measured to the nearest $\frac{1}{4}$ inch.

124 Use with Lesson 9-13.

© Pearson Education, Inc. 3

Name_____

Measuring to the Nearest $\frac{1}{2}$ and $\frac{1}{4}$ Inch

R 9-13

$\frac{1}{2}$ marks　$\frac{1}{4}$ marks

How long is the peanut to the nearest $\frac{1}{2}$ inch?

The peanut is $1\frac{1}{2}$ in. to the nearest $\frac{1}{2}$ inch.

How long is the chalk to the nearest $\frac{1}{4}$ inch?

The chalk is $2\frac{1}{4}$ in. to the nearest $\frac{1}{4}$ inch.

Measure the length of each object to the nearest $\frac{1}{2}$ and $\frac{1}{4}$ inch.

1.

3 in.; $2\frac{3}{4}$ in.

2.

1 in.; $1\frac{1}{4}$ in.

3.

$2\frac{1}{2}$ in.; $2\frac{1}{2}$ in.

4.

2 in.; 2 in.

124 Use with Lesson 9-13.

© Pearson Education, Inc. 3

Name_____

The Gift of Choice

E 9-13
DECISION MAKING

You are buying gifts for groups of children. Each group has a budgeted amount that you can spend and each child has a list of a few items he or she would like. For each group of children, choose gifts that remain within the budgeted amount for the group and then explain how you made your decision.

Price List	
Swim goggles	$3
Earrings	$5
Toy truck	$7
CD	$8
T-shirt	$10
Sweater	$12
Necklace	$15
Video game	$15

1. **Group 1** Budget amount: $30
   1 girl: Necklace or earrings
   1 girl: T-shirt
   1 boy: CD or video game

Sample answers are given.

Earrings, T-shirt, CD; I chose these because I wanted to keep the cost near $30.

2. **Group 2** Budget amount: $42
   2 girls each: T-shirt or necklace
   1 girl: Sweater or necklace

Two T-shirts, sweater; This way none of the girls would be upset because one got a necklace and the others did not.

3. **Group 3** Budget amount: $36
   1 boy: toy truck, video game, swim goggles
   1 girl: necklace, sweater, swim goggles

Video game, necklace, and 2 pairs of swim goggles; I had enough budgeted to buy them the most expensive thing they wanted, and the swim goggles.

124 Use with Lesson 9-13.

© Pearson Education, Inc. 3

Name_____

Measuring to the Nearest $\frac{1}{2}$ and $\frac{1}{4}$ Inch

PS 9-13

Segment A _____
Segment B _____
Segment C _____

1. Measure the length of segment A to the nearest $\frac{1}{4}$ inch.　　$2\frac{3}{4}$ in.

2. Measure the length of segment B to the nearest $\frac{1}{4}$ inch.　　1 in.

3. Measure the length of segment C to the nearest $\frac{1}{2}$ inch.　　2 in.

4. Measure the length of segment B to the nearest $\frac{1}{2}$ inch.　　1 in.

5. Draw a square that is $1\frac{1}{4}$ inches long.

6. **Writing in Math** Explain why a measurement to the nearest $\frac{1}{4}$ inch could be 3 in. even though 3 is a whole number.

Sample answer: You can think of the number 3 as $3\frac{0}{4}$. It is the $\frac{1}{4}$ inch that is between $2\frac{3}{4}$ in. and $3\frac{1}{4}$ in.

124 Use with Lesson 9-13.

© Pearson Education, Inc. 3

Name_____

Length in Feet and Inches

P 9-14

Write each measurement in inches. You may make a table to help.

1. 3 ft, 3 in. **39 in.**   2. 1 ft, 9 in. **21 in.**   3. 2 ft, 7 in. **31 in.**

4. 5 ft, 6 in. **66 in.**   5. 4 ft, 8 in. **56 in.**   6. 1 ft, 11 in. **23 in.**

7. Finish the table to find how many inches are in 7 ft, 8 in.
   Write the answer in a complete sentence.

Feet	1	2	3	4	5	6	7
Inches	12	24	36	48	60	72	84

There are 92 in. in 7 ft, 8 in.

African elephant	13 ft tall
Whale shark	41 ft 6 in. long
Stick insect	1 ft 3 in. long
Giraffe	19 ft tall

8. How many inches long is the stick insect? **15 in.**

9. How many inches taller is a giraffe than an African elephant? **72 in.**

10. List the animals in order from largest to smallest.

Whale shark, giraffe, African elephant, stick insect

Test Prep

11. Which measurement is equal to 3 ft, 7 in.?

   A. 37 in.   Ⓑ 43 in.   C. 44 in.   D. 73 in.

12. **Writing in Math** Name something you would not measure in feet and inches. Tell why.

Sample answer: The distance from home to school because it is too far

Name_____

Length in Feet and Inches

R 9-14

Longer lengths can be measured in feet. 1 ft is 12 in. long.

To change a measurement from feet into inches, you can multiply the number of feet by 12.

2 ft = _____ in.?

$2 \times 12 = 24$

So, 2 ft = 24 in.

How many inches are in 4 ft, 2 in.?

First multiply.

4×12 in. = 48 in.

Then add the extra inches.

48 in. + 2 in. = 50 in.

So, 4 ft, 2 in. = 50 in.

Write each measurement in inches. You may make a table to help.

1. 1 foot, 3 inches **15 inches**   2. 5 feet, 6 inches **66 inches**

3. 2 feet **24 inches**   4. 3 feet, 2 inches **38 inches**

5. 1 foot, 9 inches **21 inches**   6. 6 feet, 3 inches **75 inches**

7. 8 feet **96 inches**   8. 4 feet, 8 inches **56 inches**

9. 7 feet, 7 inches **91 inches**

10. **Number Sense** Marsha broad jumped 5 ft, 1 in. How many inches did she jump? **61 inches**

Name_____

Hide and Seek

E 9-14
VISUAL THINKING

Somewhere inside the figure on the right, the figure on the left is hidden. See if you can find the hidden figure and outline it. The figure may be larger, smaller, turned, or flipped. There may be more than one correct answer.

1.

2.

3.

4.

Name_____

Length in Feet and Inches

PS 9-14

Use the table to find the height of each person in inches.

Evan	4 feet, 6 inches
Nadia	5 feet, 1 inch
Lucas	4 feet, 10 inches
Serena	4 feet, 8 inches

1. Lucas **58 in.**

2. Evan **54 in.**

3. Serena **56 in.**

4. Nadia **61 in.**

5. Marnie, Andrew, and Sara each planted a pine tree in their neighborhood park. After one year, they measured their trees. Marnie's tree was 33 inches tall, Andrew's tree was 3 feet tall, and Sara's tree was 3 feet, 4 inches tall. List the tree heights in order from greatest to least.

3 ft 4 in., 3 ft, 33 in.

6. Female polar bears grow to about 6 feet long. How many inches is that? **About 72 in.**

7. A Komodo dragon can grow to be 9 feet long. How many inches is that? **108 in.**

8. A stick insect can grow up to 15 inches long. How long is that in feet and inches? **1 ft 3 in.**

9. **Writing in Math** Which measurement is longer, 25 inches or 2 feet, 4 inches? Explain.

2 ft 4 in.; Sample answer:
25 in. = 2 ft 1 in., so 2 ft 4 in. is longer.

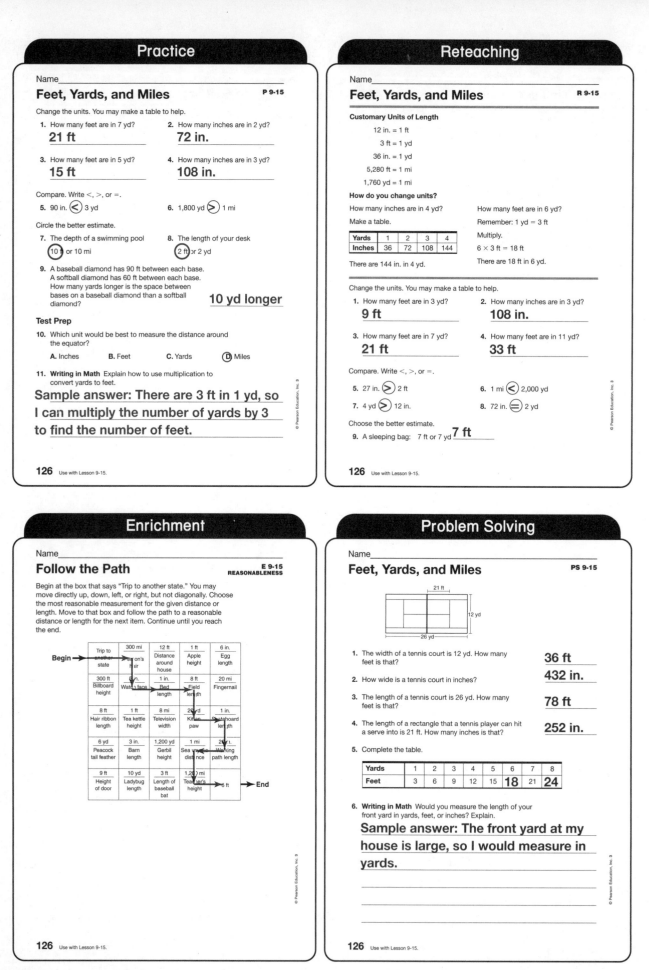

Practice

Name_____

Feet, Yards, and Miles

P 9-15

Change the units. You may make a table to help.

1. How many feet are in 7 yd?

   21 ft

2. How many inches are in 2 yd?

   72 in.

3. How many feet are in 5 yd?

   15 ft

4. How many inches are in 3 yd?

   108 in.

Compare. Write <, >, or =.

5. 90 in. $<$ 3 yd

6. 1,800 yd $>$ 1 mi

Circle the better estimate.

7. The depth of a swimming pool

   (10 ft) or 10 mi

8. The length of your desk

   (2 ft) or 2 yd

9. A baseball diamond has 90 ft between each base. A softball diamond has 60 ft between each base. How many yards longer is the space between bases on a baseball diamond than a softball diamond?

   10 yd longer

Test Prep

10. Which unit would be best to measure the distance around the equator?

   A. Inches   B. Feet   C. Yards   (D) Miles

11. **Writing in Math** Explain how to use multiplication to convert yards to feet.

   Sample answer: There are 3 ft in 1 yd, so I can multiply the number of yards by 3 to find the number of feet.

126 Use with Lesson 9-15.

© Pearson Education, Inc. 3

Reteaching

Name_____

Feet, Yards, and Miles

R 9-15

Customary Units of Length

12 in. = 1 ft

3 ft = 1 yd

36 in. = 1 yd

5,280 ft = 1 mi

1,760 yd = 1 mi

How do you change units?

How many inches are in 4 yd?

Make a table.

Yards	1	2	3	4
Inches	36	72	108	144

There are 144 in. in 4 yd.

How many feet are in 6 yd?

Remember: 1 yd = 3 ft

Multiply.

$6 \times 3 \text{ ft} = 18 \text{ ft}$

There are 18 ft in 6 yd.

Change the units. You may make a table to help.

1. How many feet are in 3 yd?

   9 ft

2. How many inches are in 3 yd?

   108 in.

3. How many feet are in 7 yd?

   21 ft

4. How many feet are in 11 yd?

   33 ft

Compare. Write <, >, or =.

5. 27 in. $>$ 2 ft

6. 1 mi $<$ 2,000 yd

7. 4 yd $>$ 12 in.

8. 72 in. $=$ 2 yd

Choose the better estimate.

9. A sleeping bag: 7 ft or 7 yd   **7 ft**

126 Use with Lesson 9-15.

© Pearson Education, Inc. 3

Enrichment

Name_____

Follow the Path

E 9-15
REASONABLENESS

Begin at the box that says "Trip to another state." You may move directly up, down, left, or right, but not diagonally. Choose the most reasonable measurement for the given distance or length. Move to that box and follow the path to a reasonable distance or length for the next item. Continue until you reach the end.

Begin →

Trip to another state	300 mi Aaron's hair	12 ft Distance around house	1 ft Apple height	6 in. Egg length
300 ft Billboard height	6 in. Watch face	1 in. Bed length	8 ft Field length	20 mi Fingernail
8 ft Hair ribbon length	1 ft Tea kettle height	8 mi Television width	26 yd Kitten paw	1 in. Skateboard length
6 yd Peacock tail feather	3 in. Barn length	1,200 yd Gerbil height	1 mi Sea waves distance	26 in. Walking path length
9 ft Height of door	10 yd Ladybug length	3 ft Length of baseball bat	1,200 mi Teacher's height	6 ft

→ End

126 Use with Lesson 9-15.

© Pearson Education, Inc. 3

Problem Solving

Name_____

Feet, Yards, and Miles

PS 9-15

21 ft

12 yd

26 yd

1. The width of a tennis court is 12 yd. How many feet is that?

   36 ft

2. How wide is a tennis court in inches?

   432 in.

3. The length of a tennis court is 26 yd. How many feet is that?

   78 ft

4. The length of a rectangle that a tennis player can hit a serve into is 21 ft. How many inches is that?

   252 in.

5. Complete the table.

Yards	1	2	3	4	5	6	7	8
Feet	3	6	9	12	15	**18**	21	**24**

6. **Writing in Math** Would you measure the length of your front yard in yards, feet, or inches? Explain.

   Sample answer: The front yard at my house is large, so I would measure in yards.

126 Use with Lesson 9-15.

© Pearson Education, Inc. 3

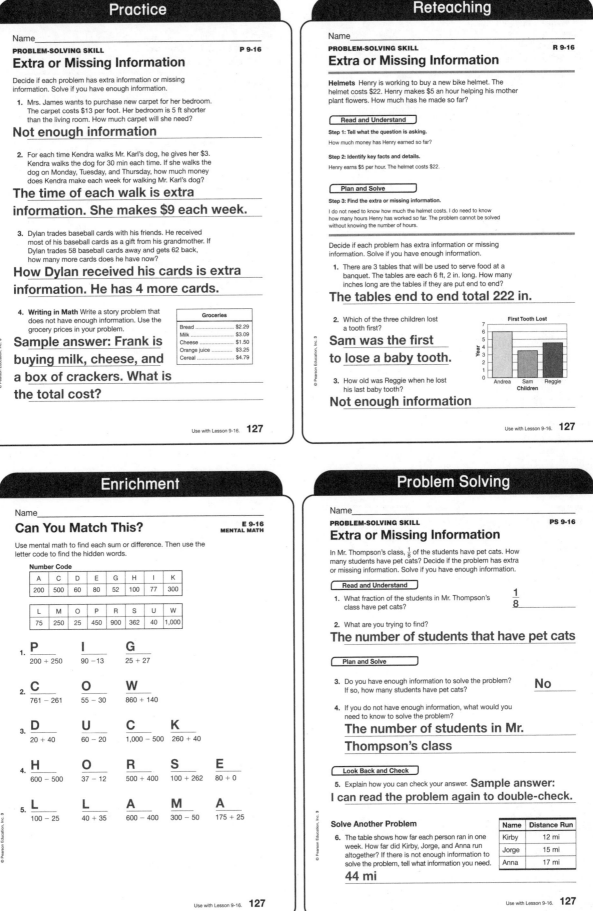

Practice

Name_____

PROBLEM-SOLVING SKILL   P 9-16

Extra or Missing Information

Decide if each problem has extra information or missing
information. Solve if you have enough information.

1. Mrs. James wants to purchase new carpet for her bedroom.
The carpet costs $13 per foot. Her bedroom is 5 ft shorter
than the living room. How much carpet will she need?

Not enough information

2. For each time Kendra walks Mr. Karl's dog, he gives her $3.
Kendra walks the dog for 30 min each time. If she walks the
dog on Monday, Tuesday, and Thursday, how much money
does Kendra make each week for walking Mr. Karl's dog?

The time of each walk is extra

information. She makes $9 each week.

3. Dylan trades baseball cards with his friends. He received
most of his baseball cards as a gift from his grandmother. If
Dylan trades 58 baseball cards away and gets 62 back,
how many more cards does he have now?

How Dylan received his cards is extra

information. He has 4 more cards.

4. **Writing in Math** Write a story problem that
does not have enough information. Use the
grocery prices in your problem.

Groceries	
Bread	$2.29
Milk	$3.09
Cheese	$1.50
Orange juice	$3.25
Cereal	$4.79

Sample answer: Frank is
buying milk, cheese, and
a box of crackers. What is
the total cost?

Use with Lesson 9-16. **127**

Reteaching

Name_____

PROBLEM-SOLVING SKILL   R 9-16

Extra or Missing Information

Helmets Henry is working to buy a new bike helmet. The
helmet costs $22. Henry makes $5 an hour helping his mother
plant flowers. How much has he made so far?

[**Read and Understand**]

Step 1: Tell what the question is asking.
How much money has Henry earned so far?

Step 2: Identify key facts and details.
Henry earns $5 per hour. The helmet costs $22.

[**Plan and Solve**]

Step 3: Find the extra or missing information.
I do not need to know how much the helmet costs. I do need to know
how many hours Henry has worked so far. The problem cannot be solved
without knowing the number of hours.

Decide if each problem has extra information or missing
information. Solve if you have enough information.

1. There are 3 tables that will be used to serve food at a
banquet. The tables are each 6 ft, 2 in. long. How many
inches long are the tables if they are put end to end?

The tables end to end total 222 in.

2. Which of the three children lost
a tooth first?

Sam was the first
to lose a baby tooth.

First Tooth Lost

(bar graph with Year on y-axis 0–7, Children on x-axis: Andrea, Sam, Reggie)

3. How old was Reggie when he lost
his last baby tooth?

Not enough information

Use with Lesson 9-16. **127**

Enrichment

Name_____

Can You Match This?   E 9-16
                                                 MENTAL MATH

Use mental math to find each sum or difference. Then use the
letter code to find the hidden words.

Number Code

A	C	D	E	G	H	I	K
200	500	60	80	52	100	77	300

L	M	O	P	R	S	U	W
75	250	25	450	900	362	40	1,000

1. **P**   **I**   **G**
   200 + 250   90 − 13   25 + 27

2. **C**   **O**   **W**
   761 − 261   55 − 30   860 + 140

3. **D**   **U**   **C**   **K**
   20 + 40   60 − 20   1,000 − 500   260 + 40

4. **H**   **O**   **R**   **S**   **E**
   600 − 500   37 − 12   500 + 400   100 + 262   80 + 0

5. **L**   **L**   **A**   **M**   **A**
   100 − 25   40 + 35   600 − 400   300 − 50   175 + 25

Use with Lesson 9-16. **127**

Problem Solving

Name_____

PROBLEM-SOLVING SKILL   PS 9-16

Extra or Missing Information

In Mr. Thompson's class, $\frac{1}{8}$ of the students have pet cats. How
many students have pet cats? Decide if the problem has extra
or missing information. Solve if you have enough information.

[**Read and Understand**]

1. What fraction of the students in Mr. Thompson's
class have pet cats? $\frac{1}{8}$

2. What are you trying to find?

The number of students that have pet cats

[**Plan and Solve**]

3. Do you have enough information to solve the problem?
If so, how many students have pet cats?   **No**

4. If you do not have enough information, what would you
need to know to solve the problem?

The number of students in Mr.

Thompson's class

[**Look Back and Check**]

5. Explain how you can check your answer. **Sample answer:**
I can read the problem again to double-check.

Solve Another Problem

6. The table shows how far each person ran in one
week. How far did Kirby, Jorge, and Anna run
altogether? If there is not enough information to
solve the problem, tell what information you need.

Name	Distance Run
Kirby	12 mi
Jorge	15 mi
Anna	17 mi

44 mi

Use with Lesson 9-16. **127**

© Pearson Education, Inc. 3

Name_____

PROBLEM-SOLVING APPLICATION   P 9-17
Food Servings

The table shows an example of one serving of each of the food groups in the food pyramid.

Group	Example of 1 Serving
Milk, yogurt, and cheese	$1\frac{1}{2}$ oz of cheese
Meat, beans, eggs, and nuts	$\frac{2}{3}$ c of nuts
Vegetables	$\frac{3}{4}$ c vegetable juice
Fruit	1 medium apple
Bread, cereal, and pasta	1 slice of bread

Solve. Write your answer in a complete sentence.

1. Patsy and Kyle each drank 1 serving of carrot juice. How many cups of carrot juice did they drink altogether?

Patsy and Kyle drank $1\frac{1}{2}$ c of carrot juice altogether.

2. Alex has $\frac{4}{5}$ c of walnuts. Does he have enough for 1 serving? Explain.

Yes, 1 serving of nuts is $\frac{2}{3}$ c and $\frac{4}{5}$ c is greater than $\frac{2}{3}$ c.

3. Luke has $1\frac{3}{6}$ oz of cheese. He says that is enough for one serving. Do you agree? Explain.

Yes, $1\frac{3}{6}$ c is equal to $1\frac{1}{2}$ c, the amount in 1 serving of cheese.

4. A loaf of bread will provide 1 serving each for Julia and her brother for 5 days. How many slices of bread are in the loaf?

There are 10 slices in the loaf of bread.

© Pearson Education, Inc. 3

Name_____

PROBLEM-SOLVING APPLICATION   R 9-17
The Family Reunion

The Angelo family had a reunion. Over 200 family members from all over the country attended.

Donna Angelo made special pies for the family members to eat. One pie was divided into 5 pieces. Bill Angelo ate $\frac{2}{5}$ of the pie. How many pieces were left?

Remember to subtract fractions with the same denominators. First, subtract the numerators. Leave the denominators the same.

$$\frac{5}{5} - \frac{2}{5} = \frac{3}{5}$$

So, 3 pieces of pie were left.

1. Diana Angelo is 36 years old. Her son Ted is $\frac{1}{4}$ of her age. How old is Ted?

Ted is 9 years old.

2. When George Angelo was born he was 16 in. tall. When he was 10, he was 4 ft, 10 in. tall. As an adult George is 6 ft, 2 in. tall. How many inches did George grow from when he was born until he became an adult? Give your answer in inches.

George grew 58 in.

3. Heidi Angelo is making a friendship bracelet for her cousin Mara. She has 3 beads on the bracelet. Two of the beads are $\frac{3}{8}$ in. wide. The other bead is $\frac{1}{8}$ in. wide. How much room will the beads take up altogether on her bracelet?

The beads will take up $\frac{7}{8}$ in. on her bracelet.

4. The family ate two kinds of submarine sandwiches. The turkey sub was 4 ft, 2 in. long. The beef sub was 53 in. long. Which sub was longer?

Beef sub

© Pearson Education, Inc. 3

Name_____

Counting Change   E 9-17
                                          NUMBER SENSE

In Papua New Guinea (PNG), one *kina* is valued at about $\frac{1}{4}$ of a U.S. dollar. To find the value of a PNG paper bill in U.S. dollars, you must multiply the number of *kinas* by $\frac{1}{4}$.

For each of the following values of PNG paper money, find the value in U.S. dollars.

1. 2 *kina* = **$0.50**
2. 5 *kina* = **$1.25**
3. 10 *kina* = **$2.50**
4. 20 *kina* = **$5.00**
5. 50 *kina* = **$12.50**

To find how many *kinas* U.S. paper money is worth, you must multiply by 4.

6. 1 dollar = **4** *kina*
7. 5 dollars = **20** *kina*
8. 10 dollars = **40** *kina*
9. 20 dollars = **80** *kina*
10. 50 dollars = **200** *kina*

© Pearson Education, Inc. 3

Name_____

PROBLEM-SOLVING APPLICATION   PS 9-17
Orange Slices

Arman divided an orange into 8 equal slices. Then he cut each slice in half. He ate 12 slices. How many slices were left?

Read and Understand

1. How many slices did Arman have after he divided the orange the first time?   **8 slices**

2. How did Arman cut the slices after that?

He cut each slice in half.

3. How many slices of orange did he eat?   **12 slices**

4. What are you trying to find?

How many slices were left

Plan and Solve

5. How many slices of orange did Arman have after he cut each slice in half?   **16 slices**

6. Solve the problem. Write your answer in a complete sentence.

There were 4 orange slices left.

Look Back and Check

7. Explain how you can check your answer.

Sample answer: I can add 4 + 12 = 16.

Solve Another Problem

8. Sergio had 18 marbles. He got 12 more marbles for his birthday. Then he gave 16 marbles to Pamela. How many marbles did he have left?   **14 marbles**

© Pearson Education, Inc. 3

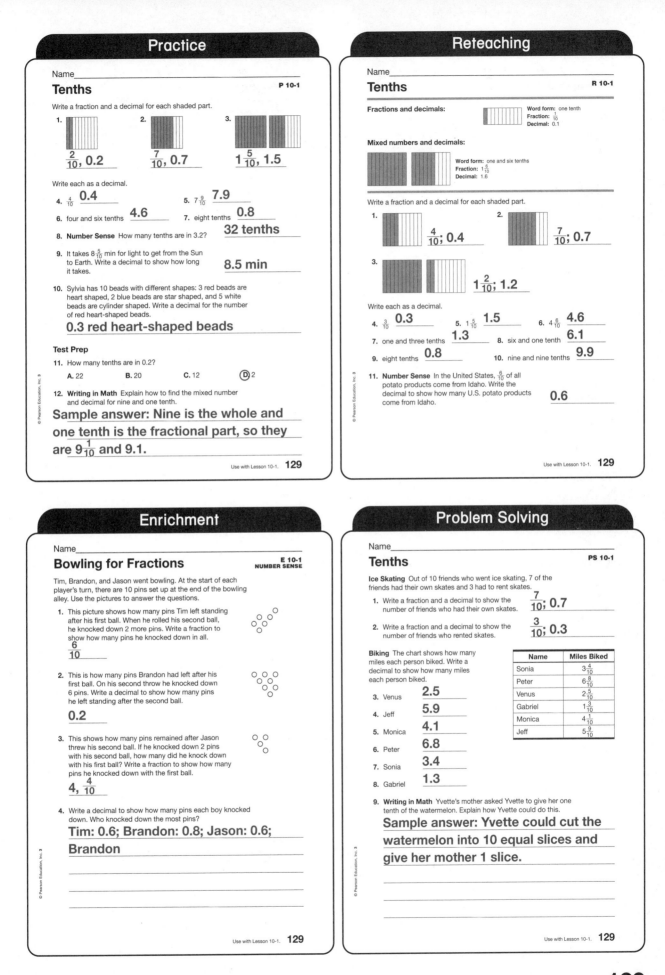

Practice

© Pearson Education, Inc. 3

Name_____

Tenths
P 10-1

Write a fraction and a decimal for each shaded part.

1. $\frac{2}{10}$, 0.2

2. $\frac{7}{10}$, 0.7

3. $1\frac{5}{10}$, 1.5

Write each as a decimal.

4. $\frac{4}{10}$ 0.4

5. $7\frac{9}{10}$ 7.9

6. four and six tenths 4.6

7. eight tenths 0.8

8. **Number Sense** How many tenths are in 3.2? 32 tenths

9. It takes $8\frac{5}{10}$ min for light to get from the Sun to Earth. Write a decimal to show how long it takes. 8.5 min

10. Sylvia has 10 beads with different shapes: 3 red beads are heart shaped, 2 blue beads are star shaped, and 5 white beads are cylinder shaped. Write a decimal for the number of red heart-shaped beads.
0.3 red heart-shaped beads

Test Prep

11. How many tenths are in 0.2?

    A. 22   B. 20   C. 12   (D) 2

12. **Writing in Math** Explain how to find the mixed number and decimal for nine and one tenth.
Sample answer: Nine is the whole and one tenth is the fractional part, so they are $9\frac{1}{10}$ and 9.1.

Use with Lesson 10-1. **129**

Reteaching

Name_____

Tenths
R 10-1

Fractions and decimals:

Word form: one tenth
Fraction: $\frac{1}{10}$
Decimal: 0.1

Mixed numbers and decimals:

Word form: one and six tenths
Fraction: $1\frac{6}{10}$
Decimal: 1.6

Write a fraction and a decimal for each shaded part.

1. $\frac{4}{10}$; 0.4

2. $\frac{7}{10}$; 0.7

3. $1\frac{2}{10}$; 1.2

Write each as a decimal.

4. $\frac{3}{10}$ 0.3

5. $1\frac{5}{10}$ 1.5

6. $4\frac{6}{10}$ 4.6

7. one and three tenths 1.3

8. six and one tenth 6.1

9. eight tenths 0.8

10. nine and nine tenths 9.9

11. **Number Sense** In the United States, $\frac{6}{10}$ of all potato products come from Idaho. Write the decimal to show how many U.S. potato products come from Idaho. 0.6

© Pearson Education, Inc. 3

Use with Lesson 10-1. **129**

Enrichment

Name_____

Bowling for Fractions
E 10-1
NUMBER SENSE

Tim, Brandon, and Jason went bowling. At the start of each player's turn, there are 10 pins set up at the end of the bowling alley. Use the pictures to answer the questions.

1. This picture shows how many pins Tim left standing after his first ball. When he rolled his second ball, he knocked down 2 more pins. Write a fraction to show how many pins he knocked down in all.
$\frac{6}{10}$

2. This is how many pins Brandon had left after his first ball. On his second throw he knocked down 6 pins. Write a decimal to show how many pins he left standing after the second ball.
0.2

3. This shows how many pins remained after Jason threw his second ball. If he knocked down 2 pins with his second ball, how many did he knock down with his first ball? Write a fraction to show how many pins he knocked down with the first ball.
$4, \frac{4}{10}$

4. Write a decimal to show how many pins each boy knocked down. Who knocked down the most pins?
Tim: 0.6; Brandon: 0.8; Jason: 0.6;
Brandon

© Pearson Education, Inc. 3
© Pearson Education, Inc. 3

Use with Lesson 10-1. **129**

Problem Solving

Name_____

Tenths
PS 10-1

Ice Skating Out of 10 friends who went ice skating, 7 of the friends had their own skates and 3 had to rent skates.

1. Write a fraction and a decimal to show the number of friends who had their own skates. $\frac{7}{10}$; 0.7

2. Write a fraction and a decimal to show the number of friends who rented skates. $\frac{3}{10}$; 0.3

Biking The chart shows how many miles each person biked. Write a decimal to show how many miles each person biked.

Name	Miles Biked
Sonia	$3\frac{4}{10}$
Peter	$6\frac{8}{10}$
Venus	$2\frac{5}{10}$
Gabriel	$1\frac{3}{10}$
Monica	$4\frac{1}{10}$
Jeff	$5\frac{9}{10}$

3. Venus 2.5

4. Jeff 5.9

5. Monica 4.1

6. Peter 6.8

7. Sonia 3.4

8. Gabriel 1.3

9. **Writing in Math** Yvette's mother asked Yvette to give her one tenth of the watermelon. Explain how Yvette could do this.
Sample answer: Yvette could cut the watermelon into 10 equal slices and give her mother 1 slice.

© Pearson Education, Inc. 3

Use with Lesson 10-1. **129**

Name_____

Hundredths

P 10-2

Write a fraction or mixed number and a decimal for each shaded part.

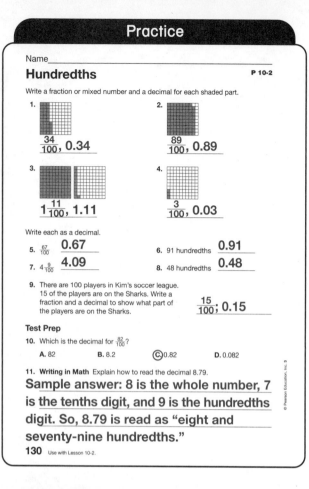

1. $\frac{34}{100}$, 0.34

2. $\frac{89}{100}$, 0.89

3. $1\frac{11}{100}$, 1.11

4. $\frac{3}{100}$, 0.03

Write each as a decimal.

5. $\frac{67}{100}$ **0.67**

6. 91 hundredths   **0.91**

7. $4\frac{9}{100}$ **4.09**

8. 48 hundredths   **0.48**

9. There are 100 players in Kim's soccer league. 15 of the players are on the Sharks. Write a fraction and a decimal to show what part of the players are on the Sharks. $\frac{15}{100}$; 0.15

Test Prep

10. Which is the decimal for $\frac{82}{100}$?

    A. 82   **B.** 8.2   **C.** 0.82   **D.** 0.082

11. **Writing in Math** Explain how to read the decimal 8.79.

Sample answer: 8 is the whole number, 7 is the tenths digit, and 9 is the hundredths digit. So, 8.79 is read as "eight and seventy-nine hundredths."

130 Use with Lesson 10-2.

Name_____

Hundredths

R 10-2

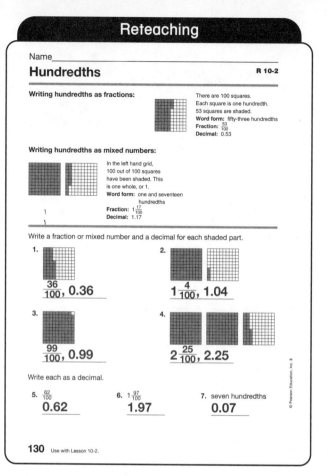

Writing hundredths as fractions:

There are 100 squares. Each square is one hundredth. 53 squares are shaded.
Word form: fifty-three hundredths
Fraction: $\frac{53}{100}$
Decimal: 0.53

Writing hundredths as mixed numbers:

In the left hand grid, 100 out of 100 squares have been shaded. This is one whole, or 1.
Word form: one and seventeen hundredths
Fraction: $1\frac{17}{100}$
Decimal: 1.17

Write a fraction or mixed number and a decimal for each shaded part.

1. $\frac{36}{100}$, 0.36

2. $1\frac{4}{100}$, 1.04

3. $\frac{99}{100}$, 0.99

4. $2\frac{25}{100}$, 2.25

Write each as a decimal.

5. $\frac{62}{100}$ **0.62**

6. $1\frac{97}{100}$ **1.97**

7. seven hundredths   **0.07**

130 Use with Lesson 10-2.

Name_____

Money Matters

E 10-2
NUMBER SENSE

Money amounts that are less than one dollar are written using decimals. Draw lines to match the following money amounts with the correct decimal amounts written in words.

1. $0.16   a. forty-one hundredths
2. $0.59   b. fifty-nine hundredths
3. $0.78   c. forty-two hundredths
4. $0.41   d. one hundredth
5. $0.66   e. seventy-eight hundredths
6. $0.01   f. ten hundredths
7. $0.42   g. sixty-six hundredths
8. $0.99   h. sixteen hundredths
9. $0.63   i. ninety-nine hundredths
10. $0.10   j. thirty-eight hundredths
11. $0.22   k. sixty-three hundredths
12. $0.84   l. twelve hundredths
13. $0.38   m. sixty-five hundredths
14. $0.65   n. twenty-two hundredths
15. $0.07   o. fifty hundredths
16. $0.12   p. eighty-four hundredths
17. $0.88   q. seven hundredths
18. $0.50   r. eighty-eight hundredths

130 Use with Lesson 10-2.

Name_____

Hundredths

PS 10-2

CD Collection Sachi has 100 CDs. The chart shows how many she has of each type. Write a fraction and a decimal to show what part of her CD collection is each type of music.

1. Country $\frac{23}{100}$; 0.23
2. Rock $\frac{56}{100}$; 0.56
3. Reggae $\frac{14}{100}$; 0.14
4. Classical $\frac{7}{100}$; 0.07

Sachi's CD Collection

Classical	7
Rock	56
Country	23
Reggae	14

Paint Colors Hanson is an artist. He keeps his paint tubes in a large case. The chart shows how many shades of each color are in the case. Write a fraction and a decimal to show what part of his paints are shades of each color.

5. Blue $\frac{27}{100}$; 0.27
6. Red $\frac{21}{100}$; 0.21
7. Green $\frac{16}{100}$; 0.16
8. Yellow $\frac{6}{100}$; 0.06
9. Brown $\frac{15}{100}$; 0.15
10. Orange $\frac{4}{100}$; 0.04
11. Purple $\frac{11}{100}$; 0.11

Color	Number of Tubes
Red	21
Orange	4
Yellow	6
Green	16
Blue	27
Purple	11
Brown	15

12. **Writing in Math** Explain how you could use a hundredths grid to show how 7 hundredths is different from 7 tenths.

Sample answer: The grid showing 7 hundredths would have 7 squares out of 100 shaded. The grid showing 7 tenths would have 70 squares out of 100 shaded.

130 Use with Lesson 10-2.

© Pearson Education, Inc. 3

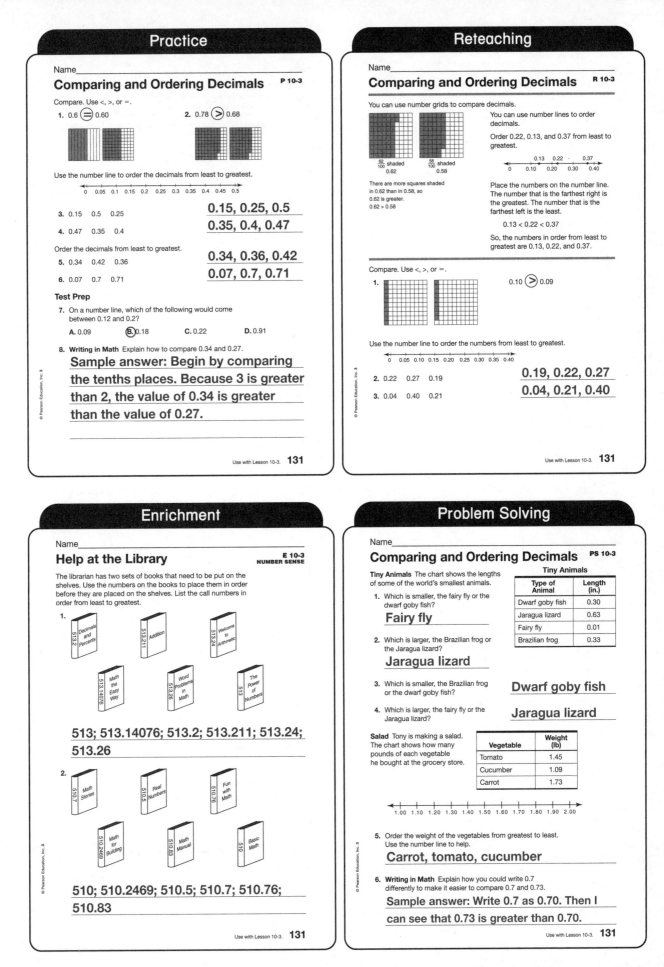

Practice

Name_____

Comparing and Ordering Decimals P 10-3

Compare. Use <, >, or =.

1. 0.6 $=$ 0.60

2. 0.78 $>$ 0.68

Use the number line to order the decimals from least to greatest.

0   0.05 0.1 0.15 0.2 0.25 0.3 0.35 0.4 0.45 0.5

3. 0.15   0.5   0.25   **0.15, 0.25, 0.5**

4. 0.47   0.35   0.4   **0.35, 0.4, 0.47**

Order the decimals from least to greatest.

5. 0.34   0.42   0.36   **0.34, 0.36, 0.42**

6. 0.07   0.7   0.71   **0.07, 0.7, 0.71**

Test Prep

7. On a number line, which of the following would come between 0.12 and 0.2?

A. 0.09   B. 0.18   C. 0.22   D. 0.91

8. Writing in Math Explain how to compare 0.34 and 0.27.

Sample answer: Begin by comparing the tenths places. Because 3 is greater than 2, the value of 0.34 is greater than the value of 0.27.

© Pearson Education, Inc. 3

Use with Lesson 10-3. **131**

Reteaching

Name_____

Comparing and Ordering Decimals R 10-3

You can use number grids to compare decimals.

$\frac{62}{100}$ shaded   0.62

$\frac{58}{100}$ shaded   0.58

There are more squares shaded in 0.62 than in 0.58, so 0.62 is greater.

0.62 > 0.58

You can use number lines to order decimals.

Order 0.22, 0.13, and 0.37 from least to greatest.

0.13   0.22   0.37

0   0.10   0.20   0.30   0.40

Place the numbers on the number line. The number that is the farthest right is the greatest. The number that is the farthest left is the least.

0.13 < 0.22 < 0.37

So, the numbers in order from least to greatest are 0.13, 0.22, and 0.37.

Compare. Use <, >, or =.

1.   0.10 $>$ 0.09

Use the number line to order the numbers from least to greatest.

0   0.05 0.10 0.15 0.20 0.25 0.30 0.35 0.40

2. 0.22   0.27   0.19   **0.19, 0.22, 0.27**

3. 0.04   0.40   0.21   **0.04, 0.21, 0.40**

© Pearson Education, Inc. 3

Use with Lesson 10-3. **131**

Enrichment

Name_____

Help at the Library E 10-3 NUMBER SENSE

The librarian has two sets of books that need to be put on the shelves. Use the numbers on the books to place them in order before they are placed on the shelves. List the call numbers in order from least to greatest.

1.

513.2 Decimals and Percents
513.211 Addition
513.24 Welcome to Arithmetic
513.14076 Math the Easy Way
513.26 Word Problems in Math
513 The Power of Numbers

513; 513.14076; 513.2; 513.211; 513.24; 513.26

2.

510.7 Math Stories
510.5 Real Numbers
510.76 Fun with Math
510.2469 Math for Building
510.83 Math Manual
510 Basic Math

510; 510.2469; 510.5; 510.7; 510.76; 510.83

© Pearson Education, Inc. 3

Use with Lesson 10-3. **131**

Problem Solving

Name_____

Comparing and Ordering Decimals PS 10-3

Tiny Animals The chart shows the lengths of some of the world's smallest animals.

Tiny Animals	
Type of Animal	Length (in.)
Dwarf goby fish	0.30
Jaragua lizard	0.63
Fairy fly	0.01
Brazilian frog	0.33

1. Which is smaller, the fairy fly or the dwarf goby fish?

Fairy fly

2. Which is larger, the Brazilian frog or the Jaragua lizard?

Jaragua lizard

3. Which is smaller, the Brazilian frog or the dwarf goby fish?

Dwarf goby fish

4. Which is larger, the fairy fly or the Jaragua lizard?

Jaragua lizard

Salad Tony is making a salad. The chart shows how many pounds of each vegetable he bought at the grocery store.

Vegetable	Weight (lb)
Tomato	1.45
Cucumber	1.09
Carrot	1.73

1.00 1.10 1.20 1.30 1.40 1.50 1.60 1.70 1.80 1.90 2.00

5. Order the weight of the vegetables from greatest to least. Use the number line to help.

Carrot, tomato, cucumber

6. Writing in Math Explain how you could write 0.7 differently to make it easier to compare 0.7 and 0.73.

Sample answer: Write 0.7 as 0.70. Then I can see that 0.73 is greater than 0.70.

© Pearson Education, Inc. 3

Use with Lesson 10-3. **131**

Name_____

Adding and Subtracting Decimals   P 10-4

Add.

1.   0.9
   + 0.4
   ____
   1.3

2.   3.47
   + 1.14
   ____
   4.61

3.   3.1
   + 2.7
   ____
   5.8

4.   4.72
   + 5.81
   ____
   10.53

Subtract.

5.   5.2
   − 2.2
   ____
   3

6.   9.51
   − 3.9
   ____
   5.61

7.   3.8
   − 2.9
   ____
   0.9

8.   8.78
   − 5.30
   ____
   3.48

9. It is 3.41 mi from Kyle's house to the library. Michelle's house is 2.78 mi from the library. How much farther from the library is Kyle's house than Michelle's house?

0.63 mi farther

10. Sam bought a book at the bookstore for $6.97. Jasmine bought the same book for $3.74 on the Internet. How much more did Sam pay for the book than Jasmine?

$3.23 more

Test Prep

11. Which is the sum of 52.62 + 6.71?

   A. 45.91   **B.** 53.29   Ⓒ 59.33   **D.** 119.72

12. **Writing in Math** Without subtracting, tell which is greater, 2.3 − 1.7 or 1. Explain.

Sample answer: 2.3 − 1.7 is less than 1 because 2 − 1 is equal to 1 and 0.7 is greater than 0.3.

Name_____

Adding and Subtracting Decimals   R 10-4

You can use what you know about adding and subtracting whole numbers to add and subtract decimals. Just remember to line up the decimal points before adding or subtracting, and to place the decimal point in the answer.

Find 8.21 + 5.89.

Step 1	Step 2	Step 3	Step 4
Line up the decimal points.	Add the hundredths.	Add the tenths.	Add the ones. Write a decimal point in the sum.
8.21 + 5.89	1 8.21 + 5.89 0	1 1 8.21 + 5.89 10	1 1 8.21 + 5.89 14.10

Find 7.45 − 1.18.

Step 1	Step 2	Step 3	Step 4
Line up the decimal points.	Subtract the hundredths. Regroup if needed.	Subtract the tenths. Regroup if needed.	Subtract the ones. Write a decimal point in the difference.
7.45 − 1.18	3 15 7.4̶5̶ − 1.18 7	3 15 7.4̶5̶ − 1.18 27	3 15 7.4̶5̶ − 1.18 6.27

Add.

1.   3.4
   + 6.2
   ____
   9.6

2.   0.47
   + 1.61
   ____
   2.08

3.   7.1
   + 4.8
   ____
   11.9

4.   2.50
   + 1.23
   ____
   3.73

Subtract.

5.   5.7
   − 2.3
   ____
   3.4

6.   7.92
   − 5.18
   ____
   2.74

7.   9.6
   − 5.4
   ____
   4.2

8.   1.56
   − 1.02
   ____
   0.54

9. Terry has $1.46 and Cindy has $1.64. How much money do they have altogether?

$3.10

Name_____

Is the Earth Shaking?   E 10-4
DATA

The Richter scale is used to measure the magnitude, or strength, of earthquakes. It measures the seismic waves, or vibrations, caused by the earthquake. The vibrations are caused when cracks in the earth move and shift. The table shows some of the major earthquakes that have occurred during the past 100 years. Use the table to answer the questions below.

Date of Earthquake	Location	Magnitude
January 31, 1906	Colombia and Ecuador	8.8
April 18, 1906	San Francisco, California	7.8
December 16, 1920	Ningxia–Konsu, China	8.6
October 22, 1926	Monterey Bay, California	6.1
January 15, 1934	Bihar, India	8.1
April 1, 1946	Unimak Island, Alaska	7.3
November 4, 1952	Kamchatka, Russia	9.0
December 16, 1954	Fairview Peak, Nevada	7.2
November 30, 1987	Gulf of Alaska	7.9
August 17, 1999	Izmit, Turkey	7.6
February 28, 2001	Olympia, Washington	6.8
June 23, 2001	Coastal Peru	8.4

1. There are two earthquakes that occurred in the 1920s listed on the table. What is the total magnitude of these two quakes?   **14.7**

2. There are two earthquakes that occurred in the 1950s on the table. What is the difference in magnitude between these two quakes?   **1.8**

3. What is the difference between the two earthquakes that occurred in California?   **1.7**

4. There are five quakes that measured higher than 8 on the Richter scale. List these by their magnitude in order from least to greatest.

8.1, 8.4, 8.6, 8.8, 9.0

Name_____

Adding and Subtracting Decimals   PS 10-4

Exercise Phoebe likes to take long walks. The chart shows how far she walked each day.

Day	Distance (in mi)
Monday	2.24
Tuesday	1.78
Wednesday	1.33
Thursday	2.02
Friday	0.96

1. How far did Phoebe walk on Monday and Wednesday combined?

3.57 mi

2. How much farther did Phoebe walk on Thursday than on Tuesday?

0.24 mi

3. How far did Phoebe walk on Tuesday and Friday combined?   **2.74 mi**

4. How much farther did Phoebe walk on Wednesday than on Friday?   **0.37 mi**

5. If Omar walked 2.14 mi on Tuesday, how much farther did he walk than Phoebe on Tuesday?   **0.36 mi**

6. How far did Phoebe walk on Tuesday and Thursday combined?   **3.8 mi**

7. On which two days did Phoebe walk a total of 2.98 mi?

Thursday and Friday

8. **Writing in Math** Which is farther, the distance Phoebe walked on Monday and Wednesday combined or the distance she walked on Tuesday and Thursday combined? Explain.

Sample answer: Phoebe walked 3.57 mi on Monday and Wednesday combined and 3.8 mi on Tuesday and Thursday combined. She walked farther on Tuesday and Thursday combined.

Name_____

PROBLEM-SOLVING STRATEGY   P 10-5

Make an Organized List

Solve. Write the answer in a complete sentence.

1. How many ways can you arrange the letters A, B, C, and D? Continue the list to find all the ways.

```
A B C D    B A C D    C A B D    D A B C
A B D C    B A D C    C A D B    D A C B
A C B D    B C A D    C B A D    D B A C
A C D B    B C D A    C B D A    D B C A
A D B C    B D A C    C D A B    D C A B
A D C B    B D C A    C D B A    D C B A
```

The letters can be arranged in 24 different ways.

2. Three marbles are in a jar: 1 red marble, 1 blue marble, and 1 green marble. In how many different orders can you take the marbles out of the jar?

I can take the marbles out of the jar in 6 different orders.

3. Beth's mother told her that she can choose 4 books from the book fair. There are 6 books that Beth would like to have. How many different combinations of 4 books could Beth choose from those 6?

There are 15 different combinations of books that Beth can choose.

4. Jim and Sarah are running for class president. Cayla and Daniel are running for vice president. How many combinations of students can be elected as class president and vice president?

There can be 4 combinations of students elected as president and vice president.

Name_____

PROBLEM-SOLVING STRATEGY   R 10-5

Make an Organized List

Posters Lisa has three posters that she would like to put on her door, but only two will fit, one above the other. One is green, one is red, and one is blue. How many different ways can she arrange the two posters on her door?

Read and Understand

Step 1: What do you know?

Two posters will fit on the door. Lisa has three posters. One poster will be above the other.

Step 2: What are you trying to find?

The number of ways two of the posters can be arranged on Lisa's door

Plan and Solve

Step 3: What strategy will you use?

Strategy: Make an organized list

```
B B R R G G
R G B G B R
```

There are 6 ways the posters can be arranged.

Look Back and Check

Step 4: Is your work correct?

Yes; there are no repeats, and all of the posters have been in the top position with each of the others, and the bottom position with each of the others.

Solve. Write the answer in a complete sentence.

1. Jenna, Mac, and Emily are having their picture taken for the yearbook. How many different ways can they line up in a straight line for the picture?

Jenna, Mac, and Emily can line up in 6 different ways.

Name_____

Discover the Pattern

E 10-5
NUMBER SENSE

Find the pattern in each table. Then complete the pattern by filling in the empty boxes.

1.

21	**57**	30	30	11	32	**0**	75
9	29	14	**15**	7	**1**	0	57
12	28	**16**	15	4	31	0	**18**

2.

9	12	6	10	7	3	**4**	5
7	**3**	3	**5**	8	13	1	5
63	36	**18**	50	56	**39**	4	**25**

3.

45	1	**2**	8	21	13	9	10
45	11	5	8	19	**10**	**0**	**7**
90	12	7	**16**	40	23	9	17

4.

6	9	8	4	**2**	3	7	5
2	3	**8**	2	9	**8**	**6**	5
12	**27**	64	8	18	24	42	**25**

5.

27	6	14	**21**	64	45	**24**	16
3	**6**	7	3	8	9	6	**8**
9	1	**2**	7	**8**	5	4	2

Name_____

PROBLEM-SOLVING STRATEGY   PS 10-5

Make an Organized List

Getting Dressed Jackie is deciding what to wear. She needs to choose one top and one bottom. How many different outfits can she wear?

Tops	Bottoms
T-shirt	Pants
Sweater	Shorts
Blouse	Skirt

Read and Understand

1. How many tops and bottoms can she choose from?

3 tops; 3 bottoms

2. What are you trying to find?

The number of different outfits she can wear

Plan and Solve

3. Make a list of all the possible outfits.

T-shirt and pants, T-shirt and shorts, T-shirt and skirt, sweater and pants, sweater and shorts, sweater and skirt, blouse and pants, blouse and shorts, blouse and skirt

4. How many different outfits can she wear? Write your answer in a complete sentence.

Jackie can wear 9 different outfits.

Look Back and Check

5. Explain how you can check your answer.

Sample answer: I can check my list to make sure I included every possible combination.

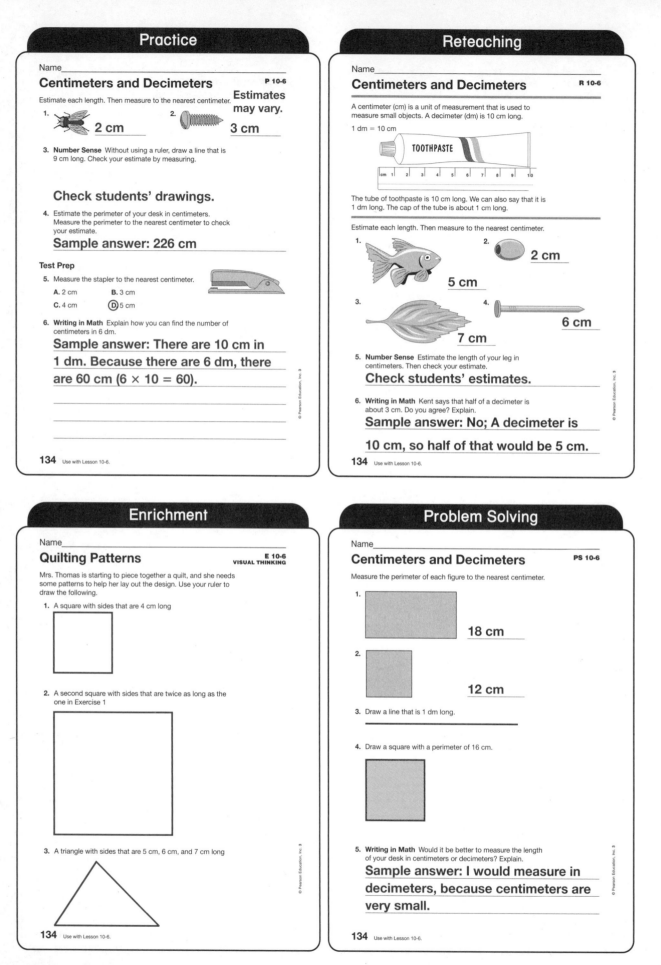

Practice

Name_____

Centimeters and Decimeters

P 10-6

Estimate each length. Then measure to the nearest centimeter.

Estimates may vary.

1. **2 cm**

2. **3 cm**

3. **Number Sense** Without using a ruler, draw a line that is 9 cm long. Check your estimate by measuring.

Check students' drawings.

4. Estimate the perimeter of your desk in centimeters. Measure the perimeter to the nearest centimeter to check your estimate.

Sample answer: 226 cm

Test Prep

5. Measure the stapler to the nearest centimeter.

   A. 2 cm   B. 3 cm
   C. 4 cm   (D) 5 cm

6. **Writing in Math** Explain how you can find the number of centimeters in 6 dm.

Sample answer: There are 10 cm in 1 dm. Because there are 6 dm, there are 60 cm (6 × 10 = 60).

134 Use with Lesson 10-6.

© Pearson Education, Inc. 3

Reteaching

Name_____

Centimeters and Decimeters

R 10-6

A centimeter (cm) is a unit of measurement that is used to measure small objects. A decimeter (dm) is 10 cm long.

1 dm = 10 cm

TOOTHPASTE

The tube of toothpaste is 10 cm long. We can also say that it is 1 dm long. The cap of the tube is about 1 cm long.

Estimate each length. Then measure to the nearest centimeter.

1. **5 cm**

2. **2 cm**

3. **7 cm**

4. **6 cm**

5. **Number Sense** Estimate the length of your leg in centimeters. Then check your estimate.

Check students' estimates.

6. **Writing in Math** Kent says that half of a decimeter is about 3 cm. Do you agree? Explain.

Sample answer: No; A decimeter is 10 cm, so half of that would be 5 cm.

134 Use with Lesson 10-6.

© Pearson Education, Inc. 3

Enrichment

Name_____

Quilting Patterns

E 10-6
VISUAL THINKING

Mrs. Thomas is starting to piece together a quilt, and she needs some patterns to help her lay out the design. Use your ruler to draw the following.

1. A square with sides that are 4 cm long

2. A second square with sides that are twice as long as the one in Exercise 1

3. A triangle with sides that are 5 cm, 6 cm, and 7 cm long

134 Use with Lesson 10-6.

© Pearson Education, Inc. 3

Problem Solving

Name_____

Centimeters and Decimeters

PS 10-6

Measure the perimeter of each figure to the nearest centimeter.

1. **18 cm**

2. **12 cm**

3. Draw a line that is 1 dm long.

4. Draw a square with a perimeter of 16 cm.

5. **Writing in Math** Would it be better to measure the length of your desk in centimeters or decimeters? Explain.

Sample answer: I would measure in decimeters, because centimeters are very small.

134 Use with Lesson 10-6.

© Pearson Education, Inc. 3

© Pearson Education, Inc. **3**

Name_____

Meters and Kilometers

P 10-7

Choose the best estimate for each.

1. a key __C__   A. 3 km

2. height of a door __B__   B. 3 m

3. distance to the store __A__   C. 3 cm

Tell if you would use meters or kilometers for each.

4. diameter of Earth   **Kilometers**

5. length of a store aisle   **Meters**

6. distance of a bus route   **Kilometers**

7. The northern border of the United States is about 6,416 km. The Great Wall of China is 6,350 km long. Which is longer, and by how many kilometers?

The northern border of the United States is about 66 km longer.

8. Complete. Use patterns to find the missing numbers.

m	1,000	3,000	5,000	7,000	9,000
km	1	**3**	**5**	**7**	**9**

Test Prep

9. Which is the best estimate for the length of a person's nose?

A. 5 ft   (B) 5 cm   C. 5 m   D. 5 km

10. **Writing in Math** Is the length of your pencil greater than or less than 1 m? Explain.

Less than; Sample answer: 1 m = 100 cm and the pencil is less than 100 cm

Use with Lesson 10-7. **135**

© Pearson Education, Inc. 3

Name_____

Meters and Kilometers

R 10-7

A meter is 100 cm. A kilometer is 1,000 m.

- Centimeters, meters, and kilometers are the most commonly used metric measurements for length or distance.
- Centimeters are used to measure small items, like pencils and paper clips.
- Meters are used to measure larger items, like pieces of lumber. They are also used to measure small distances, such as the distance from the house to the garage.
- Kilometers are used to measure long distances, such as the distance between two towns.

Choose the best estimate for each.

1. the length of a truck __B__   A. 4 cm

2. a screw __A__   B. 4 m

3. a bike trail __C__   C. 4 km

Tell if you would use meters or kilometers for each.

4. the distance to the next door neighbor's house   **Meters**

5. the perimeter of a basketball court   **Meters**

6. the length of a road   **Kilometers**

7. the length of a playground   **Meters**

8. the distance from Seattle to Chicago   **Kilometers**

Complete. Use patterns to find the missing numbers.

9.

m	10,000	7,000	5,000	1,000
km	**10**	**7**	**5**	1

10. **Number Sense** If you drove 8,000 m, how many kilometers did you drive?   **8 km**

Use with Lesson 10-7. **135**

© Pearson Education, Inc. 3

Name_____

Find the Route

E 10-7
DATA

Use the map of Ted's neighborhood to answer the questions.

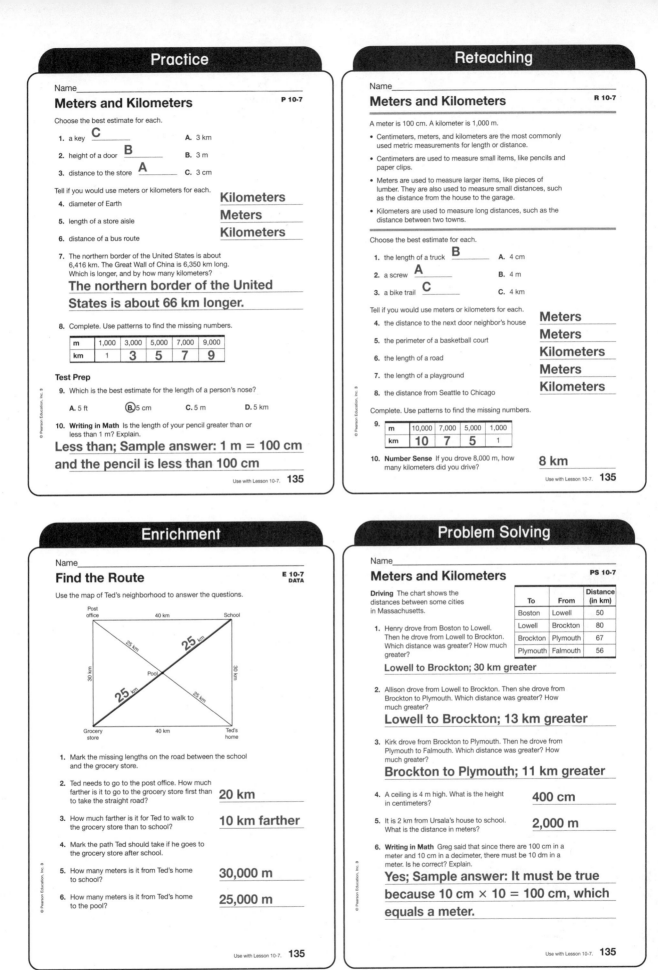

1. Mark the missing lengths on the road between the school and the grocery store.

2. Ted needs to go to the post office. How much farther is it to go to the grocery store first than to take the straight road?   **20 km**

3. How much farther is it for Ted to walk to the grocery store than to school?   **10 km farther**

4. Mark the path Ted should take if he goes to the grocery store after school.

5. How many meters is it from Ted's home to school?   **30,000 m**

6. How many meters is it from Ted's home to the pool?   **25,000 m**

Use with Lesson 10-7. **135**

© Pearson Education, Inc. 3

Name_____

Meters and Kilometers

PS 10-7

Driving The chart shows the distances between some cities in Massachusetts.

To	From	Distance (in km)
Boston	Lowell	50
Lowell	Brockton	80
Brockton	Plymouth	67
Plymouth	Falmouth	56

1. Henry drove from Boston to Lowell. Then he drove from Lowell to Brockton. Which distance was greater? How much greater?

Lowell to Brockton; 30 km greater

2. Allison drove from Lowell to Brockton. Then she drove from Brockton to Plymouth. Which distance was greater? How much greater?

Lowell to Brockton; 13 km greater

3. Kirk drove from Brockton to Plymouth. Then he drove from Plymouth to Falmouth. Which distance was greater? How much greater?

Brockton to Plymouth; 11 km greater

4. A ceiling is 4 m high. What is the height in centimeters?   **400 cm**

5. It is 2 km from Ursala's house to school. What is the distance in meters?   **2,000 m**

6. **Writing in Math** Greg said that since there are 100 cm in a meter and 10 cm in a decimeter, there must be 10 dm in a meter. Is he correct? Explain.

Yes; Sample answer: It must be true because 10 cm × 10 = 100 cm, which equals a meter.

Use with Lesson 10-7. **135**

© Pearson Education, Inc. 3

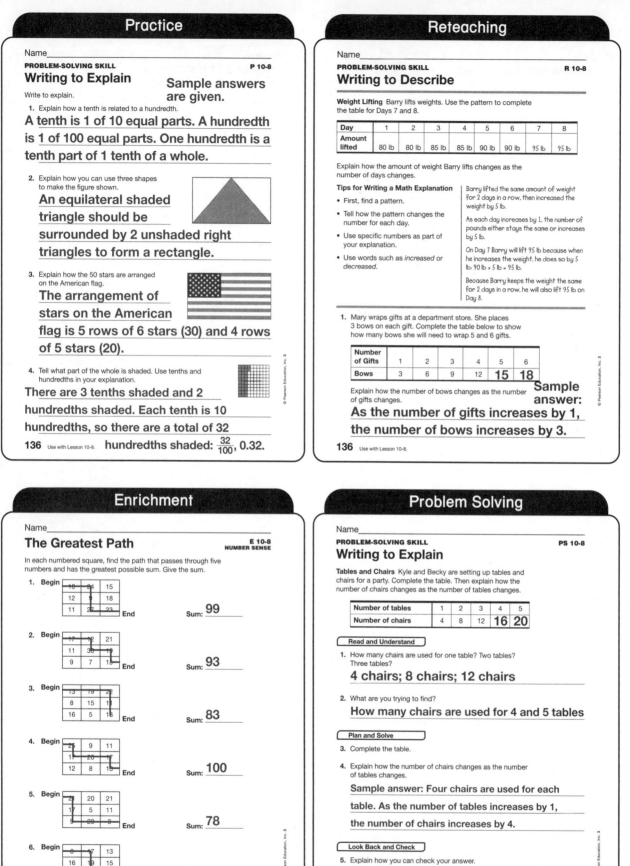

Practice

Name_____

PROBLEM-SOLVING SKILL   P 10-8

Writing to Explain

Write to explain.   **Sample answers**
                                     are given.

1. Explain how a tenth is related to a hundredth.

   A tenth is 1 of 10 equal parts. A hundredth
   is 1 of 100 equal parts. One hundredth is a
   tenth part of 1 tenth of a whole.

2. Explain how you can use three shapes
   to make the figure shown.

   An equilateral shaded
   triangle should be
   surrounded by 2 unshaded right
   triangles to form a rectangle.

3. Explain how the 50 stars are arranged
   on the American flag.

   The arrangement of
   stars on the American
   flag is 5 rows of 6 stars (30) and 4 rows
   of 5 stars (20).

4. Tell what part of the whole is shaded. Use tenths and
   hundredths in your explanation.

   There are 3 tenths shaded and 2
   hundredths shaded. Each tenth is 10
   hundredths, so there are a total of 32

136 Use with Lesson 10-8.   hundredths shaded: $\frac{32}{100}$, 0.32.

© Pearson Education, Inc. 3

Reteaching

Name_____

PROBLEM-SOLVING SKILL   R 10-8

Writing to Describe

Weight Lifting Barry lifts weights. Use the pattern to complete
the table for Days 7 and 8.

Day	1	2	3	4	5	6	7	8
Amount lifted	80 lb	80 lb	85 lb	85 lb	90 lb	90 lb	95 lb	95 lb

Explain how the amount of weight Barry lifts changes as the
number of days changes.

Tips for Writing a Math Explanation

- First, find a pattern.
- Tell how the pattern changes the number for each day.
- Use specific numbers as part of your explanation.
- Use words such as *increased* or *decreased*.

Barry lifted the same amount of weight
for 2 days in a row, then increased the
weight by 5 lb.

As each day increases by 1, the number of
pounds either stays the same or increases
by 5 lb.

On Day 7 Barry will lift 95 lb because when
he increases the weight, he does so by 5
lb: 90 lb + 5 lb = 95 lb.

Because Barry keeps the weight the same
for 2 days in a row, he will also lift 95 lb on
Day 8.

1. Mary wraps gifts at a department store. She places
   3 bows on each gift. Complete the table below to show
   how many bows she will need to wrap 5 and 6 gifts.

Number of Gifts	1	2	3	4	5	6
Bows	3	6	9	12	15	18

Explain how the number of bows changes as the number   **Sample**
of gifts changes.   **answer:**

As the number of gifts increases by 1,
the number of bows increases by 3.

136 Use with Lesson 10-8.

© Pearson Education, Inc. 3

Enrichment

Name_____

The Greatest Path   E 10-8
                                               NUMBER SENSE

In each numbered square, find the path that passes through five
numbers and has the greatest possible sum. Give the sum.

1. Begin
   | 18 | 24 | 15 |
   | 12 | 9 | 18 |
   | 11 | 27 | 23 | End
   Sum: **99**

2. Begin
   | 17 | 12 | 21 |
   | 11 | 36 | 19 |
   | 9 | 7 | 15 | End
   Sum: **93**

3. Begin
   | 13 | 19 | 22 |
   | 8 | 15 | 1 |
   | 16 | 5 | 18 | End
   Sum: **83**

4. Begin
   | 25 | 9 | 11 |
   | 17 | 20 | 17 |
   | 12 | 8 | 15 | End
   Sum: **100**

5. Begin
   | 21 | 20 | 21 |
   | 17 | 5 | 11 |
   | 3 | 28 | 8 | End
   Sum: **78**

6. Begin
   | 6 | 17 | 13 |
   | 16 | 19 | 15 |
   | 12 | 21 | 11 | End
   Sum: **74**

136 Use with Lesson 10-8.

© Pearson Education, Inc. 3

Problem Solving

Name_____

PROBLEM-SOLVING SKILL   PS 10-8

Writing to Explain

Tables and Chairs Kyle and Becky are setting up tables and
chairs for a party. Complete the table. Then explain how the
number of chairs changes as the number of tables changes.

Number of tables	1	2	3	4	5
Number of chairs	4	8	12	16	20

Read and Understand

1. How many chairs are used for one table? Two tables?
   Three tables?

   4 chairs; 8 chairs; 12 chairs

2. What are you trying to find?

   How many chairs are used for 4 and 5 tables

Plan and Solve

3. Complete the table.

4. Explain how the number of chairs changes as the number
   of tables changes.

   Sample answer: Four chairs are used for each
   table. As the number of tables increases by 1,
   the number of chairs increases by 4.

Look Back and Check

5. Explain how you can check your answer.

   Sample answer: I can add. 12 + 4 = 16;
   16 + 4 = 20.

136 Use with Lesson 10-8.

© Pearson Education, Inc. 3

---

136   Use with Chapter 10, Lesson 8

Name_____

PROBLEM-SOLVING APPLICATION P 10-9

Friends of the Forests

1. The boundary of the forest near Steven's house is 7 km long. How many meters long is the boundary?

The boundary of the forest is 7,000 m.

2. The park in Cecilia's neighborhood has 3 different forest paths. Each path is about 400 m. Is the total of the 3 paths greater than or less than 1 km? Explain.

Greater than; Sample answer: The total length is 400 + 400 + 400 = 1,200 m, which is > 1 km (or 1,000 m).

In the United States, forests and woodlands make up three tenths of the land.

3. Write a decimal and fraction to show how much of the United States is forests and woodlands. $0.3; \frac{3}{10}$

4. Henry is cutting a 120 cm long watermelon into equal slices for his family's picnic. Each slice is 5 cm. Complete the table.

Number of Slices	0	1	2	3	4
Watermelon Length	120	115	110	105	100

Explain how the length of the watermelon changes as the number of slices cut from the watermelon changes.

Sample answer: As the number of slices increases by 1, the length of the watermelon decreases by 5 cm.

Name_____

PROBLEM-SOLVING APPLICATION R 10-9

Gudren's Quilts

Gudren sews quilts. The quilt she is currently sewing is made of 100 pieces of fabric. Each piece is the same size. How many dark pieces of fabric will she need? Write a fraction and a decimal for the shaded part of the quilt.

There are 64 dark pieces of fabric.

There are 100 squares, and 64 are shaded. So, sixty-four hundredths are shaded.

Fraction: $\frac{64}{100}$ Decimal: 0.64

1. How many dark pieces of fabric will Gudren need for the quilt at the right? Write a fraction and a decimal for the shaded part.

56; $\frac{56}{100}$; 0.56

2. Gudren is deciding which rectangles to use for her next quilt. She has rectangles that are 0.32 in. long, 0.35 in. long, and 0.23 in. long. Write the lengths in order from least to greatest.

0.23, 0.32, 0.35

3. Gudren wants to make a quilt for her nephew, who is 5 years old. He loves alligators, so she wants to sew little alligator patches onto the quilt. How many centimeters long is each alligator patch?

7 cm long

Name_____

Graphing Help

E 10-9
DECISION MAKING

Mr. Mancuso owns the corner store and has asked you for some help. He wants to put the information below into a graph so he can easily find the information he needs. Make a graph for the set. Then write two sentences explaining the information Mr. Mancuso will find in your graph and how he might use the information.

1. On Monday, the store sold 6 cases of bottled water. On Tuesday it sold 4 cases. On both Wednesday and Thursday it sold 10 cases on each day. On Friday there were 9 cases sold. Saturday was the highest for the week with 15 cases sold. On Sunday, there were only 3 cases of bottled water sold.

Bottled Water Sold

(bar graph: y-axis Number of Cases 0 to 20; x-axis Day of the Week: Monday, Tuesday, Wednesday, Thursday, Friday, Saturday, Sunday)

Sample answer: Mr. Mancuso can see how many cases he sold each day, or a total for the week. He can use this to plan a sale on bottled water.

Name_____

PROBLEM-SOLVING APPLICATION PS 10-9

Lunch Choices

You can have one juice choice and one food choice for lunch. How many different lunches can you choose?

Juice	Food
Apple juice	Sandwich
Orange juice	Burrito

Read and Understand

1. How many juice choices do you have?

2 juice choices

2. How many food choices do you have?

2 food choices

3. What are you trying to find?

How many lunch choices there are

Plan and Solve

4. What strategy can you use to solve the problem?

Make an organized list

5. Make a list of all the possible lunches.

Apple juice and sandwich, apple juice and burrito, orange juice and sandwich, orange juice and burrito

6. How many different lunches can you choose? Write your answer in a complete sentence.

I can choose four different lunch choices.

Look Back and Check

7. Explain how you can check your answer.

Sample answer: I can check my list and make sure I included all possible choices.

Name_____

Mental Math: Multiplication Patterns

P 11-1

Use mental math to find each product.

1. $3 \times 10 =$ **30**

2. $6 \times 100 =$ **600**

3. $9 \times 1,000 =$ **9,000**

4. $80 \times 3 =$ **240**

5. $4 \times 700 =$ **2,800**

6. $2,000 \times 5 =$ **10,000**

7. $6 \times 400 =$ **2,400**

8. $800 \times 8 =$ **6,400**

9. $600 \times 9 =$ **5,400**

Algebra Find the missing number in each number sentence.

10. $9 \times$ **80** $= 720$

11. **8** $\times 5,000 = 40,000$

12. The average workweek is 40 hr. How many hours are there in 4 workweeks? **160 hr**

13. There are 2,000 lb in 1 T. How many pounds are there in 16 T? **32,000 lb**

14. Lightning strikes the earth about 200 times each second. How many times does lightning strike the earth in 1 min? **12,000 times**

Test Prep

15. How many hundreds are there in 2,000?

A. 2,000   B. 200   C. 20   D. 2

16. **Writing in Math** Explain how to use mental math to find 700×8.

Sample answer: 700 is the same as 7 hundreds, so 700×8 is 7 hundreds $\times 8 = 56$ hundreds, or 5,600.

Name_____

Mental Math: Multiplication Patterns

R 11-1

You can use multiplication patterns to help multiply multiples of 10 and 100.

When one of the factors you are multiplying has zeros on the end, you can multiply the nonzero digits, and then add on the extra zeros.

9×100

$9 \times 1|0\,0|$

non-zero digits   extra zeros

$9 \times 1 = 9$ add extra zeros

$9|0\,0|$

$9 \times 100 = 900$

$12 \times 2,000$

$12 \times 2|,0\,0\,0|$

non-zero digits   extra zeros

$12 \times 2 = 24$

$24|,0\,0\,0|$

$12 \times 2,000 = 24,000$

Use mental math to find each product.

1. $8 \times 10 =$ **80**

2. $7 \times 100 =$ **700**

3. $4 \times 1,000 =$ **4,000**

4. $3 \times 50 =$ **150**

5. $600 \times 3 =$ **1,800**

6. $4,000 \times 7 =$ **28,000**

Find the missing number in each number sentence.

7. **6** $\times 100 = 600$

8. $40 \times$ **9** $= 360$

9. **Number Sense** Karen says, "When I have a factor with exactly 2 zeros at the end, my answer will always have exactly 2 zeros at the end." Do you agree? Explain.

Sample answer: No, if the product of the nonzero digits ends in a zero, like $6 \times 5 = 30$, then there will be more zeros.

Name_____

Tattle Tell

E 11-1
MENTAL MATH

Each of the 15 student council members of Blakemore Elementary School is responsible for telling exactly 2 other students about the upcoming school pep assembly. Each of those 2 is then responsible for telling 2 other students. It takes 15 min for each round of students to be told. How many minutes will it take for 1,000 students to receive the information about the pep assembly? Fill in the chart to help find the answer.

Number of Minutes	Number of Students Told Each Round	Total Number of Students Told
0	15	15
15	30	15 + 30 = 45
30	60	45 + 60 = 105
45	120	105 + 120 = 225
60	240	225 + 240 = 465
75	480	465 + 480 = 945
90	960	945 + 960 = 1,905

90 min

Name_____

Mental Math: Multiplication Patterns

PS 11-1

Coins are often distributed in rolls. Coins are counted and put into a paper tube. Each tube then has a value, determined by the number and type of coin it holds.

1. If a roll of dimes is worth 500 cents, how much are 3 rolls of dimes worth?

1,500 cents

2. If a roll of pennies is worth 50 cents, how much are 7 rolls of pennies worth?

350 cents

3. If a roll of nickels is worth 200 cents, how much are 4 rolls of nickels worth?

800 cents

4. If a roll of quarters is worth 1,000 cents, how much are 9 rolls of quarters worth?

9,000 cents

5. **Writing in Math** There are 40 quarters in a roll, and 1 roll of quarters is worth 1,000 cents. Merle is 3 quarters short of having 6 rolls of quarters. Explain how you can use mental math to find how much money Merle has in cents.

Sample answer: 6 rolls $\times$ 1,000 cents = 6,000 cents. 3 quarters is 75 cents: $6,000 - 75 = 5,925$.

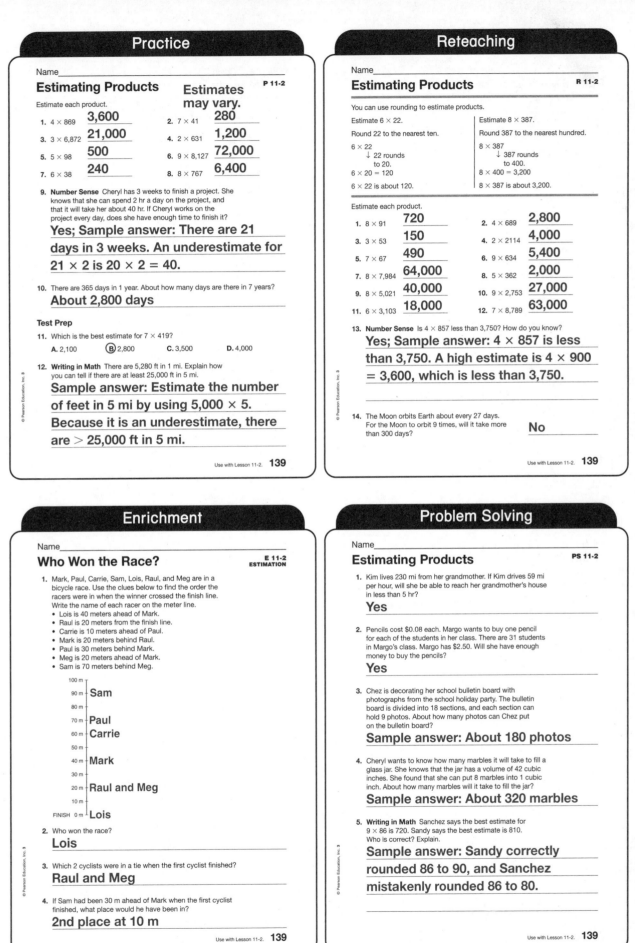

Practice

Name_____

Estimating Products

Estimates may vary.

P 11-2

Estimate each product.

1. 4×869 **3,600**
2. 7×41 **280**
3. $3 \times 6,872$ **21,000**
4. 2×631 **1,200**
5. 5×98 **500**
6. $9 \times 8,127$ **72,000**
7. 6×38 **240**
8. 8×767 **6,400**

9. **Number Sense** Cheryl has 3 weeks to finish a project. She knows that she can spend 2 hr a day on the project, and that it will take her about 40 hr. If Cheryl works on the project every day, does she have enough time to finish it?

   Yes; Sample answer: There are 21 days in 3 weeks. An underestimate for 21×2 is $20 \times 2 = 40$.

10. There are 365 days in 1 year. About how many days are there in 7 years?

    About 2,800 days

Test Prep

11. Which is the best estimate for 7×419?

    A. 2,100   **B** 2,800   C. 3,500   D. 4,000

12. **Writing in Math** There are 5,280 ft in 1 mi. Explain how you can tell if there are at least 25,000 ft in 5 mi.

    Sample answer: Estimate the number of feet in 5 mi by using $5,000 \times 5$. Because it is an underestimate, there are $> 25,000$ ft in 5 mi.

© Pearson Education, Inc. 3

Use with Lesson 11-2. **139**

Reteaching

Name_____

Estimating Products

R 11-2

You can use rounding to estimate products.

Estimate 6×22.

Round 22 to the nearest ten.

6×22
   ↓ 22 rounds
     to 20.
$6 \times 20 = 120$
6×22 is about 120.

Estimate 8×387.

Round 387 to the nearest hundred.

8×387
   ↓ 387 rounds
     to 400.
$8 \times 400 = 3,200$
8×387 is about 3,200.

Estimate each product.

1. 8×91 **720**
2. 4×689 **2,800**
3. 3×53 **150**
4. 2×2114 **4,000**
5. 7×67 **490**
6. 9×634 **5,400**
7. $8 \times 7,984$ **64,000**
8. 5×362 **2,000**
9. $8 \times 5,021$ **40,000**
10. $9 \times 2,753$ **27,000**
11. $6 \times 3,103$ **18,000**
12. $7 \times 8,789$ **63,000**

13. **Number Sense** Is 4×857 less than 3,750? How do you know?

    Yes; Sample answer: 4×857 is less than 3,750. A high estimate is $4 \times 900 = 3,600$, which is less than 3,750.

14. The Moon orbits Earth about every 27 days. For the Moon to orbit 9 times, will it take more than 300 days?

    No

© Pearson Education, Inc. 3

Use with Lesson 11-2. **139**

Enrichment

Name_____

Who Won the Race?

E 11-2
ESTIMATION

1. Mark, Paul, Carrie, Sam, Lois, Raul, and Meg are in a bicycle race. Use the clues below to find the order the racers were in when the winner crossed the finish line. Write the name of each racer on the meter line.
   - Lois is 40 meters ahead of Mark.
   - Raul is 20 meters from the finish line.
   - Carrie is 10 meters ahead of Paul.
   - Mark is 20 meters behind Raul.
   - Paul is 30 meters behind Mark.
   - Meg is 20 meters ahead of Mark.
   - Sam is 70 meters behind Meg.

100 m	
90 m	**Sam**
80 m	
70 m	**Paul**
60 m	**Carrie**
50 m	
40 m	**Mark**
30 m	
20 m	**Raul and Meg**
10 m	
FINISH 0 m	**Lois**

2. Who won the race?

   Lois

3. Which 2 cyclists were in a tie when the first cyclist finished?

   Raul and Meg

4. If Sam had been 30 m ahead of Mark when the first cyclist finished, what place would he have been in?

   2nd place at 10 m

© Pearson Education, Inc. 3

Use with Lesson 11-2. **139**

Problem Solving

Name_____

Estimating Products

PS 11-2

1. Kim lives 230 mi from her grandmother. If Kim drives 59 mi per hour, will she be able to reach her grandmother's house in less than 5 hr?

   Yes

2. Pencils cost $0.08 each. Margo wants to buy one pencil for each of the students in her class. There are 31 students in Margo's class. Margo has $2.50. Will she have enough money to buy the pencils?

   Yes

3. Chez is decorating her school bulletin board with photographs from the school holiday party. The bulletin board is divided into 18 sections, and each section can hold 9 photos. About how many photos can Chez put on the bulletin board?

   Sample answer: About 180 photos

4. Cheryl wants to know how many marbles it will take to fill a glass jar. She knows that the jar has a volume of 42 cubic inches. She found that she can put 8 marbles into 1 cubic inch. About how many marbles will it take to fill the jar?

   Sample answer: About 320 marbles

5. **Writing in Math** Sanchez says the best estimate for 9×86 is 720. Sandy says the best estimate is 810. Who is correct? Explain.

   Sample answer: Sandy correctly rounded 86 to 90, and Sanchez mistakenly rounded 86 to 80.

© Pearson Education, Inc. 3

Use with Lesson 11-2. **139**

© Pearson Education, Inc. 3

Mental Math: Division Patterns

P 11-3

Use patterns to find each quotient.

1. $18 \div 3 =$ **6**

$180 \div 3 =$ **60**

$1,800 \div 3 =$ **600**

2. $36 \div 4 =$ **9**

$360 \div 4 =$ **90**

$3,600 \div 4 =$ **900**

Use mental math to find each quotient.

3. $200 \div 5 =$ **40**

4. $3,600 \div 6 =$ **600**

5. $2,700 \div 3 =$ **900**

6. $490 \div 7 =$ **70**

7. $1,200 \div 2 =$ **600**

8. $630 \div 9 =$ **70**

Algebra Use mental math to find the missing numbers.

9. $810 \div$ **9** $= 90$

10. **1,600** $\div 2 = 800$

11. **3,500** $\div 7 = 500$

12. $4,200 \div$ **7** $= 600$

13. There are 5 reams of paper in a box. There are 2,500 pages total in the box. How many sheets of paper are in 1 ream of paper?

500 sheets

Test Prep

14. Use mental math to find the quotient of $480 \div 8$.

A. 6   B. 8   C. 60   D. 80

15. Writing in Math Explain how you can find the quotient for $120,000 \div 3$ using mental math.

Sample answer: 12 ÷ 3 = 4; There are four zeros after the 12 in 120,000, so there will be four zeros after the 4 in the quotient: 120,000 ÷ 3 = 40,000.

Mental Math: Division Patterns

R 11-3

When there are zeros at the end of the dividend, you can move them aside and use a basic division fact to divide the nonzero digits.

For example:

$120 \div 4$

12 0 ÷ 4   extra zero

nonzero digits

$12 \div 4 = 3$ add extra zero **30**

So, $120 \div 4 = 30$.

Remember to add the same number of zeros back to the quotient that you removed from the dividend.

$6\,0 \div 3 = 2\,0$ 1 zero

$6\,0\,0 \div 3 = 2\,0\,0$ 2 zeros

$6,0\,0\,0 \div 3 = 2,0\,0\,0$ 3 zeros

Use patterns to find each quotient.

1. $24 \div 4 =$ **6**

2. $240 \div 4 =$ **60**

3. $2,400 \div 4 =$ **600**

Use mental math to find each quotient.

4. $250 \div 5 =$ **50**

5. $180 \div 6 =$ **30**

6. $3,200 \div 8 =$ **400**

7. $900 \div 3 =$ **300**

8. $800 \div 8 =$ **100**

9. $280 \div 7 =$ **40**

10. Number Sense There are 200 school days that are divided into 4 equal grading periods. How many school days are in each grading period?

50 school days

A Colorful Solution

E 11-3
VISUAL THINKING

Color the following figures using the fewest colors possible: Do not use the same color on any two adjacent (touching) areas.

1.

2.

3.

Sample answers are given.

Students should use 3 colors.

Students should use 4 colors.

Students should use 4 colors.

Mental Math: Division Patterns

PS 11-3

At a festival, firefighters set up a booth to make children aware of fire safety. The firefighters handed out buttons.

Firefighter	Number of Buttons
Frank	600
Jacob	360
Janet	4,800
Ken	3,000
Sylvia	400

1. Janet worked in the booth all 6 days of the festival. On average, how many buttons did she hand out each day?

800 buttons

2. Frank worked in the booth 3 days. On average, how many buttons did he hand out each day?

200 buttons

3. Sylvia worked in the booth 4 days of the festival. On average, how many buttons did she hand out each day?

100 buttons

4. Writing in Math Janet worked in the booth for 8 hr each day. Use your answer to Exercise 1 to find how many buttons Janet passed out each hour on average. Explain.

Sample answer: On average Janet handed out 800 buttons each day, and 800 ÷ 8 = 100.

Name_____

Estimating Quotients

Estimate each quotient.   **Estimates may vary.**

1. $66 \div 8$ **8**
2. $31 \div 6$ **5** (r)
3. $19 \div 2$ **9 or 10**
4. $23 \div 4$ **6**
5. $22 \div 6$ **4**
6. $43 \div 7$ **6**
7. $70 \div 8$ **9**
8. $19 \div 4$ **5**

9. A group of students is sharing 62 markers. If there are 7 students, about how many markers will each student have?

About 9 markers

10. James has 6 pencils. His father has 44 pencils. About how many times more pencils does James's father have?

About 7 times

11. **Number Sense** Without finding the exact answer, how do you know that $41 \div 5$ is greater than $40 \div 5$?

Sample answer: A greater dividend will always have a greater quotient.

Test Prep

12. Which is the best estimate for $37 \div 5$?

A. 5   B. 6   **C.** 7   D. 8

13. **Writing in Math** Frances has 37 c of apples to make loaves of apple bread. If each loaf uses 4 c of apples, explain how Frances can find about how many loaves she can make.

Sample answer: Frances can estimate the number of loaves she can make by using the division fact $36 \div 4 = 9$.

Name_____

Estimating Quotients

When you know the basic division facts, you can estimate the quotient of a division problem.

Estimate $19 \div 3$.

First, think about the basic facts that you know that use the same divisor, 3.

For example:

$12 \div 3 = 4$ $15 \div 3 = 5$
$18 \div 3 = 6$ $21 \div 3 = 7$

Then choose the basic fact that has the closest dividend to the problem you are solving.

19 is between the dividends of 18 and 21. It is closer to 18, so use the basic fact $18 \div 3 = 6$.

So, $19 \div 3$ is about 6.

Estimate each quotient.

1. $34 \div 8$ **4**
2. $22 \div 3$ **7**
3. $46 \div 5$ **9**
4. $15 \div 8$ **2**
5. $17 \div 6$ **3**
6. $58 \div 7$ **8**
7. $43 \div 9$ **5**
8. $35 \div 4$ **9**
9. $74 \div 24$ **3**

10. **Reasoning** There are 12 eggs and 5 people. If each person eats the same number of eggs, did each person eat at least 3 eggs? Explain.

No; Sample answer: $12 \div 5$ is between 2 and 3. That means more than 2, but less than 3.

Name_____

Games, Games, Games

Julian has invented a game that would help review basic multiplication facts. The game board contains one space for every possible product that results from multiplying together any two whole numbers from 1 through 10. (Example: $3 \times 4 = 12$, so 12 is on the game board.)

1. How many spaces are on Julian's game board?

42 spaces (1–9, 12, 14–16, 18, 21, 24, 25, 27, 28, 32, 25, 36, 42, 45, 48, 49, 54, 56, 63, 64, 73, 81, all 10s)

2. Draw a picture of what you think the game board might look like. Make sure to include all of the correct products.

Sample answer:

M	A	T	H	O		
1	2	3	4	5	6	7
8	9	12	14	15	16	18
21	24	25	27	28	32	35
36	42	45	48	49	54	56
63	64	73	81	10	20	30
40	50	60	70	80	90	100

3. Using the game board you drew, create the rules for a multiplication game.

Sample answer: Game is MATHO; Choose numbers arranged like Bingo. Master numbers are used to cross off numbers on a card.

Name_____

Estimating Quotients

A pet shelter keeps kittens where people can see and play with them. Last week 26 cat toys were donated to the shelter to divide among the kittens.

1. About how many toys can each kitten have if there are 6 kittens in the shelter?

About 4 toys

2. If each kitten receives 3 toys, about how many kittens are there in the shelter?

About 8 kittens

3. A worker decided that since there are only 4 kittens in the shelter right now, she would store half of the toys and give the other half of the toys to the kittens. About how many toys will each of the 4 kittens have to play with?

About 3 toys each

4. If there were 10 kittens in the shelter and each already had 1 toy, about how many toys will each have after the 26 new toys are passed out?

About 3 toys each

5. **Writing in Math** A small box of raisins has about 37 raisins in it. Bart is making snacks and uses 5 raisins for each snack. About how many snacks can Bart make with a small box of raisins? Explain how you found your answer.

About 8 snacks; Sample answer: 37 rounded to the nearest ten is 40, and $40 \div 5 = 8$.

Name_____

Multiplication and Arrays
P 11-5

Find each product. You may draw a picture to help.

1. $3 \times 17 = $ **51**

□□□□□□□□ □□□□□□□
□□□□□□□□ □□□□□□□
□□□□□□□□ □□□□□□□

2. $2 \times 22 = $ **44**

□□□□□□□□□□ □□□□□□□□□□ □□
□□□□□□□□□□ □□□□□□□□□□ □□

3. $5 \times 34 = $ **170**   4. $4 \times 13 = $ **52**   5. $3 \times 57 = $ **171**

6. **Reasoning** Draw an array to show the number of eggs in 3 dozens.   **36 eggs**

□□□□□□□□□□ □ □
□□□□□□□□□□ □ □
□□□□□□□□□□ □ □

Each worker is paid $8 per hour of work.

Worker	Hours Worked
Bob	19
Josh	35
Marvin	13

7. How many dollars did Bob earn?

$152

8. How many dollars did Josh earn?

$280

9. How much more did Bob earn than Marvin?

$48 more

Test Prep

10. Which is the product of 52×6?

A. 42   B. 302   C. 312   D. 402

11. **Writing in Math** Explain how to use an array to find 3×19.

Sample answer: Draw place-value blocks for 19 three times. Count the total number of blocks to find $3 \times 19 = 57$.

© Pearson Education, Inc. 3

Name_____

Multiplication and Arrays
R 11-5

You can draw a picture of an array to show multiplication.

For example:

4×21

What You Show	What You Think
□□□□□□□□□□ □□□□□□□□□□ □	4 rows of 2 tens = 8 tens
□□□□□□□□□□ □□□□□□□□□□ □	4 rows of 1 ones = 4 ones
□□□□□□□□□□ □□□□□□□□□□ □	
□□□□□□□□□□ □□□□□□□□□□ □	80 + 4 = 84

To find the product, count the tens and the ones, then add them together.

There are 8 tens and 4 ones.

8 tens = 80, 4 ones = 4

80 + 4 = 84

So, $4 \times 21 = 84$.

Find each product. You may draw a picture to help.

1. $3 \times 14 = $ ▨▨▨ ▨▨▨ **42**
   ▨▨▨ ▨▨▨
   ▨▨▨ ▨▨▨

2. $2 \times 23 = $ **46**   3. $4 \times 17 = $ **68**

4. $3 \times 18 = $ **54**   5. $2 \times 34 = $ **68**

6. **Number Sense** Suppose you wanted to draw an array for 21×3. How many ones would you draw?

3 ones

© Pearson Education, Inc. 3

Name_____

Sticks and Stones
E 11-5
VISUAL THINKING

1. Remove only one stick from the picture to leave exactly three squares of the same size.

2. Find a way to make the number 10 using only two sticks.

Form an "X," the Roman numeral for the number 10.

Aaron is skipping stones across a pond. (A "skip" is a short bounce in the water.) The first stone skips 1 time, the second skips 2 times, the third stone skips 4 times, and the fourth stone skips 8 times.

3. If this pattern continues, how many total skips will the 10th stone make? How many total skips will have been made?

512 skips for the 10th stone; 1,023 total

4. What is the pattern? If you knew the number of the stone, such as 11th, or n, how would you figure out how many skips it would take?

Each skip is double the one before; Sample answer: Set up a table with the number of the stone in the top row and the number of skips in the bottom row.

© Pearson Education, Inc. 3

Name_____

Multiplication and Arrays
PS 11-5

Evelyn likes to take gifts to people who are in the hospital. She knows there are 6 floors at the hospital that are for patients. On each floor there are 4 nurses' stations, and each nurses' station is in charge of 12 patient rooms. You may draw a picture to help for 1–6.

1. How many patient rooms are there on each floor?

48 patient rooms

2. How many patient rooms are there altogether?

288 patient rooms

3. Two of the floors only allow one patient in each room. These are called private rooms. How many private rooms are there in the hospital?

96 private rooms

4. Four of the floors are set up to have two patients per room. These are called semiprivate rooms. How many semiprivate rooms are there in the hospital?

192 semiprivate rooms

5. If each of the semiprivate rooms is full, how many patients are in the semiprivate rooms?

384 patients

6. **Writing in Math** How many tens would there be in an array for 3×22? Explain.

6 tens; Sample answer: There would be 3 rows with 2 tens each, and $2 \times 3 = 6$.

© Pearson Education, Inc. 3

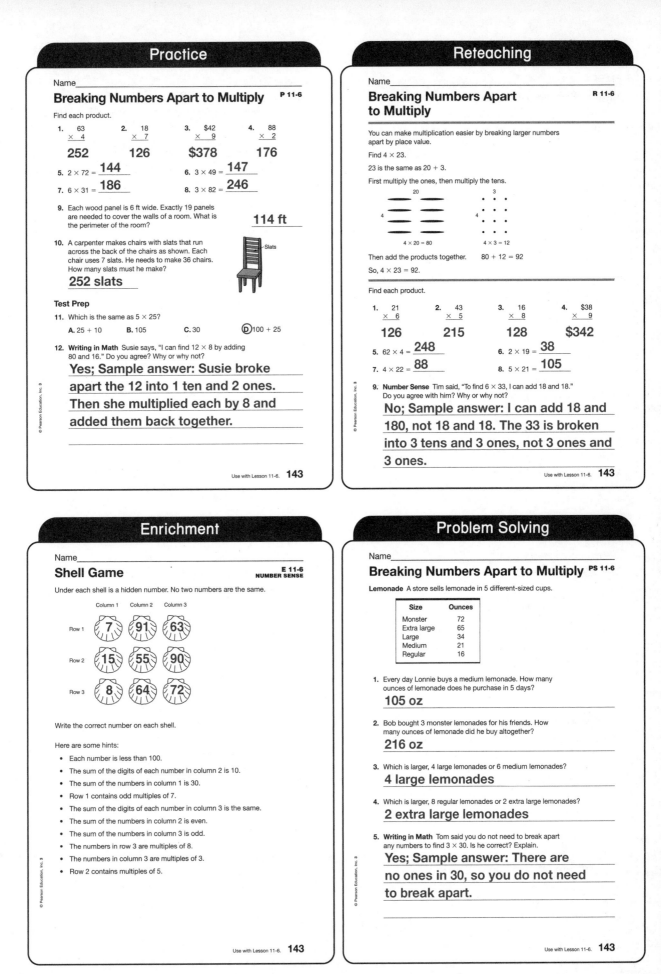

Practice

Name_____

Breaking Numbers Apart to Multiply   P 11-6

Find each product.

1.	63	2.	18	3.	$42	4.	88
	× 4		× 7		× 9		× 2
	252		**126**		**$378**		**176**

5. 2 × 72 = __144__   6. 3 × 49 = __147__

7. 6 × 31 = __186__   8. 3 × 82 = __246__

9. Each wood panel is 6 ft wide. Exactly 19 panels are needed to cover the walls of a room. What is the perimeter of the room?

114 ft

10. A carpenter makes chairs with slats that run across the back of the chairs as shown. Each chair uses 7 slats. He needs to make 36 chairs. How many slats must he make?

—Slats

252 slats

Test Prep

11. Which is the same as 5 × 25?

A. 25 + 10   B. 105   C. 30   D. 100 + 25

12. **Writing in Math** Susie says, "I can find 12 × 8 by adding 80 and 16." Do you agree? Why or why not?

Yes; Sample answer: Susie broke apart the 12 into 1 ten and 2 ones. Then she multiplied each by 8 and added them back together.

© Pearson Education, Inc. 3

Use with Lesson 11-6. **143**

Reteaching

Name_____

Breaking Numbers Apart to Multiply   R 11-6

You can make multiplication easier by breaking larger numbers apart by place value.

Find 4 × 23.

23 is the same as 20 + 3.

First multiply the ones, then multiply the tens.

20
4
4 × 20 = 80

3
4
4 × 3 = 12

Then add the products together.   80 + 12 = 92

So, 4 × 23 = 92.

Find each product.

1.	21	2.	43	3.	16	4.	$38
	× 6		× 5		× 8		× 9
	126		**215**		**128**		**$342**

5. 62 × 4 = __248__   6. 2 × 19 = __38__

7. 4 × 22 = __88__   8. 5 × 21 = __105__

9. **Number Sense** Tim said, "To find 6 × 33, I can add 18 and 18." Do you agree with him? Why or why not?

No; Sample answer: I can add 18 and 180, not 18 and 18. The 33 is broken into 3 tens and 3 ones, not 3 ones and 3 ones.

© Pearson Education, Inc. 3

Use with Lesson 11-6. **143**

Enrichment

Name_____

Shell Game   E 11-6
NUMBER SENSE

Under each shell is a hidden number. No two numbers are the same.

	Column 1	Column 2	Column 3
Row 1	7	91	63
Row 2	15	55	90
Row 3	8	64	72

Write the correct number on each shell.

Here are some hints:

- Each number is less than 100.
- The sum of the digits of each number in column 2 is 10.
- The sum of the numbers in column 1 is 30.
- Row 1 contains odd multiples of 7.
- The sum of the digits of each number in column 3 is the same.
- The sum of the numbers in column 2 is even.
- The sum of the numbers in column 3 is odd.
- The numbers in row 3 are multiples of 8.
- The numbers in column 3 are multiples of 3.
- Row 2 contains multiples of 5.

© Pearson Education, Inc. 3

Use with Lesson 11-6. **143**

Problem Solving

Name_____

Breaking Numbers Apart to Multiply   PS 11-6

Lemonade A store sells lemonade in 5 different-sized cups.

Size	Ounces
Monster	72
Extra large	65
Large	34
Medium	21
Regular	16

1. Every day Lonnie buys a medium lemonade. How many ounces of lemonade does he purchase in 5 days?

105 oz

2. Bob bought 3 monster lemonades for his friends. How many ounces of lemonade did he buy altogether?

216 oz

3. Which is larger, 4 large lemonades or 6 medium lemonades?

4 large lemonades

4. Which is larger, 8 regular lemonades or 2 extra large lemonades?

2 extra large lemonades

5. **Writing in Math** Tom said you do not need to break apart any numbers to find 3 × 30. Is he correct? Explain.

Yes; Sample answer: There are no ones in 30, so you do not need to break apart.

© Pearson Education, Inc. 3

Use with Lesson 11-6. **143**

Name_____

Multiplying Two-Digit Numbers

P 11-7

Find each product. Decide if your answer is reasonable.

1. 12×9	2. 19×4	3. $\$22 \times 7$	4. 45×6
108	**76**	**$154**	**270**

5. 96×3	6. 27×5	7. 12×8	8. $\$55 \times 4$
288	**135**	**96**	**$220**

9. $9 \times \$36$	10. 37×4	11. 82×6	12. $\$71 \times 7$
$324	**148**	**492**	**$497**

13. $14 \times 5 =$ **70**

14. $6 \times 51 =$ **306**

15. $63 \times 4 =$ **252**

16. $\$47 \times 2 =$ **$94**

17. An area in Norway gets sunlight all day for 14 weeks straight during the summer. How many days of continuous sunlight is this?   **98 days**

18. The length of a parking lot is 92 yd. How many feet long is the parking lot?   **276 ft**

Test Prep

19. Which is the product of $82 \times \$7$?

A. $434   B. $494   C. $564   (D) $574

20. **Writing in Math** Explain how an array of 5×46 can help you find the product of 5×46.

Sample answer. An array can show how to find that 5 groups of 4 tens and 5 groups of 6 ones is 230. So, $5 \times 46 = 230$.

Name_____

Multiplying Two-Digit Numbers

R 11-7

You can regroup tens and ones to multiply two-digit numbers.

Find 36×3.

	What You Think	What You Write
Step 1	Multiply the ones. Regroup if necessary. $6 \times 3 = 18$ ones. Regroup 18 ones as 1 ten 8 ones.	$\begin{array}{r} 1 \\ 36 \\ \times\ 3 \\ \hline 8 \end{array}$
Step 2	Multiply the tens. Add any regrouped tens. 3×3 tens $= 9$ tens. 9 tens $+ 1$ ten $= 10$ tens.	$\begin{array}{r} 1 \\ 36 \\ \times\ 3 \\ \hline 108 \end{array}$

So, $36 \times 3 = 108$.

Find each product. Decide if your answer is reasonable.

1. 21×6	2. 14×3	3. 32×4
126	**42**	**128**

4. 57×5	5. 62×8	6. 33×5
285	**496**	**165**

7. $43 \times 8 =$ **344**

8. $28 \times 6 =$ **168**

9. $43 \times 2 =$ **86**

10. **Number Sense** The largest snowman on record was almost 38 yd tall. There are 3 ft in a yard. How many feet are in 38 yd?   **114 ft**

Name_____

Tee-Zee Numbers

E 11-7
NUMBER SENSE

1. Place the numbers 2, 3, 4, 6, and 26 in the circles that form **T** so that the product of the numbers is the same in each direction.

the product: 312

2. Place the numbers 2, 4, 5, 7, 8, 59, and 65 in the circles that form **Z** so that the sum of the numbers is the same in all directions.

the sum: 71

3. Place the numbers 1, 2, 3, 4, 5, 6, 7, 8, and 9 in the circles that form **E** so that the sum is the same in all directions.

the sum: 15

Name_____

Multiplying Two-Digit Numbers

PS 11-7

For 1–5, find the total number of things that are in the containers.

1. A carton of eggs contains 12 eggs. How many eggs are there in 5 cartons?

60 eggs

2. Lori bought 6 bags with 21 ladybug pins in each bag. How many ladybug pins are there in all?

126 ladybug pins

3. A bottle of perfume contains 19 oz of perfume. There are 8 bottles of perfume in a box. How many ounces of perfume does a full box contain?

152 oz of perfume

4. The cafeteria ordered 6 crates of chocolate milk and 2 crates of regular milk. Each crate contains 27 cartons of milk. How many cartons of milk were ordered altogether?

216 cartons of milk

5. Joe bought 7 packs of baseball cards that had 22 cards in each pack. How many cards in all did he buy?

154 cards

6. **Writing in Math** Marcus delivers 47 newspapers every day from Monday through Saturday. On Sunday, he delivers three times that many. Explain how to find the number of papers that Marcus delivers on Sunday.

Sample answer: You can multiply $47 \times 3 = 141$.

Name_____

Multiplying Three-Digit Numbers   P 11-8

Find each answer. Estimate to check reasonableness.

1. 231 $\times$ 2	2. 420 $\times$ 3	3. 613 $\times$ 5	4. 122 $\times$ 8
462	**1,260**	**3,065**	**976**

5. 308 $\times$ 7	6. 501 $\times$ 8	7. 727 $\times$ 4	8. 914 $\times$ 9
2,156	**4,008**	**2,908**	**8,226**

9. $444 \times 4 =$ **1,776**   10. $121 \times 6 =$ **726**

11. There are 365 days in 1 year. How many days are there in 3 years?   **1,095 days**

12. A board is 144 in. long. How many inches long are 8 boards?   **1,152 in.**

13. **Number Sense** Is 721×3 the same as $2,100 + 60 + 3$? Explain.

Yes; Each place is multiplied separately and then the products are added.

Test Prep

14. Which is the product of 828×5?

   A. 4,040   **B.** 4,100   **C.** 4,140   **D.** 4,840

15. **Writing in Math** Larry multiplied 362×4. Explain Larry's error and give the correct answer.

$$\begin{array}{r} ^{2}362 \\ \times\ 4 \\ \hline 1,248 \end{array}$$

Sample answer: Larry did not add his regrouped hundreds back into the answer. The correct answer is 1,448.

Name_____

Multiplying Three-Digit Numbers   R 11-8

A three-digit factor is multiplied the same way a two-digit factor is.

Find 523×7.

Step 1	Step 2	Step 3
Multiply the ones. Regroup if needed.	Multiply the tens. Add any extra tens. Regroup if needed.	Multiply the hundreds. Add any extra hundreds.
$\begin{array}{r} 2 \\ 523 \\ \times\ 7 \\ \hline 1 \end{array}$	$\begin{array}{r} 1\ 2 \\ 523 \\ \times\ 7 \\ \hline 61 \end{array}$	$\begin{array}{r} 1\ 2 \\ 523 \\ \times\ 7 \\ \hline 3,661 \end{array}$

Estimate to check. $523 \times 7 = 500 \times 7 = 3,500$.
3,661 is close to 3,500, so the answer is reasonable.

Remember, it is important to always start with the ones place, and work from the least place value to the greatest. Any regrouping needs to be done going from least to greatest.

Find each answer. Estimate to check reasonableness.

1. 221 $\times$ 4	2. 342 $\times$ 5	3. 402 $\times$ 4
884	**1,710**	**1,608**

4. 610 $\times$ 2	5. 531 $\times$ 3	6. 213 $\times$ 8
1,220	**1,593**	**1,704**

7. $392 \times 6 =$ **2,352**   8. $104 \times 9 =$ **936**

9. **Number Sense** The Tonga micro-plate near Samoa moves at a rate of 240 mm each year. At that rate, how many millimeters will the plate have moved in 5 years?

The plate will have moved 1,200 mm in 5 years.

Name_____

Wow!   E 11-8 REASONING

A palindrome is a word or number that reads the same way backward and forward. Words such as "wow" and "dad" are palindromes. Numbers such as "252" and "70,107" are also palindromes.

1. What palindrome number is the product when you multiply 409×2?   **818**

2. Put the palindrome number into a calculator, and turn it upside down. What palindrome word does the calculator show?   **BIB**

3. What is the palindrome number for $(397 \times 2) + 14$?   **808**

4. Put the palindrome number into a calculator. What is the word that describes what you would do in a game where apples float in water?   **BOB**

5. A palindrome word fits into the blank space in the sentence: Mark ____ the house through the fog. What is the word? Turned upside down, what palindrome number is created? Write a math problem that will result in that palindrome number.

Sees; Sample answer: $1,067 \times 5 = 5,335$

6. Not your brother but your "$(3 \times 161) + 32$" is your parent's other child. What is the palindrome number? What is the palindrome word?

515; SIS

7. Make up your own palindrome riddle.

Checks students' riddles.

Name_____

Multiplying Three-Digit Numbers   PS 11-8

The table shows the distances between four major cities.

	Chicago, IL	Detroit, MI	New York City, NY	Pittsburgh, PA
Chicago, IL	0	308	787	460
Detroit, MI	308	0	614	286
New York, NY	787	614	0	370
Pittsburgh, PA	460	286	370	0

1. Joann and her family drove from Pittsburgh to New York City and then back again. How many miles did they drive?   **740 mi**

2. If a businessperson drives from Detroit to Chicago and back 3 times for a total of 6 one-way trips between the cities, how many miles did the person drive in all?   **1,848 mi**

3. If a businessperson makes 4 trips from New York to Detroit and back for a total of 8 one-way trips between the cities, how many miles did the person drive in all?   **4,912 mi**

4. Which is farther, 7 times the distance between New York City and Pittsburgh or 4 times the distance between New York City and Detroit?

7 times the distance between New York City and Pittsburgh

5. **Writing in Math** To multiply 4×302, how many times do you have to regroup? Explain.

None; Sample answer: 4×2 is only 8, and there is a 0 in the tens place.

© Pearson Education, Inc. 3

Practice

Name_____

Multiplying Money
P 11-9

Find each product. Estimate to check reasonableness.

1. $1.32 × 6	2. $4.67 × 4	3. $6.04 × 9	4. $4.21 × 2
$7.92	**$18.68**	**$54.36**	**$8.42**

5. $7.49 × 3	6. $5.08 × 7	7. $8.29 × 3	8. $5.65 × 8
$22.47	**$35.56**	**$24.87**	**$45.20**

9. $6.78 × 1 = **$6.78**

10. $7.90 × 4 = **$31.60**

11. $3.22 × 5 = **$16.10**

12. How much is 4 gal of milk? **$9.96**

13. How much is 6 bagels? **$5.67**

14. How much is 7 gal of gas? **$9.59**

Fast Gas

Gas/gallon	$1.37

Come inside!
Milk gallon $2.49
Bread $0.99
Bagels .... 2/$1.89

Test Prep

15. If wallpaper is $8.27 a roll, which is the cost of 8 rolls?

A. $48.62   B. $62.76   **C.** $66.16   D. $78.22

16. **Writing in Math** Explain how to find the product of $7.50 × 8.

Sample answer: 8 × 7 = 56, and 8 × 5 = 40. 40 tenths is equal to 4.0. 56 + 4.0 = $60.00

146 Use with Lesson 11-9.

Reteaching

Name_____

Multiplying Money
R 11-9

The only difference between multiplying money and whole numbers is the final step. The answer must be written in the form of money. Make sure you put in the dollar sign ($) and the decimal point.

For example:

Find $7.36 × 7.

Step 1	Step 2
Multiply the same way as with whole numbers.	Write the answer in dollars and cents.
2 4 $7 . 3 6 × 7 5 1 5 2	2 4 $7 . 3 6 × 7 $5 1 . 5 2

Estimate to check. 7 × $7.36 = 7 × 7 = 49
$51.52 is close to 49, so the answer is reasonable.

Find each product. Estimate to check reasonableness.

1. $1.25 × 3	2. $6.98 × 2	3. $4.24 × 5	4. $3.42 × 8
$3.75	**$13.96**	**$21.20**	**$27.36**

5. Kirk bought 3 roast beef sandwiches. How much did it cost? **$15.45**

Lunch Menu	
Tuna Sandwich	$4.53
Roast Beef Sandwich	$5.15
Chips	$1.28
Drink	$1.14

6. If you bought 7 tuna sandwiches, how much would it cost? **$31.71**

7. **Number Sense** Write a multiplication sentence with a 3-digit number that does not require regrouping.

Sample answer: 232 × 3 = 696

146 Use with Lesson 11-9.

Enrichment

Name_____

Healthy Living
E 11-9
DECISION MAKING

1.

Admission Costs	
Adults	$7.00
Children	$4.25
Senior citizens	$3.75

The chart shows the admission costs to the Riverside Hospital Health Fair. Twelve people paid a total of $55.50 for admission. If 8 children attended the fair, how many adults and senior citizens attended?

2 adults and 2 senior citizens

2.

Cafeteria	
Adult lunch	$4.50
Child lunch	$3.25
Fruit	$0.50
Drink	$1.00
Health snack bar	$0.25

This same group of twelve people has $60.00 to spend on food at the cafeteria. What would be the best way to split the $60.00 between them?

Sample answer: Give the adults and seniors each $6.00 and the children each $4.50 so the children can have lunch, a drink, and snacks.

146 Use with Lesson 11-9.

Problem Solving

Name_____

Multiplying Money
PS 11-9

Jill is shopping for school supplies. The chart shows the prices of some items.

Pens	$0.99 each
Folders	$1.49 each
Paper	$2.79 each
Binders	$3.99 each

1. How much would 4 pens cost? **$3.96**

2. How much would 6 folders cost? **$8.94**

3. How much would 3 packs of paper cost? **$8.37**

4. How much would 5 binders cost? **$19.95**

5. How much would 2 binders and 2 folders cost? **$10.96**

6. **Writing in Math** Jill has $20.00 to spend. Can she buy 3 folders, 3 packs of paper, and 2 binders with the money? Explain.

No; Sample answer: The total cost would be $20.82.

146 Use with Lesson 11-9.

© Pearson Education, Inc. **3**

Name_____

Choose a Computation Method

P 11-10

Find each product. Tell which computation method you used.

1.	$9.07	2.	500	3.	3,678	4.	619
	× 4		× 3		× 9		× 7

$36.28   **1,500**   **33,102**   **4,333**

Computation methods may vary.

5. $7,234 \times 7 = $ __50,638__   6. $8,000 \times 4 = $ __32,000__

7. **Number Sense** Explain which computation method you would choose to multiply 4.32×6.

Sample answer:

I would use paper and pencil because there are lots of regroupings.

8. Celia sent 4 packages out through the mail. Three of them had postage of $6.32 and one was $7.51. How much was the postage altogether?   **$26.47**

Test Prep

9. Which is the product of 811×9?

A. 72,990   **(B)** 7,299   C. 7,209   D. 7,200

10. **Writing in Math** Explain when it is best to use a calculator to solve a problem.

Sample answer: When the problem has a lot of regroupings or uses large numbers, or when the answer has to be exact

© Pearson Education, Inc. 3

Name_____

Choose a Computation Method

R 11-10

If the answer is easy to find, you can use mental math. Use mental math for problems like:

$90 \div 9$ or $3,000 \times 7$.

If the answer is not too difficult to find, and there are not many regroupings, use paper and pencil. Use paper and pencil for problems like:

$912 \div 3$ or 62×4 or $615 + 88$.

For problems that have a lot of regroupings, a calculator is a good choice. Some problems that you might choose a calculator to solve are:

$15,328 \times 37$ or $8,921,320 \div 8$.

Find each product. Tell which computation method you used.

1.	3,000	2.	189	3.	$302
	× 4		× 2		× 9

12,000, mental math   **378, paper and pencil**   **$2,718, paper and pencil**

4. $5,887 \times 6 = $ **35,322, calculator**

5. $421 \times 3 = $ **$1,263, paper and pencil**

6. $500 \times 7 = $ **$3,500, mental math**

7. **Writing in Math** Why is mental math not a good method to use when finding $6,789 \times 5$?

Sample answer: It is not a good method because there are too many regroupings.

© Pearson Education, Inc. 3

Name_____

Number Puzzles

E 11-10
NUMBER SENSE

Solve each puzzle.

1. Arrange the digits 2, 3, 5, and 9 in the boxes so that you get the greatest possible product.

Method of computation may vary.

```
   [5] [3] [2]
 ×     [9]
   4, 7  8  8
```

2. Each different letter in this multiplication problem represents one of these digits: 0, 2, 3, 4, 6, 7, and 8. What is the value of each letter?

```
  W H A T
×       A
  G A M E
```

A: 3, E: 8, G: 7, H: 4, M: 0, T: 6, W: 2; $2,436 \times 3 = 7,308$

3. How many cubes are in this display? (Hint: 4 layers are the same.)

101 cubes

© Pearson Education, Inc. 3

Name_____

Choose a Computation Method

PS 11-10

Steller's sea lions live in the north Pacific Ocean. The chart below lists some facts about Steller's sea lions.

Steller's Sea Lion Facts

	Average Weight	Average Length
Sea lion pup	23 kg	112 cm
Adult male sea lion	566 kg	282 cm
Adult female sea lion	263 kg	228 cm

Computation methods may vary.

1. If a female sea lion gives birth to 2 average-sized pups, about how much is their combined weight? Tell what computation method you used.

About 46 kg; Mental math

2. About how much would a group of 8 adult male sea lions weigh? Tell what computation method you used.

About 4,528 kg; Calculator

3. If 5 female sea lions lay down head to tail, about what would their total length be? Tell what computation method you used.

About 1,140 cm; Paper and pencil

4. About how much would 10 adult males weigh? Tell what computation method you used.

About 5,660 kg; Mental math

5. **Writing in Math** Miles said that paper and pencil is the best method to find 13×3. Do you agree? Explain.

No; Sample answer: Because there are no regroupings, it is easy to do in your head.

© Pearson Education, Inc. 3

Name_____

PROBLEM-SOLVING STRATEGY   P 11-11

Use Logical Reasoning

Solve. Write the answer in a complete sentence.

1. Complete the table. Then use the table to find what color uniform the Wolves wear.

The Wolves have green uniforms.

- The Bears do not wear red or green.
- The Cougars wear white.
- There is no green on the Pumas' uniforms.

	Bears	Cougars	Pumas	Wolves
Blue	Yes	No	No	No
Green	No	No	No	Yes
Red	No	No	Yes	No
White	No	Yes	No	No

2. Sally has an appointment on Thursday. The first appointment of the day is at 9 A.M. and the final one is at 3 P.M. Sally's appointment is not the first of the day or the last. Her appointment is on the hour. The sum of the digits in the hour is 3. What time is Sally's appointment?

Sally's appointment is at 12:00 P.M.

3. I am an odd number with 3 digits. The sum of my digits is 5. My first and last digits are the same. What number am I?

The number is 131.

4. Ben's grandfather is 5 times as old as Ben. Ben's father is 22 years younger than his grandfather. If Ben is 12 years old, how old is Ben's father?

Ben's father is 38 years old.

Name_____

PROBLEM-SOLVING STRATEGY   R 11-11

Use Logical Reasoning

Age Carla is 18 years old. Her father is 4 years older than her mother. Carla's mother is twice as old as Carla. How old is Carla's father?

Read and Understand

Step 1: What do you know?

Carla's age is 18. Carla's mother is twice Carla's age. Her father is 4 years older than her mother.

Step 2: What are you trying to find?

Carla's father's age

Plan and Solve

Step 3: What strategy will you use?

Strategy: Use logical reasoning

Draw a picture to help organize what you know.

Carla 18 → ×2 → Carla's mom → +4 → Carla's dad

Carla's mother is twice Carla's age, or 2 × 18 = 36. So, Carla's mother is 36. Carla's father is 4 years older than her mother, or 36 + 4 = 40. So, Carla's father is 40 years old.

Look Back and Check

Step 4: Is your work correct?

Yes, all the clues match the answer.

Solve. Write the answer in a complete sentence.

1. Complete the table to decide what color house Peter lives in.

Clues:
- Tom does not live in a blue house.
- Willis likes his white house.

	Peter	Tom	Willis
Blue	Yes	No	No
Green	No	Yes	No
White	No	No	Yes

Peter lives in a blue house.

Name_____

E 11-11
REASONING

Just in Time

Justin usually keeps a record of the number of hours he spends each day mowing lawns in the summer. But he forgot to write down the hours for this week.

Day	Number of Hours
Monday	6
Tuesday	12
Wednesday	6
Thursday	3
Friday	1
Total for the week	28

1. Use the following facts to complete the table for Justin.

- Justin remembers that on Friday he only worked for 1 hr.
- Monday's time was one half of Tuesday's time.
- Tuesday's time was twice as much as Wednesday's.
- Wednesday's time was twice as much as Thursday's.
- On Thursday, Justin mowed 2 more hours than on Friday.

2. If Justin earned $3.00 per hour in an 8 hr day and $4.00 per hour past 8 hr in a day, how much did he earn for the week?

$88

Name_____

PROBLEM-SOLVING STRATEGY   PS 11-11

Use Logical Reasoning

Street Smart On Megan's block, the first house number on her side of the street is 501. The next house on her side of the street is 503, and the one next to that is 505. The last house is 517. How many houses are there on Megan's side of the street?

Read and Understand

1. What do you know?

The house numbers begin at 501, end at 517, and are all odd numbers in between.

2. What are you trying to find?

How many houses there are on Megan's side of the street

Plan and Solve

3. What strategy will you use?

Logical reasoning; Draw a picture and fill in the information then draw a conclusion

4. Solve the problem. Write the answer in a complete sentence.

There are 9 houses on Megan's side of the street.

Look Back and Check

5. Is your answer reasonable?

Yes, there are 9 odd numbers from 501 to 517.

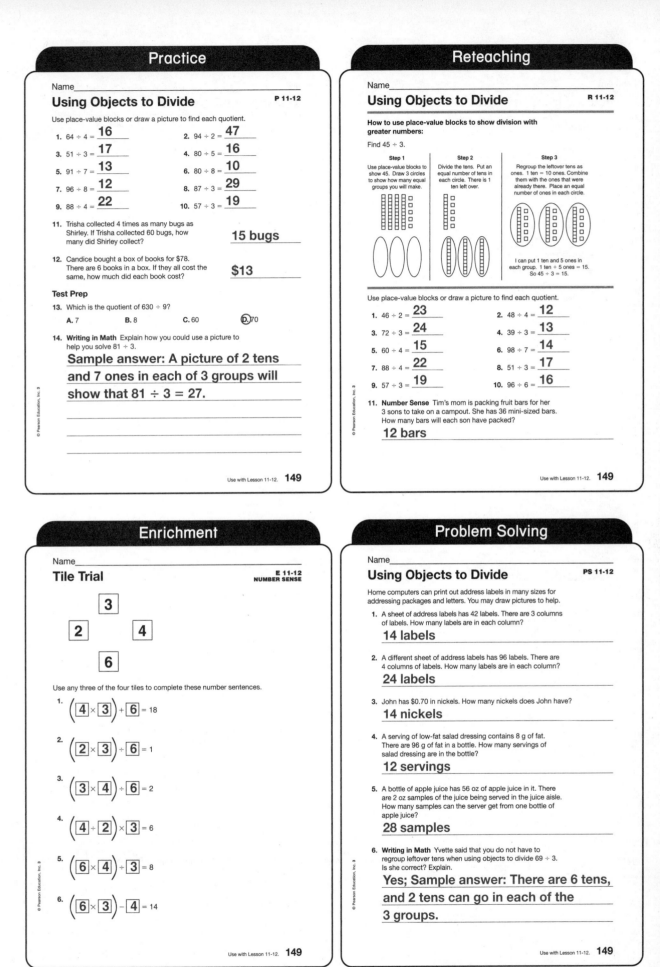

Practice

Name

Using Objects to Divide

P 11-12

Use place-value blocks or draw a picture to find each quotient.

1. $64 \div 4 =$ __16__
2. $94 \div 2 =$ __47__
3. $51 \div 3 =$ __17__
4. $80 \div 5 =$ __16__
5. $91 \div 7 =$ __13__
6. $80 \div 8 =$ __10__
7. $96 \div 8 =$ __12__
8. $87 \div 3 =$ __29__
9. $88 \div 4 =$ __22__
10. $57 \div 3 =$ __19__

11. Trisha collected 4 times as many bugs as Shirley. If Trisha collected 60 bugs, how many did Shirley collect?

__15 bugs__

12. Candice bought a box of books for $78. There are 6 books in a box. If they all cost the same, how much did each book cost?

__$13__

Test Prep

13. Which is the quotient of $630 \div 9$?
   A. 7   B. 8   C. 60   (D.) 70

14. **Writing in Math** Explain how you could use a picture to help you solve $81 \div 3$.

__Sample answer: A picture of 2 tens and 7 ones in each of 3 groups will show that $81 \div 3 = 27$.__

Reteaching

Name

Using Objects to Divide

R 11-12

How to use place-value blocks to show division with greater numbers:

Find $45 \div 3$.

Step 1	Step 2	Step 3
Use place-value blocks to show 45. Draw 3 circles to show how many equal groups you will make.	Divide the tens. Put an equal number of tens in each circle. There is 1 ten left over.	Regroup the leftover tens as ones. 1 ten = 10 ones. Combine them with the ones that were already there. Place an equal number of ones in each circle.

I can put 1 ten and 5 ones in each group. 1 ten + 5 ones = 15. So $45 \div 3 = 15$.

Use place-value blocks or draw a picture to find each quotient.

1. $46 \div 2 =$ __23__
2. $48 \div 4 =$ __12__
3. $72 \div 3 =$ __24__
4. $39 \div 3 =$ __13__
5. $60 \div 4 =$ __15__
6. $98 \div 7 =$ __14__
7. $88 \div 4 =$ __22__
8. $51 \div 3 =$ __17__
9. $57 \div 3 =$ __19__
10. $96 \div 6 =$ __16__

11. **Number Sense** Tim's mom is packing fruit bars for her 3 sons to take on a campout. She has 36 mini-sized bars. How many bars will each son have packed?

__12 bars__

Enrichment

Name

Tile Trial

E 11-12
NUMBER SENSE

3
2   4
6

Use any three of the four tiles to complete these number sentences.

1. $\left(\boxed{4} \times \boxed{3}\right) + \boxed{6} = 18$

2. $\left(\boxed{2} \times \boxed{3}\right) \div \boxed{6} = 1$

3. $\left(\boxed{3} \times \boxed{4}\right) \div \boxed{6} = 2$

4. $\left(\boxed{4} \div \boxed{2}\right) \times \boxed{3} = 6$

5. $\left(\boxed{6} \times \boxed{4}\right) \div \boxed{3} = 8$

6. $\left(\boxed{6} \times \boxed{3}\right) - \boxed{4} = 14$

Problem Solving

Name

Using Objects to Divide

PS 11-12

Home computers can print out address labels in many sizes for addressing packages and letters. You may draw pictures to help.

1. A sheet of address labels has 42 labels. There are 3 columns of labels. How many labels are in each column?

__14 labels__

2. A different sheet of address labels has 96 labels. There are 4 columns of labels. How many labels are in each column?

__24 labels__

3. John has $0.70 in nickels. How many nickels does John have?

__14 nickels__

4. A serving of low-fat salad dressing contains 8 g of fat. There are 96 g of fat in a bottle. How many servings of salad dressing are in the bottle?

__12 servings__

5. A bottle of apple juice has 56 oz of apple juice in it. There are 2 oz samples of the juice being served in the juice aisle. How many samples can the server get from one bottle of apple juice?

__28 samples__

6. **Writing in Math** Yvette said that you do not have to regroup leftover tens when using objects to divide $69 \div 3$. Is she correct? Explain.

__Yes; Sample answer: There are 6 tens, and 2 tens can go in each of the 3 groups.__

Breaking Numbers Apart to Divide
P 11-13

Name_____

Use the break apart method to find each quotient. You may draw a picture to help.

1. $60 \div 3 = $ **20**   **2.** $60 \div 4 = $ **15**

3. $72 \div 3 = $ **24**   **4.** $95 \div 5 = $ **19**

5. $4\overline{)64}$ **16**   **6.** $2\overline{)64}$ **32**   **7.** $2\overline{)32}$ **16**   **8.** $3\overline{)48}$ **16**

9. Jennifer has 57 fish in one tank. She wants to move them to 3 smaller tanks. If she puts the same number of fish in each of the 3 smaller tanks, how many fish will be in each tank?   **19 fish**

10. There is enough room for 5 rows of chairs in a room. There are 75 people to be seated. How many chairs must be in each row?   **15 chairs**

Test Prep

11. Which has the greatest quotient?

 A. $75 \div 3$ **B.** $96 \div 4$ Ⓒ $82 \div 2$ **D.** $48 \div 3$

12. Writing in Math Explain how using the break apart method can help you solve $84 \div 4$.

Sample answer: I can break 84 into 8 tens and 4 ones. 8 tens ÷ 4 = 2 tens, and 4 ones ÷ 4 = 1 one. 2 tens + 1 one = 21, so 84 ÷ 4 = 21.

Breaking Numbers Apart to Divide
R 11-13

Name_____

You can break apart numbers into groups of tens and ones to divide.

Find $42 \div 2$.

Step 1 Break apart 42 into tens and ones.	**Step 2** Divide the tens, then divide the ones.	**Step 3** Add the two quotients.
42 is the same as 4 tens and 2 ones. $42 = 40 + 2$	Tens: $40 \div 2 = 20$ Ones: $2 \div 2 = 1$	$20 + 1 = 21$ So, $42 \div 2 = 21$.

Use the break apart method to find each quotient. You may draw a picture to help.

1. $55 \div 5 = $ **11**   **2.** $48 \div 4 = $ **12**   **3.** $82 \div 2 = $ **41**

4. $3\overline{)93}$ **31**   **5.** $2\overline{)46}$ **23**   **6.** $3\overline{)66}$ **22**

7. $63 \div 3 = $ **21**   **8.** $88 \div 4 = $ **22**   **9.** $24 \div 2 = $ **12**

10. $4\overline{)44}$ **11**   **11.** $3\overline{)96}$ **32**   **12.** $6\overline{)66}$ **11**

13. Number Sense Niko has 28 pencils. He is putting them evenly into two drawers. How many pencils will be in each drawer?

14 pencils

Divide and Conquer
E 11-13
NUMBER SENSE

Name_____

1. Mary has an 800-word book report due today. She types 20 words per minute, and it takes the printer 5 min to print the paper. How long will it take her to type the report? If Mary begins typing at 9:00 A.M., at what time will her paper be complete, including printing?

40 min; 9:45 A.M.

2. The total area of the United States is about 3,600,000 sq mi. If every state had an equal share of the total area, how many square miles would each state be?

72,000 sq mi

3. Find four ways to draw a straight line between the dots so they are equally divided.

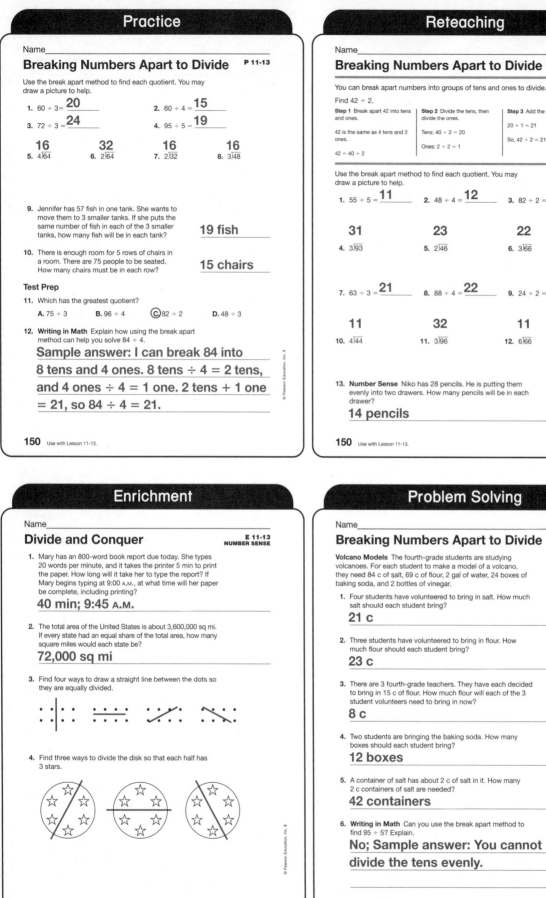

4. Find three ways to divide the disk so that each half has 3 stars.

Breaking Numbers Apart to Divide
PS 11-13

Name_____

Volcano Models The fourth-grade students are studying volcanoes. For each student to make a model of a volcano, they need 84 c of salt, 69 c of flour, 2 gal of water, 24 boxes of baking soda, and 2 bottles of vinegar.

1. Four students have volunteered to bring in salt. How much salt should each student bring?

21 c

2. Three students have volunteered to bring in flour. How much flour should each student bring?

23 c

3. There are 3 fourth-grade teachers. They have each decided to bring in 15 c of flour. How much flour will each of the 3 student volunteers need to bring in now?

8 c

4. Two students are bringing the baking soda. How many boxes should each student bring?

12 boxes

5. A container of salt has about 2 c of salt in it. How many 2 c containers of salt are needed?

42 containers

6. Writing in Math Can you use the break apart method to find $95 \div 5$? Explain.

No; Sample answer: You cannot divide the tens evenly.

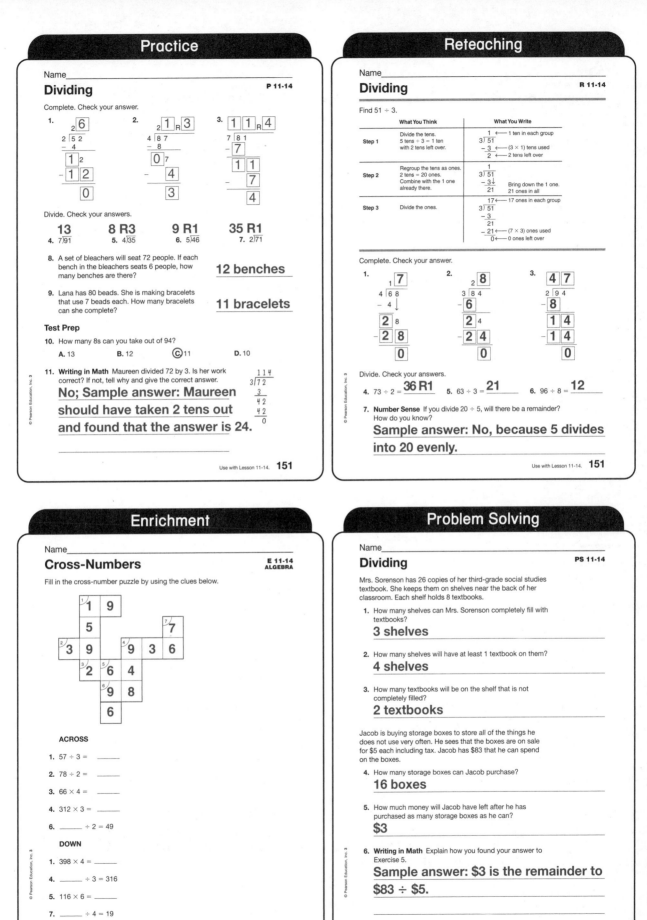

Practice

Name_____

Dividing
P 11-14

Complete. Check your answer.

1.
```
    6
2)5 2
  2 5
  - 4
   1 2
  -1 2
     0
```

2.
```
   2 1 R3
4)8 7
  - 8
    0 7
    - 4
      3
```

3.
```
   1 1 R4
7)8 1
 - 7
   1 1
  - 7
    4
```

Divide. Check your answers.

4. **13** 7)91

5. **8 R3** 4)35

6. **9 R1** 5)46

7. **35 R1** 2)71

8. A set of bleachers will seat 72 people. If each bench in the bleachers seats 6 people, how many benches are there?

12 benches

9. Lana has 80 beads. She is making bracelets that use 7 beads each. How many bracelets can she complete?

11 bracelets

Test Prep

10. How many 8s can you take out of 94?

A. 13   B. 12   Ⓒ 11   D. 10

11. **Writing in Math** Maureen divided 72 by 3. Is her work correct? If not, tell why and give the correct answer.

```
   1 1 4
3)7 2
  3
  4 2
  4 2
    0
```

No; Sample answer: Maureen should have taken 2 tens out and found that the answer is 24.

Use with Lesson 11-14. **151**

Reteaching

Name_____

Dividing
R 11-14

Find 51 ÷ 3.

	What You Think	What You Write
Step 1	Divide the tens. 5 tens ÷ 3 = 1 ten with 2 tens left over.	1 ← 1 ten in each group 3)51 -3 ← (3 × 1) tens used 2 ← 2 tens left over
Step 2	Regroup the tens as ones. 2 tens = 20 ones. Combine with the 1 one already there.	1 3)51 -3↓ Bring down the 1 one. 21 21 ones in all
Step 3	Divide the ones.	17 ← 17 ones in each group 3)51 -3 21 -21 ← (7 × 3) ones used 0 ← 0 ones left over

Complete. Check your answer.

1.
```
   1 7
4)6 8
 - 4
   2 8
  -2 8
     0
```

2.
```
   2 8
3)8 4
 - 6
   2 4
  -2 4
     0
```

3.
```
   4 7
2)9 4
 - 8
   1 4
  -1 4
     0
```

Divide. Check your answers.

4. 73 ÷ 2 = **36 R1**

5. 63 ÷ 3 = **21**

6. 96 ÷ 8 = **12**

7. **Number Sense** If you divide 20 ÷ 5, will there be a remainder? How do you know?

Sample answer: No, because 5 divides into 20 evenly.

Use with Lesson 11-14. **151**

Enrichment

Name_____

Cross-Numbers
E 11-14
ALGEBRA

Fill in the cross-number puzzle by using the clues below.

```
1 9
5       7
3 9   9 3 6
2 6 4
9 8
6
```

ACROSS

1. 57 ÷ 3 = _____

2. 78 ÷ 2 = _____

3. 66 × 4 = _____

4. 312 × 3 = _____

6. _____ ÷ 2 = 49

DOWN

1. 398 × 4 = _____

4. _____ ÷ 3 = 316

5. 116 × 6 = _____

7. _____ ÷ 4 = 19

Use with Lesson 11-14. **151**

Problem Solving

Name_____

Dividing
PS 11-14

Mrs. Sorenson has 26 copies of her third-grade social studies textbook. She keeps them on shelves near the back of her classroom. Each shelf holds 8 textbooks.

1. How many shelves can Mrs. Sorenson completely fill with textbooks?

3 shelves

2. How many shelves will have at least 1 textbook on them?

4 shelves

3. How many textbooks will be on the shelf that is not completely filled?

2 textbooks

Jacob is buying storage boxes to store all of the things he does not use very often. He sees that the boxes are on sale for $5 each including tax. Jacob has $83 that he can spend on the boxes.

4. How many storage boxes can Jacob purchase?

16 boxes

5. How much money will Jacob have left after he has purchased as many storage boxes as he can?

$3

6. **Writing in Math** Explain how you found your answer to Exercise 5.

Sample answer: $3 is the remainder to $83 ÷ $5.

Use with Lesson 11-14. **151**

PROBLEM-SOLVING SKILL   P 11-15

Interpreting Remainders

Use the table for 1–4.

Gail is a plumber. She is going to buy some supplies at the hardware store.

Item	Number in Package	Cost per Package
Nails	50	$3.00
Screws	25	$6.00
1 in. copper elbow	3	$2.50
1 in. pipe – 6 ft	1	$5.00

1. How many packages of copper elbows should Gail buy if she needs 41 elbows?

   Gail should buy 14 packages.

2. How many packages of nails can Gail buy with $74.00?

   Gail can buy 24 packages.

3. How many packages of screws can Gail buy with $52.00?

   Gail bought 8 packages.

4. If Gail started with $76.00 and bought as many pipes as she could, how much money would she have left?

   Gail would have $1.00 left.

5. Skyler has 47 apples. There are 3 people in his family. If each person ate the same number of apples, how many have they each eaten? How many apples are left?

   Each person ate 15 apples.
   There are 2 apples left.

PROBLEM-SOLVING SKILL   R 11-15

Interpreting Remainders

Window Repair Sam repairs broken windows. It takes him about 4 hr to repair 1 window. He works 25 hr each week.

How many windows are repaired in 1 week?	How many windows will be worked on in 1 week?	How many hours will be spent working on the seventh window in 1 work week?
Plan and Solve $$4\overline{)25} \quad 6\ R1$$ $$\underline{-24}$$ $$1$$ 6 windows can be repaired.	**Plan and Solve** $$4\overline{)25} \quad 6\ R1$$ $$\underline{-24}$$ $$1$$ 7 windows will be worked on.	**Plan and Solve** $$4\overline{)25} \quad 6\ R1$$ $$\underline{-24}$$ $$1$$ 1 hr will be spent on the last window.
Look Back and Check The 1 hr left over is not enough to repair another window.	**Look Back and Check** He will begin working on the seventh window in the remaining 1 hr.	**Look Back and Check** 4 windows are repaired in 24 hr. There is 1 more hour in the work week.

Solve. Write the answer in a complete sentence.

1. Tanya is knitting baby sweaters. Each sweater needs 5 balls of yarn. She has 34 balls of yarn. How many sweaters can she make?

   Tanya can make 6 sweaters.

2. José had $34. He bought as many packages of socks as he could. The socks cost $5 a package. How much money did José have left after he bought the socks? How much more money does he need to buy another package of socks?

   José has $4 left. He needs $1 to buy
   another package of socks.

Leftovers   E 11-15
                                    REASONABLENESS

1. Rhonda is in charge of buying food for a school picnic. All of the items are packaged differently.

   - hot dogs—48 to a package
   - buns—18 to a package
   - ketchup—12 serving packets per box
   - mustard—15 serving packets per box
   - relish—10 serving packets per box

   Each student receives one of each item and Rhonda has purchased enough food to feed 32 people.

   How many packages of each item did Rhonda buy and how many of each item will be left over?

   Hot dogs: 1 package, 16 left over; buns:
   2 packages, 4 left over; ketchup: 3
   packages, 4 left over; mustard: 3
   packages, 13 left over; relish: 4
   packages, 8 left over

2. Lisa and her 7 friends went apple picking. They picked 52 Red Delicious, 19 Golden, and 12 Green Granny Smith. They each took an equal amount and put the leftover apples in a basket for their teacher. Draw the apples that are in the basket for their teacher.

   Sample answer:

PROBLEM-SOLVING SKILL   PS 11-15

Interpreting Remainders

Garden Vince is constructing a wall of rocks around his garden. He needs 73 rocks and can carry 3 rocks at a time. How many trips will it take Vince to carry 73 rocks to his garden?

Read and Understand

1. How many rocks does Vince need? How many rocks can he carry at a time?

   73 rocks; 3 rocks

2. What are you trying to find?

   The number of trips Vince needs to make
   to move all of the rocks to his garden

Plan and Solve

3. What equation do you need to solve?

   73 ÷ 3 = 24 R1

4. What does the remainder represent in the answer?

   The number of rocks Vince will carry
   on his last trip

5. Solve the problem. Write the answer in a complete sentence.

   Vince will need to make 25 trips.

Look Back and Check

6. Is your answer reasonable?

   Yes; Sample answer: 25 × 3 = 75, and
   Vince needs to carry 73 rocks.

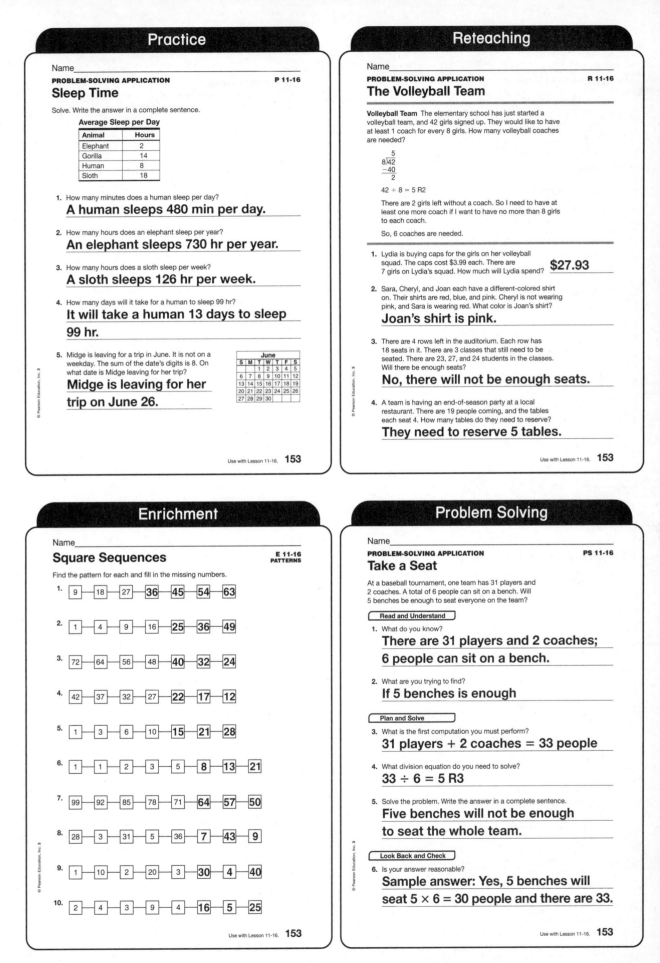

Practice

Name_____

Sleep Time

Solve. Write the answer in a complete sentence.

Average Sleep per Day

Animal	Hours
Elephant	2
Gorilla	14
Human	8
Sloth	18

1. How many minutes does a human sleep per day?

   A human sleeps 480 min per day.

2. How many hours does an elephant sleep per year?

   An elephant sleeps 730 hr per year.

3. How many hours does a sloth sleep per week?

   A sloth sleeps 126 hr per week.

4. How many days will it take for a human to sleep 99 hr?

   It will take a human 13 days to sleep 99 hr.

5. Midge is leaving for a trip in June. It is not on a weekday. The sum of the date's digits is 8. On what date is Midge leaving for her trip?

   June

S	M	T	W	T	F	S
			1	2	3	4	5
6	7	8	9	10	11	12
13	14	15	16	17	18	19
20	21	22	23	24	25	26
27	28	29	30

   Midge is leaving for her trip on June 26.

© Pearson Education, Inc. 3

Reteaching

Name_____

The Volleyball Team

Volleyball Team The elementary school has just started a volleyball team, and 42 girls signed up. They would like to have at least 1 coach for every 8 girls. How many volleyball coaches are needed?

$$\begin{array}{r} 5 \\ 8\overline{)42} \\ -40 \\ \hline 2 \end{array}$$

$42 \div 8 = 5 \text{ R2}$

There are 2 girls left without a coach. So I need to have at least one more coach if I want to have no more than 8 girls to each coach.

So, 6 coaches are needed.

1. Lydia is buying caps for the girls on her volleyball squad. The caps cost $3.99 each. There are 7 girls on Lydia's squad. How much will Lydia spend? **$27.93**

2. Sara, Cheryl, and Joan each have a different-colored shirt on. Their shirts are red, blue, and pink. Cheryl is not wearing pink, and Sara is wearing red. What color is Joan's shirt?

   Joan's shirt is pink.

3. There are 4 rows left in the auditorium. Each row has 18 seats in it. There are 3 classes that still need to be seated. There are 23, 27, and 24 students in the classes. Will there be enough seats?

   No, there will not be enough seats.

4. A team is having an end-of-season party at a local restaurant. There are 19 people coming, and the tables each seat 4. How many tables do they need to reserve?

   They need to reserve 5 tables.

© Pearson Education, Inc. 3

Enrichment

Name_____

Square Sequences

Find the pattern for each and fill in the missing numbers.

1. 9 — 18 — 27 — **36** — **45** — **54** — **63**

2. 1 — 4 — 9 — 16 — **25** — **36** — **49**

3. 72 — 64 — 56 — 48 — **40** — **32** — **24**

4. 42 — 37 — 32 — 27 — **22** — **17** — **12**

5. 1 — 3 — 6 — 10 — **15** — **21** — **28**

6. 1 — 1 — 2 — 3 — 5 — **8** — **13** — **21**

7. 99 — 92 — 85 — 78 — 71 — **64** — **57** — **50**

8. 28 — 3 — 31 — 5 — 36 — **7** — **43** — **9**

9. 1 — 10 — 2 — 20 — 3 — **30** — 4 — **40**

10. 2 — 4 — 3 — 9 — 4 — **16** — 5 — **25**

© Pearson Education, Inc. 3

Problem Solving

Name_____

Take a Seat

At a baseball tournament, one team has 31 players and 2 coaches. A total of 6 people can sit on a bench. Will 5 benches be enough to seat everyone on the team?

Read and Understand

1. What do you know?

   There are 31 players and 2 coaches; 6 people can sit on a bench.

2. What are you trying to find?

   If 5 benches is enough

Plan and Solve

3. What is the first computation you must perform?

   31 players + 2 coaches = 33 people

4. What division equation do you need to solve?

   $33 \div 6 = 5 \text{ R3}$

5. Solve the problem. Write the answer in a complete sentence.

   Five benches will not be enough to seat the whole team.

Look Back and Check

6. Is your answer reasonable?

   Sample answer: Yes, 5 benches will seat 5 × 6 = 30 people and there are 33.

© Pearson Education, Inc. 3

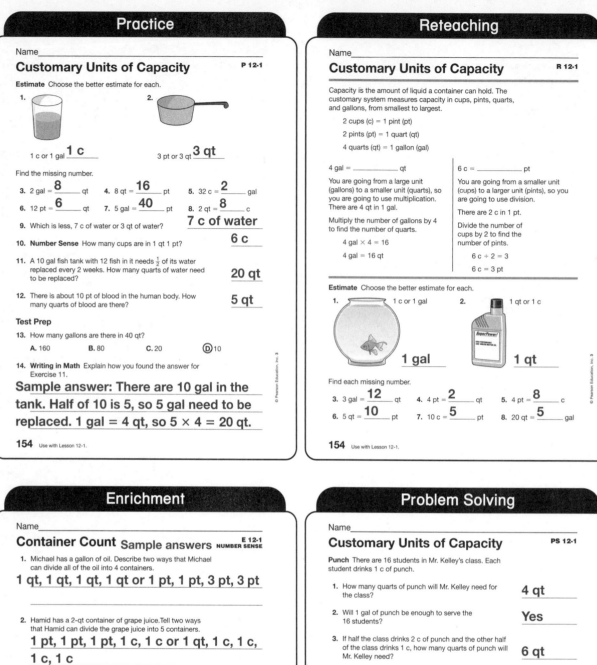

Practice

Name

Customary Units of Capacity

P 12-1

Estimate Choose the better estimate for each.

1.

1 c or 1 gal __1 c__

2.

3 pt or 3 qt __3 qt__

Find the missing number.

3. 2 gal = __8__ qt
4. 8 qt = __16__ pt
5. 32 c = __2__ gal
6. 12 pt = __6__ qt
7. 5 gal = __40__ pt
8. 2 qt = __8__ c

9. Which is less, 7 c of water or 3 qt of water? __7 c of water__

10. **Number Sense** How many cups are in 1 qt 1 pt? __6 c__

11. A 10 gal fish tank with 12 fish in it needs $\frac{1}{2}$ of its water replaced every 2 weeks. How many quarts of water need to be replaced? __20 qt__

12. There is about 10 pt of blood in the human body. How many quarts of blood are there? __5 qt__

Test Prep

13. How many gallons are there in 40 qt?

A. 160   B. 80   C. 20   (D) 10

14. **Writing in Math** Explain how you found the answer for Exercise 11.

Sample answer: There are 10 gal in the tank. Half of 10 is 5, so 5 gal need to be replaced. 1 gal = 4 qt, so 5 × 4 = 20 qt.

Reteaching

Name

Customary Units of Capacity

R 12-1

Capacity is the amount of liquid a container can hold. The customary system measures capacity in cups, pints, quarts, and gallons, from smallest to largest.

2 cups (c) = 1 pint (pt)

2 pints (pt) = 1 quart (qt)

4 quarts (qt) = 1 gallon (gal)

4 gal = _____ qt

You are going from a large unit (gallons) to a smaller unit (quarts), so you are going to use multiplication. There are 4 qt in 1 gal.

Multiply the number of gallons by 4 to find the number of quarts.

4 gal × 4 = 16

4 gal = 16 qt

6 c = _____ pt

You are going from a smaller unit (cups) to a larger unit (pints), so you are going to use division.

There are 2 c in 1 pt.

Divide the number of cups by 2 to find the number of pints.

6 c ÷ 2 = 3

6 c = 3 pt

Estimate Choose the better estimate for each.

1.

1 c or 1 gal   __1 gal__

2.

1 qt or 1 c   __1 qt__

Find each missing number.

3. 3 gal = __12__ qt
4. 4 pt = __2__ qt
5. 4 pt = __8__ c
6. 5 qt = __10__ pt
7. 10 c = __5__ pt
8. 20 qt = __5__ gal

Enrichment

Name

Container Count Sample answers

E 12-1
NUMBER SENSE

1. Michael has a gallon of oil. Describe two ways that Michael can divide all of the oil into 4 containers.

1 qt, 1 qt, 1 qt, 1 qt or 1 pt, 1 pt, 3 pt, 3 pt

2. Hamid has a 2-qt container of grape juice. Tell two ways that Hamid can divide the grape juice into 5 containers.

1 pt, 1 pt, 1 pt, 1 c, 1 c or 1 qt, 1 c, 1 c, 1 c, 1 c

3. Isaac has a quart of milk. Tell a way that Isaac can divide all of the milk into 3 containers.

1 pt, 1 c, 1 c

4. Tell two possible ways that Mitchell can divide a gallon of apple cider into 3 different containers.

3 pt, 3 pt, 1 qt or 4 pt, 2 pt, 1 qt

5. Eight people shared a pitcher of iced tea. Two people poured tea into 1-pt glasses, four people poured tea into cup containers, and two people poured tea into 1-qt mugs. How much iced tea was there in the original pitcher?

1 gal

6. Alice made a pitcher of lemonade. She poured 1 c of lemonade for each of her twin boys. She poured the rest into a 1 pt glass for her husband. How much lemonade was there in the original pitcher?

1 qt

Problem Solving

Name

Customary Units of Capacity

PS 12-1

Punch There are 16 students in Mr. Kelley's class. Each student drinks 1 c of punch.

1. How many quarts of punch will Mr. Kelley need for the class? __4 qt__

2. Will 1 gal of punch be enough to serve the 16 students? __Yes__

3. If half the class drinks 2 c of punch and the other half of the class drinks 1 c, how many quarts of punch will Mr. Kelley need? __6 qt__

Humidifier Mr. Janis refills his humidifier with 2 qt of water every day.

4. How many cups of water does Mr. Janis put into the humidifier each day? __8 c__

5. How many gallons of water does Mr. Janis put in the humidifier over 4 days? __2 gal__

6. How many pints of water does he use in 3 days? __12 pt__

7. **Writing in Math** Explain how you found the answer to Exercise 6.

Sample answer: There are 2 pt in 1 qt and Mr. Janis used 6 qt in 3 days.

2 × 6 = 12 pt

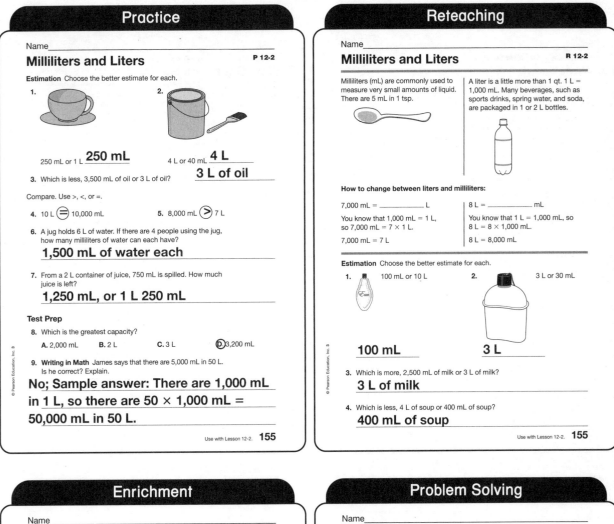

Practice

Name_____

Milliliters and Liters

P 12-2

Estimation Choose the better estimate for each.

1.
250 mL or 1 L **250 mL**

2.
4 L or 40 mL **4 L**

3. Which is less, 3,500 mL of oil or 3 L of oil?
3 L of oil

Compare. Use >, <, or =.

4. 10 L $=$ 10,000 mL

5. 8,000 mL $>$ 7 L

6. A jug holds 6 L of water. If there are 4 people using the jug, how many milliliters of water can each have?
1,500 mL of water each

7. From a 2 L container of juice, 750 mL is spilled. How much juice is left?
1,250 mL, or 1 L 250 mL

Test Prep

8. Which is the greatest capacity?

A. 2,000 mL   B. 2 L   C. 3 L   D. 3,200 mL

9. **Writing in Math** James says that there are 5,000 mL in 50 L. Is he correct? Explain.
No; Sample answer: There are 1,000 mL in 1 L, so there are 50 × 1,000 mL = 50,000 mL in 50 L.

Use with Lesson 12-2. **155**

Reteaching

Name_____

Milliliters and Liters

R 12-2

Milliliters (mL) are commonly used to measure very small amounts of liquid. There are 5 mL in 1 tsp.

A liter is a little more than 1 qt. 1 L = 1,000 mL. Many beverages, such as sports drinks, spring water, and soda, are packaged in 1 or 2 L bottles.

How to change between liters and milliliters:

7,000 mL = _____ L
You know that 1,000 mL = 1 L, so 7,000 mL = 7 × 1 L.
7,000 mL = 7 L

8 L = _____ mL
You know that 1 L = 1,000 mL, so 8 L = 8 × 1,000 mL.
8 L = 8,000 mL

Estimation Choose the better estimate for each.

1. 100 mL or 10 L
100 mL

2. 3 L or 30 mL
3 L

3. Which is more, 2,500 mL of milk or 3 L of milk?
3 L of milk

4. Which is less, 4 L of soup or 400 mL of soup?
400 mL of soup

Use with Lesson 12-2. **155**

Enrichment

Name_____

Conversion Fun

E 12-2
MENTAL MATH

1. 1,525 mL + 1 L = how many milliliters? **2,525 mL**

2. 4 L − 2,000 mL = how many liters? **2 L**

3. 8,000 mL + 3 L = how many liters? **11 L**

4. 6,500 mL − 2 L = how many milliliters? **4,500 mL**

5. 5 L + 3,900 mL = how many milliliters? **8,900 mL**

6. 14,000 mL − 8 L = how many liters? **6 L**

7. 2,590 mL + 2 L = how many milliliters? **4,590 mL**

8. 7 L − 3,526 mL = how many milliliters? **3,474 mL**

9. 11,000 mL + 9 L = how many liters? **20 L**

10. 4,286 mL + 5 L = how many milliliters? **9,286 mL**

11. 10 L − 3 L − 2,000 mL = how many milliliters? **5,000 mL**

12. 2,500 mL + 1,500 mL + 3,000 mL = how many liters? **7 L**

13. 1,386 mL + 4,614 mL − 1 L = how many liters? **5 L**

14. 15,212 mL − 3,201 mL + 2 L = how many milliliters? **14,011 mL**

15. 863 mL + 17,916 mL − 5 L = how many milliliters? **13,779 mL**

Use with Lesson 12-2. **155**

Problem Solving

Name_____

Milliliters and Liters

PS 12-2

Bird Care Carrie has a pet bird. She also enjoys taking care of the birds that visit her backyard.

1. Carrie gives her pet bird fresh water each day. Do you think she gives the bird more than or less than 1 L of water?
Less than

2. Carrie refills the birdbath each week with fresh water. Do you think the birdbath holds 4 L or 4 mL of water?
4 L of water

3. Every other week, Carrie scrubs the birdbath with soap and water. Do you think the bucket of water holds 8 mL or 8 L of water?
8 L of water

Water Alan has 3 containers filled with water. Each container holds 250 mL of water.

4. Will all of the water fit in a 1 L container?
Yes

5. If Alan has 2 L of water, how many 250 mL containers can he fill?
Eight 250 mL containers

6. If Alan has 2 L of water and then drank two 250 mL containers of water, how many milliliters of water does he have left?
1,500 mL of water

7. **Writing in Math** Walter said that 500 mL is the same as 5 L. Is he correct? Explain.
No; Sample answer: 5 L equals 5,000 mL, not 500 mL.

Use with Lesson 12-2. **155**

Name_____

Work Backward

Solve each problem. Write the answer in a complete sentence.

1. This morning 50 mL was poured out of a container of water. Then 1 L of water was added, making the total amount of water 1,500 mL. How much water was in the container before any was poured?

There was 550 mL of water in the container.

2. Marty has $6.25 at the end of the day. Today he bought lunch for $8.50, a bagel for breakfast for $1.25, a newspaper for $2.25, and a necklace for his mother for $37.75. He was paid $12.50 for delivering two boxes of paper to his uncle's office. How much money did Marty have when he started his day?

Marty had $43.50 when he started this morning.

3. Cindy drank 4 c of fruit punch from a pitcher. Jackie drank 2 c and Lauren drank 2 more. There are 2 qt of punch left in the pitcher. How many quarts of punch were there before the girls drank some?

There were 4 qt of punch before the girls drank some.

4. It took Will 30 min to walk from his house to the grocery store. He was in the store for 45 min, and then walked for 15 min more to his grandmother's house. It was 3 P.M. when he arrived at his grandmother's. What time did Will leave his house?

Will left his house at 1:30 P.M.

Name_____

Work Backward

Larry's Dog When Larry was in fourth grade, his dog gained 7 lb. The dog was sick over the summer and lost 3 lb. When Larry started fifth grade, his dog weighed 81 lb. How much did Larry's dog weigh when Larry started fourth grade?

Read and Understand

Step 1: What do you know?

The dog weighed 81 lb when Larry started fifth grade. The dog gained 7 lb when Larry was in fourth grade, and lost 3 lb over the summer.

Step 2: What are you trying to find?

How much Larry's dog weighed when Larry started fourth grade

Plan and Solve

Step 3: What strategy will you use?

Strategy: Work backward

Draw a picture to show each change.

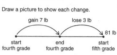

Start at the end, work backward using the opposite operation of each change.

Where the dog gained weight, I subtract. Where the dog lost weight, I add.

81 lb + 3 lb = 84 lb

84 lb − 7 lb = 77 lb

The dog weighed 77 lb when Larry started fourth grade.

Look Back and Check

Step 4: Is your answer reasonable?

Yes, I worked backward using the weights that were known.

1. Cristie spent $6.50 on food and $22.50 on a haircut. She had $5.00 left. How much money did she have before she spent any?

Cristie had $34.00 before she spent any money.

Name_____

Find the Way Back

1. Princeton started at the corner of Broad and High Street. He walked 2 blocks north, turned left and walked 4 blocks, turned right, and walked 1 block. Using the same path, how can Princeton get back to Broad and High?

1 block south, turn left, walk 4 blocks, turn right, walk 2 blocks

2. Blaine drove to Molly's house. He drove 1 mi west, then 5 mi north, and 1 mi east. How can Blaine drive home from Molly's house using the same path?

1 mi west, 5 mi south, and 1 mi east

3. Marshall left his house by car. He drove 3 mi north, turned west and drove twice as far. He turned south and drove 1 more mile. Tell Marshall how to return home using the same path.

1 mi north, 6 mi east, 3 mi south

4. Sally hiked part of the Appalachian Trail, starting at Katahdin, Maine. She went 2 km east, 4 km south, and 1 km west. How can Sally return to Katahdin using the same path?

1 km east, 4 km north, and 2 km west

5. Joshua ran in a city marathon. He ran 8 mi south, 12 mi east, 3 mi south, and 3 mi west. His friend, Tom, was waiting for him at the finish line with a car. Tom wants to drive the same route back. Tell Tom how to drive back to the starting line using the same path.

3 mi east, 3 mi north, 12 mi west, and 8 mi north

Name_____

Work Backward

Note Cards Marsha had some note cards. She gave 21 note cards to her mother and 15 to her teacher. She then had 31 note cards left. How many note cards did Marsha begin with?

Read and Understand

1. How many note cards did Marsha give to her mother? To her teacher?

21 to her mother; 15 to her teacher

2. How many note cards did Marsha have left?

31 note cards

3. What are you trying to find?

The number of note cards Marsha began with

Plan and Solve

4. What strategy will you use?

Work backward

5. Solve the problem. Write the answer in a complete sentence.

Marsha began with 67 note cards.

Look Back and Check

6. Is your answer reasonable?

Yes, because 21 + 15 + 31 = 67

Name_____

Customary Units of Weight

P 12-4

Choose the better estimate for each weight.

1. 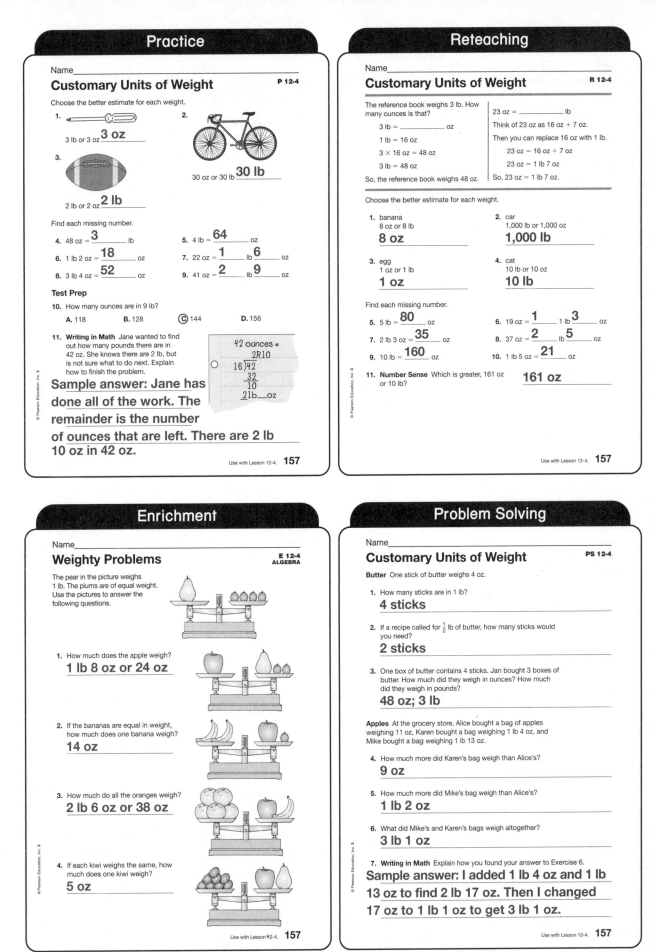 3 lb or 3 oz **3 oz**

2. 30 oz or 30 lb **30 lb**

3. 2 lb or 2 oz **2 lb**

Find each missing number.

4. 48 oz = **3** lb

5. 4 lb = **64** oz

6. 1 lb 2 oz = **18** oz

7. 22 oz = **1** lb **6** oz

8. 3 lb 4 oz = **52** oz

9. 41 oz = **2** lb **9** oz

Test Prep

10. How many ounces are in 9 lb?

A. 118   B. 128   Ⓒ 144   D. 156

11. **Writing in Math** Jane wanted to find out how many pounds there are in 42 oz. She knows there are 2 lb, but is not sure what to do next. Explain how to finish the problem.

```
42 ounces =
        2R10
   16)42
      32
      10
      21 lb___oz
```

Sample answer: Jane has done all of the work. The remainder is the number of ounces that are left. There are 2 lb 10 oz in 42 oz.

© Pearson Education, Inc. 3

Use with Lesson 12-4. **157**

Name_____

Customary Units of Weight

R 12-4

The reference book weighs 3 lb. How many ounces is that?

3 lb = _____ oz
1 lb = 16 oz
3 × 16 oz = 48 oz
3 lb = 48 oz

So, the reference book weighs 48 ounces.

23 oz = _____ lb

Think of 23 oz as 16 oz + 7 oz.

Then you can replace 16 oz with 1 lb.

23 oz = 16 oz + 7 oz
23 oz = 1 lb 7 oz

So, 23 oz = 1 lb 7 oz.

Choose the better estimate for each weight.

1. banana
8 oz or 8 lb
8 oz

2. car
1,000 lb or 1,000 oz
1,000 lb

3. egg
1 oz or 1 lb
1 oz

4. cat
10 lb or 10 oz
10 lb

Find each missing number.

5. 5 lb = **80** oz

6. 19 oz = **1** lb **3** oz

7. 2 lb 3 oz = **35** oz

8. 37 oz = **2** lb **5** oz

9. 10 lb = **160** oz

10. 1 lb 5 oz = **21** oz

11. **Number Sense** Which is greater, 161 oz or 10 lb?

161 oz

© Pearson Education, Inc. 3

Use with Lesson 12-4. **157**

Name_____

Weighty Problems

E 12-4
ALGEBRA

The pear in the picture weighs 1 lb. The plums are of equal weight. Use the pictures to answer the following questions.

1. How much does the apple weigh?
1 lb 8 oz or 24 oz

2. If the bananas are equal in weight, how much does one banana weigh?
14 oz

3. How much do all the oranges weigh?
2 lb 6 oz or 38 oz

4. If each kiwi weighs the same, how much does one kiwi weigh?
5 oz

© Pearson Education, Inc. 3

Use with Lesson 12-4. **157**

Name_____

Customary Units of Weight

PS 12-4

Butter One stick of butter weighs 4 oz.

1. How many sticks are in 1 lb?
4 sticks

2. If a recipe called for $\frac{1}{2}$ lb of butter, how many sticks would you need?
2 sticks

3. One box of butter contains 4 sticks. Jan bought 3 boxes of butter. How much did they weigh in ounces? How much did they weigh in pounds?
48 oz; 3 lb

Apples At the grocery store, Alice bought a bag of apples weighing 11 oz, Karen bought a bag weighing 1 lb 4 oz, and Mike bought a bag weighing 1 lb 13 oz.

4. How much more did Karen's bag weigh than Alice's?
9 oz

5. How much more did Mike's bag weigh than Alice's?
1 lb 2 oz

6. What did Mike's and Karen's bags weigh altogether?
3 lb 1 oz

7. **Writing in Math** Explain how you found your answer to Exercise 6.
Sample answer: I added 1 lb 4 oz and 1 lb 13 oz to find 2 lb 17 oz. Then I changed 17 oz to 1 lb 1 oz to get 3 lb 1 oz.

© Pearson Education, Inc. 3

Use with Lesson 12-4. **157**

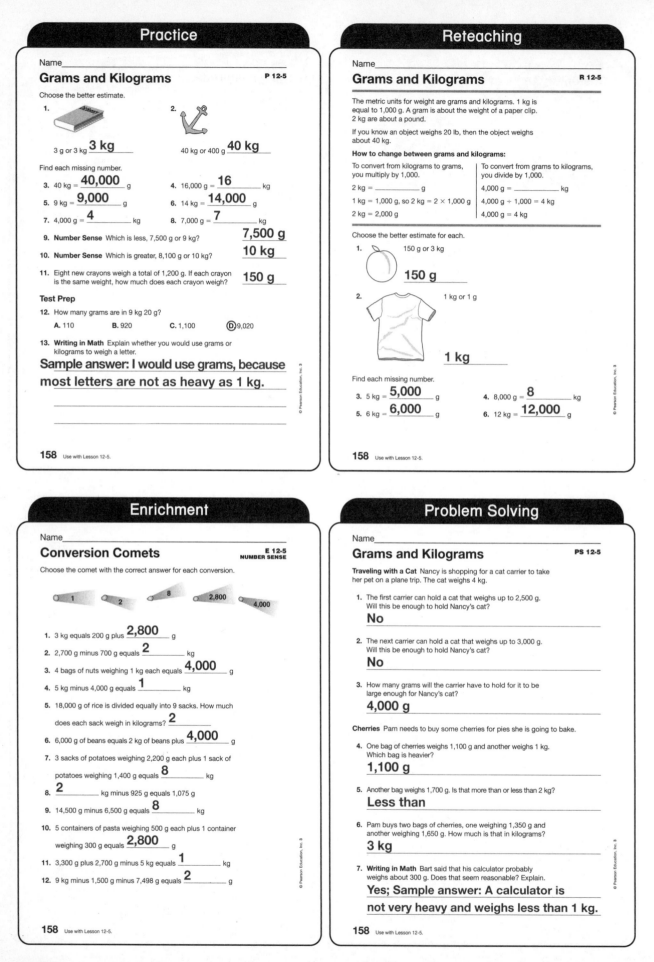

Practice

Grams and Kilograms

Choose the better estimate.

1. **3 kg**
3 g or 3 kg

2. **40 kg**
40 kg or 400 g

Find each missing number.

3. 40 kg = **40,000** g

4. 16,000 g = **16** kg

5. 9 kg = **9,000** g

6. 14 kg = **14,000** g

7. 4,000 g = **4** kg

8. 7,000 g = **7** kg

9. **Number Sense** Which is less, 7,500 g or 9 kg? **7,500 g**

10. **Number Sense** Which is greater, 8,100 g or 10 kg? **10 kg**

11. Eight new crayons weigh a total of 1,200 g. If each crayon is the same weight, how much does each crayon weigh? **150 g**

Test Prep

12. How many grams are in 9 kg 20 g?

A. 110   B. 920   C. 1,100   (D) 9,020

13. **Writing in Math** Explain whether you would use grams or kilograms to weigh a letter.

Sample answer: I would use grams, because most letters are not as heavy as 1 kg.

_____

_____

Reteaching

Grams and Kilograms

The metric units for weight are grams and kilograms. 1 kg is equal to 1,000 g. A gram is about the weight of a paper clip. 2 kg are about a pound.

If you know an object weighs 20 lb, then the object weighs about 40 kg.

How to change between grams and kilograms:

To convert from kilograms to grams, you multiply by 1,000.	To convert from grams to kilograms, you divide by 1,000.
2 kg = _____ g	4,000 g = _____ kg
1 kg = 1,000 g, so 2 kg = 2 × 1,000 g	4,000 g ÷ 1,000 = 4 kg
2 kg = 2,000 g	4,000 g = 4 kg

Choose the better estimate for each.

1. 150 g or 3 kg   **150 g**

2. 1 kg or 1 g   **1 kg**

Find each missing number.

3. 5 kg = **5,000** g

4. 8,000 g = **8** kg

5. 6 kg = **6,000** g

6. 12 kg = **12,000** g

Enrichment

Conversion Comets

Choose the comet with the correct answer for each conversion.

1   2   8   2,800   4,000

1. 3 kg equals 200 g plus **2,800** g

2. 2,700 g minus 700 g equals **2** kg

3. 4 bags of nuts weighing 1 kg each equals **4,000** g

4. 5 kg minus 4,000 g equals **1** kg

5. 18,000 g of rice is divided equally into 9 sacks. How much does each sack weigh in kilograms? **2**

6. 6,000 g of beans equals 2 kg of beans plus **4,000** g

7. 3 sacks of potatoes weighing 2,200 g each plus 1 sack of potatoes weighing 1,400 g equals **8** kg

8. **2** kg minus 925 g equals 1,075 g

9. 14,500 g minus 6,500 g equals **8** kg

10. 5 containers of pasta weighing 500 g each plus 1 container weighing 300 g equals **2,800** g

11. 3,300 g plus 2,700 g minus 5 kg equals **1** kg

12. 9 kg minus 1,500 g minus 7,498 g equals **2** g

Problem Solving

Grams and Kilograms

Traveling with a Cat Nancy is shopping for a cat carrier to take her pet on a plane trip. The cat weighs 4 kg.

1. The first carrier can hold a cat that weighs up to 2,500 g. Will this be enough to hold Nancy's cat? **No**

2. The next carrier can hold a cat that weighs up to 3,000 g. Will this be enough to hold Nancy's cat? **No**

3. How many grams will the carrier have to hold for it to be large enough for Nancy's cat? **4,000 g**

Cherries Pam needs to buy some cherries for pies she is going to bake.

4. One bag of cherries weighs 1,100 g and another weighs 1 kg. Which bag is heavier? **1,100 g**

5. Another bag weighs 1,700 g. Is that more or less than 2 kg? **Less than**

6. Pam buys two bags of cherries, one weighing 1,350 g and another weighing 1,650 g. How much is that in kilograms? **3 kg**

7. **Writing in Math** Bart said that his calculator probably weighs about 300 g. Does that seem reasonable? Explain.
Yes; Sample answer: A calculator is not very heavy and weighs less than 1 kg.

© Pearson Education, Inc. 3

Name_____

Temperature

P 12-6

Write each temperature using °F.

1. **40°F**

2. **85°F**

Write each temperature using °C.

3. **0°C**

4. **25°C**

Estimate Choose the better outdoor temperature for each activity.

5. jogging

(20°C) or 40°C

6. sledding

(17°F) or 40°F

7. gardening

10°C or (25°C)

8. If it is 84°F at noon on Monday and 70°F at 11 P.M. on Monday, how much did the temperature drop?

The temperature has dropped 14°F.

Test Prep

9. Which is the best temperature for snow skiing?

A. 40°C   B. 10°C   C. 40°F   (D) 10°F

10. **Writing in Math** Would you describe the temperature as cold, warm, or hot if it were 35°C? Explain.

Sample answer: I would describe a temperature of 35°C as hot because it is between 90°F and 100°F.

Name_____

Temperature

R 12-6

On the Fahrenheit scale, water freezes at 32°F and boils at 212°F. At 32°F you would need a winter parka, gloves, and a warm hat if you were planning to go outdoors.

On the Celsius scale, water boils at 100°C and freezes at 0°C. At 32°C, you would wear shorts and a T-shirt.

How to read a thermometer

The top of the column is at 80 on the Fahrenheit scale, so the temperature is 80°F. The top of the column is at about 28 on the Celsius scale, so the temperature is about 28°C.

Write each temperature using °C.

1. **10°C**

2. **40°C**

Write each temperature using °F.

3. **60°F**

4. **75°F**

Name_____

Hit or Miss

E 12-6
REASONABLENESS

Tell whether the person HIT the true temperature or MISSED and made an error in reporting Celsius or Fahrenheit.

1. Cindy went on a vacation to Florida in August. She wrote a postcard to her mother stating that the temperature was 32°C.

Hit

2. Leslie wrote that during the month of December in Anchorage, Alaska, the temperature reached 212°F.

Missed

3. Margaret told her friend that she swam in 27°C ocean water in the Gulf of Mexico last June.

Hit

4. Sheila told her father that icicles could form when the temperature was less than 0°C.

Hit

5. Richard told his sister that his car slid on the ice on a night when the temperature was 20°C.

Missed

6. Robin told his mother that he needed a blanket to keep warm on a 104°F evening.

Missed

7. Jay said he went skiing when it was 20°F.

Hit

8. Mark said he slept outside without a sleeping bag in 20°C.

Hit

9. Carlos said he went sledding when the temperature was 72°F.

Missed

10. Marcy said an ice cube would melt outside when it was 23°F.

Missed

11. Gaby planned to go water skiing on a day when the temperature was 31°C.

Hit

12. Alexa wore sandals outside when it was 27°F.

Missed

Name_____

Temperature

PS 12-6

Highs and Lows Justin charted the high and low temperatures for a week. Use the chart for 1–5.

	Mon	Tues	Wed	Thur	Fri	Sat	Sun
High	60°F	58°F	50°F	41°F	51°F	36°F	30°F
Low	40°F	39°F	35°F	28°F	35°F	21°F	18°F

1. What was the difference between the high and low temperatures on Monday?

20°F

2. On which two days of the week was there exactly a 15°F difference between the high and low temperatures?

Wednesday and Saturday

3. On Tuesday, about how high was the temperature in °C?

About 14°C

4. On Thursday, about how high was the temperature in °C?

About 8°C

5. **Writing in Math** On Sunday, was it cold enough for water to freeze? Explain.

Yes; Sample answer: The high temperature was only 30°F, which is below 32°F.

© Pearson Education, Inc. 3

Name_____

Describing Chances

Sarah is an adult with a dog named Fred. Describe each event as certain, likely, unlikely, or impossible.

1. Fred will sleep tonight.   **Likely**

2. Fred will weigh more than Sarah.   **Unlikely**

3. Fred will eat.   **Certain**

4. Fred will learn to play the accordion.   **Impossible**

Describe each spin as certain, impossible, likely, or unlikely.

5. Spinning a square   **Likely**

6. Spinning a triangle   **Unlikely**

7. Spinning an even number   **Unlikely**

8. Spinning an odd number   **Impossible**

Test Prep

9. Which is the best description of the event that a cat will become a doctor?

   A. Likely   **B.** Unlikely   **C.** Certain   **(D)** Impossible

10. **Writing in Math** Explain the difference between a likely and an unlikely event.

Sample answer: Both likely and unlikely events are possible. If there is a good chance, it is likely. If there is not a good chance, it is unlikely.

160 Use with Lesson 12-7.

Name_____

Describing Chance

You can use the words **certain**, **likely**, **unlikely**, or **impossible** to describe the chance that something will happen.

If you were to toss the number cube to the right:

It is **certain** that you would toss a number from 1 to 6, because all of the numbers are between 1 and 6.

It is **likely** that you would toss a number greater than 1. There are 5 numbers that are greater than 1, and there is 1 number that is not greater than 1.

It is **unlikely** that you will toss a 6. There are 5 numbers that are not 6, and one number that is 6. The event does not have a good chance of happening, but it could.

It is **impossible** that you would toss the number 7, because there are no 7s on the cube.

Describe each event as certain, likely, unlikely, or impossible.

1. There are no pencils in the school.   **Unlikely**

2. Moe the cat can play the trumpet.   **Impossible**

3. Next week will have 7 days.   **Certain**

4. Janet's dog has 4 legs.   **Likely**

Suppose you pick a card from the hat without looking. Describe each pick as certain, impossible, likely, or unlikely.

5. Picking a shaded card   **Likely**

6. Picking a round card   **Impossible**

7. Picking a card that is not a black card   **Likely**

160 Use with Lesson 12-7.

Name_____

Possible or Impossible?

A scrap of paper is covering part of an equation in each problem. Tell whether it is possible or impossible for the equation to be true. If it is possible, tell what the hidden numbers are.

1. $1,250 = 1,200 + 4 \square - 375$ **Possible; 25**

2. $374 = 200 + 4 \square - 150$ **Impossible**

3. $175 = 1 \square + 350$ **Impossible**

4. $\square 24 = 520 - 96$ **Possible; 4**

5. $6 \square 11 = 41 + 70 + 6,000$ **Possible; 1**

6. $\square 02 = 822 - 320$ **Possible; 5**

7. $8,365 = 2,144 + 72 \square 1$ **Impossible**

8. $999 = 6 \square 6 + 332$ **Impossible**

9. $430 = 1 \square + 800 - 499$ **Possible; 29**

10. $7,654 = 1,123 + 65 \square$ **Possible; 31**

11. $2,138 = 937 + 3 \square - 428$ **Impossible**

12. $579 = 623 - 200 + 1 \square$ **Possible; 56**

160 Use with Lesson 12-7.

Name_____

Describing Chances

Marbles Greg and Tom are going to play marbles. They have the 10 marbles shown to choose from. Describe each event as likely, unlikely, certain, or impossible.

1. Choosing a marble
   Certain

2. Choosing a red marble
   Likely

3. Choosing a green marble
   Unlikely

4. Choosing a black marble
   Impossible

5. Paula's father bought her a balloon. Paula picked it from a bundle that included 7 red-and-white-striped balloons, 2 blue balloons, and 2 yellow balloons. Is choosing a blue or yellow balloon likely, unlikely, certain, or impossible?
   Unlikely

6. **Writing in Math** What would you have to change about the balloon bundle to make it certain that Paula would choose a blue balloon?
   Sample answer: All of the balloons would have to be blue.

160 Use with Lesson 12-7.

© Pearson Education, Inc. 3

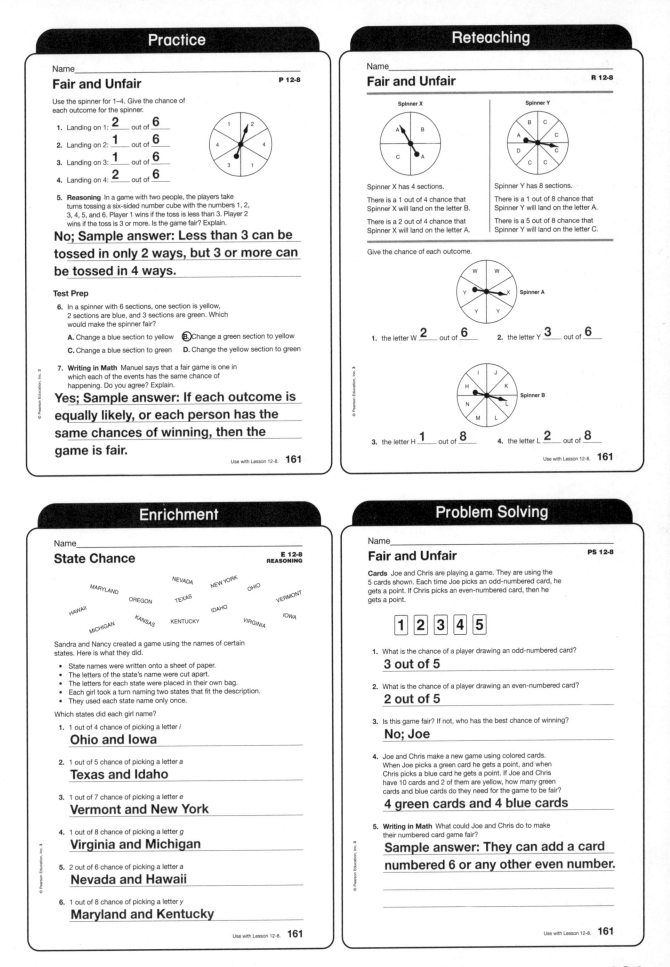

Practice

Name_____

Fair and Unfair
P 12-8

Use the spinner for 1–4. Give the chance of each outcome for the spinner.

1. Landing on 1: **2** out of **6**

2. Landing on 2: **1** out of **6**

3. Landing on 3: **1** out of **6**

4. Landing on 4: **2** out of **6**

5. **Reasoning** In a game with two people, the players take turns tossing a six-sided number cube with the numbers 1, 2, 3, 4, 5, and 6. Player 1 wins if the toss is less than 3. Player 2 wins if the toss is 3 or more. Is the game fair? Explain.

No; Sample answer: Less than 3 can be tossed in only 2 ways, but 3 or more can be tossed in 4 ways.

Test Prep

6. In a spinner with 6 sections, one section is yellow, 2 sections are blue, and 3 sections are green. Which would make the spinner fair?

   A. Change a blue section to yellow   (B.) Change a green section to yellow

   C. Change a blue section to green   D. Change the yellow section to green

7. **Writing in Math** Manuel says that a fair game is one in which each of the events has the same chance of happening. Do you agree? Explain.

Yes; Sample answer: If each outcome is equally likely, or each person has the same chances of winning, then the game is fair.

Use with Lesson 12-8. **161**

Reteaching

Name_____

Fair and Unfair
R 12-8

Spinner X   **Spinner Y**

Spinner X has 4 sections.   Spinner Y has 8 sections.

There is a 1 out of 4 chance that Spinner X will land on the letter B.   There is a 1 out of 8 chance that Spinner Y will land on the letter A.

There is a 2 out of 4 chance that Spinner X will land on the letter A.   There is a 5 out of 8 chance that Spinner Y will land on the letter C.

Give the chance of each outcome.

Spinner A

1. the letter W **2** out of **6**   2. the letter Y **3** out of **6**

Spinner B

3. the letter H **1** out of **8**   4. the letter L **2** out of **8**

Use with Lesson 12-8. **161**

Enrichment

Name_____

State Chance
E 12-8
REASONING

MARYLAND   NEVADA   NEW YORK   OHIO

OREGON   TEXAS   VERMONT

HAWAII   IDAHO   IOWA

MICHIGAN   KANSAS   KENTUCKY   VIRGINIA

Sandra and Nancy created a game using the names of certain states. Here is what they did.

- State names were written onto a sheet of paper.
- The letters of the state's name were cut apart.
- The letters for each state were placed in their own bag.
- Each girl took a turn naming two states that fit the description.
- They used each state name only once.

Which states did each girl name?

1. 1 out of 4 chance of picking a letter *i*

   Ohio and Iowa

2. 1 out of 5 chance of picking a letter *a*

   Texas and Idaho

3. 1 out of 7 chance of picking a letter *e*

   Vermont and New York

4. 1 out of 8 chance of picking a letter *g*

   Virginia and Michigan

5. 2 out of 6 chance of picking a letter *a*

   Nevada and Hawaii

6. 1 out of 8 chance of picking a letter *y*

   Maryland and Kentucky

Use with Lesson 12-8. **161**

Problem Solving

Name_____

Fair and Unfair
PS 12-8

Cards Joe and Chris are playing a game. They are using the 5 cards shown. Each time Joe picks an odd-numbered card, he gets a point. If Chris picks an even-numbered card, then he gets a point.

1 2 3 4 5

1. What is the chance of a player drawing an odd-numbered card?

   3 out of 5

2. What is the chance of a player drawing an even-numbered card?

   2 out of 5

3. Is this game fair? If not, who has the best chance of winning?

   No; Joe

4. Joe and Chris make a new game using colored cards. When Joe picks a green card he gets a point, and when Chris picks a blue card he gets a point. If Joe and Chris have 10 cards and 2 of them are yellow, how many green cards and blue cards do they need for the game to be fair?

   4 green cards and 4 blue cards

5. **Writing in Math** What could Joe and Chris do to make their numbered card game fair?

   Sample answer: They can add a card numbered 6 or any other even number.

Use with Lesson 12-8. **161**

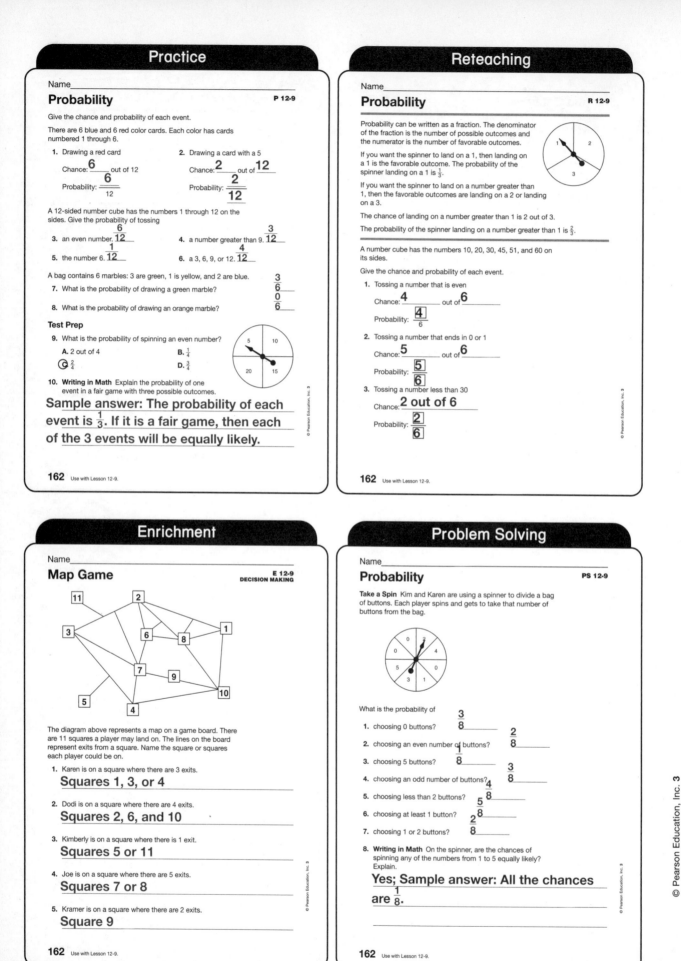

Practice

Name_____

Probability
P 12-9

Give the chance and probability of each event.

There are 6 blue and 6 red color cards. Each color has cards numbered 1 through 6.

1. Drawing a red card

Chance: $\frac{6}{}$ out of 12

Probability: $\frac{6}{12}$

2. Drawing a card with a 5

Chance: $\frac{2}{}$ out of 12

Probability: $\frac{2}{12}$

A 12-sided number cube has the numbers 1 through 12 on the sides. Give the probability of tossing

3. an even number. $\frac{6}{12}$

4. a number greater than 9. $\frac{3}{12}$

5. the number 6. $\frac{1}{12}$

6. a 3, 6, 9, or 12. $\frac{4}{12}$

A bag contains 6 marbles: 3 are green, 1 is yellow, and 2 are blue.

7. What is the probability of drawing a green marble? $\frac{3}{6}$

8. What is the probability of drawing an orange marble? $\frac{0}{6}$

Test Prep

9. What is the probability of spinning an even number?

A. 2 out of 4

B. $\frac{1}{4}$

C. $\frac{2}{4}$

D. $\frac{3}{4}$

10. Writing in Math Explain the probability of one event in a fair game with three possible outcomes.

Sample answer: The probability of each event is $\frac{1}{3}$. If it is a fair game, then each of the 3 events will be equally likely.

Reteaching

Name_____

Probability
R 12-9

Probability can be written as a fraction. The denominator of the fraction is the number of possible outcomes and the numerator is the number of favorable outcomes.

If you want the spinner to land on a 1, then landing on a 1 is the favorable outcome. The probability of the spinner landing on a 1 is $\frac{1}{3}$.

If you want the spinner to land on a number greater than 1, then the favorable outcomes are landing on a 2 or landing on a 3.

The chance of landing on a number greater than 1 is 2 out of 3.

The probability of the spinner landing on a number greater than 1 is $\frac{2}{3}$.

A number cube has the numbers 10, 20, 30, 45, 51, and 60 on its sides.

Give the chance and probability of each event.

1. Tossing a number that is even

Chance: $\frac{4}{}$ out of 6

Probability: $\frac{4}{6}$

2. Tossing a number that ends in 0 or 1

Chance: $\frac{5}{}$ out of 6

Probability: $\frac{5}{6}$

3. Tossing a number less than 30

Chance: 2 out of 6

Probability: $\frac{2}{6}$

Enrichment

Name_____

Map Game
E 12-9
DECISION MAKING

The diagram above represents a map on a game board. There are 11 squares a player may land on. The lines on the board represent exits from a square. Name the square or squares each player could be on.

1. Karen is on a square where there are 3 exits.

Squares 1, 3, or 4

2. Dodi is on a square where there are 4 exits.

Squares 2, 6, and 10

3. Kimberly is on a square where there is 1 exit.

Squares 5 or 11

4. Joe is on a square where there are 5 exits.

Squares 7 or 8

5. Kramer is on a square where there are 2 exits.

Square 9

Problem Solving

Name_____

Probability
PS 12-9

Take a Spin Kim and Karen are using a spinner to divide a bag of buttons. Each player spins and gets to take that number of buttons from the bag.

What is the probability of

1. choosing 0 buttons? $\frac{3}{8}$

2. choosing an even number of buttons? $\frac{2}{8}$

3. choosing 5 buttons? $\frac{1}{8}$

4. choosing an odd number of buttons? $\frac{3}{8}$

5. choosing less than 2 buttons? $\frac{4}{8}$

6. choosing at least 1 button? $\frac{5}{8}$

7. choosing 1 or 2 buttons? $\frac{2}{8}$

8. Writing in Math On the spinner, are the chances of spinning any of the numbers from 1 to 5 equally likely? Explain.

Yes; Sample answer: All the chances are $\frac{1}{8}$.

Name_____

PROBLEM-SOLVING SKILL   P 12-10

Writing to Explain

Sample answers are given.

Write to explain.

1. Explain why the spinner is not fair.

The spinner is not fair because it is more likely to land on 3 because it is much larger than 1 or 2.

2. A bag contains tiles with the letters shown. Explain how to find the probability of drawing a letter tile that is not a vowel.

There are 5 tiles. Two are vowels, and three are not vowels. So, the probability of a non-vowel being drawn is $\frac{3}{5}$.

3. Is it likely, unlikely, certain, or impossible that the sun is shining somewhere? Explain your decision.

It is certain that somewhere the sun is shining. There must be one place in the world where there are no clouds.

4. Are you more likely to swim at 30°F or 30°C? Explain how you decided.

I am more likely to swim at 30°C, because 30°F is very cold. 30°C is more than 80°F, so it is warm.

Use with Lesson 12-10. **163**

Name_____

PROBLEM-SOLVING SKILL   R 12-10

Writing to Explain

Which Cube? Joe and Mona each took 10 turns tossing the number cubes below. Use the results of their tosses to predict which of the two number cubes below they most likely used. Explain how you made your prediction.

Number Cube A: 2, 4, 7, 13, 16, 21   Number Cube B: 6, 12, 16, 24, 30, 31

Results of Number Cube Experiment

Name	Times even number was tossed	Times odd number was tossed
Joe	9	1
Mona	8	2

Writing a Math Explanation

- State your prediction.
- Use information from the problem to help explain your prediction.
- When a problem has choices for the answer, explain why some of the answers are not chosen.
- Use specific examples or numbers to explain why something makes sense.

Example

I think the children used Number Cube B.

The table tells me that most of the tosses were even numbers. Number Cube B has more even numbers on it than Number Cube A. More tosses would be even using Number Cube B.

1. Karl predicted that if he spun the spinner to the right 100 times, it would land on the letter X about the same number of times as it landed on the letter Z. Do you agree?

Sample answer: Disagree. There are more spaces with the letter X than with Z. If Karl spins the spinner 100 times, it will likely land on X more often than on Z.

Use with Lesson 12-10. **163**

Name_____

Permutations   E 12-10 PATTERNS

1. Francis has two colors, red and blue. She wants to write them in order in two different ways. What are the two ways?

Red blue or blue red

2. Charo has three colors, red, blue, and white. List the six different ways Charo can arrange the letters. What pattern did you use to organize your answer so that you did not repeat any combinations?

Rbw, rwb, brw, bwr, wbr, wrb: Sample answer: Two different combinations of the 2 colors after the first one has been chosen

3. Eva, Lisa, and Maria ride to school together and sit in the back seat of a car. List the different ways they can sit if Eva sits in the middle. Why is this a different pattern than the pattern in Exercise 2?

Lisa, Eva, Maria or Maria, Eva, Lisa; Sample answer: This time there was a special condition about Eva.

4. A bookstore has book covers in red, green, orange, and yellow. The owner wants to set up a display with two different book colors on a shelf. How many different ways can he arrange the books?

12 ways; RO, OR, RY, YR, RG, GR, OY, YO, OG, GO, YG, GY

Use with Lesson 12-10. **163**

Name_____

PROBLEM-SOLVING SKILL   PS 12-10

Writing to Explain

Number Cube Carly tossed a number cube five times and got the numbers 2, 6, 4, 6, and 2. Predict whether it was more likely that Carly was using a cube numbered 1, 2, 3, 4, 5, and 6 or a cube numbered 2, 2, 4, 4, 6, and 6.

Read and Understand

1. How many times did Carly toss the number cube? **5 times**

2. What were the results? **2, 6, 4, 6, and 2**

3. What are you trying to find?

If Carly was using a cube numbered 1, 2, 3, 4, 5, and 6 or a cube numbered 2, 2, 4, 4, 6, and 6

Plan and Solve

4. How can you solve the problem? Explain.

I can find the chances of tossing the numbers using each of the cubes.

5. Write your answer in a complete sentence.

I predict the cube numbered 2, 2, 4, 4, 6, and 6 was used.

Look Back and Check

6. Is your answer reasonable?

Yes, since all of the numbers were even, it is unlikely the cube was numbered 1, 2, 3, 4, 5, and 6.

Use with Lesson 12-10. **163**

Name_____

PROBLEM-SOLVING APPLICATION   P 12-11
Marble Probability

Suppose you pick a marble from the bag shown
at the right without looking.

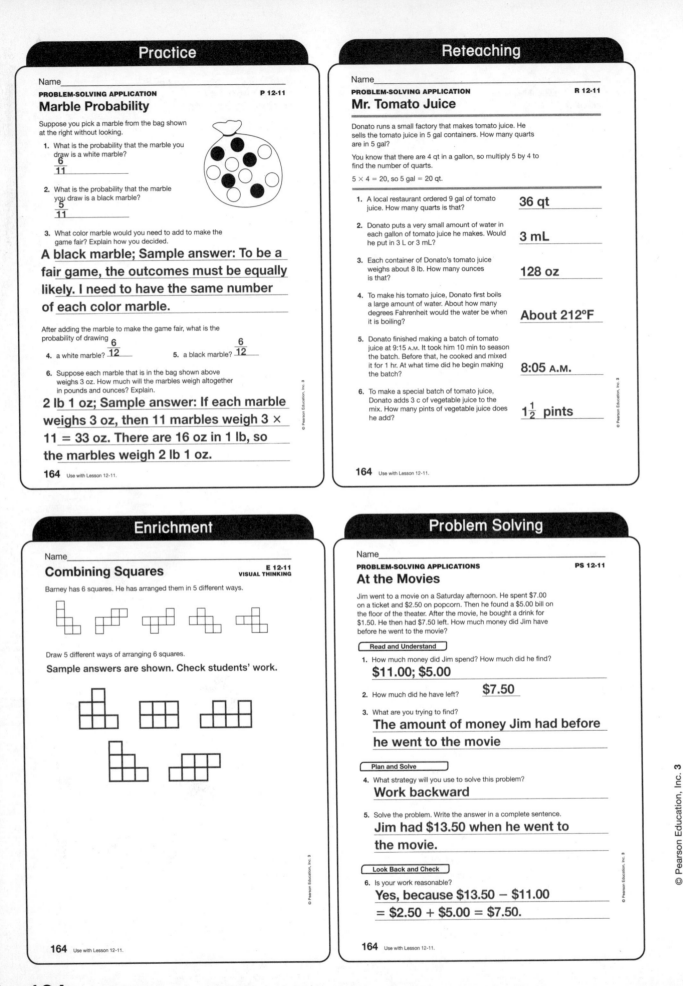

1. What is the probability that the marble you
   draw is a white marble?
   $\frac{6}{11}$

2. What is the probability that the marble
   you draw is a black marble?
   $\frac{5}{11}$

3. What color marble would you need to add to make the
   game fair? Explain how you decided.

   A black marble; Sample answer: To be a
   fair game, the outcomes must be equally
   likely. I need to have the same number
   of each color marble.

After adding the marble to make the game fair, what is the
probability of drawing

4. a white marble? $\frac{6}{12}$ 5. a black marble? $\frac{6}{12}$

6. Suppose each marble that is in the bag shown above
   weighs 3 oz. How much will the marbles weigh altogether
   in pounds and ounces? Explain.

   2 lb 1 oz; Sample answer: If each marble
   weighs 3 oz, then 11 marbles weigh 3 ×
   11 = 33 oz. There are 16 oz in 1 lb, so
   the marbles weigh 2 lb 1 oz.

164 Use with Lesson 12-11.

Name_____

PROBLEM-SOLVING APPLICATION   R 12-11
Mr. Tomato Juice

Donato runs a small factory that makes tomato juice. He
sells the tomato juice in 5 gal containers. How many quarts
are in 5 gal?

You know that there are 4 qt in a gallon, so multiply 5 by 4 to
find the number of quarts.

$5 \times 4 = 20$, so 5 gal = 20 qt.

1. A local restaurant ordered 9 gal of tomato
   juice. How many quarts is that?   **36 qt**

2. Donato puts a very small amount of water in
   each gallon of tomato juice he makes. Would   **3 mL**
   he put in 3 L or 3 mL?

3. Each container of Donato's tomato juice
   weighs about 8 lb. How many ounces   **128 oz**
   is that?

4. To make his tomato juice, Donato first boils
   a large amount of water. About how many   **About 212°F**
   degrees Fahrenheit would the water be when
   it is boiling?

5. Donato finished making a batch of tomato
   juice at 9:15 A.M. It took him 10 min to season
   the batch. Before that, he cooked and mixed   **8:05 A.M.**
   it for 1 hr. At what time did he begin making
   the batch?

6. To make a special batch of tomato juice,
   Donato adds 3 c of vegetable juice to the $1\frac{1}{2}$ **pints**
   mix. How many pints of vegetable juice does
   he add?

164 Use with Lesson 12-11.

Name_____

                                          E 12-11
Combining Squares   VISUAL THINKING

Barney has 6 squares. He has arranged them in 5 different ways.

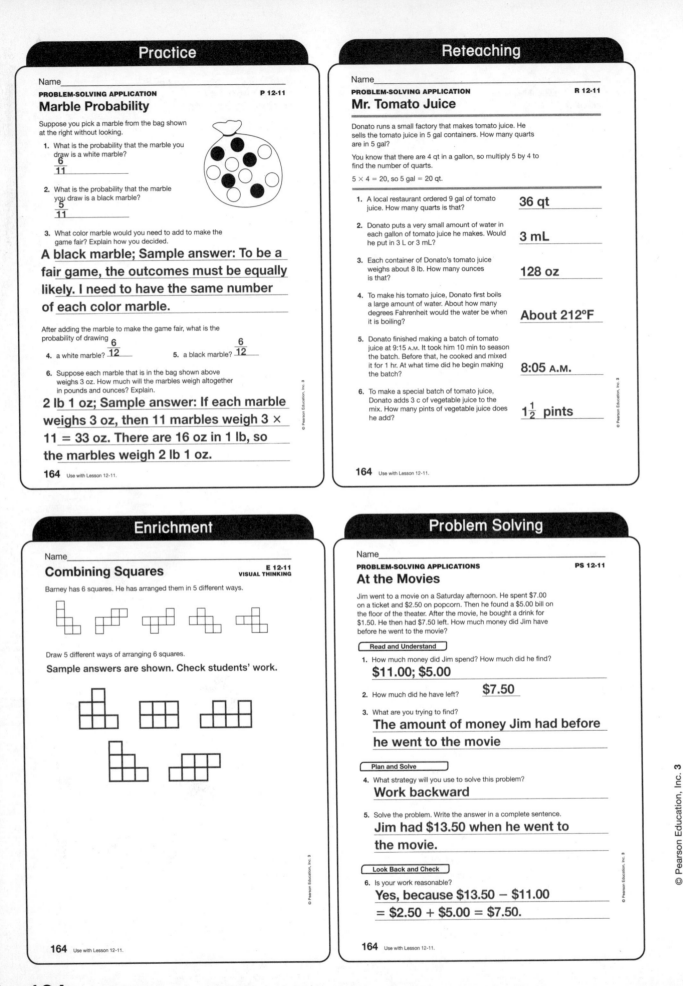

Draw 5 different ways of arranging 6 squares.

Sample answers are shown. Check students' work.

164 Use with Lesson 12-11.

Name_____

PROBLEM-SOLVING APPLICATIONS   PS 12-11
At the Movies

Jim went to a movie on a Saturday afternoon. He spent $7.00
on a ticket and $2.50 on popcorn. Then he found a $5.00 bill on
the floor of the theater. After the movie, he bought a drink for
$1.50. He then had $7.50 left. How much money did Jim have
before he went to the movie?

Read and Understand

1. How much money did Jim spend? How much did he find?
   $11.00; $5.00

2. How much did he have left?   **$7.50**

3. What are you trying to find?

   The amount of money Jim had before
   he went to the movie

Plan and Solve

4. What strategy will you use to solve this problem?
   Work backward

5. Solve the problem. Write the answer in a complete sentence.
   Jim had $13.50 when he went to
   the movie.

Look Back and Check

6. Is your work reasonable?
   Yes, because $13.50 − $11.00
   = $2.50 + $5.00 = $7.50.

164 Use with Lesson 12-11.

© Pearson Education, Inc. 3
